THE VOICES

Author of *The Cosmos and the Creeds*
and
Glimpses of the Next State

THE VOICES

by

VICE-ADMIRAL
WILLIAM USBORNE MOORE

www.whitecrowbooks.com

SOLITUDE

Laugh and the world laughs with you
Weep and you weep alone;
For the sad old earth must borrow its mirth,
But has trouble enough of its own.
Sing, and the hills will answer;
Sigh, it is lost on the air;
The echoes bound to a joyful sound,
But shrink from voicing care.
Rejoice, and men will seek you;
Grieve, and they turn and go;
They want full measure of all your pleasure,
But they do not need your woe.
Be glad, and your friends are many;
Be sad, and you lose them all.
There are none to decline your nectar'd wine,
But alone you must drink life's gall.
Feast and your halls are crowded;
Fast and the world goes by,
Succeed and give, and it helps you live,
But no man can help you die.
There is room in the halls of pleasure
For a large and lordly train,
But one by one we must all file on
Through the narrow aisles of pain

ELLA WHEELER WILCOX

To Those Who Weep, This Record of the
Return of the Dead Is
Dedicated With Respect and Sympathy
By the Author

"God is not the God of the dead, but of the living" -Matt. xxii, 32

"In my fathers house there are many mansions." -John xiv, 2

Contents

PREFACE

This book is divided into two parts; the first containing records of 1912, the second those of 1913. It includes the testimony of Mr. James Coates of Rothesay, who writes his own account of the excellent sittings held in his hospitable house at Ardbeg in 1913. His experiences of 1912 are to be found in *LIGHT*.

In part 1, I have reprinted a number of articles in *LIGHT*, written by myself and others, with the kind permission of the editor of that journal.

The object of the work is to present to those who have neither the leisure, the opportunity, nor the means to investigate for themselves, a compact story of the exhibition of what is called the "direct voice" through the mediumship of Mrs. Etta Wriedt of Detroit, Michigan, U.S.A., when she visited England in the spring and summer of 1912 and 1913 at my invitation. In 1911 she was at Wimbledon under the care of the late Mr. W.T. Stead, and also in Glasgow, where she held one or two Séances; these Séances are referred to, but not discussed at length. Some details will be found in my epilogue to Chapter X in *Glimpses of the Next State*, published in October, 1911.

I address myself specially to those that mourn, who may, by these pages, which give evidence of the return of the dead, be, in some measure, consoled by reflecting on the proximity of the spirits of those they have lost, and who, they may rest assured, are watching over them and awaiting re-union.

The communications from the spirits to the sitters are usually made through an aluminium trumpet which magnifies the voices, the spirit talking into the mouth, and the sound emanating from the smaller end. The trumpet is made in three lengths of thirteen inches each. These are put one inside the other, and gently pulled out until fixed. When it is on the floor ready for use, the trumpet stands thirty-two inches; the small orifice being from one half to three-quarters of an inch in diameter, the mouth five inches. Some spirits do not require the trumpet; it is a common occurrence for two spirits to talk to two people at different positions in a circle, one with, and the other without, its assistance. The weight of the trumpets varies from eight to thirteen ounces.

In 1912 Mrs. Wriedt had her own light trumpet in the circle; in 1913 she preferred to place one or both of mine , though they are slightly heavier. In 1912 a cabinet was left in the room which Mr. Stead had set up in previous years for materialisation experiments; in 1913 it was removed.

The room where we always sat in Cambridge House, known as "Julia's Bureau," is twenty-two feet long by fourteen feet broad. It contained a musical box of the disk type (symphonion), twelve chairs, a bookcase, and two tables. Plenty of flowers were provided by the sitters. It was lighted by electric light, one of the globes being covered with red paper.

I desire to express my thanks to my publishers' press reader for suggestions and corrections.

W. U. M.
8 WESTERN PARADE, SOUTHSEA.
October 1, 1913

INTRODUCTION

Every attempt, such as the one I am making to bring home to mortals the knowledge of the proximity of their beloved dead must, owing to the very nature of the subject, be only partially successful. There are five difficulties with which I have to contend, (1) the reluctance of people to write at all: (2) their special reluctance to put on paper details which may sooner or later give pain or offence to living friends or relatives; (3) the national habit of reserve which causes many a man to become an oyster when he thinks he may be betrayed into revealing his innermost feelings – that which deeply stirs his heart; (4) the fear of ridicule, diminution of income, loss of position, or respect of his fellow men; (5) the apprehension of appearing more credulous than his associates (perhaps the most powerful motive for silence). Thus, after all, the man who aims at obtaining the true opinions of investigators into this sacred subject only receives the rind of the fruit; the fruit itself remains untouched.

To some extent I, the author- or, more properly, the editor- of this collection of narratives am "cribbed, cabined, and confined" by one or other of the above restrictions. Neither in *Glimpses of the Next State*, nor in this sequel, have I given the whole evidence for the faith that is in me. I have submitted all I can with propriety, but there is much behind that is suppressed which, if known, would be absolutely convincing to the few, but become the subject of ignorant buffoonery to the many, to the great majority who are tied and bound by sacerdotalism or materialism.

However the requests I have made to those who have had sittings with this highly- privileged woman, Mrs. Etta Wriedt, have been met with as willing a response as one can expect, considering the age in which we live; and the narratives which have been furnished me I earnestly hope may assist the weary and dispirited to take up their lives again and bravely face the future in the sure and certain hope that they will meet, at no great distance of time, with those they have lost awhile; or, at any rate, encourage them to seek assurance for themselves by personal investigation on the same lines.

That noble soul W.T. Stead, conceived a plan for giving comfort to the bereaved which was perfect of its kind; but the form that it took rendered it liable to extinction directly its founder passed to the higher life. But the spirit of "Julia's Bureau" still lives. It is in the power of every man and woman in comfortable circumstances to carry out the idea in their own person. Let us each do what we, individually, can to assist, with our purse, those whom we know to be in trouble to find consolation by investigation through competent psychics. If we do this, have we not accomplished in detail, what Stead and his guide, Julia, did in wholesale fashion? In these days of general education it is futile to tell a man of any intelligence that he will meet his child again some millions of years hence on a day of Judgement, when he may again part with him. He wants to know if his child is alive now; if he is happy or likely to become so; if he will be restored to him; if he will again hold him in his arms, and be to him what he was before his transition to the Next State. Whether his child was good, or whether he was bad, the parent's mind cannot grasp that he is eternally lost to him. His sense of justice revolts against the decree of the Church, and he will have none of it. It is to this man that spiritism appeals; and it is this man that all should desire to help.

And help is at hand. This American woman has a mysterious gift which enables those who sit in the same room with her to learn of the continued existence of those whose physical bodies have perished. The possession of this strange power is acquired by no virtue of her own; she was born with it. Unlike the gifts of poesy, art, oratory, or song, it demands from her no effort; and, with proper precautions, it causes no strain upon her physical constitution. To exhibit it, all she has to do is to sit passively in a chair, preferably in pitch darkness. It is, indeed, difficult to know what her personality has to do with the phenomena, for she never goes into the trance condition, and talks naturally throughout. What we do know is that we cannot hear a whisper when she is out of the house, but that, if she is in the room, we can distinguish voices in full light or in darkness; if in the latter, they speak louder, longer, clearer, and, in every way, more satisfactorily than in light. When the room is made pitch dark we can not only hear the voices, but can see, as phantasms, those to whom they belong.

We are told by Dr. Sharp that the power to speak is obtained from the sitters, and that they succeed or fail according to what "they are able to give out"; that some people give out freely, others not at all, and that his medium is not "drawn upon" more than is absolutely necessary. He includes me in the first category, and, if I am to judge by my feelings after a good private séance, he is correct, for I am depleted, and cannot continue investigations without long periods of rest. That Mrs. Wriedt is not drained is proved to my satisfaction by the following incident:- In 1913, owing to her suddenly announcing her intention to leave Cambridge House twenty-four hours before the time agreed upon, I found myself obliged to put four more sitters than was customary into the last day of her visit. In the morning she gave four private sittings; in the afternoon four; and in the evening she held a general circle of twelve people. All these séances were successful. At 10 p.m. one of the party took her to Euston in his motor, and forty-five hours later she began a series of excellent séances in Glasgow.

Mrs. Wriedt is controlled by Dr. John Sharp, who was born in Glasgow in the eighteenth century, lived all his life in the United States as an apothecary farmer, and died in Evansville, Indiana. He states that he was taken over to America by his parents when he was two months old. I have never known him say an unkind word, nor express any feeling but benevolence and desire to assist all who seek the help of his medium. He frequently straightens out obscure messages, and invariably endeavours to manage the sittings to the best advantage of those present. Very often he talks what, in a mortal, I should call nonsense; but I think he is limited in expression – in some curious way – by the absence of any sort of culture in his medium.

John King (Sir Henry Morgan), the control of Cecil Husk, the blind medium, frequently managed Mrs. Wriedt's séances in England. It was explained that he was better acquainted with English people than Dr. Sharp, who, however, was always in the background. He only put in a word or two at Rothesay.

Grayfeather, a North American Indian medicine chief when in life, the control of J. B. Jonson, the materialisation medium of Toledo, Ohio, U.S.A., visited me several times at Cambridge House, and often came to the circles; he seldom manifested when I was absent. He did not come to Rothesay at all.

Mimi and Blossom were casual visitors. The former we know nothing about. Blossom states that in life she belonged to the Seminole tribe of Indians, who lived in the Everglades, South Florida, and that she died as a child. It is as a noisy fractious, but extremely witty child that she now manifests. Her talk, engaging manner, and lively

repartee always created a diversion, causing much laughter, which benefited conditions.

Now and then Dr. Sharp, John King, Grayfeather, and Blossom all manifested at the same circle.

When there was not sufficient power, or the proper sort of power, present for the more refined manifestation of the direct voice the controls resorted to the exhibition of the coarser physical phenomena of telekinesis, moving a table with a vase of flowers upon it, throwing trumpets about, and so forth. Occasionally these things occurred at the best of séances when the direct voices were also abundant.

There were many blank séances in both years, and also some very poor ones. This is only what reasonable investigators expect in the presence of all powerful mediums; it is as provoking to the psychic as to the sitters, and some people, of whom I am one, consider it evidence of the genuineness of the proceedings.

In 1913 a curious fact was observed. I spent thirteen or fourteen days at Cambridge House, and in the garden, from 10 a.m. to 4 or 5 p.m. On these days there were no blanks, and only two or three indifferent sittings. I am not conscious of my mind being occupied in the slightest degree with what was going on in the séance-room, nor have I any pretensions to the possession of psychic powers. But it has occurred to Miss Harper, the hostess, and to me, that it is possible that my absolute conviction, after over a hundred experiments, of the genuineness of Mrs. Wriedt's extraordinary gift may have, in some occult manner, found its way into the séance-room and assisted the controls. I make no assertion, but throw this speculation out to my readers as one worth consideration.

That W.T. Stead was at the back of us, and gave us his assistance, I have no doubt whatever. In 1912 Mrs. Wriedt arrived on the evening of May 5, twenty days after his death. After her supper she proposed a séance. Stead manifested, and gave three admirable tests of his identity – two to Mr. Harper, and one to me; he also directly instructed us where his daughter was to sit on the following evening. The test he gave to me was unmistakable; he alluded to the conversation we had at bank buildings the last time I saw him. This conversation had lasted half an hour, and ranged over a variety of subjects; but the chief topic was the approaching visit of Mrs. Wriedt to his house. He desired that certain conditions should be observed, and it was to one of these that his spirit referred, with emphasis, on this evening. (See Light, May 18, 1912, page 239.)

The spirit called Iola in these pages is that of a lady who passed over forty years ago in the prime of her life. She was a near and dear relation of my own, and has proved herself to be so closely in touch with me that I am justified in calling her my "guide."

PART 1

RECORDS OF 1912

TWO SÉANCES WITH MRS. WRIEDT
MR. W. T. STEAD MATERIALISESS

By M. Chedo Miyatovich

After some hesitation, from personal reasons, I have arrived at the conclusion that it is my duty to the undying memory of my dear friend, William T. Stead, and my duty to a great cause, to address this letter to you for *publicat*ion in Light.

By profession I am a diplomatist, having had the honour to represent my country (Servia) at the court of the King of Roumania, at the sublime porte of the Sultan of Turkey, and three times at the court of Queen Victoria, and once at the court of King Edward VII, besides having been entrusted by my Government with several important diplomatic missions and representations at international conferences. I am a member of several learned societies on the Continent, and an honorary member of the Royal Historical Society in London. I mention these personal facts to claim from your readers the credit that I am a man accustomed to weigh the facts and my own words in full consciousness of my responsibility. I ought to add that for many years I have been interested in the scientific study of occult phenomena, but was not yet a convinced Spiritist.

Having heard that at Mr. W.T. Stead's house at Wimbledon the remarkable American medium, Mrs. Wriedt, with whom Vice-Admiral Moore experimented, was staying, I asked that lady for permission to pay her my respects, and eventually to have a séance with her. She gave me an appointment for Thursday, May 16, at 10.30 in the morning. I went there accompanied by my friend, Mr. H. Hinkovitch, doctor of law and a distinguished barrister at Agram (Croatia), who had just arrived in London.

Mrs. Wriedt took us to Julia's Bureau, and told us that she is what is called a voicing medium, but that under good conditions the materialised spirits may also show themselves. She asked us to examine the cabinet and the room if we liked. As I have been on a previous occasion in that room, and examined the cabinet with several German Doctors, I did not think it necessary to do that on this occasion.

I and Dr. Hinkovitch took seats near each other in the centre of the room, facing the cabinet. Mrs. Wriedt did not enter the cabinet, but sat all the time on a chair near me. She placed a tin speaking-tube (megalophon) in front of my friend. She started an automatic musical clock and put all the lights out, so that we sat in perfect darkness.

When a beautiful melody of a somewhat sacred character was finished by the clock, Mrs. Wriedt said to us that the conditions were very good, and that we should be able not only to hear, but also to see some spirits. "Yes," she continued, "here is the spirit of a young woman. She nods to you, Mr. Miyatovich; do you not see her?" I did not see her, but my friend saw a piece of oblong and illuminated fog. "she whispers to me," continued Mrs. Wriedt, "that her name is Mayell – Adela or Ada Mayell," I was astounded. Only three weeks ago died Miss Ada Mayell, a very dear friend of mine to whom I was deeply attached. But in that moment there was no other manifestation of her. She disappeared without saying anything more except her name.

Next moment a light appeared from behind the medium, and moved from the left to the right of the cabinet, as if carried slowly by a soft breeze. There, in that slowly moving light, was not the spirit but the very person of my friend William T. Stead, not wrapped in white wrappers, as I have seen spirits at other séances, but in his usual walking costume! We both, I and Mrs. Wriedt, exclaimed loudly from joy. My friend Hinkovitch, who only knew M r. Stead from photos, said: "Yes, that is Mr. Stead!"

Mr. Stead's spirit nodded to me in a friendly manner and disappeared. Half a minute later he appeared again and stood opposite me (but somewhat higher above the floor), looking at me and bowing to me. And a little later he appeared again, for the third time, seen by us all three still more clearly than before. After his third disappearance I felt that the speaking-tube was moved towards my face, and then we all three heard distinctly these words:

"Yes, I am Stead—William T. Stead! And, my dear friend Miyatovich, I am so pleased you came here. I myself came here expressly to give you a fresh proof that there is life after death, and that Spiritism is true. I tried to persuade you of that while here, but you always hesitated to accept that truth."

There I interrupted him by saying: "But you know I always believed what you said to me!" "Yes" he continued, "you believed because I was telling you something about it, but now I come here to bring you proof of what I was telling you—that you should not only *believe*, but know [pronouncing that word with great emphasis], that there is really a life after death, and that Spiritism is true! Now, goodbye my friend! Yes, here is Adela Mayell, who wishes to speak to you!"

Stead never knew Miss Ada Mayell in his life, nor had he ever heard her name before. She then spoke to me in her affectionate and generous manner, trying to reassure me on certain questions which have sadly preoccupied my mind since her death, and telling me that she is happy now. There is no need to report here all she said to me. Mrs. Wriedt and Mr. Hinkovitch heard every word she said.

Then, to my own and my Croatian friend's astonishment, a loud voice began to talk to him in the Croatian language. It was an old friend, a physician by profession, who died suddenly from heart disease. My friend Hinkovitch could not identify who that might have been, but they continued for some time the conversation in their native tongue, of which, naturally, I heard and understood every word. Mrs. Wriedt, for the first time in her life, heard how the Croatian language sounds.

Mr. Hinkovitch accidentally overturned the speaking tube, and although he tried to replace it in the original position, and thought he had succeeded in doing so, the talking manifestations were not continued. When the light was turned on, Mrs. Wriedt found that the speaking tube was not placed properly, and that circumstance, according to her, explained the cessation of further manifestations.

I and my Croatian friend were deeply impressed by what we witnessed on that day, May 16, between 11 and 12 o'clock at noon. I spoke of it to many of my friends as the most wonderful experience of my life. I spoke of it to the most scientific woman of Germany, Frau Professor Margarette Selenka, Who had just returned from Tenerife, where she was establishing a station for scientific observation of apes. Mme. Selenka came to London to hear all the *details* of the Titanic catastrophe, in which her great friend W.T. Stead had perished. We arranged to have a private séance with Mrs. Wriedt on Friday, May 24, at one o'clock. That séance was held in Julia's Bureau, but excepting for a voice shouted once, "Sit quiet in the chair!" no other manifestation took place. By arrangement with Mrs. Wriedt, I and Mme. Selenka returned in the evening, and at eight o'clock we had a séance, at which, besides me and Mme. Selenka, Mrs. And Miss Harper and a very charming lady, whose name I did not ascertain, were present. After a short time from the beginning of the séance we all saw Mr. Stead appear, but hardly for more than ten seconds. He disappeared, to reappear again somewhat more distinctly, but not so clearly as he appeared to me on May 16. That was the only materialisation phenomenon of that evening, but as compensation we had wonderful and various voicing manifestations. Mr. Stead had a long conversation with Mme. Selenka and a short one with me, reminding me of an incident which, two years ago, took place in his office at Mowbray House. Then, again, Miss Ada Mayell spoke to me, telling me, among other things, that she knew that her sisters and her niece wrote to me, as she wished them to do. After her my own mother came and spoke to me in our own Servian language most affectionately. Mme. Selenka had a very affecting conversation with her husband, Professor Lorentz Selenka, of the Munich University, and also with her own mother, who died last year in Hamburg; both these conversations were carried on in German. A friend of Mme. Selenka came singing a German song, and asked her to join him, as they used to sing together in old times, and Mme. Selenka did join him singing. Then we had an Irishman, once a naval officer, who had a long, cheerful and. Indeed, quite a sparkling talk with the charming lady, whose name I unfortunately do not know, but with whom the brilliant Irishman seemed to be everlastingly in love. Naturally, although I heard clearly all the conversations in German and in English, I am not justified in reporting them here. Not even the long statement which Julia made concerning certain suggestions to keep the Cambridge House as a centre for psychic research in memory of Stead, can I properly reproduce here. All I wish to state publicly is that I am deeply grateful to the wonderful gift of Mrs. Wriedt for having enabled me to obtain from my unforgettable friend, William T. Stead, a convincing proof that there is a life after death, and that Spiritism is true, and for having given me almost a heavenly joy in hearing the affectionate words of my dear mother in our own tongue, and in getting another and sacred proof of the continuance of the living individuality of one of the most charming, most selfless, and generous women whom I have ever known so far in my life.

Royal Societies Club,
St. James's S.W.
By Vice Admiral W. Usborne Moore

The versatile genius of W. T. Stead was never directed to a better object nor one more worthy of the highest admiration than when he instituted "Julia's Bureau." No mortal has ever schemed out a saner or more altruistic plan. He claimed to be guided from the next state of consciousness, and I believe he was, and by his friend in spirit-life, Julia Aimes. The general idea was that men and women who wished to come into touch with their relatives who had passed the change called death were to come to him, register their names, and to be *taken to* mediums incognito, who would probably be able to put them in touch with those from whom they wished to hear. Free of cost, these visitors received more or less consolation, and enjoyed the use of Mr. Stead's psychic library.

As far as money went Stead was "Julia's bureau," and Julia's Bureau was Stead. It was a very costly experiment. Except for certain insignificant contributions which he received, the whole of the expenses were borne by the founder alone. He dropped some thousands of pounds over this beneficent project.

It was a noble scheme, and it was successful. Many a sorrowing man and woman found peace and comfort through the agency of the bureau; but, like all one man undertakings, it was bound to fail when its originator passed over. On July 4, 1912, the Bureau ceased its labours. If a philanthropist comes forward with a thousand a year to spend upon it, the useful work may still flourish in different hands. Unfortunately, on this plane we can do nothing without cash, and I see no prospect of either the man or the money being found.

Mr. Stead had a custom of holding a weekly religious service at his country house with a small circle of friends, one of whom was a medium; it was followed by a séance. Julia generally manifested in some way or another. But these Wednesday evening meetings did not constitute in themselves the "Bureau," though pleasing to the few who joined in them. They were merely incidents in a far larger and more comprehensive plan of benefit to the general public. These little gatherings may still be continued, but the grand work of obtaining consolation for those who need it has ceased to exist, and there is little chance of its being revived.

Early in 1911 Stead wrote to me in America asking whom I could recommend as a suitable psychic for "Julia's Bureau." I knew exactly what he required, and named Mrs. Wriedt, of Detroit, who, in fact is the very person of all others whose gift is most active and conspicuous for the purpose he desired to achieve. She came to England at his invitation, and, through her mediumship, much good was done during the two and a half months she was able to remain. She was again invited this year, and agreed to come for two months and to return with Mr. Stead. On the morning of Monday, April 15, she heard the ghastly intelligence *of the* loss of the Titanic, and hurried down to New York to stop with kind friends in 61st Street. At this time, and, indeed, until Wednesday, the 17th, the extent of the catastrophe was not known. Rumours and false Marconigrams were flying about all over the place; it was not till the 17th that it was accepted in New York that the majority of the crew and passengers had perished. The following letter was received by me by the next return voyage of the Mauretania, from Mrs. Wridet's host; date, New York, April 23, 1912:-

Mrs. Wriedt came in from Detroit Tuesday morning, 16th, and was to return with Mr. Stead for London. The sad end of poor Mr. Stead was a great shock to her, and she was very much discouraged. At a séance on the same night of her arrival Dr. Sharp gave us the full details of the Titanic's encounter with the berg; also assured us of the passing of Mr. Stead, and gave us names of many prominent persons who went down with the ship. The following night, Wednesday, Mr. Stead came (just three days after his passing). He was weak in his articulation, but we quite understood him; his stay was short. The next night, Thursday, Mr. Stead came again; his articulation and personality were much stronger, and he went into details of his passing. The following night, Friday, he came again very strong and clear, again gave us full details of his passing.........He particularly desired that Mrs. Wriedt go over to London to fulfil her engagement, which she is now about doing.

On Friday this gentleman wired to me for instructions, and on Sunday, 21st, I directed that Mrs. Wriedt should come over, and then took charge myself of the financial and other details of her visit. The ladies and gentlemen who had guaranteed Mr. Stead for the expenses of the undertaking, just as I expected, cordially supported my action. The psychic arrived at Wimbledon on Sunday, May 5. Proper arrangements were made for her times of sitting and periods of diversion and rest, and séances were held throughout nine weeks, ending on Friday, July 5.

The results of this visit were, on the whole, satisfactory. More power was exhibited than last year, and much good was achieved; but during June there were many blank séances, owing, in my opinion, to Mrs. Wriedt, against my express wishes, holding sittings for her own friends at times allotted by me for her rest and amusement. I found it was quite impossible to stop these irregular proceedings; any attempt to thwart the determination of the psychic resulted in a painful scene and consequent "bad conditions"; remonstrance's only defeated their own object. My own failures were very few; no more than I ought to expect in any case (the last sitting was the best), but I had my finger on the pulse of Cambridge House all the time, and knew of many disappointments, though not one sitter complained to me. They appeared to appreciate that in all such cases the psychic was as disappointed as they were, also that these blanks afforded good evidence of her entire genuineness. Of the thorough honesty of the proceedings in the séance room no sitter has ever hinted a doubt. As trustee for the guarantors I only regret that many casual visitors enjoyed sittings with Mrs. Wriedt who took no part in bringing her to England or maintaining her while here.

I propose to give an account of some of the séances with this privileged instrument of the higher powers —enough to demonstrate to your readers the value of her unique gift, which is not in the least dimmed and which I hope will continue for many years. I will first give a brief résumé of my own experiences alone with Mrs. Wriedt in the dark.

We were in the habit of sitting at some distance from one another; by leaning forward in our chairs as far as possible and stretching out our right arms to their fullest extent we were just able to clasp hands. I do not remember that we were ever closer than that. When the sitting began we sat upright in our chairs in an easy posture; a trumpet, mouth downwards, on the floor between us; plenty of flowers in bowls and vases on either side of me. Generally within five minutes voices could be heard, and conversation would last for periods of between thirty and fifty minutes. On many occasions there were beautiful spirit lights and etherealisations—i.e., heads and forms brightly illumined, but features not plainly visible. When the room appeared to me pitch dark the phenomena were poor; when, to my partially clairvoyant sight, the room was lighter and psychic clouds could be seen we always had a good sitting.

My guide always appeared as a phantasm, but could not always speak. It was curious to see her move back from me to the psychic or to the flowers to gather strength, and then return. That the forms were not hallucinations of my own was quite clear, for they moved their arms and could be seen crossing and recrossing each other. I soon found that Iola had developed a new power. She could appear to me without being seen by the psychic, and talk to me without trumpet and without a single articulate word being heard by Mrs Wriedt. I could just catch the words, which appeared to emanate from a distance of six inches from my ear; but Mrs. Wriedt heard nothing at all, or only a slight swishing sound. On the other hand, the psychic often saw lights and spirit forms which I was unable to see. All this shows that our friends on the other side can present a dark half and manifest only to those whom they desire shall see them or hear them.

Several of my relatives came to talk to me through the trumpet, but only one or two friends. The chief communicator was Iola, who told me many new truths and evinced the most extraordinary memory for events ranging over a period of from forty to fifty years. She recalled to me circumstances that occurred during my voyages about Australia, showing a familiarity with numerous events that did not take place till four years after her death. These I shall not relate, as they would not interest your readers.

One feature of the conversations with my relatives should be noted. On some twenty occasions they alluded to a lady friend of mine who is in a home for those who are mentally distressed. I trust that the affliction is only of a temporary nature; but, whether temporary or permanent, it is obviously the proper course to separate her from her children for a considerable time. To do otherwise would be to invite a tragedy. The children are at present in the care of their nearest relatives, tenderly cared for and happy in constantly seeing their father, who also visits his wife whenever his professional duties allow of his doing so. No sane man could possibly adopt any other course than that which he has found himself obliged, reluctantly to follow. Yet those on the other side have been endeavouring to influence me to induce the lady's relatives to restore her to her children. Apparently all these spirits can see and feel is divine sympathy with the sufferer; the common-sense precautions which we discern so clearly are nothing to them; anything in the nature of sternness or firmness is abhorrent to their thoughts. To me this is inexplicable, but it is a very useful lesson. We are not intended while on this plane to regulate our lives by advice from people in the next state; they do not know all the circumstances, and have only commiseration and loving kindness for those who are in distress. They, apparently, are incapable of understanding that there are conditions in our sphere where sternness is kindness and true wisdom.

I was surprised that Greyfeather, the old Indian medicine chief, was equally indulgent. The persistence of the latter and my relatives can only be *compared to the* story in David Copperfield of the constant repetition of Charles the First's head in Mr. Dick's Memorial. I asked my relative, A., a psychic, what he thought of all this. He replied: "Well, what do you think would happen if Mrs. —— were to be put in command of a battleship?" It is a fair Analogy. The lady he mentioned is remarkable for her sympathy, selflessness, and spirituality. Most certainly, if she were transferred to the grotesque situation he named, there would be no punishments; crime and offences against discipline would go unchecked; and in three months, at latest, the ship would be in a state of mutiny.

This little experience of mine blows to atoms the overstretched theory that our subliminal self is responsible for the information we receive in many ways through mediums. For every utterance of these spirits on the subject of the restoration of her children to the invalid is opposed to my judgement. I have not the least intention of seriously considering them, nor of obtruding advice on the husband, who is acting in the best interests of his wife and family.

During the time Mrs. Wriedt was our guest, Grayfeather, the control of J. B. Jonson, the materialisation medium at Toledo, Ohio, was a frequent visitor. He only manifested once, so far as I know, when I was not present. I asked him one day; "Grayfeather, will you come to my friends Colonel L. and Major and Mrs. R. next Tuesday at 8 o'clock?" He said: "Are you coming Chief?" I replied: "No" he said: "I only come when you are here. I not come to make laugh, I come to do good." I told him that he was doing good to come to my friends, and he finally replied, "I see." On the Tuesday morning I repeated my request: "I hope you will come to my friends this afternoon, Grayfeather." Again he grunted "I see." That evening Mrs. R. kindly wrote to me an account of her séance in which she said that Grayfeather had manifested, shouting: "Chief Usborne send me: what you want?" He had a friendly talk with the circle, and then departed. During these last two months the old Indian has repeatedly told me that he is treating the invalid lady I mentioned above "in her topknot," and that he has magnetised me several times so that I shall be fit to sit frequently. That I have been magnetised often I do not doubt, for I have sat six times a week for three periods, with gaps between, without any depletion worth mentioning. I only hope he has been equally successful with the patient.

As regards "conditions," the best, of course, were in dry weather and when the sitters were harmonious. Rain always had a depressing effect, and the voices were low in the room. When the conditions were at their best the voices were high, level with or above our heads; when

9

conditions were bad, and the controls found it impossible to draw from the throats of the sitters, the voices failed, and they resorted to the exhibition of coarser physical phenomena. These consisted of movements of a small table and large vases of flowers, flowers taken out of vases and bowls which were given to the sitters, and upsetting of chairs, all done noiselessly.

John King (the Sir Henry Morgan of the past) was active in assisting all phenomena. I think he might be called the "control-in-charge" at Cambridge House. Dr. Sharp (Mrs. Wriedt's own control) came often and talked in a loud, clear voice; his visits were more frequent when those people were present who knew him and had talked with him during the psychic's visit last year.

Before closing my brief record of my séances alone with Mrs. Wriedt I ought to mention two rather curious evidential sittings. A Mrs. H. had a private séance one day which she did not consider satisfactory, because none of her relatives were able to make their identity clear to her, but Iola (whom she neither expected nor desired to see) came to her and sent a significant private message to her sister, who, she asserted, was a friend of Mrs. H. (this last statement was true). On the following morning I had a private sitting. After the visits of some of my relatives a voice was heard, Admiral, I am Mrs. H's nephew." He then gave his Christian and surname correctly, and expressed his great regret that he had not been able to make himself known to his Aunt clearly on the previous day; and requested that I would tell her. An expression was used in the message which sealed his identity beyond doubt. On acquainting the lady I found that it was this relative she had specially hoped would manifest during her sitting. I had known this spirit myself when he was in earth life; he passed over twelve years ago.

It is very rare, indeed, for my guide to manifest in any way to strangers when I am not present. She has only done so three times in England, and four times in America (through another medium). On each of these seven visits there has been a special reason; on four it has been at my own request.

During this visit (1912) I did not sit with Mrs. Wriedt in the light, though many of the guarantors did so. I have done this so often as a scientific experiment that it was, for me, wholly unnecessary. Sittings in the dark are better in every way on account of the extraordinary lights, etherealisations and phantasmal forms; the voices are more numerous and clear.

I will now proceed to give an account of some of the sittings held on Wednesdays, generally known as "Julia's circles."

Mr. Stead's manifestations.

The first appearance of W. T. Stead at Cambridge House, Wimbledon, his country residence when in life, was at 11.30a.m., May 6, when I was sitting in the dark alone with Mrs. Wriedt. This phenomenon has been mentioned in your journal in the issue of May 18, p. 239 [Light, 1912}, and also in Miss Estelle Stead's *article* in the July number of Nash's magazine. On the same evening a meeting of Julia's Circle was organised to welcome Mrs. Wriedt; it was attended by Miss Stead, who has recorded briefly what she saw and heard from her father, in the magazine above mentioned. The first spirit that manifested was Cardinal Newman, who recited a Latin benediction; Dr. Sharp made himself known in a loud, clear voice; Grayfeather followed; then Mr. Stead; he was followed by the son of two of the sitters and by Iola. Finally, Mr. Stead came again.

The séance lasted one hour and a quarter, and was replete with incident. The voice of the Cardinal was heard the instant the lights were put out. At least forty minutes were taken up by Stead talking to his daughter. I could not help hearing every word. It was the most painful and, at the same time, the most realistic, convincing conversation I have ever heard during my investigations. The first time he came it was chiefly to give directions to his daughter as to the disposal of his private papers. Miss Estelle was, naturally, much agitated, and her grief at last reacted upon her father, who uttered a loud shout, "Oh my God!" and dropped the trumpet, which fell to the floor with a crash. The second visit, which was at the end of the séance, was a calmer manifestation; this time the speaker was much assisted by Dr. Sharp, who sometimes interpreted what he wanted to say.

On Wednesday, May 8, the members of Julia's circle met again. This time Mr. Robert King was one of the party, and sat, as he always has done when Mrs. Wriedt has been present, opposite to her at a distance of eight feet. The reason that I am relating in some detail what happened in Julia's circles is because, speaking generally, the sitters were the same every time, and occupied the same places. Psychic history has proved that when this is done the best results are obtained. I have attended these meetings only when Mrs. Wriedt was present, and have never known a blank séance. Some have been better than others, owing, no doubt, to superior atmospheric conditions, and partly to the presence of Mr. Robert King, whose gift has materially assisted in the results obtained through the American medium. All the members of Julia's circle were mediumistic, except three men.

The séance was a very good one. A few seconds after the lights were switched off phenomena commenced, and they lasted without interruption for one hour and forty minutes. At least fifteen different spirits identified themselves to their friends, and there was an unknown entity making comments on what went on from under a chair. For quite an hour a spirit was slapping me, at intervals, on the back with a trumpet (Mr. King described him as a tall, big man); the noise of sawing wood was going on at the end of the room, ten feet outside the circle. About the middle of the séance W. T. Stead came, talking loudly, and insisting upon Julia's sittings going on. He said "Ladies and gentlemen, I beg to propose that these sittings be continued, at any rate as long as Mrs. Wriedt is here. Those in favour hold up their hands. If any money is required I will see to it." (Pause.) "Admiral Moore, you have not held up your hand." (Pitch Dark.) To humour him I then raised my hand; my head was struck twice with a trumpet. The voice continued; "I was hit in this room once in the same way."

(I must here explain that the Julia meetings involved a small extra expense. At the time I did not see how this was to be met, and discouraged the idea. But for three weeks after this séance subscriptions of expectant sitters poured in, and it was evident that there would be no difficulty; the amount finally received amounted to one-fourth more than the sum estimated, and enabled me to give the psychic a substantial gift from the guarantors. As to my friends allusion to being hit on the head the previous year, the story was this. One night Stead came up to his house determined to be very scientific; he directed the two trumpets to be painted near the big end with luminous paint. This was done, and they were stood up in the centre of the circle. The lights were put out, Stead took both Mrs. Wriedt's hands in his, and the séance began. Presently one trumpet was seen to be rising, but, instead of any voice coming from it, it was thrown at his head and hit him a sharp blow. The second trumpet behaved in a similar manner. Stead was mildly indignant, and exclaimed: "This to me! Take those trumpets away and have them washed." When brought back clean and put down in the circle phenomena went on as usual, and there was a satisfactory séance.)

There was a long talk by the spirits about the work of Julia's bureau being carried on as a fitting memorial to Mr. Stead, and all the members of the circle, except myself, joined in a chorus of approval. As it was certain that not one-fiftieth part of the annual sum required could have been raised by those present for the purpose, and the most modest estimate for carrying out such a project is one thousand pounds a year, this seemed to me futile; so little do those in the next state appreciate the material facts of earthly conditions.

The ladies of the party were ejaculating, "Yes, dear chief, it shall be done," and so forth. With all my respect for Mr. Stead I have never regarded him as my "chief," so I sat tight, knowing well that the "Bureau" was quite defunct.

Grayfeather came and made himself known to each sitter; Dr. Sharp, as usual loud, clear, and in his best form. Cardinal Newman manifested, and Iola. An Admiral St. C. came to me and told me he had been present when I was talking to a friend at Southsea, giving the man's name, and recalling some details of the conversation. (They were true) Each member of the circle received some test. Two or three times three spirit voices were speaking at the same moment. The Captain of the Titanic made himself known, and, through Dr. Sharp, assumed full blame for the disaster. Dr. Sharp explained that Mr. Stead could not etherealise that evening. Julia addressed the circle. Miss Estelle was not present on this occasion.

I may mention that Stead's talk on every occasion that he came was characteristic of him. Nobody who heard it and who had enjoyed the privilege of knowing him in life could doubt that he was before us.

Wednesday, May 15. Julia's circle. There was one stranger present, a physician much interested in psychic research. He was well known to the psychic, who asked him to sit next to her. As usual, phenomena began very quickly, and continued throughout the séance with but few gaps. Two spirits came to speak to Dr. ——. One was a lady whom he had attended last year. Dr. Sharp assisted her to make her identity known, and then said: "She wants to ask you a question." A voice asked: "Doctor, did you get your fee?" and went on to indicate that the speaker had been troubled about it.

The Doctor told me afterwards that this was, to him, a remarkable test. Before an operation he had made special arrangements with this poor lady, whose means he knew were very limited, and had agreed to a very reduced fee. After her death, owing to some foolish misunderstanding on the part of one of the executors, his account was disputed, and the payment was delayed for some time; in fact he was actually asked to reduce his minimised charge, which, of course he declined to do. Eventually the sum for which he had originally agreed was sent to him, and apologies tendered. Now, talking to him from the next state, was the lady herself, earnestly inquiring if her debt had been paid. He reassured his visitor, and she departed after a short conversation, apparently relieved.

His other visitor was a foreigner, who asked the Doctor if he would do something for his brother. He made his own identity clear, and there was no ambiguity about the request. Dr. Sharp then intervened, and, addressing the doctor, said: "Don't do it; if people who are born with five senses use only four, you cannot do anything with them." The doctor told me he quite understood the message of the spirit, and that the control's advice was good.

Mr. Stead spoke. He welcomed the doctor to the circle, and greeted me and other members. Iola manifested, and addressed a few words to all. Mrs. Anker's child came to her, talking in the Norwegian tongue; also her father-in-law, whom she had never seen in life. As I sat next to Mrs. Anker, I heard the prattle of the child very distinctly. The cloak of a lady sitting opposite to me, and distant about five feet, was brought from the back of her chair, and thrown over the back of the lady next on my left and over my left arm. Many spirit friends of the sitters spoke during the evening. Two voices, occasionally three, talked simultaneously.

Wednesday, May 22. A minute or two after the lights were switched off the white form of a man appeared in front of me, and was sensed by the lady on my left. Mrs. Wriedt said: "There is someone here of the name of ——." This was the surname of a military man, a friend of mine, who died some five or six years ago after many years of great suffering. I asked him to speak, but he was unable to do so. (He came to me afterwards at one of my private séances, and talked for some little time. There was a decided significance, to me, in his making himself known just at this time.) Cardinal Newman manifested, and gave a Latin benediction. Again Mrs. Anker's child came to her and talked in their own language. Some three or four friends of different sitters came to them, after which Grayfeather talked in loud and lively tones.

Q. (from my neighbour): "Do you build houses the other side, and do you need sleep?" A.: "No; no shutte eye always wake." Q.: Do you get tired?" A.: "No get tired, because me no walke with bones." Q.: "Do you need food?" A.: "Where I put it?"

The Indian told Mrs. Wriedt that her husband in Detroit, Michigan, had slipped on the outer steps leading up to the house and strained his ankle. (A letter received a month later confirmed this.) He also gave good tests to four members of the circle.

On several occasions the spirits sang through the trumpet or joined in when we sang. Iola came to me, but could not speak. She was not seen by the ladies right and left of me. Neither Julia nor Stead manifested. As a Wednesday evening sitting it was inferior.

Wednesday, May 29. Dr. Sharp came first, and greeted all the members of the circle. Mrs. Wriedt complained bitterly that none of her relatives ever came to her. Could not Dr. Sharp bring her father to see her? He was a Welshman, who had many relatives residing in this country. Sharp said, I will tell him what you have said," but made no promise.

William Stead Jr., who passed over several years before his father, came and talked to his sister, who told him that she recognised his voice as the same she had heard last year. I can support Miss Estelle in this statement. There are a few spirit voices, I have noticed, which never alter, and one is young Stead's. I have often talked to him; the voice and manner of talking are always precisely the same. He is an excellent communicator. When in this life he did not believe in Spiritism.

Grayfeather burst in: "Me here! Me heapy much glad to see you" (Trumpet banged on the floor). He then greeted each sitter individually, paying special attention to Miss Estelle, and threw the trumpet out of the circle. Sir Henry Irving manifested for a minute, saying in the same voice I heard last year, "'Tis well, 'tis well," and singing a few bars of a song. He was followed by three spirits, who came to different sitters and were identified. I related to the circle a curious phenomenon I had been shown the previous morning; the trumpet had been twice removed from the floor, and twice, noiselessly, replaced in exactly the same position. The first time this happened Mrs. Wriedt thought that, in sweeping round my hand in the dark, I might have missed it. I knew this to be extremely improbable, because it was standing within six or eight inches of a table, and the small end three inches above it; I had the table as a guide. On the second experiment we clasped hands (which we could just do by both reaching forward to the full extent of our arms), swept towards the table, touched it, lowered our arms one and a half feet, and then swept outwards an arc of about forty degrees. No trumpet! On lighting up, there it was, standing precisely where I had found it after the first experiment. The trumpet is always kept damp inside, and one damp ring only was visible on the floor coinciding exactly with the rim of the mouth of the trumpet, Joined as our arms were, it was absolutely impossible to miss any object within the arc I have mentioned.

A voice, Iola: "Dematerialization is suspension. It was suspended out of reach and sight." Q.: "What do you mean? There was no question of sight, for we were in the dark." Iola: Do you remember that a trumpet has fallen several times from the ceiling?" [Correct. I have seen this phenomenon at least eight times] That is dematerialization; the light was so strong that it fell." [Every time it happened it was at the instant of switching on the lights.] "This is suspension. In our case yesterday morning the trumpet was lifted up; it was not actually dematerialised." Q.: "It was in exactly the same place when the lights were switched on.. Was it simply lifted up out of our reach, or was it dematerialised?" Iola; "Dematerialised."

Dr. Sharp now intervened, and gave an explanation in almost the same words as those used by my guide. I could not make head or tail of it; but I find that I seldom can when spirits try to explain to us how these mysterious physical phenomena are performed. They appear to be unable to explain these wonders in terms that mortals can understand. It was no use pursuing the subject.

A husband and wife were visited by their son, who talked to them for several minutes. The lady on my left got into touch with *young* Brailey, who was drowned in the Titanic; then Mrs. Anker, on my right, was visited by a distinguished Norwegian authoress, who conversed with her for some time in their own language. Mrs. Anker told me that the last time she saw this lady in life was in Rome; she was much attached to her. She added: "I asked her just now if she knew my husband [in spirit life}, and she replied: 'Yes, yes; he is here now!' I wrote of her in Norway after her death." All that I could make out in the talk of the spirit were the words "Ella Anker, Ella Anker," in most affectionate tones.

Mrs. Wriedt: "Things seem to be a little queer in my head. I must go outside." She left the room for a few minutes. I gathered that she had taken on the dying condition of the spirit who had just been talking to my neighbour. On her return, Dr. Sharp gave an address on the developing customs of the fakirs in India, in clear, loud tones that anybody might have heard outside the room. It lasted several minutes, and wound up with, "Remember, friends, this is not for publication.

The control then went on to say that most mortals had not developed their brain cells, and referred to the superior development of distinguished men like Mr. Stead. I tried hard to follow this discourse, but failed, and other sitters were no more fortunate. The enunciation was perfect; but he could not explain his meaning, nor answer questions put to him by the sitters, in such a way that we could find out what he meant. The voice was firm, and loud enough to have been heard down-stairs; he must have talked for thirty minutes in the aggregate. Julia now manifested, and greeted Miss Estelle Stead and all the members of the circle.

I did not attend the séance of Wednesday, June 5. Wednesday June 12. Atmospheric conditions bad. As soon as the lights went out, I saw a white form approaching me. Iola whispered for a second or two, and said: "You have dropped a flower." The lady on my right did not see the form, but the lady on my left sensed a presence and heard the words; she most kindly picked up the flower from the floor that had been brought by the spirit. Dr. Sharp then made himself known, and greeted each sitter by name. Then Grayfeather exclaimed: "Me here! me here! Me heap much glad to come to big chief across pond." That morning the Indian had come to a private circle of mine, and accosted an old lady sitting next to me who was wearing a turquoise brooch, asking her in what month she was born. She replied "February"; and he then said, "Turquoise no good for February." It seemed appropriate, therefore, to ask him this evening what precious stones represented the months of the year. His answers to various questions of the sitters were: March, catseye; September, moonstone: June, topaz: December, turquoise; April, amethyst. We could not make much of it. Then he had quite interesting conversations with the ladies to the right and left of me about their respective occupations; they seemed to think that his knowledge of their affairs was remarkable. All this time a second had been ejaculating remarks from the floor not far from Mr. King, and at rare intervals a third voice intervened.

The voice which we have been accustomed to associate with Sir Henry Irving now spoke: "'Tis well, 'tis well." He could not make us understand what he wished to say. A son of two of the sitters now manifested, and talked with his parents for some minutes. Here William Stead, junr., had a long talk with his sister, and made an appointment to meet her and another brother at a private sitting the following week.

Grayfeather came again to give a prophecy to a sitter about a friend of his who, he declared, would have an accident in a motor-car in a month or two if he did not take care. His description of the gentleman (whom I afterwards met) was excellent. After this I heard a voice close to the floor near my feet. It was clear that the spirit wanted to speak to me; but the words were not distinguishable. Grayfeather said: "You remember, chief, where once you go in your ship to line Islands, the first Island you come to you go ashore to big meeting you meet a tall man with black moustache; he not a black man. When you come back, you find no clapper on bell. You hunt around to find out who did it, and no one tell."

Admiral Moore: "I have a sort of dim remembrance of the tongue of the ship's bell being removed, Grayfeather; but I cannot clearly recollect anything about it. I will ask my brother officers."

Dr. Sharp: "You got off the ship and went to the meeting house, and that was when it was done. This man here [spirit] is the man who did it. He did it for a purpose." Admiral Moore: "It was a very curious voyage." Dr. Sharp: "You had to be very careful, and it's a wonder you ever returned. You had treachery behind and in front of you."

The next day I enquired of a captain in the Navy who had served with me for some years. He laughed and said: "I remember hearing about that having happened when you commanded the Dart, but not when I was with you." I am now making further inquiries. This much is certain: that twenty-nine years ago I did command a ship which made two long and arduous voyages among the remote islands in the Pacific at and near the Equator; that during these voyages I was faced with difficulties of no ordinary kind (not inaptly described by Dr. Sharp); and that I did go to several meeting-houses of the Polynesians. Unfortunately, the first lieutenant of the Dart is dead; but I hope to find out more about it, and, if I am successful, will report in a future letter.

A Voice: "Power up, power done."

Julia now came in and talked briefly to Miss Estelle and the members of the circle in her refined English tones, finishing with "Sweet rest to all, good night."

Wednesday, June 19. The members of Julia's circle assembled in the drawing-room, where they examined a photograph taken that day in the séance room, in the dark, by a lady. The picture is unquestionably of psychic origin. It shows a cabin with door open and apparently broken, a porthole, ropes hanging about, and, in relief against the porthole, a face which is very like W. T. Stead. We then went upstairs to the séance-room. The psychic switched off the lights, and before she had time to regain her chair Dr. Sharp's voice was heard. He greeted the sitters by name, and carried on a conversation in a clear voice with three of them. Other spirits then manifested. One was Wilbur Wright, the airman, who conversed with Mrs. Wriedt for a short time; then Grayfeather, who shouted: "Me here, me here! How do, chief from across big pond? Me heap much glad you got letter." Admiral Moore: "I got a letter from Mr.—— ——[Mrs. Wriedt's host in New York] today."

Grayfeather: "You got your scratchem from little squaw?" [meaning my wife]. Admiral Moore: "Not yet, but I expect to when I get back to-night" [which I did]. The Indian addressed another sitter and left. Then came another Indian spirit a girl, to judge by the voice; we had heard this voice last year. Admiral Moore: "Is that you Mimi? How old are you?" Mimi: "Two hundred years! Miss Scatcherd [addressing the lady on my left], I going to play with your beads." [The lady had some beads about her.] Mimi talked for some minutes very clearly; the voice was close to me, and sometimes above my head.

The spirit of a young man manifested to his parents; he also gave a message to a sitter near to them. A flower from his mothers dress was taken to another sitter. The members of the circle sang, and a voice joined in through a trumpet. Iola then spoke to me, and afterwards greeted the sitters in a little speech. She was instantly followed by Mr. Stead, who spoke rapidly to his daughter upon private matters, and then said, with reference to the narrative of his life, which was to be written by his private secretary: "I want to get right on. I want Edith to write it as I want it." A sitter: "He is in a hurry." W.T. Stead: Did you ever know me take my time over anything?" There was a chorus of "No!" from all present. W. T. Stead: "How are you Admiral?" Admiral Moore: De-lighted to hear you again." A few final words to his daughter followed. Admiral Moore: "Will you tell us about the photograph?" W. T. Stead: "The photograph represents what took place in the Titanic as near as I can give it to you." Admiral Moore: "Is that your cabin door?" W. T. Stead: "yes, and the porthole."

A voice on the floor kept on, at intervals, complaining "his trumpet had been taken away from him."

Another spirit came and talked intelligently to the lady on my left; and a man's hand was put into that of Mrs. Anker. He spoke to her in the Norwegian language. She told me after the séance that it was her husband.

Julia now manifested, as usual, to close the séance, and talked in eu-logistic terms of Mr. Stead. While she was speaking there was a shout, "Stained Glass Julia." This last utterance of Mr. Stead was to me the most striking evidential fact of the séance. He was, in life, surrounded by a knot of women who adored him for his kindly sympathy. When one of them approached him with some complimentary speech he would good-naturedly turn it off by saying "Stained Glass."

When the lights were switched on a vase of lilies from a small table was found in the centre of the circle four feet from where it was seen before the séance commenced. Phenomena had gone on with scarcely a gap for nearly two hours.

Wednesday, July 3. Farewell to Mrs. Wriedt.

Directly the lights were out Dr. Sharp gave a general greeting to the sitters; then a great number of spirit lights, a flash of light in the ceiling of the room, and a partial etherealisation were seen; there was an illuminated head and some white stuff underneath, but the features were not distinguishable. Then a voice, Iola: "That was Mr. Stead." I made an appointment with her for Friday, July 5; she then gave a few words of address to the members of the circle and departed. Many spirits manifested to their friends. The feature of the evening was the clear talk of an Indian girl who called herself "Blossom." She gave tests to at least half of the circle. One sitter was especially insistent that she should spell out the name of the spirit who had just before been trying to make himself known. She made an attempt, but failed, and then said (apparently to someone in the background), "Come here and do your own talking," causing a roar of laughter from us all.

Grayfeather came for a short time, and told me I had received a letter from a friend in America (quite correct; I had received it the day before). W. Stead, junior, spoke for a long time with his sister Estelle. I asked him to give my kindest regards to his father. Hr replied, "He hears you Admiral." Julia manifested last, as is her custom, and gave a farewell address to Mrs. Wriedt; after which Dr. Sharp broke in with thanks to all for their kindness to his medium; the speech of the old control was most effective.

This closes my abridged account of those "Julia circles" which were held in 1912 while Mrs. Wriedt was at Cambridge House. It is very far from being complete. I am not justified in revealing the hundred private details which came out and gave conviction to individual sitters. But it may be sufficient to confirm the reiterated statements of all serious investigators during the last forty years that the best results can only be achieved by the circle being composed of the same people, sitting on the same day of the week at the same time. W. T. Stead rightly valued these weekly meetings; but, as I said before, he only regarded them as pleasant periodical incidents in his magnificent plan of eventually enabling all, young and old, the strong and the weak, rich and poor, to get in touch with those whom they loved and feared they had lost.

Some remarkable physical phenomena occurred on two or three occasions after the Wednesday evening séances, in another room downstairs; but, as I left at once after each séance was over, I am not competent to report them.

The following account, written by Mr. and Mrs. J. Maybank, is a typical "Bureau" case.

Mr. Maybank served under my command in H.M.S. Rambler on the China station as a private of the Royal Marine Light Infantry, 1885-1889. He holds now a responsible civil post. I sat with him at one circle séance and one private séance; his account of these sittings is correct.

I notice one rather important omission in his narrative of his private sitting of Monday, May 20. There was one bright etherealisation. It was a simulacrum of the chaplain of H.M.S. Tamar, 1889, the troopship which brought home the crew of the Rambler, Maybank had often talked with the chaplain on the voyage. I knew him well, not only on board the Tamar, but afterwards up to the time of his death, which occurred three years ago at Southsea. Mr. Maybank writes:—

Having suffered bereavement through the loss of our only child, who passed away on February 24, 1911, from consumption, at the age of nearly twenty-one years, my wife and I were drawn to the help and comfort afforded by Spiritualism at Christmas-time of the same year. We were first made curious by the conversations we had and reading the literature lent us by some old friends, who, themselves pronounced

Spiritualists, had suffered bereavement like ourselves, and had found much consolation in this beautiful doctrine. An advertisement which appeared in Light drew our attention to a publication by Vice-Admiral W. Usborne Moore, called *Glimpses of the Next State*, and as I had been to sea and served on board H.M.S. Rambler, whose Captain was W. Usborne Moore, I thought it not unlikely they were one and the same person. So I determined to write and ask the Admiral if he could assist me in my investigations respecting Spiritualism. I was not greatly surprised to find my surmise was correct, and that the Captain I had served under years ago was the author of the work quoted. His letters were most kind and helpful, and I should like to say here how thankful my wife and I are for the many kindnesses we have experienced since asking advice about Spiritualism, and how much we appreciate what he has been able to accomplish for us. Words do not seem adequate, and expressions fall flat when we remember the amount of consolation that we have obtained through his instrumentality and goodness of heart.

In replying to me, the Admiral sent a copy of *Glimpses of the Next State*, which, by the way, is most interesting and fascinating, with a request that I should lend it to anyone whom it would help, and who could not afford to purchase it, and further stated that in May of this year (1912) Mrs. Wriedt, a famous medium from America, was coming to England to stay at the late W. T. Stead's place at Wimbledon, and I should hear from him again. Further correspondence resulted in the Admiral kindly arranging a series of sittings for us with Mrs. Wriedt at Wimbledon, two private sittings and two in the general circle, and on the invitation of the Admiral I propose to place on record our experiences at these sittings, so that others may be led to know of the consolation and comfort given by Spiritualism.

My wife and I arrived at Cambridge House, Wimbledon, on Thursday, May 16, 1912. As arranged we were met by the Admiral, who was pleased to see us, and made us very welcome and quite at home. After he had given us a few directions relating to the sittings, we were introduced to Mrs. Wriedt, the medium, and in company with six others, all strangers to us, we proceeded to the room where the sittings were to take place. This room was the one that is known as "Julia's Bureau," and is a large room, comfortably furnished and bright, with many flowers——an ideal room for that purpose. On the floor were two aluminium trumpets, through which the spirits were expected to speak.

We sat in a semi-circle, Mrs. Wriedt sitting at one end of the arc, and after taking our seats all light was excluded by heavy curtains over the windows etc. The Lord's prayer was then repeated aloud, and then one verse of that beautiful hymn, "Lead Kindly Light," was sung by all present, and lovely voices from all parts of the room were heard joining in the singing. A voice then pronounced the benediction, individually, in Latin, and we were told it was Cardinal Newman who was speaking. The hymn, "There are angels hovering round," was next sung, and my wife and I were conscious of bright forms floating about the room. These forms were not recognised by us, but we undoubtedly saw them. I propose to omit all that happened which did not directly concern us, and only mention the facts we experienced and can vouch for. We were all sitting quietly and expectantly when Mrs Wriedt exclaimed, "There is someone at the roses!" and a lady next to me said, "I have a rose," and another and another said the same. I then felt a splash of water on my forehead, and immediately after a rose with a long stem dropped into my hand, which I passed to my wife.

Directly after this an uncle and a great uncle and great aunt of my wife came and spoke through one of the trumpets previously mentioned. The conversation that ensued was purely personal and private, and would not be of interest to the general reader, but it left no doubt in my mind that I was actually conversing with those who had departed from this life many tears ago.

Those who have read *Glimpses of the Next State* will remember the Grayfeather who is described there so well. He was the next to manifest. He did not use the trumpet, but spoke direct—first to the Admiral, and then to my wife and me. Iola, who is the Admiral's spirit guide, also came and blessed the circle generally. Next came one singing and whistling as happy as any schoolboy. He sang Annie Laurie in a powerful voice, and then whistled beautifully. When he had finished he spoke to me and said: "Don't you know me. Maybank?" I replied, "No I don't." He repeated the question, and I answered as before. "What!" he exclaimed, "don't you know Tommy Mahone?" I was with you on the Rambler." He then referred to several incidents that happened on the ship when on the China station, and I am certain it was the same Tommy Mahone that I knew on that ship. The Admiral remarked, "Who is that? Do I know him Mr. Maybank?" and I described who he was and mentioned several small items in connection with Mahone that had happened when he was with us on the ship, and I am pleased to say I fully established his identity with the Gallant Admiral.

Our dear boy next had possession of the trumpet and spoke to us, and I want to emphasise this point—immediately he commenced to speak we (his mother and I) recognised his voice. We did not see him, but we knew his dear voice again; it was our loved one returned and speaking to us. He greeted us with, "Hulloa, mum! Hulloa, dad! How are you? I am so pleased you are here tonight through the kindness of Admiral Moore." He then told us he was perfectly sound now, and was very happy, and was with his mother's grandmother. Then, speaking to his mother, he said: "Did you get your rose, mum? I gave it to dad to pass to you."

I should say that before I passed the rose to Mrs. Maybank she was disappointed at not having received one, she not knowing or being able to see that I had already got it. We both distinctly heard our son make the sound of kissing through the trumpet three times, we heard his fingernails in contact with the metal. He promised to return on the following Saturday, when we were to sit at the next circle. This concluded the sitting, and we left deeply impressed, and oh! So thankful for what we had listened to.

On Saturday we met at 7 p.m. in the same room, this being another general circle; those present, with the exception of Mrs. Maybank and me, being entirely different from the sitters on Thursday. Mr. W. T. Stead came and spoke to some in the circle for quite a long time. Then our dear boy Harold came and spoke to us. He said: "Hulloa, mother hulloa father! I am glad you are here." Then followed a short conversation which would not interest anyone other than his parents. Now although not in the least doubting that it was my son speaking to me, it flashed upon me suddenly to put a test question—one that would be absolutely convincing to anyone at that time, and one that I could mention when endeavouring to try and teach the truth about Spiritualism. So I said: "Harold, do you remember poor old Cyril?" He replied: "Of course I do dad; didn't I tease him?" I agreed that he had teased him, when he went on: "And didn't he growl?" And he caused a laugh among the sitters by imitating the noise that a cat would make when angry. It is reasonable to assume that, when the name "Cyril" was mentioned, not one of the people sitting there would suppose it referred to a cat. This, to my mind, was convincing and unique, as under no circumstances whatever could anyone present have possibly known that we had a cat named "Cyril." Mrs. Maybank then spoke to Harold, and said: "You know Harold dear, I have had a letter from Mrs. Sainty today, and she wants to know if you can bring Bernie Sainty to speak to me on Monday next." He said he would try and do this. I then said: "What did he pass over with Harold? Do you know?" He replied: "Of course I do dad; but we never speak about that here." We then asked if he knew we visited the Sainty's, and he said: "Yes, Bernie and I often see you there, and we are glad you are friends." He further said: "You know, his mother does worry so, and it does upset the poor chap." We then inquired if he (Harold) could help us at home to get automatic writing, or some other means whereby we could communicate with him. His reply was that he did not know, as it was all so new and strange to him yet. I asked him if he had met Florrie Allen (another friend of ours), and whether he could bring her, and also my grandmother, on Monday next, when we were to have a private sitting. He then bade us goodbye, saying. "Goodbye; God Bless you"; and again we heard the sound of kissing. Others came and spoke to others in the circle, and then we came away from the second sitting, deeply grateful for what had been sent us.

On the following Monday (May 20) we had a private sitting at 11 a.m., and at our request Admiral Moore sat with us, there being present Mrs. Wriedt, Admiral Moore, my wife and myself. This was, to us, the best sitting we had, being the most convincing and absolutely reliable so far as concerned tests and the giving of proofs of the life beyond.

Grandmother was the first to come, and I plainly saw and recognised her. She spoke through the trumpet, and her voice was strong and quite distinct. She told us both that our boy was with her, and quite happy, and she had grandfather with her too. Harold then came and was clearly visible to Mrs. Maybank and myself, and I must emphasise this—we both distinctly saw and recognised him. He expressed his pleasure at seeing us, and thanked the Admiral for his kindness in affording us this opportunity to come into communication with him. The Admiral, who was delighted, said "Don't mention it Mr. Maybank; this is one of the greatest pleasures of my life that your parents are so successful in this experience."

A voice then suddenly said: "I'm Flossie, I'm Flossie!" and Mrs. Maybank cried: "What, my little sister?" when the voice replied: "Little sister indeed! I'm a woman now." I said: "Do you remember, Flossie, what I said to you when I was going away that Sunday ever so long ago?" She replied: "Yes, you said, 'Goodbye, dear, I'm off to China, and when I return you will be quite well." The Admiral here remarked: "Dear me, this is marvellous, and she was well, Mr. Maybank." I should state here that the Flossie referred to was a sister of Mrs. Maybank who passed away twenty- seven years ago at the age of three years.

She told us how nice it was to have her bonnie nephew with her, and Mrs. Maybank remarked, "I suppose you are looking after him," when the reply came quick and sharp: "No, indeed, he looks after us!" which greatly amused both the Admiral and Mrs. Wriedt.

Mrs. Wriedt then said: "I see a young man standing here with an empty sleeve; he is showing that to me." I inquired if she could describe his hair, when she said: "He has very bushy hair." A voice said: "I'm Bernie Sainty! I'm Bernie Sainty!" Neither Mrs.

Maybank nor I saw him; but he spoke to us, and gave us messages to give to his parents, which messages were of a purely private character. He promised to come again the next day, when we were to have another private sitting. I should explain here that Bernie Sainty was the elder son of the friends mentioned as having first brought Spiritualism to our notice. He had had his right arm amputated for sarcoma, and passed away nearly twelve months before our son. It was simply impossible for either Mrs. Wriedt or the Admiral to know this, which fact speaks for itself when considering the genuineness of these sittings. Grayfeather then came and spoke, greeting Admiral Moore with a cheery "Good morning Chief Moore across the big pond"; then to me "Good Morning Chief Bankies." I replied: "Good morning; are you going to help me in

25

my search for light and truth in Spiritualism?" He answered, "Yes, me help you"; and on my inquiring how he proposed to help me I was requested to keep my eyes open, and I should see. Further conversation ensued between Grayfeather and myself, which proved to me conclusively that he was cognisant of facts which were known to no one else present beside myself, such as points about my daily duties, which at the time I am quoting were hardly known to me, and the knowledge expressed by Grayfeather was simply astounding.

Iola came next, and spoke to the Admiral for a few minutes, and then to Mrs. Maybank and myself. My wife asked if she had brought our boy to us. She replied: "No dear friend; your own presence brought him." After Iola had gone Julia blessed us, and the private sitting concluded, and we had reached another point, and had gained more information about Spiritualism.

Next day, Tuesday, May 21, at 11 a.m., my wife and I and Mrs. Wriedt held our last sitting. Immediately we had taken our seats, our dear son Harold spoke, his voice being much stronger than it had been at either of the previous sittings. After a short conversation of a private nature, Mrs. Maybank asked him if he knew what it was she had tucked in the front of his shirt as he lay in his coffin. He replied, without any hesitation: "Of course I do, mum; it was that piece of gold you gave me." The explanation of this incident, which is quite true, is that about five years ago Harold's mother gave him a small nugget of gold which she had had for some time. He was very pleased with it, and told her he would always keep it, and so would never be without a piece of gold in his purse. He had retained it till he passed away, and as he lay in his coffin his mother took it from his purse and tucked it in the front of his shirt. He now went on to mention things that had happened at home since his passing, such as the framing and hanging of two small pastels, which he had purchased a short while ago, and other matters of a domestic nature which, while being convincing and of deep interest to us personally, would only weary the reader if given in detail.

Bernie Sainty came again, as he had promised, and we all remarked what a strong and beautiful voice he had. He sent loving messages to his parents which were calculated to cheer them up. Mrs. Maybank's grandmother came and spoke to us, touched us both with the trumpet, expressed her delight at our being there, and proved by her knowledge of events in our lives that it was indeed our grandmother who was speaking. Mrs. Maybank's sister Flossie again manifested, sending her love to her mother, who is still in the earth life, and requested us to inform her about these sittings and the possibilities of Spiritualism.

Our dear boy came to us twice more and spoke to us, the conversations being very, very dear and beautiful to us. He especially mentioned that we were not to worry, it was all for the best, and even if he could, he would not like to return to earth life, the life in the spirit world being so lovely, so beautiful, and he was so well and strong, never tired, always happy, and love was so abundant. This concluded our sittings with this remarkable medium, and both my wife and I have had ample proof that our dear boy still lives, that he is often with us, that our happiness is his happiness and our sorrow his sorrow. And now let me say how thankful both Mrs. Maybank and I are for the kindness we experienced at the hands of Mrs. Wriedt. We were total strangers, but we felt from the first moment we were together that here was one whose sole aim in life was to make things brighter and better for her sorrowing brothers and sisters, to console, to cheer, to reason, and, lastly, to convince. May she long be spared to use her wonderful gifts, and so lessen the grief of wounded hearts and brighten the lives of those who mourn over their departed.

LIGHT REPRESENTATIVES AT "JULIA'S BUREAU"

A Good Séance with Mrs. Wriedt.

On June 17 Mr. And Mrs. F. W. South, Mr. And Mrs. Bernard D. Godfrey, and Miss Evans, from the offices of Light and the London Spiritualist Alliance, at the invitation of Vice-Admiral W. Usborne Moore, attended a Séance at "Julia's Bureau," Wimbledon, with Mrs. Etta Wriedt as medium. There were five other sitters present. The sitting was mainly interesting because of the evidential character of the communications which were given to Mr. and Mrs. South. We have received a full report of the Séance, from which we extract the following salient points:—

Twelve persons, including Mrs. Wriedt, were present. After Dr. John (Mr. Percy Street's healing control) and John King had spoken in loud, clear voices, Mrs. Wriedt said: "Would anyone recognise the name of Priest? He seems to go near Mr. South,"

Mr. South: "I used to know a man named Priest."

Mrs. Wriedt: "I see something in his hand, and it looks like tools. They are very small things; and I see small articles that he is putting on a counter or table, and he is picking them up."

Mr. South: "Yes, he was the overseer *of the* composing department at the firm that printed Light years ago."

After some more talk, a voice said, "George—South."

Mr. South: "Yes I know you. I am glad to meet you."

Voice: "We have never had an opportunity like this before, and we may never have again, and I want you to know that I am happy to meet you here and have that pleasure."

Mr. South, explaining: "That was my fathers brother, the last one that passed on."

Mrs. Wriedt: "He wanted you to know he was always round you. He wanted to speak to you daily."

A Voice: "I am Mary South"(sound of kisses). Mr. South: "I am glad to hear of you again."

Voice: "How are you? You were very, very fond of me. I am here, dear, and I love you still. I am always watching over you."

Mr. South: "That was my uncle's wife."

A Voice: "What in the world are you doing here? I am William South. I am glad to see you. My God, I was never so surprised in my life as when I heard George talking to you. I am glad to meet you and yours. Thank God I have got my wish."

Mr. South: "That is remarkable. William is the brother of George, and Mary is William's wife."

John King's voice: "That is the way to do it—talk to them when you can."

Mr. South: "George and William were my father's brothers, and Mary South was like a mother to me. It was a correct loud voice of William, and 'My God' was a characteristic expression."

Mrs. Wriedt: "You have a strong mediumistic power round you."

Mr. South: "They are just the people who would be watching round me, but of whom I was not thinking; and no one in the room even knew their names, or that I had such relatives."

Mrs. Wriedt: "There is a lady standing by you, Mrs. T., and her name is Alice. She died of consumption."

Mrs. South: "I think it must be for me."

Voice: "Yes, I have been waiting all night to talk to you. I was by that lady drawing power from her."

Some other personal conversation followed between Mrs. South and Alice, who was her sister.

After some further conversation with other sitters, the trumpet dropped. Then john King's voice was heard again saying:—

"You cannot go away and say it is mind reading. When you meet people in your neighbourhood they will say it is mind-reading, but we want to give all the good folks that loved you when you were little the opportunity to say, how do you do? The people that died today are liable to come any time. God bless you. We want those who nursed you when you were little to come to you. I had a mother and an aunt, and a whole lot of people, when I was Governor. My name is really Henry Morgan. I was Governor of Jamaica."

More conversation with other sitters. Then Julia's voice was heard. She said:—

"Dear friends,—It is a very great pleasure to meet you all on this occasion. I love to be with you. I love to see you with your spiritual friends when you meet those you love and those who love you. I want this Bureau to be a lasting remembrance of dear Mr. Stead. Mr. Stead's best wishes to all from Light Office and this company. He is perfectly satisfied with his transformation, and he will meet you in the sweet Creator's office face to face as he met you here. May the good be with you always in all your works; may it travel with you. Good night."

As the circle ended, and the light was turned on, the trumpet fell from the ceiling.

I will now give a few instances of good evidence obtained by my friends who attended circles and private sittings at Cambridge House.

The following account is written by a clergymen of the Established Church:—

(1) May 30, 1912, at 7 p.m., general circle. Accompanied by my daughter. First voice, Mr. W. T. Stead. Addressed us all collectively, and my daughter and me, as well as others present, by name, with words of welcome "to 'Julia's Bureau.'" His manner was that of a host to his guests. I said how greatly he and his work in this world were missed, and asked him to tell me how he was occupied now. He replied emphatically and abruptly, "Why, talking to you." He said no more than how glad he was to see us all, etc.

Voices came for many in the circle, but I have only specially noted those that were meant for my daughter and myself. There were persons whom I had not given a thought to previously; whereas those I had tried to "will" to come, and thought of intensely with that object, did not come at all.

A name was given for me, which I recognised as that of a lady recently passed over at an advanced age, and by whose decease I had received a small legacy. The voice was so feeble that we could gather only a little of what she said, a great deal being inaudible. It was to the effect that she had known many members of my family(correct), but that I was the only one to whom she could now gain access. My daughter asked, "Do you know me?"

Answer: "Why should I not?" Here John King interposed in his deep voice: "This poor soul has come to you as the only one of the family that she knew of to come to."

The next voice that came to me announced itself as my "uncle." I asked: "Which uncle?" Answer: "Your mother's brother." (I have had uncles on each side—all now passed over.)

Question: "Which?"

Answer: "Edward." (correct.)

Question: "Where did you and I first meet?"

Answer: "At the gate."

Question: "What gate?"

Answer: "Why, of the cottage—the cottage covered with roses." (I could only think of the lodge belonging to his house.) I failed to elicit more on this point. Then my daughter asked: "What cottage?"

Answer: "You know nothing about it, child; I am talking to your father." Here, and throughout, the manner was very characteristic, and especially the laugh which he constantly gave. I then asked, "Do you remember the violets?"

Answer: "Oh yes."

Question: "What used you to do with them?"

Answer: "Why we tied them up in bundles and sent them away." (Correct. He used to cultivate them for sale in London.) I then asked if he remembered his dogs.

Answer: "Yes—a short, wire-haired terrier called——" (name inaudible); and he added: "Do you remember Jack?" (This not verified.) I asked him what he was doing now. Answer, "I see: you want to know about my experiences." I got nothing more: he had departed.

A clergyman sitting next to me had several voices, none of which he could identify, although specific indications were given him. I suggested to him, in one case, that he should ask test questions, as I observed he always kept silent. The voice then speaking remarked here: "He [i.e., myself] knows more about Spiritualism than you do."

At this séance I was greatly impressed by the voices which came to a Dutch lady in the circle, and conversed with her fluently in that language, these being her husband, "Frederick," an "Uncle Pat," and her child, "Yvonne" names all correctly given. The child's prattle especially was most fascinating, and was interspersed with sounds of kissing. There was no doubt whatever about the genuineness of the language; spoken also, I should say, as only a native could, although the language itself, being unknown to me, I did not understand what was actually said. Duration of séance, two and a quarter hours.

May 31, 1912, at 3.30 p.m., private sitting. Present; Wife, self, and medium (only). First of all, under the red light, Mrs. Wriedt asked my wife to hold the trumpet to her ear. As she did so she heard continuous taps, and a whispering sound as if a voice struggling to speak: Mrs. W. and I hearing nothing. After total darkness a voice came for my wife especially, which we recognised under the name of an acquaintance between whose daughter and a member of our family there had been a friendship which had fallen off since the marriage of the former. The voice said that he could not understand this cessation of intercourse. We said it had naturally come about by absence through marriage. He replied he was not satisfied, that this should not have made the difference. Here John King interposed, to say that our acquaintance had "worried" considerably about this estrangement, as it seemed to be, and that he would be relieved to be sure that it meant nothing in particular. (I regard this incident, for certain reasons, as a good test.)

The next name given was also for my wife especially, and was that of a former parishioner, of whose family we had nearly lost sight since our disconnection with the parish in question. This lady spoke to my wife of the latter's kindness to her when ill, in bringing her fruit, etc. (all correct), and of my own visits to her. She added: "But you are greatly changed now." My wife replied she was so much older: but the voice did not seem to mean it in this sense; hoped my wife would come to see her again when on the other side: ended by saying: "I want to tell you that I could not make Mr.——[myself] and your daughter understand that we came to them last night." (we had no recollection of the name being then given} The husband of the preceding then came; and, in allusion to the independence of his still living daughters, remarked how little one is missed on earth after once leaving it. As a test I asked: "Do you remember the name of the vicar I was working with?" The name came at once: "Vicar——"; and I could not have had a better proof of identity than this.

The next voice was one who was announced to my wife by John King as her mother- in-law. She began by saying: "You have never seen me" (my mother died when I was three years old); "But I know you, and love you, and admire all your endeavours." My wife said: "We have your picture at home—one with long curls" (the then fashionable side ringlets). She replied: "I have those curls still." She then spoke of "the sweetness" of her grandchild, but confused the number of our children. After saying goodbye to my wife, she sent many kisses through the trumpet towards myself. My uncle of the previous evening then came, and said he wanted to give my wife "some Violets," and expressed his particular fondness for her. He said to me "Do you know how fond I am of her?" I replied: "I know you were." He repeated: "Do you know how fond I am of her—now?" emphasising the last word. Then he asked me: "Do you know about my son—how well he is doing?" I asked which son (there are two); and he at once gave the correct name, "Ted." I then asked: "What did he do last week?" and he replied at once with his characteristic, hearty laugh: "Got married at last!" (He was, in fact married on the previous Saturday, having long been regarded as a confirmed bachelor.) An interval of laughter. Question (by me): "Were you pleased?" Answer: "Very much." Question: "Is she a nice girl—a suitable match?" Answer: "Yes a beautiful young woman—will make a nice wife." My wife remarked: "You were always so kind to us." Answer: "Not half kind enough." I then pressed him about "The cottage" he mentioned on the previous evening. He replied "It is the cottage by the sea, where you live." Question: "Where is that?" Answer "Southsea." (This did not accord with his previous statement, "the cottage covered with roses"; nor had he ever seen us at Southsea.) After laying a hand on my head he departed. The séance ended by Mrs. Wriedt, "as a test for what might follow," holding one of my hands in both of hers; when, almost immediately, a wet leaf fell upon my imprisoned hand. Then my forehead was stroked by what felt like a similar leaf. I at once put up my free hand to take it, but found nothing. The same thing happened a second time. An object like a wet branch then fell on our clasped hands; I exclaimed that it was a "branch," and John King then uttered some quotation about lilies, which I forget. "They have all gone," he then said: and the light being turned up revealed a stalk of fine Madonna lilies. They, and the leaves, had evidently been taken from the vases standing near-by on two tables. The séance had lasted forty minutes.

The conclusion I have come to from my own experience of the Wriedt séances is that the nature of many of the communications made, and

the various foreign languages spoken, through the trumpet, afford ir-
refragable proof of genuineness. Neither by fraud, nor telepathy, nor
illusion can these be accounted for; Spirit agency is, therefore, the only
remaining explanation.

July 31, 1912 (Signed)   C. B.

The next narrative is written by Colonel E. R Johnson, a personal
friend of six or seven years' standing. He is a careful and accurate observer, interested in several branches of science, and a good draftsman.
His account may be accepted as trustworthy:—

During May, June, and July, 1912. I attended seven séances with Mrs.
Wriedt as medium. Five of these were private séances, only the medium and myself being present. The other two were circle sittings with
about ten people present.

The first séance, a private one, was in full daylight. The second, also
private, was held in the red light of two shaded electric lamps, and the
other five, including the two public séances, were in absolute darkness.
As far as I was personally aware there were no lights seen, or other appearances of an abnormal kind, at any of the séances. I have kept no
record of the number of speakers at the two public sittings, but they
were very numerous. Many of the sitters were addressed by their own
friends and relations, and I could not hear a good deal of the conversations that went on when I was not addressed, but the speakers and
sitters seemed to mutually (in most cases) understand each other. Besides these there were a few voices which addressed the sitters generally; most of these being at once recognised by the medium and some
of the others. They seemed to be perfectly at home and sang. Occasionally joked, and were often more or less amusing. One appeared to be
a kind of stage manager who arranged the séances and the sequence
of the speakers. This entity that I have called the "stage manager" was
the only one, besides friends and relatives, who spoke at the private
séances, and then he generally, but not always, said a few words at the
beginning or joined in the discussion.

At the five private séances I was only addressed by one voice that I
could not hear sufficiently well to identify him or her. This was the first
voice heard at the daylight séance. All the others were identified with
certainty. They consisted of seven relatives, some of whom spoke only
once, others on three or four occasions. Several times the individual

conversations must have lasted from twenty minutes to half an hour, and related to incidents and events which could not have been known to the medium, and in some cases to anybody now living except myself. References were made to objects that have disappeared for twenty or thirty years, which were accurately described, and, on the other hand, to conversations and events which took place between the séances.

Besides relatives, I was spoken to by seven personal friends and acquaintances, and three of these asked me to carry messages to living people. In one case an incident was referred to which was entirely unknown to me, but which I afterwards ascertained to be quite correct. I was also barked at by three of my dogs which had died more than twenty years ago, their barks being suited in tone and power to their respective sizes and breeds. This part of the séance did not convince me in the same way that the human voices did. Their barks appeared to be stagey and "to order." I do not mean to infer that there was any deception or trickery on the part of the psychic, for she seemed even more surprised than I was, and continually made observations and exclamations as this was going on, and her voice was heard at the same time as the barking of the dogs, and it was both in distance and direction from me evidently from a different place; the dogs being a little to my left and close by, while she sat at some distance to my right.

The physical phenomena, if we may so call them, for, after all, sounds or vibrations of the air are physical too, were the giving of flowers to several of the sitters (I myself was not so honoured), the placing of a small table with a bowl of roses on it into the circle and presumably over the heads of the sitters (the flowers and table having been taken from another part of the room), the sprinkling of water and the touching of the hands and faces of the sitters. In one case a small lapdog, formerly belonging to me, which had died about thirty years ago, was placed on my knee. I was not conscious of its removal, for the weight and pressure of its body, which was quite distinct at first, gradually seemed to disappear.

At one public séance an entity with a little girl's voice talked for nearly half an hour. She identified quite accurately various objects such as brooches, jewellery, miniatures, the number of coins in a pocket, etc. She foretold the route which a sitter would have to take to reach his home—he said quite correctly—and in my case said I should go to a funeral within a week. This was also quite accurate. The funeral was that of a distinguished military officer who died two days after the séance, and whose funeral I witnessed six days after the séance.

I believe I am not a particularly credulous person. In fact, I was taunted by the "Stage manager" for the long period I had been a doubter, and was asked in a somewhat sarcastic tone if I was now satisfied as to the reality of the phenomena. I may say that I had no reason at any time during these séances to doubt their genuine character; and to suppose that the psychic or any combination of persons could have manufactured the phenomena by trickery of any kind appears to me absolutely impossible.

I cannot give many occurrences referring to personal or family matters without long and tedious explanation; but the following may be of interest:—

I was conversing with a friend, late an officer of the Royal Engineers, who, according to many people, and probably to most of his friends and relations, would be regarded as dead some thirty years; and I asked after a mutual friend, a distinguished Indian civilian, who died a little over a year ago, and said I supposed the latter "was working as hard as ever." In reply I was told "No; he is amusing himself with his horses." This rather astonished me, for I knew he was by no means a horsey man. I called on his widow a few hours later in the day. She at once knew what was meant, and told me that, when alive, he visited his horses, spent some time with them, and fed them daily. I was quite unaware of this habit of his, though I knew him and his family fairly intimately.

The Royal Engineer officer above referred to died from an accident in India. I had heard how the accident was caused, but purposely did not mention it, and asked him "how it happened." He said "It was entirely due to my own carelessness." This was said with such marked emphasis and in such a loud tone that I was somewhat surprised, for at the time I saw no particular reason for the forcible manner. The explanation came when the next speaker, who had evidently been an unseen hearer of the previous conversation, introduced himself for the first time. Though in quite an indirect and entirely innocent way, the latter might have felt in some slight degree responsible for the fatal accident, and the reason for the reply of the engineer officer was at once apparent, for it was evidently intended to spare his friend's feelings.

Another incident. A man who had recently died asked me to convey a message to his widow. This I did at her house the same day as well as I remembered, but I made a slight verbal inaccuracy, which no doubt altered the tenor of the message. Shortly afterwards on my return home I wrote out the details of the séance. At the following séance the man spoke to me again, and said I had not given the message quite correctly, and repeated it. In replying, I went on to relate what the lady had answered; but before I got out the first word or two I was interrupted by his saying, "Oh I know that. I was there when you told her." On looking at my notes on my return home afterwards I found that I had written the correct message, though I had not delivered it perfectly.

The scoffer may say that all this "corroborative detail gives atristic verisimilitude to a bold and unconvincing narrative"; but the most hardened sceptic hearing, with his own ears, unimprovised conversations such as these following each other in rapid succession for a few hours would find it difficult to maintain his original position.

In talking with a number of my relatives and friends who had passed over I noticed that several had a difficulty in remembering names. Christian names seemed to be well known, but surnames were much less easily recalled, though they were at once recognised when mentioned. The names of the three dogs were forgotten, to my surprise; and their colour, sizes, and other characteristics had to be described; but this was done so accurately and instantaneously that there was not the least doubt as to their identity. I cannot give a good explanation for this rather curious phenomenon. It may possibly have been due to the tired and overworked condition of the medium. It has also occurred to me that our friends on the other side may think more than we do in visualised ideographs and less in actual words, but the material at my command is not sufficiently large for anything more than these suggestions.

VARIED PHENOMENA AT MRS. WRIEDT'S SEANCES

Possibly my experiences at the séances of Mrs. Wriedt may comfort some who are bereaved, and may help those who are "almost persuaded."

I have had the privilege of sitting in Julia's circle for nearly three years at Mr. Stead's Wimbledon house, and have never missed a service save through illness. I sat next to Mr. Stead at supper two or three weeks before his fatal journey, and heard him say that when he came back from the other side he would shake the floor and walls and stamp round the room. I was also present at supper on May 29, when the room was shaken as though by an earthquake. I had to take hold of the table as my chair rocked. I heard heavy steps round the room, and saw Mr. Steads chair moving alone. (See Miss Scaterd's account in Light of August 3.) I was present at the séance on May 6, and saw Mr.

Stead's etherealisation, and heard his conversation with his daughter. My place at the séance was always between Mr. Robert King and my husband, and about eight feet from the medium.

After the preliminary service Mrs. Wriedt turned out the light. Immediately a hand would touch me, within (I should say) ten seconds. I generally held a hand of those each side of me. The materialised hands were often placed gently on my head, and stayed there for some minutes. My back was to the wall. My hand was often firmly grasped by a hand of warm flesh and blood, which I am convinced was my son's. He passed from this life three years ago aged nineteen. Once I mentally said: "If you are my boy, give three grips." Immediately the hand gave three grips.

Sometimes Mr. King would say: "I see your boy standing by you." I only saw a pillar of faint cloud. Invariably from this light came a hand caressing my face. Once a bunch of pinks was gently unfastened from my waist, and Immediately a sitter opposite said: "I have had some flowers given to me." Afterwards we found they were my pinks. One night, being tired, I stretched my hands above my head. Two hands, coming as it were, from the ceiling, took mine and pulled me upwards till I stood on tiptoe. I felt I should have been lifted, but became agitated, and the hands melted away. I invariably told the circle of these hands, and Mr. King reached up and felt them grasping mine. My husband also felt them. I touched the forefinger of the right hand, and found it roughened, as my boy's often was by attending to his motor bicycle. At one séance a heavy satin coat was rather in my way. It was gently lifted from me, and put on the back of Admiral Moore's chair at the other side of the room. I was sitting on part of this coat. It left me like a cloud, although I had not moved. Sometimes, when the hands were placed on my head, My son's voice would say: "It is I dear." The voice did not come from behind me, where the hands were, but from high in the centre of the room.

A remarkable test is that the hands never groped. They deliberately took my hand, touched my forehead, placed flowers in my hand from the vases eight feet away. I am certain no one moved in the room. Could we do this in darkness? I once mentally asked my boy if Mrs. Ella Anker could not have the hands, and immediately she delightedly exclaimed that a little hand was caressing her. We then heard a child's voice talking to her in Norwegian for some minutes. I also felt a baby's hand pat me. I took hold of it and felt the tiny nails; they were very soft, as a baby's would be. We had been sitting for over an hour, and no child was in the room.

The best results occur when the same sitters meet and take the same places week after week. I was fortunate in being near to Mr. King, as his mediumship helped me greatly. My boys voice—a whisper at first—became stronger and more natural. He spoke to each sitter in turn, and in response to my request told each the colour of his or her aura.

I feel much compassion for those in sorrow, and earnestly wish everyone could have the comfort I have had.

I saw lately in some paper that those who come back are evil spirits. That should be a great comfort to those who say so and believe so, for if evil ones keep their identity, remember even the terms of endearment in their old home life, and give their time to comforting those in sorrow, surely the good spirits should also keep their identity and be allowed to visit their loved ones. We must make no conditions. They tell us their missionary work is terribly difficult. On this earth plane they need a medium. If they ask for a paper or aluminium tube for acoustic purposes, or darkness for the creation of simulacra, we must not imitate the savage chief who demanded a photograph without the use of camera or darkroom.

When I suffered the terrible loss of my only child three years ago I knew nothing of Spiritualism. Mr. Stead has my eternal gratitude. He told me to go patiently forward even for seven years. I am doing so, and have had the most wonderful and convincing proofs. I may say I have read every word of Light these three years.

Physical mediumship is often scorned, but Jesus of Nazareth did not despise it, and thus comforted his disciples.

I can no longer say:— Oh, for the touch of a vanished hand And the sound of a voice that is still. M. M. Kingston-on-Thames.

The following letter was written to my friend Lady Hill, the widow of a late Governor of Newfoundland, who lives at Southsea. It is from a young relative by marriage, who, on hearing that I was collecting narratives of the sittings at Wimbledon, kindly gave me permission to send it to Light for publication:—

My dear Lady Hill,—I know you will be anxious to hear all about the séance. We [i.e., the writer and her mother] were much impressed with our experiences. The first spirit that talked to us was Uncle John, which is a curious fact, as one or two members of mother's family that have attended séances with English mediums have said that Uncle John is always the first to come and speak. He said, "I have come to my sister"; and added that he was so pleased to be able to talk to us. We asked him if he would ask father and Alice to come, and he said he would send them. Later on mother was knocked with the trumpet on her face and knees; then we heard kisses, and a voice saying "I am William." He said to mother [his widow]: "I hope you are well; don't worry." Mother asked him if he was happy, and who was with him. He replied: "Yes, I am quite happy, and we are always together—seven of us." I asked him who were the seven, and he said: "Father and mother, Stevie, Alice, Willie, and the little baby." I said: "Oh yes; Gerald—that was the name of Maudie's little baby she lost." Then father said to mother: "You will come when you can, and thank you for all your tender care of me." Then mother asked him if he ever came to her. He replied: "I am with you every night. Goodbye, dearest." We asked him if he would send Alice, and he answered: "She will come." Presently mother felt three gentle knocks on her shoulder, and the trumpet knocked me on the knees; then a voice, "I am Alice" (and several kisses sounded in the trumpet); "It is nice to be able to talk to you." Mother explained: "Your children are very happy and well, and Vesey has never forgotten you." Alice replied in quite a matter-of-fact way: "I am with them always." I asked: "What message shall I give them?" She said: "Nothing, they would not understand." Then I enquired if she was happy, and what she was doing. She replied: "Yes, quite happy; I am progressing, and am teaching in a kindergarten."

This last answer is very remarkable, as I told one or two people a long time ago, soon after dear Alice passed over, that I woke up one night hearing her talking, and then saw her most vividly in a hat, coat, and skirt, just her old self, smiling. When I have mentioned this to any-one, I have always said: "It was so strange, as she seemed to be talking to a lot of children, which puzzled me." She said one or two more lit-tle things, and then, "Goodbye to all, and to you sweet mother"; then kisses were heard in the trumpet.

There were several other people there who held conversations with spirits; one conversed in German. Mr. Stead had a long conversation with one gentleman present. We saw one or two spirit-forms at the be-ginning of the séance, but not afterwards. Sir Henry Irving, Cardinal Newman, Julia, and Dr. Sharp manifested. The latter controlled the séance; he got angry twice when the sitters were dense and stupid, and raised his voice very loud, which amused me. I did not feel in the least nervous. The only time I was startled was when the trumpet touched me; it was pitch dark......I think that what impressed me most was that everything was so natural.—Yours very affectionately   N.

I have already reported the strange fact that John King, the con-trol of Husk and Williams, took charge of Mrs. Wriedt's séances at

Cambridge House, Dr. Sharp (the psychic's own control) remaining in the background when the circle was composed of sitters who did not personally know him.

My friends Major and Mrs. R., with Colonel L., attended a well-selected general circle in the middle of May, when they were much interested. Among other events, John King came and accosted Mrs. R. as "The Rose," an old joke of his band when she sat with Husk and Williams. At the end of the month this party formed a private circle one afternoon, made up of Mrs. R.'s daughter, a Mrs. F. B. and her son, a Mrs. B., and a Mr. J. In the evening Mrs. R. kindly sent me the following account:—

Dear Admiral Moore,—I am writing to tell you about today's séance, which was most interesting. Grayfeather came strong, and said "Usborne" had sent him, and asked what we wanted. He told Mr. F. B. that a "Frenchie" was there for him, (This "Frenchie," whom he does not know, came one day previously, when he had a private séance with his mother, and told him he was interesting himself greatly in his motor business, and was then "recommended" by his grandfather, who also spoke that day.) Uncle [of John King's band] came after Grayfeather, but only said: "Don't like trumpet." Joey [same band] followed, and remarked that he did not either. (Uncle had told us through the table last week that he would "Try talk trumpet.") John King moved a glass full of flowers and water, and gave it to Mr. J. to pass round the circle. A spirit came to my husband. At first we could not get his name, and he was emphatic in refusing the names we tried to give him. At last he made it quite clear that he was Colonel P., whom my husband knew at his club, and also connected with freemasonry. He passed over about a year ago. He asked my husband to repeat a toast that he used to give at freemason dinners, and which always amused him, saying. "I should like to hear it again." My husband repeated it, when Colonel P. laughed in the trumpet, and exclaimed: "we do not forget the 'Jacks' and 'Johnnies' " (My husband is called "Jack" or "Johnny.") The spirit then repeated a sort of toast in rhyme himself.

An old uncle came next, gave his name, "William," talked to my husband, and said that our son was with us yesterday, but had gone today "On a visit to——" (great attempts to say where; it sounded like "Miss Kes") "to prepare for tomorrow." (My boy has gone to Miss Keyser's officers hospital today to prepare for an operation to his leg tomorrow.) This spirit also picked out my daughter in the circle, and spoke to her; he had passed over years before she was born.

Sister Amy (Craddock's band) sang "Just a song at twilight" alone, when I asked her for her favourite song. Very strong voices joined in "Lead kindly light." Two spirits spoke a long time at the same moment—one a woman, who whispered to Mr. J., another (A South African) trying to make himself known to Colonel L. When we asked for the name of the latter, Grayfeather said: "Oh, it is as long as your arm!"

John King and Julia both spoke very clearly...... We did not get many of our particular friends for more than a moment. Mrs. F. B. and Mrs. B. had no spirit visitors. Altogether, it was a wonderful séance—I think, so far as tests go, the best we have ever attended.—Yours sincerely,   S. R.

REMARKS BY COLONEL L.

Dear Admiral,—Mrs. R. has just read out her letter to Major R. and myself. We think it is a most accurate description, with the exception of Sister Amy's manifestation. When asked by Mr J. about her favourite song, she said, "You sing it," which he did, and then she sang it alone. The voice that joined in when we sang "Lead kindly light," was very like the one we were accustomed to hear at Husk séances (Cardinal Newman's acolyte). The Cardinal himself came and blessed us in Latin, as at Husk's. We were all much pleased and impressed.—Yours Sincerely,   F. P. L.

A few days later the same party had another private sitting. This time Cheiro accompanied them, but neither Mrs. Wriedt nor the ladies of the house knew who the stranger was until after the sitting was over.

Colonel L. wrote to me the same evening:—

My Dear Admiral,—We had our last sitting with Mrs. Wriedt, this afternoon. Cheiro sat with us. We had very little, but what we had was very wonderful. First, some very bright lights and an indistinct figure; then a voice through the trumpet addressed R. and gave the name "F——." R. said: "Oh R—— F——, who used to be in the regiment?" The voice answered: "Yes." I said: "F——, you must know me, too." Answer "Of course I do."

I said: "Tell me your nickname in the regiment." Answer: "They called me D—— F——." (This was perfectly correct; he passed over about two years ago, and was always called "D——.")

He then said to Mrs. R. "How is your boy getting on?" (He F——, has a son in our old regiment, a great friend of R.'s boy, who is also in the regiment.) I said: "D——" (calling him by his nickname), "I saw your boy at our regimental dinner." Answer: "I know; you had a great spread." He went on to say he was perfectly happy, and bade us "Goodbye."

How could one have a better test than this? Cheiro had visits from two friends and his sister; the latter addressed him in very affectionate tones by his Christian name. After this the power seemed gone. Mrs. Wriedt is the most wonderful medium I have ever seen......—

Yours sincerely,   F. P. L.

Commenting on this sitting, Mrs. R. wrote:—

Major F.'s return was extraordinary, as he was able to give his nickname so readily. He also said to my husband: "It is strange to meet you here, and find you interested in this sort of thing." He asked me how my boy was getting on, thus showing he was aware of his accident (this would be likely, as his son and mine are great friends). And he addressed Colonel L. by name when he (Colonel L.) asked him if he recognised him. [Colonel L.'s name is very uncommon, and foreign.] At one time there were two voices speaking simultaneously, as well as Mrs. Wriedt. Cheiro met some old friends, who gave their names; he says he had hardly thought of them for many years, but had once known them well. Someone tried to etherealise, but it was faint.

Last night we dined with Mrs. B., and on our sitting at a table after dinner a spirit gave the name of W. T. Stead. We asked why the manifestations had not been stronger, and the answer came at once: "Too little power." Uncle was very strong, gave two messages (this was at dinner, with the lights on, a party of eight at the table), and showed great intelligence in rapping the alphabet in a new way which Colonel L. explained to him. He said he was with my husband when he was talking to you at the club yesterday.—

Yours Sincerely, S. R.

My friend Mr. W., a barrister and a member of the Civil Service, lives in Ireland; he is nearly sixty years of age, an Associate of the London S. P. R., and an active member of the S. P. R. of Dublin. He applied to me in June to be allowed to sit with Mrs. Wriedt. As all the sittings were filled up, the only thing to be done was to ask him to join me in one of my private Séances, which he did on the morning of June 22. Until the sitting was over neither the psychic nor the ladies residing in the house knew anything whatever about him. I, alone, was aware of his name, nationality, and occupation: it was impossible that anyone in touch with Cambridge House could be aware that he was a "psychical researcher"—in the sense that the words were used by Dr. Sharp.

Mr. W. has kindly permitted me to make use of his notes. I can vouch for the accuracy of his narrative:—

Admiral Usborne Moore sat on a chair at arm's length from my left. Immediately on my right was an oval table with vases of flowers, chiefly roses, with some white flowers brought by myself. In front of me, at arm's length, Mrs. Wriedt sat on a chair at right angles to my own chair. On the left front of Admiral Moore was a small table about one foot four inches square, with a large vase of lilies on it, also a telescopic aluminium speaking trumpet. There was also on this small table in front of Admiral Moore a small vase with some roses brought by him on the day previous. At the end of the room, on my left, near the door, was a small cabinet about six foot six inches in height, perfectly open in front. Before the sitting commenced I examined this cabinet, and found that there were no exits at the back—curtains hung down at each side. This cabinet was about eight feet from the table at my right, and consequently was about six feet in front of Mrs. Wriedt, and probably three or four feet from the chair on which Admiral Moore was seated. There was also a large aluminium telescopic speaking trumpet standing upright on the floor about the centre of the circle.

Lights were extinguished. Almost immediately Dr. Sharp, (Mrs. Wriedt's control) spoke in a strong, clear voice (a masculine voice) through the trumpet—presumably through that on the floor in the centre of the circle. The voice seemed to be about the level or a little above my head. Dr. Sharp saluted Admiral Moore and welcomed him.

He said he was also glad to welcome "the psychical researcher"—my name, nationality, and connection with the Society for Psychical Research were then known only to Admiral Moore. I said that great caution was required on the part of the members of the Society of Psychical Research in dealing with these phenomena. Dr. Sharp agreed, but deprecated the exhibition of unreasoning belief on the part of many of the members and their efforts to explain away the incontrovertible evidence which was often presented to their senses.

Iola (Admiral Moore's guide) then spoke in a soft, but perfectly audible, voice, through the trumpet to Admiral Moore, the matter communicated being of a private nature. Admiral Moore said to Iola: "let me introduce my friend to you." Iola replied; "I will try and help this gentleman's wife to manifest to him." Dr. Sharp said that the conditions of the circle were very good; he also said that "this gentleman's wife, a very sweet spirit, will manifest." After a short interval some very bright spirit lights appeared—about the size of a sixpence, and some of them red in colour; they approached Admiral Moore, and then appeared near the centre of the circle. Presently a beautiful, angelic, bright spirit form was gradually built up in the cabinet, clearly visible to each of the three sitters. The figure was draped, and the graceful contour was very clear, though the features were indistinct. At the time the figure appeared all three sitters exclaimed. "What a beautiful figure!" Mrs. Wriedt's voice was distinguished by me as proceeding from the chair immediately in front of me—the cabinet where the figure appeared was at least six feet distant from Mrs. Wriedt's chair. Admiral Moore, who was the sitter nearest the cabinet, thought it was the figure of a tall woman about five feet six inches to five feet eight inches in height (the latter was about the height of my wife); he said that it was not the figure of Iola, who was of slight build and about five feet one inch in height. The apparition disappeared completely in about five to ten seconds. After a short interval the same spirit figure was etherealised for several seconds, somewhat more distinctly than before; the features were still not distinguishable, but the dark hair and the general contour of the figure were very clear. Both Mrs. Wriedt and Admiral Moore declared they had never before seen a more beautiful angelic figure etherialised. Admiral Moore was quite certain that the apparition was not the figure of Iola (his guide), and Dr. Sharp said very clearly through the trumpet: "That beautiful form you saw was this gentleman's wife."

My wife did not hold any conversation with me through the trumpet, so that I have received no evidence of her identity except as to the height and contour of the figure and the assertion of Dr. Sharp that the apparition was that of my wife.

Dr. Sharp then asked me through the trumpet; "Did you know a man called Johnson or Thompson?" I said that I did not remember, except a doctor in Dublin of that name who was dead some years. Dr. Sharp said; "He is here, and wishes to speak with you." Presently a low voice addressed me through the trumpet. I asked, "What is your name?" I heard some reply, but was unable to catch the name. The voice then said, "I am the wife of a member of your society who recently passed over." I asked whether he was a member of the Modern Languages Society or of the Society for Psychical Research. The voice replied, "The

Psychical Society." I requested that the name should be pronounced more clearly, but was still unable to catch it. The voice thereupon became distressed and said, "Well, well, well, well—oh dear!" I asked the spirit to make another effort. The voice then became stronger, and I recognised the name "P——." I asked, "is the name P——." Answer, "Yes! Yes!" The spirit seamed quite pleased, and the voice became much stronger. [The name is unusual and foreign.]

Mrs. P—— was a very charming young woman in Dublin, at whose house I had been in the habit of visiting on the first Sunday evening of each month through the previous two winter seasons. The meetings at her house were generally frequented by those of advanced thought in psychical, religious, or social matters. I talked to the spirit for some minutes; she remembered sitting with me at a séance of "seven." I asked, "Was it with Mrs. Mitchell?" She said, "Yes, with Mrs. Mitchell; Mrs. Mitchell was a grand woman." She said she remembered the rather disagreeable contretemps I had with "Cissie," a Negro girl guide of Mrs. Mitchell. The spirit then said through the trumpet: "I shall never hand round cups of tea again." Mrs. P—— was a delightful hostess, and always dispensed hospitality at our Sunday evening meetings. I said "As a very strong test of your identity, I want you to tell me if you can remember my calling to see you on one particular occasion when you were convalescent." She said at once, "Yes, yes here in London." I said "Where?" The reply being somewhat indistinct, I asked, Was it in the neighbourhood of Warwick Avenue?" I thought she said something about Torrington Place, and I asked, "Was it Torrington Place?" At once the reply came, emphatically and strongly, "No, not Torrington Place; it was Warrington Crescent." This was quite correct. I once called to see her, and had dinner with her, at a house in Warrington Crescent when she was convalescent. This was very evidential, as I had completely forgotten the address of the house at which I had called to see her, it having passed out of my memory until the voice recalled it so emphatically: "No, not Torrington place, but Warrington Crescent." I next asked Mrs. P—— if she was happy in spirit life, and she replied that she was very happy. I told her I had recently seen her husband in Dublin, and she said "Give my love to him."

After the P—— incident, Dr. Sharp said to me: "Now sir, take Mrs. Wriedt's hands in yours, and your wife will try and give you a rose." I took both of Mrs. Wriedt's hands firmly in my right hand. After about two minutes a rose was put into my disengaged hand, and shortly afterwards another. Dr. Sharp then said: "You were talking just now about the physical phenomena that occurred the other morning." (Mrs. Wriedt had been telling me of the lifting of the vase full of lilies from the smaller table on to the floor, also of the movement of this table at a recent séance.) "Now, sir" (to me), "take Mrs. Wriedt's hands again in yours." Presently I was struck on the right side of the head by a bunch of roses (my face being previously stroked by flowers). The bunch fell on to my knees, and then on to the floor. These roses were afterwards found to have been taken out of a vase close to my right elbow on the table. After a few minutes of silence Dr. Sharp said: "Mrs. Wriedt, turn on the light." On the electric light being switched on, the big vase of lilies from the table near Admiral Moore's chair was found on the floor in front of me, and the bunch of roses previously mentioned was lying on the floor close to me. When we had satisfied ourselves of the altered position of the roses and of the lilies from the smaller table, the lights were again extinguished, and I put the trumpet to my right ear with my right hand pointing over the table at an angle of about sixty degrees from the direct line between the psychic and myself, at the same time holding Mrs. Wriedt's two hands firmly with my left hand. Minute taps came through the trumpet, audible to both Admiral Moore and myself, but no distinct message, though I heard a whisper once or twice, without recognising any definite words. My left hand was repeatedly touched while grasping Mrs. Wriedt's two hands. Mrs. Wriedt announced twice that her hands had been touched. Admiral Moore said he was not touched throughout the séance, and received no manifestations other than one or two sentences from Iola audible to all. Iola did not, as usual, speak to him without the trumpet. During the incidents with the flowers, which I have described, Admiral Moore was sitting in his chair to my left, and could not possibly have moved without my knowledge, my hearing being very acute.

GENERAL REMARKS

During the whole of the séances just described I was particularly careful to notice the attitude of the psychic during the phenomena. On one or two occasions I observed that Mrs. Wriedt appeared to be speaking at the same time as Dr. Sharp, and while I was holding both of the hands of the psychic in my hand. From the almost involuntary exclamations of admiration by Mrs. Wriedt while the spirit form was building up in the cabinet, and from the fact that the sound of Mrs. Wriedt's voice proceeded from a position in close proximity to my chair at this time, I can entertain no doubt that during the occurrence of these phenomena Mrs. Wriedt was sitting fully six feet from the cabinet. In my opinion there could have been no collusive action on the part of the other two sitters, as I should have been instantly aware of any movements on the part of Mrs. Wriedt and Admiral Moore while the manifestations were taking place. Several times during the séance my face and hands were stroked as if by flowers while I had a firm hold of the two hands of the psychic.

My name was not on the books of the Syndicate of the Guarantors. I accompanied Admiral Moore on one of his private sittings. He assures me that it was impossible that my name, occupation, nationality, or my connection with the Society for Psychical Research could have been known until after the séance.

It was my first experience of phenomena so remarkable , and I have no explanation of them to offer, except the extraordinary psychic power possessed by Mrs Wriedt.

C. J. W.

The following account is by a lady who only attended one private séance with Mrs. Wriedt. She was a perfect stranger to the psychic, to me, and to the inmates of the house. On this one occasion only did she enter Cambridge House. The "conditions" could scarcely have been worse, for the psychic was suffering at the time from a great feeling of annoyance; consequently I felt quite sure that the lady had drawn a blank, but I did not like to write and ask. To my great surprise and relief I received a spontaneous letter from her on August 16 telling me that she had been most successful. I can only conclude that she must herself possess some psychic power which nullified Mrs. Wriedt's mental state. Here is her epistle:——

Dear Admiral Moore—I am reading your account of Mrs. Wriedt's séances every week in Light, and think it may interest you to know that the one I had with her on the day I met you was most convincing. When in the train on the way home from Wimbledon, remembering what you say in your book, I took full notes of what had occurred, and wrote the account out in full as soon as I reached the house.

Seven of my people—my father, mother, son, daughter, cousin, a nephew, and a very old friend—came to me, one after the other, without a break, all giving their names. My mother said: "I quite thought ——(mentioning my husband by his abbreviated Christian name, by which all the family knew him) was coming over to us last week. I hope he won't get knocked about like that again." (He had a very bad fall from his horse the week before.) My daughter said she was looking after her brother (a son I have in Canada), and gave a pet name by which she always called him. My nephew gave his Christian and surname. At first I could not quite catch it; then he said "Oh auntie, auntie, you remember me; I was on the Worcester [training ship], and was drowned afterwards." Then he gave his name again quite clearly, and what he said was quite true.

My husband's cousin gave both his names. I said: "I know who you are quite well; but you did not know me in life, so how do you know who I am?" He replied: "I was at my sister's yesterday when you called, so knew then who you were." I said: "That is true; but I did not tell her I was coming here." He returned: "I followed you to the next house you called at, and there heard you were coming here today, so thought I would let you know I was alive." I considered this showed most convincingly how our friends on the other side of life are able to be in touch with us if they wish, as all he said was perfectly true.

I forgot to mention that, after my nephew had been, John King (who is an old friend of mine) said: "Oh I am glad you knew that boy; he was just crazy to come and speak to you." My old friend who came at last, said: "I see you sometimes." I replied: "I have been able to convince two of your old schoolfellows of the future life lately." He rejoined: "Yes you had —— with you yesterday" (this was correct; the gentleman named, one of the two, came to supper with us the previous evening). Then John King said: "This is all we can do; now I am coming home with you."

I hope I have not bored you with this long account, but, knowing of the interest you take in Mrs. Wriedt's work, I venture to send it.......

My correspondent has excellent reasons for concealing her identity. So far from her letter boring me, I am sure that your readers will consider this narrative as one of the most interesting and valuable testimonies ever yet given to the world in support of the belief in the next state.

A neighbour of mine writes the following:—

I had two private sittings with Mrs. Wriedt this year, both in the afternoon. I had sat with her once last year in a large general circle of eighteen people, when Admiral Usborne Moore was one of the sitters. On that occasion I brought with me three friends, two men and one woman. One of the men was a barrister, a member of Parliament, and an officer of the Territorial force; the other was an Admiral in the Navy. These men did not wish to be known, and I foolishly introduced them to the psychic under false names. As far as I was concerned this séance was a failure, as I became ill and had to leave the room in the middle of it. I was told later that two books were taken from the bookcase by some unknown power, and flung on to the knees of the member of Parliament. One was *The History of Her Majesty's Army*; the other, I think, was some legal book. This much is necessary to explain what follows.

My first séance this year did not impress me. I was over-anxious and nervous, and feel I may have suggested names instead of waiting for my spirit friends to give them. However, there could be no mistake about my brother, who came singing; he was very fond of singing in life, and would warble all day long. My guide almost made himself known unmistakably.

On my second visit my mind was more prepared for the phenomena, and I was strictly cautious in my talk to the spirits who came. The following manifested: My guide, my father, mother, brother, a cousin, and a friend; also (much to my surprise) my father-in-law, canon Hamilton. All gave their names without any suggestion from me. It is not worth while relating all that passed, but there is one evidential fact which should be specially mentioned, as it relates to the séance last year. Canon Hamilton visited me for the first time on this occasion. When in life he was vicar of a parish in county Galway; he was an ultra-strict evangelical parson of the old fashioned school. The slightest departure from truth, even in joke, was hateful to him. When the voice first came I said: "Who are you?" Answer: "I am Charley's father" (Charley is the name of my husband)."What, Canon Hamilton?" Answer: "I am." He then scolded me for what happened at the séance of last year, and spoke of his strong objection to my introducing the two gentlemen under assumed names. He went on to say that he assisted in putting the books on the knees of the M. P., and that he, on that occasion, had influenced me so unpleasantly that I had to leave the room. His tone, in speaking, was that of severe reproof, precisely as it would have been in similar circumstances when he was alive.

I must add one incident in my conversation with my mother. She asked me: "What have you got of my Jewellery? I hope you took some." I told her what articles I had appropriated, when she appeared satisfied. During the last year or two of her life it was my mother's hobby to dwell upon the division of her trinkets among my sisters and me.

My brother came singing as before, and talked of what had occurred at the previous sitting. I mentioned this, and he exclaimed: "Yes, and I am a medium here."

(signed) H. M. BUCHANAN HAMILTON.

With regard to this lady's admission about the séance of last year, I remember John King telling me, on the morning following, that two gentlemen had come under false names, and that he picked out two books from the library on Majesty and Law and placed them on the knees of one of them "to show him he was known for what he was" (sic).

BY THE REV. CHARLES L. TWEEDALE

I have read the account of the alleged "exposure" of Mrs. Wriedt published in the Frankfurter Zeitung, and referred to in Light of the 7th inst., on p. 424, with feelings of indignation and contempt. The whole article is an ignorant farrago of nonsense, which would disgrace a schoolboy in the third form, not to mention a Professor. The attempt is made in this precious article in the Zeitung to insinuate that Mrs. Wriedt holds the trumpet in her hands and speaks through it, and that the percussive sounds are the result of a mixture of lycopodium and water. As to the latter suggestion, it wanted but this to reduce the article to absurdity and cover it with ridicule. Any schoolboy dabbling in his first chemistry knows that lycopodium has to be fired by a flame or spark before it will explode; and it is almost needless to say that this flame or spark, not to mention the flash of the explosion, would instantly betray the trick to the sitters. Another report has it that "sulphur" was found in the tube. This only makes the absurdity greater. The professor evidently set out to find a mare's nest, and duly found one.

I have examined the trumpets, and so have my friends, some of them expert S.P.R. investigators, and found nothing that could in any wise account for the phenomena.

Now as to the implied suggestion that Mrs. Wriedt speaks through the trumpet herself. I have been present at four sittings. On one of these occasions I sat next to Mrs. Wriedt, and on another a friend of mine, one of the most experienced investigators connected with the Society for Psychical Research, sat next to her. At the commencement of each séance the trumpets are generally placed in the centre of the circle, and during the séance, and while the persons present are seated, these trumpets pass all round the circle in a manner in which it would be quite impossible for them to do were Mrs. Wriedt handling them, unless she rose from her seat. By means which I need not here disclose, my friend, on the occasion of his sitting, made absolutely sure of the fact that Mrs. Wriedt did not move from her chair, while on the occasion when I sat next to her I positively proved that she did not use the trumpet as a speaking tube. The "voice" was speaking through the trumpet to a person seated on the other side of the circle. The trumpet, judging by the sound, seemed to be horizontal, and at a height of about four feet from the ground. I noticed that the sound of the voice seemed to be coming out of both ends of the trumpet. I heard the voice speaking through the trumpet at the other side of the circle, and at the same time a hissing, or sound reflection, seemed to issue presumably from the small end of the trumpet, and come in the direction of Mrs Wriedt, who was sitting by my side. In fact, one might have thought, judging from this hissing sound, that the trumpet was being used by her in the manner the wretched article in the Frankfurter Zeitung insinuates. All this flashed across my mind in a moment, and I was quick to seize the opportunity afforded.

Tucking my cuff up my sleeve, so that the white should not betray my action, I stretched out my hand down nearly to the floor in front of Mrs. Wriedt; then I raised my arm steadily up in front of her face until it was higher than her head; then slowly brought it down again nearly to the ground. This I did four times, during the whole of which the loud voice was sounding through the trumpet on the other side of the circle, and the sibilant sound coming back in the direction of Mrs. Wriedt. Had she been holding the trumpet, and using it to produce the voice, I should by this action have knocked it out of her hands; but I am glad to be able to affirm that my arm encountered nothing as I passed it up and down before her face. This disposes once and for all of the fiction that at her dark Séances Mrs. Wriedt uses the trumpet as a speaking tube by placing it to her lips. Admiral Moore and others testify to the fact that, at séances held in the light, the voices come through the trumpet, under test conditions, when it is a considerable distance from the psychic. On one occasion the rim of the trumpet was placed upon my forehead with a delicacy and accuracy of touch that would have been impossible for anyone to affect in the dark. There was no fishing or bungling, but perfect precision. Others have had the trumpet placed accurately in response to mental requests.

During the whole of this séance, when I sat next to her, I listened intently for any signs of movement on Mrs. Wriedt's part. She sat very still, and I did not hear that rustling of the clothing which almost invariably accompanies even the movement of the arms. I am positive of the fact that during the séance she did not rise from her chair. At its conclusion she got up to turn on the light. However as is justly remarked, the great value of Mrs. Wriedt's mediumship lies in the personal evidence obtained by the sitters. Of this I obtained many instances which were absolutely conclusive. Details of the most private nature and of events which took place forty years ago in my own family, and which even my wife, who was present, did not know, were given, and private matters occurring seventeen years ago in my wife's life, which I did not know, were related, with correct names and details, of which it was simply impossible for any other person present to be aware. These were given with a facility that was astonishing. Details concerning one of my parishioners, who had passed over about eight months previously, and whom I had found dead in her chair by her own fireside, were also related to us, some of them private matters only known to ourselves, and in a detail connected with the grave was given which I did not know, and thought was incorrect, but which, on inquiring from the sexton who made the grave, I found to be true. But the experiences of my friend, the investigator for the S. P. R., obtained as they were under test conditions, will probably rank among the most evidential of any obtained during this last visit of Mrs. Wriedt to England. For evidential purposes, and in the interests of Mrs. Wriedt's mediumship, he was introduced unexpectedly at one séance under a name which was not his surname, and from events which afterwards occurred we have proof that his identity was unknown to any person present save ourselves. Immediately the séance began personal evidence of the most remarkable kind began to come for him, and which formed quite a feature of the sitting. Afterwards he gave me the information which enabled me to follow the evidence obtained. It was of the most striking and conclusive nature. He informed me that this was the first conclusive evidence of a personal nature that he had obtained during some twenty years of investigation, during which time he had had sittings with many noted psychics, had (and rightly so) exposed the tricks of fraudulent mediums, and had travelled thousands of miles for the purpose of investigation. None of the evidence which came for him was previously known to myself or my wife.

At these remarkable séances I witnessed many strange happenings of an evidential nature. Sometimes three voices were heard at once, and on one occasion a friend of ours had a voice whispering private details in her ear during the time that two other voices were talking through the trumpet. I also heard voices speaking volubly in Dutch and Italian, that in Italian being evidently that of a man, and quite beyond the power of Mrs. Wriedt to imitate. Mrs. Wriedt often was heard explaining or asking questions of the sitters, and the voice through the trumpet and her voice very often alternated rapidly, and were heard almost at the same instant, enabling one to compare differences of volume and timbre. This was particularly the case on one occasion when a voice talked with her for a considerable time, and the impression one obtained was that the two were absolutely different. Some of the voices I heard, one in particular, were of the deepest base, of extraordinary depth and volume.

It has been said that Mrs. Wriedt employs an army of private detectives to search out everything known about the sitters. The absurdity of such a statement can only be fully realised by those who have been present at her séances. The expense would, in the first place, make her unable to put such a plan into operation, and even if this were not a fatal objection, the theory breaks down utterly when applied to cases of persons suddenly introduced without warning under assumed names, and fails equally to explain the production of evidence, often of extreme delicacy and privacy, known only to the sitters. It is this private and personal evidence which forms the strongest testimony at once to the genuineness of Mrs. Wriedt's mediumship and to the survival of human personality.

I will now give an account of two séances in which I sat with my friends. It is better to make it clear at once that the inmates of the house were present on only two occasions when I attended sittings at Cambridge House, besides the Wednesday ("Julia") nights described in issues of Light of August 3 and 10. They were not in evidence on the two occasions about to be described.

The first was an average séance, but there were two points about it which deserve mention. The circle was composed of seven people—all, except myself, strangers to the house and Mrs. Wriedt. Atmospheric conditions poor. The séance lasted one hour.

A vicar of one of our northern towns sat on my left at the end of the semi-circle and directly opposite to the psychic, from whom he was distant eight feet. Nothing happened for ten minutes. Then Iola came with private messages about my wife and an invalid relative; she was followed by Cardinal Newman, who at once accosted the clergyman in his low, refined voice, "Brother —— Brother ——," My neighbour said, "Yes, who is it?" Answer: "Cardinal Newman." After a few words by the clergyman the voice pronounced a Latin benediction in front of him, and then turned to the remaining sitters and gave a benediction in English. It then said, "Peace be with you Brother ——, peace be with you all; good morning, good morning all."

The mother of my neighbour came to him and identified herself, calling him by his Christian name and referring to other members of the family. The most evidential feature of the séance was the visit of an old bell-ringer who spoke before Grayfeather had finished talking.

Question: "Who are you?"

Answer: "......When you first came to the village twelve years ago."

Question: "Did you live in the village?"

Answer: "No, no; but I came to the service......bell."

Question: "What name?"

Answer: "William Crookes."

Question: Are you William, who used to ring the bell?"

Answer: "Yes, yes that's it. You were very kind to me and visited me when I was ill, before I died. You were very kind to me."

Question: "Yes, I remember; but it was very little I did for you."

Answer: "No you were very kind to me indeed, and I was very grateful."

I heard all this, but I have not trusted to my own memory or notes; I have borrowed the clergyman's notes, which he made with great care. He wrote to me after he got home. He says:—

While William Crookes was speaking to me I sat with fingers intertwined, elbows on knees, leaning forward towards the point whence the voice appeared to come, which was about two feet from the floor. While in this position I was touched lightly by the trumpet first on the right eyeglass and then three or four times on the fingers. On reference to my sick-visiting book I find this entry: "1900, Dec. 4. Crookes, Win., 63 O——Lane age 72. Ailment and remarks: Old age. Idiot. Died." I came to —— in August, 1900; it was not then a parish, but a village as he named it.

William Crookes said a good deal more. He alluded among other matters to a member of the congregation "who hands the plate round." (Bags are used now; but plates for the collection were used for the collection when William Crookes was alive.) The vicar said to him; "You know we have a new church now, William?" Answer: "Yes, yes, but you still ring the curfew bell." The ancient custom is still carried on in this district, but not from my friends church. The tower in which the curfew bell rings is half a mile from 63 —— Lane.

Grayfeather came twice. The first time he talked a great deal to one of the sitters, and asked an old lady why she wore turquoise. Was she born in December? She replied, "No in February." Grayfeather: "Blue stone no good for February." And so forth.

A spirit came to a man in the centre of the circle, and said in earnest tones: "My dear Son, God bless you!" Sitter: I did not know you had passed over." Spirit: "Yes my son, may God bless you, and when you come over give you a better place than mine" (this gentleman, who is about fifty years of age, explained to me that there had been a tragedy in the family, and he literally did not know if his father was alive or dead).

Julia came and made many kind remarks to me personally, and greeted the circle. She said Mr. Stead was always busy, going from one place to another. He was still working on the Review.

A friend came to a lady and spoke gratefully of presents of fruit and flowers which she (the sitter) had brought to her during her last illness (recognised).

The vicar says in his notes; "Before my mother spoke I saw a luminous mist on my left hand, and felt my head grow very heated. When she began to speak this sensation passed away......Iola and my mother spoke in low, tender tones, full of peace and affection."

The second séance took place on May 11; it was not remarkable as a whole, but there were two features about it which make it worth recording—one a prophecy to a naval officer, the other the manifestation of Mr. Vincent N. Turvey, the famous psychic who died recently at Bournemouth.

The circle was composed of Mrs. S., of Bournemouth, her son, Lieutenant and Mrs. V. U. (her son-in-law and daughter), Miss Scatcherd, Mrs. H. (a psychic), and myself. We had to wait some ten minutes or more before anything occurred. Then Iola came to me, and went on to Lieutenant V. U. (who is my cousin). She gave to him one of her Christian names—in fact, the name by which she was called by his father when she was in life—and sent a message to his father. After reminding my cousin of the last time she had spoken to him (exactly a year before), she said: "I am helping someone who has just passed away, and I cannot bring him to talk, for he is not able" (her nephew, died the previous morning). Iola and Mrs. S. entered into conversation, and she gave the name of Mrs. V. U. and warned her to be careful of her health.

After two spirits had manifested to a sitter, Grayfeather came in with a shout, and accosted Lieutenant V. U.: "How do, tickey, tickey, tickey? U——, long chief" (Mr. U. is tall). This appeared to have some connection with a steam or motor boat. After a talk with Mrs. S.'s son during which the gentleman was rapped over the head with the trumpet several times, he turned to me and chatted; then again talked to Lieutenant V. U. Presently there was a voice—"Turvey." This spirit spoke chiefly to young Mr, S., occasionally to his mother; and while doing so coughed many times, taking on the conditions of his death. (Mr. Turvey was a friend of the S. family. He did not know young Mr. S. well, but was an intimate friend of his father, who was not present at this séance. It is possible that he mistook the son for the father.) The mother of Mrs. S. came, calling her daughter by her Christian name, and expressed her pleasure at being able to "come and talk to the two children." She addressed herself specially to young Mr. S.; then said: V ——" (giving the Christian name of Lieutenant U.), "How do you do?"

Lieutenant U.: "I am very glad to meet you."

Voice: "Thank you; I am very glad to see you in the family. I like to see you in the family. Goodbye." Then to Mrs. S.: "I hope he will be well during the rest of the summer" (a clear allusion to Mr. S., Senior). "Give him my love. It is so nice to have a chat with you. Goodbye, dear."

Grayfeather now came back to Lieutenant U., and told him he was going to Halifax, and he was soon going to get "three rings." We heard a noise of the trumpet scraping the floor, apparently making three circles. This was repeated later, and Grayfeather volunteered the information that the three rings would come "in cherry time." He also talked about U. going to Ottawa, and having something to do with the "House of top- knots" (presumably Parliament). It was rather confused, especially as he introduced a prophecy of the officer carrying with him "a box of shinem" (money). Grayfeather finally gave a lugubrious prognostication of coming trouble in the East: "Heap much trouble across water—white people, black people, all kinds of people—they go fight. Lots of heads cut off."

Admiral Moore: "We don't cut heads off nowadays."

Grayfeather made a reply which all the members of the circle understood to mean: "History repeats itself" (I have heard these dismal forebodings by Grayfeather twice since this séance).

Julia manifested, and welcomed the sitters to her "Sanctuary," and the séance terminated.

Notes.—Mr. Vincent Turvey died on May 3, 1912. Lieutenant V. U. is an officer of the Royal Navy, of considerable promise. He was promoted to the rank of Commander on June 30, 1912, seven weeks after this séance. I must explain that the Lieutenants are not promoted to this rank by seniority, but by selection; the uniform is distinguished by three gold stripes on each arm. It is true I knew that, unless some injustice was perpetrated, my cousin was bound to be in the next "Gazette." And he probably knew it too. Promotions are only made twice a year—viz, June 30 (cherry time) and December 31. But how did this old Indian spirit foresee this? It was not a certainty—far from it; his name was ninety-fourth on the list, and only twenty-four could be promoted. Let us suppose he picked my mind; how about the visit to Halifax and Ottawa? This, at any rate, was foreign to the thoughts of everybody in the circle. It so happens that the father of Lieutenant U. is a Canadian, and he has many relatives in the Dominion. Quebec was also mentioned. It remains to be seen if this visit, of which V. U. knows nothing at present, will really come off.

Sir W. F. BARRETT'S SÉANCES WITH Mrs. WRIEDT

Sir W. F. Barrett has kindly sent us, for the benefit of English readers, the following copy of a letter he has forwarded to the leading Norwegian newspapers that contained an account of the so-called exposure of Mrs. Wriedt:—[Ed. Light]

Through the kindness of my friend, Miss Ramsden, I have had an opportunity of reading a translation of the discussion that has taken place in your columns, and elsewhere, of the séances held with Mrs. Wriedt in Christiania. Miss Ramsden has also shown me the admirable letter she sent to you on the subject. As a former president of, and intimately associated with, the English Society for Psychical Research, perhaps I may be allowed warmly to support Miss Ramsden's plea for the formation of a similar society in Christiania.

Before referring to that, however, permit me to say a few words on my own experience of Mrs. Wriedt. During her visit to London this year I had the opportunity of some séances with her. Two of these were private sittings at midday with Miss Ramsden. In one of these private sittings, when no one was present but Miss Ramsden, myself, and Mrs. Wriedt, we sat for the first part in good light. I had previously, when alone, carefully examined every part of the room, and assured myself that no one was concealed and no suspicious apparatus was present; the only door opened on to a landing with a window, through which the sunlight was streaming. Any person attempting to enter the room through the door would therefore have been detected at once, when the room was darkened. When, after my examination of the room, Mrs. Wriedt and Miss Ramsden entered, the door was locked, and one of the electric lights over our head was left on to illuminate the room. We sat on chairs adjoining each other; I sat next to Mrs. Wriedt and held her hand. Miss Ramsden sat on my left. We asked Mrs. Wriedt to let us try in the light first, and at her suggestion Miss R. held the small end of a large aluminium trumpet to her ear; the larger end I supported with my left hand. My body therefore came between the trumpet and the medium. I had previously looked into the trumpet, which was perfectly bare and smooth. Presently Miss Ramsden said she heard a voice speaking to her, and entered into conversation with the voice. I only heard a faint whispering sound, but no articulate words. To avoid the possibility of Mrs. Wriedt being the source of the whispering, I engaged her in talk, and while she was speaking Miss Ramsden still heard the faint voice in the trumpet, but begged us to stop speaking, as it prevented her hearing distinctly what the voice said. Miss Ramsden assured me afterwards there could be no doubt whatever that the voice in the trumpet was independent of Mrs. Wriedt, and I can testify that I watched the medium and saw nothing suspicious in the movement of her lips. She did not move from her place, and no accomplice or concealed arrangement could possibly have produced the voice.

As I did not hear what the voice said, I have asked Miss Ramsden to add a few lines.

(NOTE BY MISS R.—The speaker claimed to be the bearer of a message from one of my relations who has died; he told me that, contrary to my expectations, I should receive a visit from a person who was named. This was fulfilled on the following Monday. Here I must add that, if this was explained by thought-transference, we must suppose it possible for Mrs. Wriedt to receive telepathic communications from people of whose existence she knows nothing; in this case the person was in a foreign country. While holding the trumpet I could feel the vibration of the little voice inside.—H. R.)

When the voice ceased speaking, the trumpet was placed with its broad end on the floor standing upright near Miss Ramsden. The electric light was now switched off, and the room became absolutely dark. A very loud man's voice almost immediately called out: "God bless you: God bless you." Mrs. Wriedt said it was the soidisant John King. I begged her to place her right hand on mine, which held her left hand. She did so, and I distinctly felt the two hands, my left hand being free.

During every séance with her Mrs. Wriedt remained perfectly normal, talking with me or others present, and not in the least excited. On this occasion, in a few moments I felt something rather cold gently stroking my face. And, as at a previous sitting when a rose was placed in my hand, the act was performed without any fumbling about. This was very curious, as the room was so dark that nothing whatever could be seen. But under these conditions of complete darkness it is impossible to arrive at any conclusive evidence concerning the supernormal character of the various physical phenomena that occurred. All I can assert is that it seemed to me impossible for Mrs. Wriedt to have produced them by trickery. A large elastic band and a card, on which were sealed the ends of a loop of string, which objects I had brought and placed by my side away from Mrs. Wriedt, were taken up and thrown over my head, and I heard the snapping of the elastic band, which was found broken and at some distance behind me when the light was turned on.

At another sitting I observed a luminous appearance resembling a man's head and beard in front of and a little above me. I put up my free hand and moved it to and fro, but felt nothing, though, as far as I could judge in the dark, my hand passed through the place where the luminosity appeared. My head was gently rapped with the small end of the trumpet, and flowers from a vase on a distant table were thrown in my lap. But, as I said before, these manifestations are of little evidential value when occurring in the dark, and I attach no importance to them.

Much more impressive were the voices; sometimes very loud, apparently through the trumpet, at other times faint and directed close to my face or that of my companion. These voices were heard often simultaneously when Mrs. Wriedt was speaking, and while I held her hand, as I did at every sitting. There is little doubt that I should have felt the movement had she attempted to get up and seize the trumpet which was not near her, or place her mouth near Miss Ramsden or Mrs. Anker, who on one occasion sat next to me and heard the voice speaking in Norwegian, as she informed me.

On one occasion the voice, like that of a man, gave me the Christian name and surname of an old Irish friend of mine, wholly unlikely to be known to Mrs. Wriedt. It was a name not common in Ireland, though a public man of that name, who died some years ago, was a well known Orangeman; but my deceased friend was a Roman Catholic and on my expressing my surprise that he should appear—though I did not allude to his religious belief—the voice said: "You know what the priests say, Once a Catholic always a Catholic; but that is not so here." Then another voice, like that of an old lady, spoke close to me and said: "How are things in Dublin?" I replied: "Who are you?" and the voice answered, "Lady Helena Newenham," emphasising the three syllables of the surname—an unusual one. I did not know any such person, but subsequently found that an Irish lady of that name, much interested in psychical research, had died a year before and was well known to some friends of mine in the South of Ireland, to whom I wrote for information.

A voice addressed itself to me, but I could not at first distinguish the name. After several trials I heard: "Sidgwick." "What is your Christian name?" I asked: at once it said: "Henry Sidgwick." Professor Sidgwick's name is, of course, well known; he was a personal friend, and the first president of the Society for Psychical Research. Mrs. Wriedt doubtless had heard his name, but he died before she visited England, and I doubt if she, or many others who knew him by name, were aware that he stammered badly. So I asked the voice: "Are you all right now?" not referring to his stammering. Immediately the voice replied: "You mean the impediment in my speech, but I do not stutter now." At another sitting the same voice, purporting to be Henry Sidgwick, came again and addressed itself to me in a long speech, in the course of which one or two rather characteristic things were said, but on the whole the speech was more commonplace than would be expected from the real Sidgwick.

I will only trespass on your space by relating another incident that occurred to a personal friend, the hon. Secretary of the Irish section of the S. P. R., a gentleman of legal knowledge who occupies a high position in Dublin. He came to Mrs. Wriedt's sitting unexpectedly with Admiral Moore, and was unknown to any present except the Admiral. The voice gave him the name a very unusual one, of an Irish friend of his who had lately lost his wife, and said she was the deceased wife, and told my friend correctly the exact address of a place in London where she had been staying, and where my friend had called on her, though at this time he had quite forgotten the address. He saw the luminous figure of a lady in front of him, though he could not distinguish the face.

I went to Mrs. Wriedt's séances in a somewhat sceptical spirit, but I came to the conclusion that she is a genuine and remarkable medium, and was given abundant proof to others besides myself that the voices and the contents of the messages given are wholly beyond the range of trickery or collusion. Like nearly all mediums through whom physical phenomena are manifested, she may, consciously or unconsciously, sometimes be obsessed with a spirit of stupid trickery, which, in several cases that I have known, appears like the projection of the fixed ideas of hostile sitters among those present. In fact, all of us project our thoughts into the unseen, and more often than we know they come back to us as objective realities. Whether I and others who have been convinced of the existence of supernormal phenomena have done so, and are suffering under a delusion of our own creation, or whether Professor Birkeland— for whom we all have the highest respect as an eminent savant—and other even more resolute sceptics than he, have done so, patient and prolonged investigation can alone determine. This is one reason why I hope the project of a Norwegian Society for Psychical Research may be carried out. And I earnestly trust that the same spirit of calm and unimpassioned inquiry, which has enabled science to solve so many problems not less hotly debated in the past, may be found to prevail among those scientific men in Norway who undertake the investigation of this difficult research—a subject where fools too often rush in "Where angels fear to tread."

The attached narrative is written by a lady in a Western county who is of a literary and philosophical turn of mind, but at the same time very practical and fond of outdoor life, fox- hunting, etc. She has only lately interested herself in occult phenomena. Though we have corresponded, I have never yet had the pleasure of meeting her, and up to June 4 she was an absolute stranger to Mrs. Wriedt and the inmates of Cambridge house.

She writes to me: "I am sorry I cannot publish my name, but from the conversation I had with my father I gathered he did not wish me to mention the séances to my relatives (his sisters specially). 'To them,' he said, 'it would be such an outlandish idea, and they would never understand.' This I know to be true."

MY FIRST EXPERIENCES WITH A MEDIUM

On June 4, 1912, I was privileged to sit with a wonderful medium (Mrs. Wriedt of Detroit) at Cambridge House, Wimbledon. I must first say I have had no experiences of mediums, but have read a great deal for some years past on occult subjects. I went to "Julia's Bureau" with an open mind, but fully prepared to test the medium. I had four sittings; June 4, at 4 p.m., being the first. I took a friend with me, and we sat alone with Mrs. Wriedt in the dark. After we had sat a few minutes, the medium saw a name apparently in the air, and she said: "I see the name 'Morley'";

to which we both replied we knew nobody of that name. She then heard the name "Mary," and said: I hear now it is 'Mary,' not 'Morley.'" I then said I knew of no one who had passed over, and would be likely to speak to me, of that name, but that I had an Aunt who died many years ago whose name was Mary. I said then: "I wonder if it is my Aunt?" To which a reply came at once, most emphatically, through the trumpet: "No! no! no! I am your grandmother." This while I was being touched on my head and knees. I was most astonished, as I had quite forgotten all about my grandmother, and then remembered her name was Mary. "Yes," came the voice, "I am your grandmother Mary. I am here dear granddaughter." I at once thought I would test her, so said; "How many sons had you?" She replied: "Five." I was not sure of this; but she stuck to it, and when I got home I found she was correct. They were a large family—nine daughters and five sons—but at the moment I could not count them up, and thought there were fewer daughters and more sons! She then told me two of her children died young, which was correct. I then asked: "Do you ever see my father?" She replied: "Yes; he is with me now, and P." (P. was an uncle who died many years ago). My father then spoke, giving me his name, which at first I could not make out. He talked at great length over private family affairs, which to me were most convincing, and reminded me of events and conversations which had taken place years ago between him and another member of our family in my presence. These events and conversations I had never, to my knowledge, had in my mind for years, and they then all came back to me. He told me to "Sit up." I was leaning over, as I had some idea I could hear better so. The trumpet being on the floor. After a long conversation with him, which I am Sorry I cannot publish (being of a very private nature), my uncle came and talked also through the trumpet. I at once asked him as a test if he had any children on the other side; to which he replied, "Yes," and named his son who had passed over. After this, John King, in a loud voice, gave us good advice, and said it had been a great comfort to my relatives to have been able to talk to me. This ended my first séance and it sent me back wondering how such things could be!

The second séance held the following day, again with only my friend and the medium present, was more or less a failure, as nothing happened except that we were touched, and the medium said she saw some spirits.

The next, and third, sitting for me was the following week, June 10. I sat this time alone with the medium. My father came immediately, which rather surprised me, and Mrs. Wriedt said: "He must have come in with you." He began: "I want to tell you more, as I could not discuss our family affairs before company" (meaning my friend who before came with me). Then came more private conversation on family affairs which I cannot repeat, and I afterwards gave him some tests. I had specially put on a broach which was once studs of his, and he had them made up for me as a broach. I asked him if he saw anything on my person which he recognised. He replied at once: "Yes, on your chain—a pin." I had it on over a chain. I said: "Yes we call them broaches." He said: "I am glad you have something of mine." I then said: "Can you see what else I have on my lap?" He again replied: "Yes, a picture." (It was a photograph of himself, with a letter of his in a sealed envelope.) I said: "Whose picture is it?" He at once said: "It is me." I then said "What else is in the envelope?" And he replied: "A letter of mine. Poor girl, poor girl! Keep it for old times' sake."

He then went on with private conversation, and, before leaving kissed me three times through the trumpet, saying: "Can you hear?" After this my uncle came again, and talked on family matters, naming aunts of mine (sisters of his) who have passed on, and whom I had not mentioned, and telling me which spheres they were all in. Soon after this John King came and said "God bless you. It has been the greatest comfort to your father to talk to you in this way," and spoke of the subject my father had dwelt upon chiefly, after which he said, "Goodbye."

I left much impressed with it all, and returned the following day at two o'clock; but, alas! The spirits came no more, and Mrs. Wriedt most patiently sat with me alone for over an hour. I think her power is most wonderful and marvellous, and hope very much that she may be spared for many years to use this extraordinary gift which has been bestowed upon her.

The next narrative is by a lady of my acquaintance who attended one of the last general circles at Cambridge House:—

My sitting was on July 1, 1912. There were ten people besides the psychic present, all of whom were women except one, a gentleman from the north of England, who sat next to me. Until half way through the séance I did not know his name, nor did I know the names of any other sitters, except the Harpers. No introduction took place in the drawing-room, and, as far as I know, Mrs. Wriedt was not aware of my name. The séance was held in pitch darkness. I think everyone was visited by some spirit whom he or she appeared to identify satisfactorily. Voices spoke in German to two German ladies in the circle. Lights floated about the room. Julia spoke at great length to Miss Harper about the maintenance of the Bureau; she stated very emphatically that too much was expected from spirits, and more force was required from earth life. A voice asked for "Cecilia." I said: "Do you mean me, Cecil?" Answer: "Yes: I am father." I replied: "Oh how are you—are you well?" Answer: "Yes, and happy." Question: "Yes; have you seen mother?" Answer "Yes." Question: "What a long time it is since you died!" Answer; "Oh good lord, it seems shorter and shorter!" There were a few other words, and he said, "Goodbye."

I had not expected to hear my father, as he passed out so many years ago, and was unprepared with anything to say. I was sixteen when he died. He very often called me "Cecilia."

Later on came a voice: "Its teeny," I said "Is that tiny?" (My sister, who died some six or seven years ago). Answer: "Yes it is; how are you?" I said: "Much better." Answer: "I am so very glad to hear that." Question: "Do you see me sometimes?" Answer "Yes, every day." Question: "Have you seen mother?" (my mother died three months ago). Answer: "Oh, yes; she is very well and very happy." Question: "Has she any message for me?" Answer: "Yes, her love." Question: "Is she vexed with me still?" Answer: "Oh, no, not at all. She asked me to say so." I then repeated my question two or three times: "Are you quite sure she is not still vexed with me or B——?" (my husband). Answer (the voice got quite impatient): "Oh, no, she thought you had done something she did not like; but she knows now she was wrong and very naughty, and says: 'Will you forgive her?'" I answered: "Of course; how is Bertie?" (my brother, who died thirty years ago at the age of two). Answer: "Oh, he is splendid, and such a dear; you wouldn't know him." Then the spirit said something about being so happy she would not return "here" for anything. I asked if my mother minded my attending the séance, and was told "No"; she loved me to be there, adding: "Where God is there is good."

The gentleman next to me had a long talk with his brother, chiefly about his business. The mother of one of the sitters came to her daughter, and, after talking to her for some time, addressed us all in a very sweet way, just as an old lady might do saying: "You must all know how happy it is where I am—no ailments, no worries, only hope." She said she and her brothers were inseparable, and very happy.

Dr. Sharp was the first to speak. He addressed us collectively, and then turned to my neighbour in a jokey way, saying: "I am sorry for you Mr.——, being the only man in the party, but I will support you."

At one time there was a spirit voice speaking in very low tones to two ladies on my right, and at the same moment an Indian spirit (whom the sitters addressed as "Blossom") was talking in a baby voice to the circle. She was rather noisy, and Mrs. Wriedt tried to check her, saying: "Don't talk so loudly; someone else is speaking as well as yourself; you are making too much noise." I noticed that the three voices were heard simultaneously.

One of the things I remarked to myself was how impatient spirits appear to be when one does not catch what they say at once, or when one asks the same question two or three times, as I did to "Tiny"."

To my surprise there was no feeling that there was anything uncanny about the proceedings; it was quite a serene atmosphere.

My husband says that, to him, the chief interest of this séance lay in the face that my sister announced herself as "Teeny" (needless to say, not her correct name). She was so called by the youngest members of the family, but I never think of her as anything but "Tiny."

The following narrative is written by a Dutch lady, whose children have been educated to speak Dutch, English, and French with equal facility.

Referring to the communication in Light, on p. 398, by the Rev. C. B., it appears that the gentleman and the Dutch lady were members of the same circle on May 30; but the clergyman has mixed up the spirit visitors of three Dutch ladies who were present. On the other hand, I observe that, in the account below, Mrs. E. F, S. has omitted to mention the visit of Uncle Pat on this occasion:—

At the request of Admiral Usborne Moore, I have much pleasure in giving an account of my sittings with Mrs. Wriedt, the direct voice medium from Detroit. On May 11 I had a private sitting with my sister and my two sons, when my little daughter, who passed over four years ago, at the age of twelve, spoke to us in a very clear voice through the trumpet. She called her brothers by their names, and said how pleased she was to see them. She asked if we remembered the "bunnies" she had in the garden some years ago. "One of them is here with me," She said. It was so nice to hear her talk in the same way as she used to do when she was on the physical plane. After a few moments of silence we heard somebody touch the flowers, which were near me in a vase. "I tried to give you a flower, mother, but I can't," she said. Before parting she gave me a kiss on my cheek. After a short while a loud voice said; "I am Pat." "He must be father's brother," remarked my son; and he was right. Pat talked a good deal about family affairs, and gave some good advice to my sons. When I asked him if he knew my daughter, he answered: "Yes; I love her—she is so sweet." None of us knew Pat in earth life; he died thirty-four years ago, at the age of thirty-two, when he was Herbert Spencer's secretary.

Without knowing that it was my daughter's birthday, Mrs. Wriedt invited us to a general meeting on May 14. As soon as the lights were out my daughters voice was heard: "Mother, I thank you for the flowers." "They are for your birthday, darling." I said "Yes, I know it," was her reply. An old aunt of mine spoke to us in Dutch, expressing her delight in being able to see us, and to talk to us. Pat came and spoke about my husband, who was on his way home from China at the time.

On May 18 I sat in a general circle with a lady friend, when several etherealised heads were seen. One of them was recognised by my friend as Sir Henry Irving. My friend's father came and spoke to her in a very distinct voice. Before leaving, he turned to me and thanked me for having brought his daughter. Pat said a few words, as also did his sister, who passed over several years after him. We also heard the voices of Mr. Stead, Cardinal Newman, Dr. Sharp, John King, and Julia.

An aunt and a friend of mine from Holland were with me at a general circle on May 19, when my daughter welcomed them in Dutch, talking with the same foreign accent as she did before she left us. The husbands of my aunt and friends came and spoke Dutch to them, also a son of my aunt, who died thirty-three years ago, at the age of six weeks.

At our final séance, on June 6, conditions were bad; my daughter was the only one who spoke to us, besides two spirits who were not recognised by anyone.

Words fail to express our feelings of gratitude towards Mrs. Wriedt for affording us the opportunity of hearing the voices of our beloved ones, who gave us such convincing proofs of life after death.   E. F. S.

The writer of the account given below, Mr. H. Dennis Taylor, is a manufacturer and an inventor of scientific instruments, and author of A System of Applied Optics. He is now engaged in perfecting a new range-finder for the Navy. He is a member of the S. P. R.:—

My experience of Mrs. Wriedt's mediumship strongly impressed me. Accompanied by Mrs. Taylor, I attended evening sittings at Cambridge House on June 15 and 17, about ten persons being present at each. Neither of us received any completely satisfactory proofs of identity or tests that are worth narrating in detail, but we were witnesses to far more remarkable tests than our own being received by other sitters.

On June 15 we heard ten or twelve distinct, and in some cases highly characteristic, voices, ranging from the feeblest whisper up to the boisterous voice of John King (the same voice that I had previously heard at a séance with Husk) and the distinctly womanly contralto voice of Julia. While one entity was conversing with me through the trumpet just in front of me, Mrs. Wriedt kept interpolating remarks to encourage me, and her voice unmistakably came from my left front, ten feet away, near the door, where she had seated herself before switching the light out. This also occurred in the case of an, at first, feeble voice manifesting to Mrs. Taylor, whose identity we made out fairly well. In some cases we heard the medium's voice and the voice of the communicating spirit within a fraction of a second of one another, and widely separated in locality, and also noticed how much more distinctly the voices emerged after some sort of recognition had been achieved. This would, of course, suggest fraud to a sceptic who has not studied the evidential experiences that have been forthcoming through Mrs. Wriedt's mediumship. It may not be remiss to remind such a sceptic that, if he is accosted in the street by some former acquaintance whom he had almost entirely forgotten, he will feel more or less tongue-tied, or at any rate, his conversation will be halting, and, perhaps, incoherent, until recognition has taken place and established a rapport between them. Nor must we forget other instances in which the communicator announces and identifies himself with an unmistakably distinct voice and a clear pronunciation of the surname without the least sign of any fishing for a clue from the sitter. We were witnesses to at least three such cases in the sitting of June 17, a partial account of which was reported in Light for July 27. This was extracted from a stenographic report taken down for me, as the events occurred, by Mr. Harper, who sat at a table on my right, just outside the circle, so that whenever quietness prevailed I could hear his slight movements and his pencil writing, to say nothing of many remarks interjected by him.

Evidentially, Mr. South's experiences were the best we heard as proofs of identity, especially as he has assured me since that nobody in the circle could have possibly known anything about his three relatives who manifested in such an unmistakable manner. The voices, especially that of William South, were full of character and individuality.

I was much impressed by the apparent fall of one of the trumpets from the ceiling when Mrs. Wriedt turned on the electric switch by the door. It fell end on and perpendicularly, about nine or ten feet away from the medium; an electric pendant or chandelier intervened between the path of the trumpet and the nearest sitter in the circle. Anyone acquainted with the trajectories of falling bodies that have been thrown will know that if the trumpet had been thrown into the middle of the room by Mrs. Wriedt at the instant before switching on the light, then, even supposing the most favourable trajectory, it would have fallen obliquely, at an angle of forty-five degrees or more with the perpendicular. But it fell perpendicularly and telescoped itself (being made of three sections not soldered together) in doing so, and subsided just where it fell. My line of vision was at right angles to the line joining the medium and the trumpet, and therefore best for seeing how it fell. On this occasion we heard two voices talking at once close by us, and Mrs. Wriedt's voice interjecting remarks perfectly naturally, and practically simultaneously, from her position near the door ten feet or more away. I also heard a voice (John King's, I think it was), joining in singing the Doxology in the middle of the circle, suddenly transferred to a position near the wall behind me. We had several little incidents proving that the entities manifesting could see perfectly well what we were doing in pitch darkness. I have often heard it asserted that darkness favours fraud, but this can be true only of certain forms of fraud, and I, for one, can conceive of no form of ventriloquial fraud or personation by a confederate which would account for what we witnessed, or for the remarkable tests which have been received by so many sitters at Mrs. Wriedt's séances. I regard as contemptible the attitude of so many sceptics who would judge mediums by their own limited experiences alone, without taking due account of those of other observers as level-headed as or more so than themselves. I noticed nothing to justify any suspicion of the integrity of this remarkable medium, whose whole mien and personality inspire confidence. As to the total darkness, I really fail to see how certain feebly self- luminous phenomena, such as lights and etherealisations, could be made perceptible to the sitters under any other condition. Nor do I see how certain of the voices, at first but feeble whisperings, could be made audible without the use of a trumpet to concentrate them towards the sitter for whom they are intended. And I know that certain reliable observers have heard and conversed with the voices in the trumpet in daylight, and although more feebly and slowly. It struck me that the louder and more practised voices did not use a trumpet at all. Finally, I would very much like to see the experiment tried of setting some conjurer and ventriloquist to carry out an analogous programme (excluding, of course, the internal evidence in the way of proofs of identity) in such a circle sitting in total darkness, and on hundreds of occasions, without ever stumbling over the furniture or the sitters, or otherwise betraying his presence by touch or sound, even supposing he could be smuggled into the room in the first place; still less is it believable that a woman in skirts could do it.

Note.—Ventriloquism is impossible in the dark, for reasons given in any good dictionary or text-book. It is true that one gentleman, who considers himself an acute observer, said that the trumpet could be thrown. He only had not noticed the disused electric globe and shade, which renders such a feat impossible without detection.

The accompanying narrative has been sent to me by a mining engineer who manages some large quarries in the North of England. On several occasions he travelled between five and six hundred miles in twenty-four hours in order to be present at the séances. I have good reasons for saying that he is an acute observer. At his first séance he was an entire stranger to Mrs. Wriedt and the inmates of the house:—

For many years I have been interested in reading all the literature I have come across on psychic phenomena, and naturally I had a strong desire to witness some manifestation of spirit return, so that when Admiral Moore offered me the opportunity of attending Mrs. Wriedt's séances at Julia's Bureau, Cambridge House, I readily accepted. I had never been to a séance of any kind before, so entered upon my experiences with my wits about me as one entering an unexplored country.

As I am a mining engineer by profession, my hearing has been trained to locate sounds in perfect darkness, and I feel, perhaps, more at home in it than do those who are unacquainted with the absolute darkness of a coal mine.

All my notes of the sittings were made immediately after leaving, usually in the train riding home, a five hours' journey by express. Some of the sittings are reported in detail by a stenographer whose services I was able to requisition, and who had a faculty of being able to write shorthand in the dark. The following may be taken as a correct record of what took place in my presence, but condensed and contracted, as there was much spoken of too private a nature to be made public, not only in my own case, but in the case of other members of the circles.

May 25, 1912. After being received along with other visitors by Mrs. Wriedt, I was asked to ascend to a room on the first floor. Although it was only 7 p.m. and still daylight, this room was lighted by electric light, the windows being heavily curtained to exclude any ray of daylight. The room itself was rectangular and, I should judge, about twenty feet long by twelve feet wide. The walls, where not covered by bookcases, were hung with pictures, for the most part photographs or portraits of people, except at one end, at which stood a cabinet—i.e., a black piece of furniture about three feet square and six feet high, standing against the wall, with two curtains hung on the open front. I looked inside this but saw nothing. Next to it in the corner stood a mechanical musical instrument, which was playing rather sweetly at the time. In front of this musical instrument stood a small square table, on which were placed vases of flowers. Ranged in a semi-circle facing the cabinet were chairs for the sitters, and behind the chairs again was another large oval table carrying bowls of roses and other flowers. Mrs. Wriedt suggested where we should sit. There were eleven of us on this occasion, including Mrs. Wriedt, who placed in the centre of the circle on the floor an aluminium trumpet standing on its bigger end. I examined this and found it to be a simple tapered tube made in three pieces to telescope; it was damp inside, and Mrs. Wriedt explained that she had been drenching it with water. The lights were extinguished, so we found ourselves sitting in complete darkness, the scent of the roses being very noticeable. The séance was opened by all repeating the Lord's Prayer and then singing a hymn, "Lead Kindly Light." Now I copy from my notes. We sat still for probably five minutes, when a lady near the small flower-table said that she was being touched on the face. Immediately afterwards the gentleman sitting next her said something had dropped on his foot, and, feeling, said it was a flower; a moment after I myself felt something with a fragrant scent touching my forehead very delicately; it was cool, as though dew was on it; I put my hand up to feel, and found the stalk of a rose placed against my fingers, and naturally took hold. I noticed that it showed no disposition to fall down whilst I was taking hold, nor did I feel anything supporting it. Mrs. Wriedt was speaking to someone at the time some distance removed from me. After that flowers were scattered over the sitters. Presently I heard a voice uttering a sort of prayer which ended with "God bless you," repeated two or three times. Mrs. Harper, who was present, said it was Cardinal Newman. Following that, several voices spoke through the trumpet to various sitters, but they were not recognised except in two cases, one being for a lady (the relationship was not disclosed, but terms of endearment passed between them, the voice being very clear), and in the other a voice spoke to a lady so distinctly that I heard every word, although the lady addressed did not hear so well. When this voice finished the trumpet fell to the floor, and some of us were about to feel for it put it up again, but Mrs. Wriedt told us to leave it alone; the spirits would find it. John King then spoke, greeting the company in a loud voice, and departed. I then heard a voice close to me, but, thinking it was meant for my neighbour, was surprised to hear her told that the voice was not speaking to her, but to Mr. M—— E—— (that is myself). My name was given clearly and distinctly, but I quite failed to identify the name given by the voice. He described himself as a friend of the family, and, seeming to be annoyed at my stupidity, ceased speaking. I now noticed ovals of light floating about above the cabinet, but could not see any detail; but those who had better psychic vision than myself described them as men's faces. Suddenly there appeared a very bright oval light above the cabinet, and I distinctly saw the face of Mr. Stead, who seemed to bow to the company and then disappear. Almost immediately after a strong voice asked: "Did you see me?" One or two ladies immediately replied: "Yes, Mr. Stead." The voice replied: "I am not speaking to the ladies, but to the gentlemen"; then, addressing me by name, he said: "How do you do? I am pleased to see you here." (I knew Mr. Stead when he lived in the North.) Voices continued to speak afterwards, but with no great success; and Mrs. Wriedt decided to close the séance, which was done by singing a closing hymn. When the lights were turned up I saw that a bowl which had contained flowers on the small table was empty, and flowers were scattered on the floor. This was about 8.30 p.m. I have gone into detail and particulars of the séance room and procedure, as it was my first experience; but will simply give practical results of further sittings, as the methods of conducting them were much the same.

May 27. There were thirteen at this Séance, eight gentlemen and five ladies. 7 p.m. For ten or fifteen minutes there was no manifestation. Then something was heard to fall on the floor in the circle; shortly after I heard a swishing sort of sound, and felt something laid on my shoulder. I took hold of it, and found it to be a long-stalked rose. I laid it on my lap, but, as it began to move away, kept it in my hand. Nothing more happened, and Mrs. Wriedt closed the sitting, and expressed disappointment at the failure. When the lights were turned up, a book, a quarto volume on the British Army, was found on the floor, which Mrs. Harper returned to its place in a bookshelf at the back part of the room. A bowl of flowers was also found on the floor in the centre of the circle.

May 31. Sitting commenced about 7 p.m. with seven ladies and five gentleman. About 8 p.m. touched on left knee with trumpet. Voice:

"E——" (myself). "Yes, who are you?" Voice: "I am your uncle, your father's brother." "Yes?" Voice: "I was with your father this morning." Question: "Is it Willie?" Voice: "I am known as William." Question: "Were you with me today?" Voice "I am with you always." Question: "Is my brother with you?" Voice: "Yes he is here now; he asked me to speak to you first, to see how the thing worked." Question: "Ask him to speak." (Interval; others speaking.) Voice: "E——." Question: "Yes who is it?" Voice: "Brother." Question: "My brother J——?" Voice: "Yes are you deaf?" "No, I hear you, and am listening." Voice: "I have been seeing mother today." Question: "How did you find her?" Voice: "Better than she was; she has not been at all well this winter, but is better now that the weather is warmer." (correct) Then followed a long conversation over the manner of his death, which occurred under tragic circumstances in a foreign country during a political upheaval; but, as the names of people still living were mentioned, I cannot, for obvious reasons, make public what was said, but I may say that what he told me threw a strong light on the mystery of his death, and made clear what had hitherto been a strange problem. At the close of the conversation I asked him: "Tell me, do you know what I am touching now?" Voice: "Yes, it is the ring I gave you. Keep it and wear it always." (Correct; I made no sign of taking hold of the ring, as it had been between my finger and thumb of the other hand all the time.) I had sufficient proof at this sitting to convince me of the genuineness of the communications.

June 18, 2 p.m. Private sitting. Soon after the lights had been lowered I saw discs of red light about the size of a half-crown floating about quite near to me. Then my brother began to speak, and from him I learned the whole story of the treacherous circumstances surrounding his death; he gave names of people and places only known to myself. In describing one room in a certain house in this distant and turbulent country, he used a term which gave a clear reason, for me, of its peculiarities, which had puzzled me when I visited the place some short time after. Towards the close of the sitting he warned me to be particularly careful in the use of my motor car at a certain period, detailing the class of trouble which would arise. Curiously enough, I had the trouble at the time predicted, due to the illness of my regular man. However, I was alert owing to the warning, and discovered the fault before anything very serious happened. My uncle then spoke and said that he had been with me the previous day in my office, describing correctly the actual work I had been engaged in. When we were about to close I felt something touch me on the foot, and, on remarking it to the psychic, John King spoke, saying that it was a small dog I used to have, come to see me. He described it well, and gave a word sounding very like its name. I had a dog similar to the one described some years ago which was poisoned by some stranger and died in my hands.

June 22, 4 p.m. Private sitting. My brother came again and spoke with me on family matters which cannot be set down here; and two other close relatives, who had passed out of this life, held conversations with me, and thereby clearly demonstrated to me the truth of spirit return. John King came and spoke to me in his strong voice, encouraging me to go on with my investigations.

At a sitting the same night, 7 o'clock, when there were eleven present in all, including Mrs. Wriedt and the stenographer, no one spoke to me except one, Blossom (a child's voice), who seemed to delight in discovering hidden trinkets or private mementoes worn by the sitters and describing them. In my case she correctly told me the number of gold coins in my pocket, the number being quite unknown to me at the time. She also told me how I proposed to spend it, and what I was going to do the next morning. (All correct.) A great deal of conversation took place between "voices" and the other sitters, but nothing which I can repeat.

June 24, 7 p.m. This was an excellent séance, lasting two hours, Admiral Moore being present. Dr. Sharp immediately spoke, greeting the company, and indeed took charge of the sitting, seeming to be always at hand to assist in identifying spirits and making explanations. He gave a lady present a minute description of the ailment of her son, and suggested a course of cure. Lights were seen in the cabinet, and there was plainly seen going round the circle the form of a child who turned out to be a little grandchild of the Admiral. Grayfeather spoke with a gentleman regarding a message of warning he had transmitted. My brother came and spoke to me about family matters. Boursnell manifested and held a short conversation with Admiral Moore respecting the taking of spirit photographs. But perhaps the most convincing part of the sitting was the display of lights. "Two brilliant crosses of light were seen in the middle of the room and a light like a full moon. All the sitters agreed that they had never seen such a wonderful phenomena of lights." (Quoted from stenographers notes.) Julia concluded the sitting by a little address in her usual sweetness of language.

June 27, 7 p.m. Failure.

July 1, 7 p.m. Dr. Sharp spoke to me, saying he was sorry that attending the séances interfered with my work, but that I should be rewarded for my labours. My brother also spoke to me and told me much about certain business which I have since found to be perfectly correct. During this sitting I saw much bright light, and once, when the trumpet fell near my feet and I stooped to pick it up, a light seemed to exist on the floor so that I saw the trumpet and picked it up. Julia spoke at great length with Miss Harper with regard to the future carrying on of the bureau, and to me this conversation was the most natural and impressive that it had been my pleasure and privilege to listen to during the whole number of sittings I had attended.

July 4, 7 p.m. A very large circle, about twenty in all. Some little time elapsed before there was any manifestation, when John King spoke his greeting. Almost immediately one of the sitters (a gentleman with a foreign name) asked John King something which he resented, and no further phenomena too place.

I should have liked to describe the impression these experiences have made on the mind of one who had seen manifestations of the above kind for the first time (and up to the present has not discovered any sign of internal Psychic powers), but space forbids.

(Signed)   M. E.

The attached narrative is furnished to me by a gentleman of independent means residing in the South of England. He had a scientific business training, but has occupied himself for some years with honorary work connected with county affairs and charitable organisations:—

The first séance I had with Mrs. Wriedt was in July, 1911, at Cambridge House, Wimbledon. It was a private sitting early in the afternoon. I was accompanied by my wife and my two eldest daughters, both of whom were over twenty-one years of age. The room was completely darkened; the medium sat near the cabinet and retained throughout her normal consciousness, talking frequently to us, sometimes describing spirits and visions which were unseen by ourselves. Immediately the lights were extinguished we were flicked with water, and soon afterwards luminosities appeared floating in the air, visible to all the party. I can but describe their shape and size as like luminous night-gowns in movement, with a head shaped top, the forms being about the size of average thin people; no features were distinguishable; they developed near the cabinet, approached to within a couple of feet of the sitters, and the faded gradually away, sometimes as if through the floor.

No sounds emanated from these forms, which came from time to time during the eighty minutes séance; and they were intangible.

After two or three had appeared, voices came from the trumpet; these varied in tone and quality, but none were recognised as resembling those of the alleged speakers when they were in earth-life. Once we heard two different voices speaking simultaneously, whilst at the same time the medium was talking to us.

The first voice that came said she was "Mary". One of us asked, "Mary Ann?" answer: "No; Mary Adams." "Mary Adams?" I repeated. Answer "Yes, yes, your guide." She gave us a welcome and greetings in a fairly distinct voice. (Mary Adams is one of my spirit guides to whom I am much indebted.)

Then a voice announced itself as "John." After some difficulty we got, "Begins end of alphabet—no, not 'Z'"; and after some guessing we obtained the name of "W——y"; the voice proceeded: "John W——y the older one. You remember Lizzie? Yes; you must. I was connected with your business." (I noticed that Christian names were given readily and clearly, but surnames nearly always seemed to present great difficulties to the speaker. We had two W——y's, father and son, connected with our business. Both passed over some time ago, but their Christian names were both James—not John; and we do not remember any Lizzie connected with them.)

Another voice announced itself as "William." One of my daughters asked," "Is it grandpa or uncle?" Answer: "Yes; grandpa." I was gently stroked on the cheek by a hand, and my wife was stroked on the knees. He said: "I am pleased to see you here. This is delightful. God bless you!" And he left with the sound of a kiss. Then a voice called clearly several times most eagerly, "Maude, Maude!" The name given by the spirit was indistinct but it sounded like Carrie. "Are you Aunt Carrie?" my wife (whose name is Maude) asked. Answer: "Yes." A long conversation ensued between them (just as if her aunt were in the flesh), during which the spirit referred to two prints she gad given us, now hanging in one of the bedrooms (correct), and to a necklace given to my eldest girl (who was present), now worn as a chain; the spirit said it was a weak chain (correct). She inquired, "Who had her brooch with the red stone in it?" (not understood); reminded us how she used to dance the children, when very young, on her foot, singing "Diddledy, diddledy" (correct); said how she always loved us (Aunt Carrie had a hard life, and we endeavoured to be kind to her); requested us to send her love to my wife's twin sister, and said I was to teach her about spiritualism (my wife is a spiritualist, but her sister knows but little about the subject); and when I mentioned how I used to chaff her sometimes, she laughed pleasantly and said "Goodbye." We all considered this conversation as a most satisfactory test and evidence of identity.

Mrs. Wriedt described several people near us whom we were unable to identify; then a voice sang "Loch Lomond," and said he often used to visit my wife when a girl and sing Scotch songs; that he was Mrs. Somebody's husband (we could not catch the name), and insisted that my wife knew him (this spirit was not recognised at all). Finally, Dr. Sharp came, and in a good clear voice talked for some time on ordinary topics of conversation. He said we ought to have ten children like those two present. "We should then be in paradise"—with which little piece if flattery the séance closed.

It will be noted that in this séance we obtained only one good test of identity, but that was so convincing and evidential that I think we are justified in looking for another explanation for the failures than that of "Humbug," or unsuccessful "helping out" by the medium. We were all perfect strangers to the medium and to everyone connected with "Julia's Bureau"; there was no "Fishing" on the part of Mrs Wriedt during the "Carrie" conversation, and not one of us gave ourselves away in any particular.

The second séance with Mrs. Wriedt took place in June this year at Cambridge House. The sitters were my mother, my wife, a married sister, my eldest daughter, and myself. As soon as the lights were switched off sundry luminosities appeared similar to those described above; then a voice claiming to be that of Julia welcomed us to the "Temple of Truth, the source of light and Wisdom," and spoke well in a serious strain for many minutes (this was my first introduction to Julia). After this a voice purporting to be that of my father spoke (I may repeat that the voices were not, in any case, like those of the persons when in earth life); my sister's knees were touched, and also my moustache, by an intangible hand. The voice inquired after my mother's health, and before she had time to reply said, "You are better" (which was the fact). Mrs. Wriedt then said she got the name of "Cross"—"a lady who died after an operation"; at the same time my sister's knees were touched. The spirit could not be identified at first. A Christian name sounding like Nellie was given through the trumpet. She said she belonged to my sister's husband's side of the family. My sister suddenly asked: "Are you Louisa L——?" (This lady died within a week of an operation.) Without replying definitely, the spirit said: "I am often with you; your boy is doing well, do not worry about him" (my sister had been anxious about her son's health and his theological views.) After some conversation I asked: "How does the name of 'Cross' come in here?" My sister suggested that it might be symbolic of the High Church views held by Louisa L—— when in the flesh, as a means of recognition. One of her sons had made Louisa L—— a cross when she was alive; the husband of the latter lady, when a churchwarden, used to carry a large cross in procession. After this spirit left John King interposed and said emphatically that "it was Louisa L——. What did it matter if she had one or a hundred and one crosses? It was the cross she carried to church that mattered." Shortly after this the medium said, suddenly, without any circumlocution. "I get the name of Josephine"; and at the same time my mother was touched on the shoulder and a voice through the trumpet said: "I am your sister. It is all happy and bright here. I will welcome you to heaven some day; jealousy and selfishness do not exist in heaven; those come from differences in position on earth. I thank your son for bringing my treasure here." She then went to my wife, calling her by name. My wife said "I never knew you on earth." The reply came, "I am glad to welcome you in the family; you have been a good wife, a good mother, and a good daughter." (I consider this visit of "Josephine" quite good evidence of identity. The somewhat uncommon name coming so pat, followed immediately by the statement of relationship and the touching of my mother's shoulder, was almost startling. The spirit had passed over a good many years; the family had never been in close touch with this relative, and she was far from all our minds. I doubt whether my children had ever heard us speak of this aunt of mine. The references to jealousy and differences of social position were peculiarly apposite to the circumstances of her life. Evidences of this character are usually more convincing than any other kind; there is something so artless and genuine about them. Thought- reading as an explanation is out of the question, because she was not in the mind of any person present who had known her in life, and the sentence she made use of came rather as a piece of self-confession.)

After some other incidents a voice greeted us as "William, I am brother and son" (correct name of my brother). He laughed several times whilst speaking (a characteristic habit of his when in the flesh). He sent his love to my daughter G—— (his godchild), and said to my daughter W——, "I will walk with you down the Dyke road" (my daughter had been staying recently in Brighton with his widow). The voice then approached my sister and said, "How is Billy?" She asked," "Do you mean the dog?" and the reply was a bark. She said, "How do you know I have a dog called Billy?" He replied, "Do you think I don't keep my eyes open when I come to see you?" My daughter asked if he had a message for anyone else (expecting he would wish to send one to his widow). After several attempts, we heard something like "Sherry." My sister asked, Do you mean 'Cherie'?" Answer: "Yes; love to 'Cherie.' Maude (my wife) ought to know" (my sister alone knew and remembered that he used to call his wife "Cherie" sometimes). My wife was asked to shake hands, which she tried to do; but, although her hand was touched, she could not grasp anything. My spectacles were touched, and the trumpet struck my head gently several times. He stayed some time talking—mostly to my wife, of whom he was very fond.

Mrs. Wriedt now said she saw a white violin coming over the table and a person dressed in violet stopping behind me. Then came a voice "Grace." My daughter inquired if her sister was meant (there is also an aunt Grace). Answer "Yes, yes." Then the voice sang two little bits of songs; one was "The harp that once through Tara's hall the sound of music shed." The spirit went on to say that Grace would play one day at the Albert hall. We replied that she was too nervous, and intended to teach music. Answer: "You cannot teach without first learning to play; no, no, she must fight against it. Encourage her, the fear will go, I will help her.

My general opinion of Mrs. Wriedt's mediumship, based upon the above experiment, may be gathered from my observations in parentheses. There are the usual failures of identification, the occasional inaccuracies mixed with truth, and sometimes that which has the appearance of guessing; but I am convinced that this woman is a powerful medium. I credit her with honesty, and assert that she has provided us with positive evidence of the survival of human personality after death and the possibility of communication with the deceased.

A lady who was born in Sydney, N.S.W., and spent all her girlhood there, and who now resides in Devonshire, sends me the following:—

I sat many times with Mrs. Wriedt both in private and in general circles, and I will tell you of one or two interesting episodes. One day in 1911, my sister and I had a private sitting at Cambridge house, and an entity announced himself through the trumpet as "George." We know several Georges who have passed over. My sister said; "Are you George Lloyd?" Answer "No." Question: "What is your other name?" The spirit seemed to find great difficulty in replying to this positive question, so I said: "Where did you know us?" Answer "At Rose Bay. My name is George Smith. Your father brought me here." I was much puzzled as the name given conveyed nothing to me; but my sister said "Did you live at Rose Bay?" Answer; "Yes, near your old home." (Our old home was at Rose Bay, one of the numerous little bays in Port Jackson; it is three miles from the city of Sydney, New South Wales.) Then the voice addressed me; "Where is your sling stone? You were a small little girl. You used to have a sling stone." Question "Do you mean a catapult?" Answer; "Yes, you were a little mischief." (I used to have a catapult when I was a small child; it is possible that I was a great nuisance to the neighbourhood.) Then turning to my sister, he said: "I should not have known you; what have you done to yourself? You were always the sedate one." (This allusion is quite correct.) When the voice no longer spoke, my sister said: "Well, I am the only one who would remember him; you were too young. George Smith did live near us at Rose Bay. He was a contractor." (This was forty-six years ago.)

The incident I am now about to describe occurred this year (1912). I went with my sister and had a private sitting with Mrs. Wriedt again in the dark. One of my objects was to obtain a test from an ancestor of ours who had manifested on previous occasions, calling himself by his abbreviated Christian name.

Before we left my sister's house for Wimbledon, and unknown to her, I had written on a piece of paper the name of the ship in which our relative was lost, and the question: "What does this convey to you?" I put the piece of paper in my handbag and did not mention it to either my sister or to Mrs. Wriedt. When the lights were switched off, and the room in total darkness, I opened my bag softly, took the paper out noiselessly, and held it in my hand. A friend of ours came and talked to my sister; he suddenly said to me: "Put that on the table." (I was sitting near the large oval table where the flowers were.) I answered: "No, it is not for you." He repeated: "Put it on the table," which I did. When the spirit finished speaking, my ancestor made himself known in his usual way by giving his abbreviated first name. Then he said: "I am going to answer this question in a peculiar way. It is the name of a ship: she was destroyed, and I went to the bottom." We heard the crumpling of paper and the flowers being touched. At the end of the séance, when the lights were switched on, we found on the floor the paper my question was written upon wrapped round the stalk of a spray of rosebuds from which a bud had been broken off.

My ancestor passed over one hundred and twenty-six years ago, at the early age of twenty-two. He was a naval officer; his ship was wrecked on the English coast. So I think we may say his life was nipped in the bud, as he tried to convey by showing us the mutilated roses.

One afternoon, on my way to a séance at Cambridge House, I was walking alone up Bond Street rather in a hurry. To my annoyance a man kept walking alongside of me, trying to attract my attention. After a time he left my side, and I was able to walk on without molestation. I had no time, before I went into the séance room, to speak of it, even if I had thought of it or wished to do so. During the sitting my mother came to my sister and myself and said: "My dear, what a horrid thing for that man to do this afternoon, to try and speak to you!" I said: "Why mother were you there?" She answered: "Yes, dear."

At every séance which my sister and I attended together different spirits talked to us simultaneously, one generally with the trumpet and one without.

(Signed)   E. R. Richards.

Mrs. Jacob, Mrs. Richard's sister Writes:——

I beg to corroborate my sister's account. I am six years older than my sister, and can certify to the fact that a contractor called George Smith did live a short distance from my fathers house at Rose Bay, Sydney. He must have known us by sight when we played about as children, and probably spoke to us now and then. My sister had a small catapult.

I agree with my sister that we cannot give details of the various conversations that we enjoyed with our deceased relatives and friends through the mediumship of Mrs. Wriedt; but I have pleasure in sending you what I consider a rather good proof of the nature of her extraordinary gift. One day in August last (1912) I called upon her at her hotel in London, and was shown up into her bedroom. She had just returned from shopping, and was packing, as she was leaving for Norway the next day. It was broad daylight, and there was considerable noise, not only from the traffic in the street outside, but from the opening of parcels and cutting up and folding of paper. I asked Mrs. Wriedt if I might hold the trumpet to my ear and try if I could get a message. She replied; "Do, but I am sorry I must finish packing, and cannot help being noisy." She then continued what she was doing, and constantly walked about the room bringing things to her trunks. I sat down on one chair, resting the big end of the trumpet on the back of another, and put the small end to my ear. Only Mrs. Wriedt and I were in the room. Very soon I heard a voice greet me. It was my father. He spoke well and strong, and I had a conversation of several minutes with him. Presently I heard another voice as if speaking to him; two voices in the trumpet simultaneously, the second very low. I asked: "Who is speaking to you?" Answer: "your sister." Question: "Is she talking to you?" Answer: "Yes." Question: "What is she saying?" My father then spoke for my sister, and gave me her message. We three then talked about old days in Australia in quite a natural way.

When my father left another relative came, and had a long talk with me.

I should tell you that my father died in Sydney in 1891, and my sister in 1909. At Cambridge House I have had a voice speaking to me without the trumpet, the latter only being used towards the end of the sitting.

When I held the trumpet to my own ear, as I did in Mrs. Wriedt's bedroom, I found it difficult to keep steady, and tiring to maintain it in place. It made me wonder at the ease with which the spirit people use it in the dark séances, and at the great patience they exercise.

I noticed that when Mrs. Wriedt was near me the spirit voice was stronger than when she was at the end of the room; so I tried to guide the trumpet towards her as she walked about. At one time John King interposed, and gave me a message for her. I said to her: "You had better hold it yourself; he wants you." She stopped packing and took the trumpet. I could hear her questions and answers to him, but not what he said to her. She told me that she could not make out what the voices were saying to me, only what I said to them.

On September 6, the night before Mrs. Wriedt left for America, I stayed with her at the Grosvenor Hotel, as she was leaving very early the next morning for Southampton by train. She had been ill and run down with a severe cold; and I was so sorry that she was going away alone, and in bad health, that I decided to see her away. She had been very busy packing and arranging all that day for her early departure next morning by the boat train, and went to bed tired, and fell asleep quickly. We shared the same bed (a large double bed). I could not sleep for hours, it seemed to me; and, after laying quietly for some time, I suddenly felt impressed to raise my head and look to where she was sleeping, still and quiet. What I saw made me sit right up. Over her sleeping form, her head being on the pillow partly turned away from me, was another Mrs. Wriedt, just her head and shoulders, looking full face at me over her own sleeping body—over her chest. A white, soft, gauzy scarf was loosely over the head, showing the hair, which seemed much brighter and lighter in colour, the eyes intensely blue and bright, complexion clear. The eyes met mine; the face had such a sweet smile, and the expression seemed wistful. As I looked, wondering at her, the thought came into my mind: You do look quite beautiful; you are not as beautiful as this in life. It was some moments before the vision faded. She was sleeping in the body peacefully through this phenomenon.

(Signed)   M. Jacob.

By Vice-Admiral W. Usborne Moore

The best general circle séance I attended at Cambridge House, apart from the "Julia" evenings (Wednesdays), was on Monday June 24. One of the sitters had come from Poole at my invitation. It was the only time he had seen Mrs. Wriedt, and the evidence he obtained of the presence of his wife and children who had passed over was, he assures me, wholly satisfactory. The stenographer's report, which is before me, is about as good as such records can be. Dr. Sharp, after greeting me and other friends, said:—

"How do you do, Mr. Osman?" [the sitter from Poole]. "I am very glad to see you." Mrs. Wriedt: "How do you know him?" Dr. Sharp: "His dear wife and children told me he was here."

I was sitting next but one to Miss M., a well known member of the S. P. R. and a psychic. The lady on my right was also a psychic. After I had introduced Miss M. to Dr. Sharp, he spoke to Mrs. Harper about one of her sons who was in hospital, giving a diagnosis of his disease and advising certain treatment. Whether his advice was good or bad I have no means of telling, but the address was delivered in a clear, firm voice without any hesitation.

A white form moved towards me, but there was no voice. Mrs. W. and Miss M. both saw forms. Then we sang, and the form of a little child was seen by psychics going round the circle. Mrs. Wriedt: "Admiral, it is your little grandchild, your Aunt E. brought her." I could hear the word "Grandpapa." (This infant would now be two years old had it lived. The relative named is the one who has always been said to be in charge of it.) A sitter entered into a conversation of some minutes with his sister, who during the talk gave the name of a living sister. Then a spirit sang a verse of "Lead Kindly Light." Cardinal Newman spoke, and bestowed upon the circle a Latin benediction. A brother came to Mr. M. E. (see Light of October 12), and talked for many minutes; among other things, he mentioned the name of a sister, also in spirit life.

Grayfeather renewed a warning he had previously given about an accident he saw as likely to happen to one of the sitters. He was introduced to the lady on my right, who had not met him before. The Indian spirit-girl called Blossom manifested to the sitters who knew her best. The room appeared to be filled with white clouds, and Miss M. was addressed by a voice which gave her a test satisfactory to herself. Several spirits manifested to sitters, and were recognised. One purporting to be Robert Boursnell, came to me and we had a brief talk. In one case Dr. Sharp intervened to assist a spirit who was apparently quite strange to this method of communication. One spirit, who gave his name as Charlie, attempted to prove his identity by whistling a tune. Asked by a sitter if he was Charlie Grimaldi, he replied: "Yes, why sure"; and added: "Do you remember who played the mocking-bird with variations of 'Home, Sweet Home'?" (Whistling again.)

Mrs. Wriedt: "There is a thin little man—smooth-faced—standing in the centre of the room." Voice: "Lincoln Cox." Mr. C.: "I know who that is." Voice: "This is a treat; what in the world are you doing here?"

Mr. C., "Because I had a great wish to come, and I thought I might meet someone who would tell me something." (Mr. C. explained to the other sitters that Mr. Cox had a place in New Burlington Street.)

Voice to Mr. Osman: "Marie. How are you, dear?" Mr. Osman: "I am very pleased to hear you; I have come a long way to meet you."

Voice: "Mother is coming to talk to you, and Reggie. Father dear, it is very lonely for you, but we are with you every day in the home. Mother is here. Leonard is not here, but mother is. Father dear, give auntie my love. Goodbye father." Mr. Osman: "Goodbye, dear."

Mrs. Wriedt announced that she saw the name of "Bee." This was recognised by the inmates of the house, who explained that she was a lady teacher many years ago. Miss Bee: "We have a lot of little evening parties in Heaven with the children. They dance, and are happy; it is fine. I still keep on teaching."

Here two sisters, Mrs. Jacob and Mrs. Richards, were visited by the spirit of an ancestor, a naval officer who was drowned in the eighteenth century (see Light of October 26, p. 507). These ladies sat on my right, between me and the psychic. I was introduced. The voice said: "I want to tell you I am J. They called me——" (using an abbreviation). Question: "What sphere are you in?" Answer: "The celestial sphere, but I have been over a long time." Question: "I heard that you were in the sixth sphere and seventh realm." Answer: "I a,, but I am also in the celestial sphere." Question: "I suppose there is no difficulty in coming here from the higher spheres?" Answer: "No, my pleasure is here till my friends come." Question: "What is the colour of the seventh realm?" Answer: "Lavender. There are thirty different colours in each sphere, but the principle ones are red, purple, blue, lavender, scarlet, white, and green." Question: "You were a sailor man: how did you come by your end?" Answer: "By a sudden dip; the ship was wrecked."

Mrs. Wriedt: "Does anyone recognise the name of Temple?" A Voice; "Chester." Admiral Moore: "Who are you for?" Answer: "Pardon me; I am not for you." (Spirit left, apparently annoyed.) A Voice: "Mrs. Osman." Mr. Osman: "Are you my wife?" Answer: "Yes I am glad to welcome you. All the children are here." Mr. Osman: "I am so glad to hear it." Answer: "I am so glad to be with you here. It is so good of you to have come. I have been looking forward to this for a long time." Mr. Osman: "It is a long time since I spoke to you." Answer: "The children and I are with you every day. I do not miss you as much as you do me, because I am there every day, and the children as well. How is auntie?" Mr. Osman: "Auntie is very well, thank you." Answer: "Give her my love. "Oh, dear, it is such a comfort to have a chat with you! God bless you for your long wait. Goodnight." (The voice turned in my direction.) "Thank you, Admiral, for your trouble." Much surprised that the spirit should be aware of the small share I had in bringing her husband there on that evening, I could only say: "It is very kind of you to speak to me. Goodnight.")

A French artist came, who was recognised immediately by the ladies on my right. He gave an explanation about a fault in the eyes of a certain picture he had painted, which they appeared to understand.

A voice to Miss M. (on my left). Miss M.: "Please cam you tell me your name? Who are you? Are you a relative?" Dr. Sharp: "My dear lady, this spirit is for a certain individual that you know very well." (The control went on and talked for a few minutes. Miss M. stated that she quite understood what was meant.) A Voice: "Reggie. Dear father, how are you?" Mr. Osman: "Are you better than you were?" Answer: "All right now — never any trouble." Mr. Osman: "I have been so anxious." Answer: "You have come a long way to see us and talk to us. We are in the house just the same." The trumpet then dropped and he was gone.

A Voice to me: "Aunt E. Did you hear the little child? She attempted to say 'grandpapa.' I am very glad, W.. to see you tonight. I was afraid I might not have another opportunity. All is well at home."

Now occurred a rare phenomenon—flashes of light. I had never seen it before. Some of the sitters saw, or thought they saw, crosses of light, and the stenographer says he saw a light like a full moon; but I only made out two or three flashes. (This phenomenon is occasionally seen when sitting with Miss Ada Besinnet.)

Julia now gave an address, consisting of one hundred and sixty words, in her usual style and refined English voice. While she was speaking, Iola called me by name, very clearly, five or six times, and gave a brief message. The voice came from a position between my neighbour on my right and myself, and about level with the top of my head. During this séance all the sitters except one were visited by more than one spirit friend. Mr. Osman has kindly sent me the following particulars:—

My daughter Marie was our only girl out of a family of eight; she passed over in January, 1896, aged thirteen years. Leonard passed over when a baby. My wife passed away three years ago without being able even to say "goodbye" to me. My son Reginald passed over in November, 1910, aged thirty-one years, after suffering for four years from consumption; he was very reluctant to go, except the last day or so; and, after passing over, he was very unhappy indeed for a time. I was so glad to hear him say, in his characteristic way: "I am all right now—never any trouble."

"Auntie is my wife's favourite sister, who lives at a farm a few miles from here. She and my children thought a great deal of one another, and it was the custom of the family to speak of her in this manner.

Marie mentions "Mother," "Reggie," and "Leonard." *There* was no person present in Cambridge House who could have connected those names together except myself.

THE VOICES OF 1912: THE TESTIMONY REVIEWED
From Light, November 23, 1912

It only remains for me to make a few remarks in summing up the various narratives in Light devoted to the voices which have been obtained through the mediumship of Mrs. Wriedt.

The truth or otherwise of spirit return is entirely a matter of evidence. If the reader does not think that there is any truth in these papers, or imagines that it is possible for a foreign medium to have become possessed of the knowledge of the various events described by the voices to the sitters who have recorded their experiences, there is nothing in them to convince him of the proximity of people in another state of consciousness; whatever value there is in the narratives depends upon their veracity, and the assurance (1) that the sounds were discarnate voices, and (2) that the utterances were not merely echoes of facts known to the psychic (and consequently to her controls or familiar spirits) , but items of information which could only be recalled by the sitters themselves, or by their friends not in the house.

The witnesses consist of a publisher in London, a physician in London, a late private of the R.M.L.I., two clergymen, an Eastern traveller, a lady from Surrey, two military men, one naval officer, a lawyer from Ireland, a distinguished Fellow of the Royal Society from Ireland, two ladies in London, a lady from Southsea, a lady from Bournmouth, a foxhunting lady from Wales, a Dutch lady, a mining engineer from Durham, a gentleman of leisure from Surrey, two ladies Australian by birth, a hotel proprietor from Poole, and a foreign diplomat. Had there been room in Light for more narratives, I could have produced testimony from many others.

The gem of the collection, in my opinion, is the first letter on page 435. The psychic was in a distressed condition of mind about a matter which had gravely disturbed her for four days, but which had nothing more to do with her than Home Rule for Ireland. Everyone knows that this is the most unfavourable circumstance under which a spirit can get through. Nevertheless, so powerful were the influences that they managed to overcome the mental storm and to introduce perfect harmony. No less than seven discarnate entities made their identities known, and in such a way as to cause it to be abundantly clear that they were aware of even the most trifling actions of the sitter. John King was the control in charge on that occasion.

A correlation proving the influence of John King in Mrs. Wriedt's séances is given on page 410. A lady who has been in the habit of sitting with the mediums Husk and Williams, enters Cambridge House for the first time. She had often been playfully addressed by John King's band as "The Rose." John King manifests and speaks to her, using the same nickname at Mrs. Wriedt's séance. On this occasion an Indian spirit visits my friends at my request, though I was not present.

Many languages were spoken by discarnate spirits; Mrs. Wriedt is unacquainted with any language except Yankee. A good instance of this is given by "E. F. S." The daughter in spirit life speaks English to her brother in earth life; both son and daughter were educated to speak Dutch, English, and French with equal facility. One day an aunt and friend from Holland accompany "E. F. S." to Cambridge House. The same spirit speaks to these ladies in Dutch, and the husbands (in spirit life) of the aunt and friend converse with their wives in their own language. As regards foreign tongues, we have the evidence of M. Chedo Miyatovich, formerly Servian Minister at the courts of Queen Victoria and King Edward VII, on page 271, that German, Servian, and Croatian were spoken during his sittings with Mrs. Wriedt.

W. T. Stead speaks to me and others at a brief séance held within two hours of the psychic's entry into Cambridge House, and alludes to the last conversation we had together when he was alive. The next morning he shows himself to me; the etherealisation, though certainly Steed, does not resemble any picture taken of him in life. He is seen and speaks frequently to his personal friends, not only in the Julia circles, but at casual séances; and he uses phrases which it was known he used when in the body.

On page 380 it is recorded that a spirit comes to a physician and inquires earnestly if he has been paid his fee for attendance upon her during her last illness. The inquiry is pertinent to the circumstances of the case. On page 381 Grayfeather and Dr. Sharp remind me of a trifling incident — a breach of discipline—which occurred on board a ship I commanded twenty-nine years ago. It happened, I know, but I can only faintly remember it; when and where it occurred I have no recollection. It is not the sort of incident which would make a lasting impression upon the mind of a commanding officer immersed in the details of a somewhat important mission.

Valuable testimony to the extraordinary nature of Mrs. Wriedt's gift is given to us by Mrs. Jacob, who records, on page 507, how she was able to obtain messages when noise was going on, and the psychic was walking about the room cutting up paper, opening parcels and packing. A deputy-lieutenant of a midland county relates how he heard voices when the psychic was downstairs in the drawing room forty feet distant, and the séance room closed. He has told me of this, and his assertion is repeated on page 490.

The attention of the reader is directed to page 429, where he will find an account by a civil servant whose work lies in Dublin. This gentleman visits Cambridge House with me as a perfect stranger. His name, nationality, and his position as a member of two societies for psychical research—indeed, everything about him—are unknown to the psychic and the inmates of the house. Yet Dr. Sharp, the spirit control, greets him as "Mr. Psychical Researcher," and lays himself out to give him certain definite proofs of the action of intelligence's which were not those of the mortals present. On this occasion a supremely beautiful spirit form appears.

On page 387 there is a letter from Mr. Maybank, formerly a private R.M.L.I., who, by way of testing the identity of his son Harold in spirit life, says: "Do you remember poor old Cyril?" The son instantly replies: "Of course I do; didn't I tease him?" and proceeds to imitate the noise that a cat would make when angry. Mr. Maybank remarks: "It is reasonable to assume that, when the name 'Cyril' was mentioned, not one of the people sitting there would suppose it referred to a cat." I think most of us would agree to that.

On page 448 will be found three good tests. The spirit of an old bell-ringer, who died an idiot, speaks to his vicar in earth life and says: "You still ring the curfew bell." I wonder in how many places in England the curfew bell is rung today. It so happens that it is rung in a tower half a mile from old Crookes's home when he was in earth life. Again: Grayfeather comes to a lieutenant R. N., and says, "I see three rings for you at cherry time." On June 30 (seven weeks later) this gentleman is promoted to the rank of commander. The distinctive mark of the new uniform is three gold rings round each arm. The third test or prophecy is not quite so clear, but, allowing for the spirit's rude manner of expression, I consider it significant. "Heap much trouble across water— white people, black people, all kinds of people, —they go to fight—lots of heads cut off." At that time no one could foresee the invasion of Turkey by the Balkan States, or the appalling slaughter which has taken place in Thrace. It would seem that the old Indian was predicting the sanguinary war now in progress. God alone knows whether it will affect the British Empire, which embraces nearly one hundred millions of Moslems, who look to the Caliph as the head of their religion. Grayfeather has repeated his dismal forebodings of great slaughter across the sea twice since May.

Sir William Barrett, who, in conjunction with Mr. Dawson Rogers, founded the S. P. R. in London, is rightly considered by most psychic investigators as the greatest expert on the subject now living, for this reason: He combines sympathy for these abnormal people we call mediums with acute observation and a cautious habit of mind—so cautious that he stated in public last winter that he did not believe any satisfactory test had ever been obtained through the exhibition of psychical phenomena—this, after over thirty years of investigation, a personal knowledge of the prominent English psychics, and a close acquaintance with fellow-scientists who had investigated them. The evidence for the existence of the phenomena of the "direct voice" through the mediumship of Mrs. Wriedt, which I gave him, produced no impression upon him, though he began to think when a Norwegian lady told him she had conversed with her relatives in her own language. He did, however, guarantee for two sittings this year. Let us see what his attitude is now. After relating some remarkable experiences, on page 459, he says: "I went to Mrs. Wriedt's séances in a somewhat sceptical spirit, but I came to the conclusion that she is a genuine and remarkable medium, and has given abundant proof to others besides myself that the voices and the contents of the messages given are wholly beyond the range of trickery or collusion."

Dr. Abraham Wallace, on page 513, gives a curious piece of information: "Those who had attended these séances knew that John King spoke with a marked English accent. But, none the less, John King once [at Cambridge House] conversed with him in broad Scotch, and, when interrogated on the subject, replied: "Why, I got it from you," explaining that he was speaking under an influence derived from the aura of Dr. Wallace.

Mr. James Robertson and Mr. Coates have borne testimony to the Scotch voices heard when Mrs. Wriedt was in Scotland. As the evidence given in Light shows conclusively, Mrs. Wriedt has often been heard to speak at the same moment as the spirits, and two spirits have frequently been heard talking simultaneously to different members of the circle, with and without the trumpet.

Of my own experiences this year I have little to report. I talked only to my guide, about five relations, and two or three friends. There was nothing of public interest. My guide, at private sittings, invariably spoke only of private matters; she did not use the trumpet, and the psychic could not hear one word. Nor did she usually see her, though I was always able to do so.

But enough! If the evidence for the voices given in these papers from people who in most cases were unacquainted with one another is not sufficient to establish their genuine character, human testimony is no good for anything whatsoever.

There is only one alternative theory to that which attributes these voices to the discarnate spirits of our dead. It is this: That surrounding us is a region inhabited only by a special breed of demons who can ascertain every thought and action of our lives, create dramatic situations at will, and who, by their dexterity, can silence any doubt as to identity by returning to us our own thought. Let those who can believe this cheerful doctrine, as the Roman Catholics undoubtedly do, hug it for all it is worth if it affords them comfort. For my own part, I cannot see how it could interest these alleged demons to give me proofs of immortality. Rather would they endeavour to teach: "Eat, drink, for tomorrow ye die." Catholics like Monsignor Benson and Mr. Raupert are a great support to Spiritists; speaking broadly, they admit all the facts, but say that these spirits who visit us are "fallen angels." I am content that they should believe so. I think differently; I believe the time has come in the evolution of the human race when the Almighty has thought fit to permit the veil to be slightly lifted, and to allow us to meet the growing materialism of the day with evidences of the senses—not alone by faith, which is inadequate; and to let us know that the phenomena recorded in the Bible did not cease with the mission of the Apostles.

In some cases psychics, after many years, lose their sense of proportion, and get to think themselves the "Gift," and not merely the instrument. I earnestly hope that Mrs. Wriedt will not be spoilt by the adulation of admiring sitters. If such a catastrophe takes place, she will, I feel confident, lost her divine gift. I sincerely trust that she will so regulate her life as to make it possible for her to retain the mysterious power which has been the means of spreading so much happiness around her.

November 9, 1912   W. Usborne Moore.

The following séances are not recorded in Light.

Lieut.-General A. Phelps sat with Mrs. Wriedt eight times. In 1911 he attended one general circle sitting and two private sittings, and in 1912 five private sittings. I was present on four of these occasions. A stenographer *was* in attendance at the General's last private sitting of 1911. and during the five private sittings in 1912. His first two sittings in 1911 have been described in Light, August 12, 1911, p. 377. During the second of these a famous homeopathic physician, Dr. Compton Burnett, manifested. I refer the reader to the above-mentioned account as an introduction to this vigorous spirit, who came again at other séances.

General Phelps for many years held a highly responsible administrative post in the Indian Army. He is the president of the Anti-Vaccination League of Great Britain, a spiritualist of some forty years' standing, and seventy-five years of age.

90

I propose to record his séances at some length, in order to show the vigour of the communicating entities, the length of time they were able to talk, and the characteristic nature of their speeches. Neither the General nor I would desire to associate ourselves with the opinions expressed. They do not say much which is profoundly wise, nor are their utterances suggestive of any new truths. They are, however, interesting as examples of attempts of strong personalities to get through and give ideas to the world they have left, if only in somewhat obstructed and imperfect language.

Most of the more interesting statements from near relatives are necessarily suppressed.

After the sitting of July 21, 1911, General Phelps asked me to find out what I could from Iola with reference to Mrs. Burnett's state of health. He knew she was very ill. My guide told me during our last interview in 1911 (late August) that her disease was hopeless—no power could save her.

After this, on August 31, 1911, the General sat again with Mrs. Wriedt. The stenographer entered the room five minutes after the séance had begun, and General Phelps said to him: "Dr. Burnett came, and he spoke about his wife, and said if there was anything to relieve her pain he would have come to some medium in this city, and told them to convey the message in a way that it would be understood, to help her; but, as there was no way possible to cure her, and an operation would kill her, it was unwise to attempt anything. A Voice (Dr. Burnett), through trumpet: "I want the General to understand that it is not wise to say anything to my brother-in-law, for he is not sufficiently educated on these lines, and it is unwise to say anything about this. There is nothing young man, that I can do to restore my wife; there is nothing I can do to build up the disease— to kill it—to cure it; death is the only thing that can help her on this side of life and the next! I have fought all these things. Cancer is one of these things; when internal, and it has eaten some of the membranes—certain lining membranes—that cannot be cured by the knife or by medicine. They can numb her consciousness. She understands—she knows; she is conscious that the medicine is doing it. And it is very good of you to try and help her; but at her age—incurable! incurable! incurable!"

General Phelps: "I am so indebted to you for what you did for my wife that I would gladly do something for yours. I believe if you had been on this side when she was ill you would have prolonged her live."

The Voice: "We are here for a long time, and it makes no difference what comes about us; we have to live out the laws of the great universal powers. We cannot live beyond our allotted time. I believe we are here born under the planetary conditions, and they rule our lives."

General Phelps: "That is a very hard thing to believe. Mdme. Blavatsky used to say that; but I never could understand its truth."

The Voice: "With the present conditions of the atmospheric wave you do not feel as brisk as you do on a bright, sharp day. Why is it? The elements form a current, a blood current, which rushes through the veins in an active way. It is the planetary conditions and the atmospheric conditions that really can govern all things that have breath. Man is a stream of gas and liquid. Yes, but the man has the brains and the woman the heart!"

General Phelps: "Mrs. Somerville had the brains, and Hypatia had the brains." The Voice: "She had the brains and the heart as well; but the ingenuity of man is far beyond the comprehension of woman!"

General Phelps: "I believe myself that woman has ingenuity much deeper than man, and it is a mere accident that man uses it much more strongly. Sir Richard Burton thought that women had a contempt for danger. Look at the women soldiers in Africa! He came to the conclusion that the women were stronger, braver, and more practical than the men, in Ashanti."

The Voice: "The women did not lose their temper, but they lost their head with their heart in their hand. I tell you man is man all the days of his life—you cannot change him! But, going back again to my wife, I feel it very keenly to say that it will not be long before she joins me."

General Phelps: "Is she anything of a spiritualist? Will she be prepared to meet you?"

The Voice: She will meet me on that rock of truth. She met me and we were one on earth, and we will be one in heaven. Well, we must all look forward to meeting. But remember one thing, there is a law—it controls all things. We spring from something. We come here unsolicited."

General Phelps: "Is that so?"

The Voice: We did; we came from the law of the great power of force, and we are going to leave this world by the law of this great force."

General Phelps: "I cannot help thinking that we pre-existed."

The Voice: "If such was the case, I have never met nor seen one over here that knew anything about it. I have not met a soul that could tell me one thing about reincarnation."

General Phelps: "Negative evidence is outweighed by positive!"

The Voice: "Nonsense, it is only a descension from another descendant. And when we come down to this pillar of truth, what did we emanate from—the Power, the law, the Light, the force of nature!"

General Phelps: "Nature in that case is a synonym for the Creator?"

The Voice: "Supposing we were all men, where does your reincarnation come from?"

General Phelps: "When we were in a certain state the two sexes were in one, and reproduction was conducted by fission, and there was no need for sex. It gradually arrived, and the two sexes have been evolved; but they are not essential to life, because if we go back to the spherical animals—the Rotifers, reproduced by fission— we find they are produced without sex."

The Voice: "I never saw a tree, a bush, or a flower without the two sexes, and so with the birds that soar in the air, and so with light, and so with the moon, and so with sunshine—Oh, my boy, my boy!"

General Phelps: "But if we carry our minds back to the genesis of the human race, we come to a time before their bodies were human!"

The voice: "If we were not human in those days, my dear boy, then what education came before us to give us the intelligence, the power, the wisdom, the hope? Why are we not covered with hair like the savages, or think and see like the animal? We are the proper mechanism of the great mundane sphere!"

General Phelps: "At one time we occupied bodies which were not human. Evolution is that of the physical, and not of the spiritual body. It has been very wide."

The Voice: I met a man over here who lived in—; he told me that there were stronger men and women, stronger intellects longer lives than there are at the present day; and he said they were human beings— ate, slept as we do, lived and worked, only in a different manner."

General Phelps: "That is a story of historical times. The Grecian architects arrived at results—they went forward, beyond us! But still we go forward and back; but going back one million years we come to the bodies which were not human. We find that from the annals of the Jesuits. The Jesuits tell us——"

The Voice (interrupting): "If you believe that, what do you suppose came before that? My dear man, my dear General, when you come over here I will take you round and show you something that will open your eyes. But every man will change his opinion when he comes into this land of reincarnation. Mdme. Blavatsky is not reincarnated yet, and no more am I, nor will I; I will always be the same old chap, looking after the boys and taking care of the women. Speaking again about my wife, there is nothing I can do to cure her or help her. The doctors are doing all they can for her. Give her the medical treatment she has had;

it is not helping her, but it is giving her a little relief, because at times she has terrible spells, and again she is quite easy. After the effect of morphine wears off, it is worse than ever again."

General Phelps: "Is there anything wrong with her diet?"

The Voice: "Her stomach is so weak that it is hard to give her food to digest; but once she begins to vomit, then the time is not far distant.

General Phelps: "I remember a case of that kind in one of your books."

The Voice: "The minute the gasses form and she spits water, then look out; the worst is there. I wish it were tomorrow that she comes to me, but life is sweet to some of us."

General Phelps: "And useful. It was not given to us by mistake."

The Voice: "And when a man is low down in life it is because of his own negligence. You know what a happy chap I was; and when I saw a woman grumbling, and nothing was right, many a time I gave her a little salt water, and she was all right next day" (here the spirit laughed).

General Phelps: "By the by, I have to give you a message from Mrs. W. She wants me to thank you for your address (paper) on the 'Super-salinity of the Blood'—she fears too much salt in the body for the kidneys. I think I read it in your book on Natrum Muriaticum, which I enjoyed reading very much."

The Voice: "I am glad you enjoyed it—I wrote that from my own experience. The best thing to treat the subject of bad circulation is salt. Give injections of one kind of salt, and it sets the heart going immediately.

General Phelps: "I have been treating my brother lately and successfully with Natrum. It affected his heart at first, but it has got right to the chilliness. He is older than I."

The Voice: "Yes, age is the difficulty. You have to be guided by age and pulsation, and you have to understand your patient."

General Phelps: "You said if you wanted to keep a thing to yourself you must publish it."

The Voice: "Yes but I had another meaning for that.

General Phelps: "I have been trying your recommendations for diseases of the skin. There is the lady of seventy who is about cured by taking 30 12" (Stenographer did not understand).

The Voice: "It is different when you look at a person; you can tell what is good for him. I used to look at the person and tell what was wanted."

The spirit then gave some medical advice to the stenographer, which was as useful as it was unexpected. It consisted of one hundred and eighteen words. After a few more remarks about his wife's condition and his approval of her present treatment, Dr. Compton Burnett left.

Hypatia came and stated that she was a guide to Dr. John King of Toronto. She alluded to Dr. John of Ontario, and to Iola.

Iola manifested, and had a conversation with the General and Mrs. Wriedt. Then Mrs. Phelps came and conversed with her husband for several minutes about their children and grandchildren. John King wound up the séance. Hs spoke of his medium, Cecil Husk, and said he was going to keep him as long as he could, and ended by saying: "I don't believe you can do anything to this lady [meaning Mrs Burnett] to cure her, there is nothing can help her."

General Phelps: "When I got Admiral Moore's letter saying that, I lost all hope. I suspected it myself before."

Mrs. Wriedt: "My head goes round."

John King: "Tell him [Mrs. B.s Brother] the doctors are doing all they can; but there is no cure for her: if they cannot relieve the pain, they cannot relieve the pain. To give her this hypodermic morphine is not cure."

The next of General Phelps séances was on May 31, 1912. Present Mrs. Wriedt (medium), General Phelps, Admiral Usborne Moore, and a stenographer.

There was a good deal of talk at first about the phenomenon of the trumpet being taken away and put back in exactly the same spot, which occurred a few days before (see Light, page 380), and also about the present condition of an invalid lady. After sitting about twenty minutes we heard a voice: "William." General Phelps said:

"Which one?" answer: "Brother William; I am glad to see you again." General Phelps: "I am glad to see you."

Admiral Moore: "It is the brother I knew; I am delighted to meet you. You did not think much of this in your lifetime."

The Voice: "You know I had a great admiration for my brother and his views; but I would not accept it as he did, and so I consequently left it alone."

General Phelps: "Do you know the house is to be sold on the fourth of next month?" Answer: "I am very glad of it." General Phelps: "It is possible our Nephew might buy it." Answer: "I should like to have it in the family, but it is a great load to carry. You can quite understand it. And I fear when the owner of the home has gone that the head has gone."

Admiral Moore: "I hear you had a beautiful garden and were very proud of it." Answer: "Yes, yes, I was proud in my heart and soul to see things grow that we could cherish." General Phelps: "And to give away the fruit and flowers to your neighbours!" Answer: "Yes, but I had not half enough. But I had to give it up and go on to something different. I had to give it up. I would like to see it with my relatives, who would appreciate it as I did. But under the circumstances let it go cheerfully to the one that can hold it. God bless you and the step you have taken. My religion would not allow me to perforate the laws."

Admiral Moore: "I hope you are quite happy?" The Voice: "What I mean by perforate is that I always thought that looking into the unseen was too dangerous, and not right. I did not want to perforate the deep veil called death. I loved the thought of seeing my blessed mother, my cherished father, and loved ones; but I was fearful that the law of God would punish me, so I would not look. Feed it to the mutes, feed it to the sensitives, feed it to those who look into darkness. You have taught me a lesson that no book could do. My dear brother, you have taught me the better way; but I was so dense I could not see." General Phelps: "Have you met our parents?" The voice: "Mother showed herself to you a spell ago when you thought you saw a scull. You remember the little bonnet she used to wear on her head? That was what you saw."

A spirit here came in who called himself "Brennen," and said he had been invalided when serving with the General. He implied that he had been sent home from Gibraltar suffering from dysentery a very long time ago (not recognised). He was followed by the mother of Iola, who greeted me and General Phelps, then said to me, "Grayfeather is helping you remarkably." I said, "I hope you feel better towards him than you did?" (This relative had previously expressed a great dislike to the old Indian.) Answer: "You understand I am getting accustomed to these things. I did not like the earth element......My dear W., I wish you would ask this man Sharp about this other dimension. He claims there is a fourth. Well, I don't know what the fourth is, so if you would just ask him." Admiral Moore: "We do not understand." Answer: "Well, he does, and I wish you would just ask him." Admiral Moore: "The thing could not be done in three dimensions, for we swept well over where the trumpet stood, and there was nothing there; when the lights were switched on, there it was in the same place where I had originally placed it." (Nobody has been able to understand Dr. Sharp's explanation of this phenomenon . We have been obliged to give it up.

General Phelps's mother now came in and talked of a member of the family who had caused trouble in his life. She was followed by the relative himself. General Phelps: "Well, I hope you have come to your right mind now?" Answer: "There are no excuses for me to make. It is done, and you cannot make it over again. We all do certain things which we wish that we had not done, but when we do them we think we are quite right. The biggest mistake a man can make is when he punishes another man for vengeance. We carry it too far in flesh and blood." After a few remarks by the General, he went on to say: "I was represented to have done a great deal more than I did. I should have worshipped my mother. I see a lot of people coming over here, and they are troubled. They say, 'I did this, that, and the other, and I must make it right.'" General Phelps said: I don't understand that; what you did wrong was due to ——" (his second wife). The Voice: "There is not a woman on the face of the earth who could make me do a thing if I did not want to." Question: "You were as obstinate as a mule when you liked." Answer: "I am sorry for it, and my mother knows it." Question: "Which of your wives is with you now?" Answer: "I loved my first wife, and there is no one living on the face of the earth who can love two women like their first love." Question: "Where is the second one?" Answer: "She is not with me; I found the girl of my love; I cannot love two and love them alike." Here the trumpet dropped to the floor.

Iola, my guide, now came in: "I am happy to see you this morning. Down in Wales she is feeling splendid [my wife was at Llandrindod Wells]. She would love to know how you are; I am trying to impress her that you are very well and happy, and I will go down with you." I said I was going next day by the 1.15 train from Euston, and the spirit repeated that she would accompany me.

Enter John King: "How do you do, God bless you?" General Phelps: "I am old and——."

John King (interrupting): "Then come over here and we will make you new. Grayfeather is away this morning; he is working hard." The control then addressed a few words to the stenographer, and the séance terminated.

June 1, 1912. Present Mrs. Wriedt, General Phelps, Admiral Usborne Moore, and a stenographer.

John King manifested, speaking very loudly, and held a conversation of several minutes with General Phelps, of no particular interest to the reader. I remarked that his voice was unusually loud that morning, when he said; "Three men against one woman; more men, more power, more women, more fine vibration; clearer and more distinct voices through the female organism." He then handed me the trumpet, which I stood up on the floor.

Iola then came in and said: "Good morning; how do you do? I was with——[my wife] this morning: you will have a nice time today and tomorrow. You will return home with her......I will go down with you." We were then very pleased to hear the voice of Dr. Burnett. General Phelps: "Pleased to hear you again. Since you were here your beloved wife has joined you." Dr. Burnett: "I told you nothing would save her. You know how the brilliant young man expressed himself to you; you remember the message I gave you that my wife—you know to whom you gave it, and what sarcasm there was in connection with it. I knew perfectly well she could not be cured." After some further remarks: "You know, my dear good friend, that I would do anything to assist you mentally, physically, and spiritually."

General Phelps: "Taking a hint from your book, *Fifty Reasons*, I have been using Vanadium. It has done me a great deal of good, but it leaves a horrible taste in my mouth."

Doctor Burnett: "That is the stomach—the liver parts solely; and in your condition the weakness of the flesh does not carry off the saliva. You understand the depressed feeling which comes over you occasionally? That is the weakness of the liver, not the heart. Your heart is as sound as a bell." General Phelps: "Thank you; but I sometimes feel a pain underneath the breast-bone."

Dr. Burnett: "That is not the heart; it is the pleural lining of the lower part of the lungs." After a question from me about Turkish baths the doctor said to me: "A Turkish bath is a good thing if you have nicotine in the system, or gout." Question "I thought you left something behind in drawing from us." Answer: "No, not at all. You have a certain amount of nicotine in your system, and there is a little chalk in your bones; and understand, the kidneys do not operate right; that is due to the uric acid in the system...... I want to say a word to the reporter." (Here the voice approached much closer and spoke more deliberately.) "I want you to put in your notes that I was gifted with the sixth part of the sixth sense of medicine. For instance, if I was baffled and did not know just how my case was—did not know the real cause of my patient's trouble —in the evening, just before I retired, I sat in my office. Took notes in my brain that such might be the case with this patient. I worked upon it from inspiration, but did not know about the law of spiritualism. But it is true through spiritualism in an unknown way that I made a success of my medicines. I knew that something was telling me what to do, but I did not know what it was."

General Phelps: And who was your inspiring spirit? Hahnemann?"

Dr. Burnett: "Yes, and we have inspiring spirits for every person living."

A brief talk then ensued about the new discovery of "Crookes's Collsoles" and the advisability of drinking out of silver vessels. General Phelps said that Dr. Burnett had been cured once too quickly of a cold, and it brought on an attack of jaundice.

Dr. Burnett: "Will you allow me to suggest—just a moment—I was listening to your conversation. Jaundice comes in this form—the gall duct overflows. It is not from any other reason. And why does it overflow? Do you know that?" Answer: "No." Dr. Burnett: "Take a note of this, because these gentlemen are at an age when they might forget. [Laughter.] The gall duct overflows from the liver being chilled. Then it goes all over the whole system, and you are pretty near as yellow as a copper-coloured man." Later on the spirit said: "Another thing I want to say, gentlemen. I may never get another opportunity. My wife one time was quite ill, and I did not know what under the living canopy of heaven to do for her. I thought the only thing I could do was to give her an injection in the arm of salt and water, and in three hours she was herself again. I gave her an injection of solution of salt water, and it strengthened and revived her. Salt is an excellent thing if you know how to use it, but you can take too much of anything. I gave it to a great many others who did not know what I was giving them."

Mrs. Phelps now manifested, and talked with her husband about their children and grandchildren. She was followed by Iola. General Phelps remarked that he thought that the two voices of his wife and Iola sounded very much alike; but Iola exclaimed "Oh, oh no, I am much younger; she is older than I; the voices are not at all the same." Then came the member of General Phelps's family whom he criticised the previous day. He said to me; "That lady who has just left forgot something. She intended to congratulate you upon your new suit." (This little pleasantry was very apt.) The travelling suit I had on was precisely the same cut as that which I had worn for weeks, but it was entirely new.)

John King: "I hope everyone is well here today. I think the doctor thought he was in a medical college the way he spouted it. But he is a good chap." I asked, "Where is Grayfeather?" Answer: "He is with the lady that is sick in the institution. [A relative of mine]......She is going to get well. It is just a little pressure on the veins that lead from one brain to the another. Good luck to you all—God bless you. I always like to come to you, whether I say a little or a lot."

The lights were switched on, and the trumpet fell from the ceiling between the General and myself.

The following notes are necessary to explain the personalities of the spirits who manifested at General Phelps's séances:—

Dr. Compton Burnett, a descendant of the famous bishop of Salisbury, was born July 20, 1840, and passed over April 2, 1901. He made a profound study of anatomy as a young man. He practised at Chester and Birkinhead, and finally in London, where he had a large consulting practice for twenty-three years. Latterly he lived at Brighton. In middle life he adopted Homeopathy. His cures were very remarkable, and gained him the soubriquet of "the Magician." He wrote a book called *Fifty Reasons for being a Homeopath*, and edited *The Homeopath World* for fifteen years. Those who wish to know more of this remarkable man should read *Life and Work of James Compton Burnett, M. D., by D. J. H. Clarke* (Homeopathic Publishing Company). General Phelps says: "I did not know him in private life, unfortunately, so only formed opinions of him from visits to his consulting-room......He very soon convinced me on July 21, 1911, that it was verily himself who was speaking; it was quite his own free idiomatic style, and his description of my own condition and symptoms was characteristic."

Captain William Phelps passed over on December 24, 1911, aged seventy-six years. He was a Church of England ritualist, and avoided any discussion of the subject of spiritism. He lived at Droxford, Hampshire, devoted to his house and to his garden, where he grew a large quantity of fruit. General Phelps, in writing to me, says: "I think there is no room to doubt that his was the intelligence which spoke to me through Mrs. Wriedt's trumpet."

Mrs. Burnett passed over October 5, 1911.

June 4, 1912. Present Mrs. Wriedt, General Phelps and a stenographer.

Dr. Sharp came in first and chatted. Mrs. Wriedt asked him to get Mr. Stead to speak to General Phelps that morning. Dr. Sharp: I will go right up to the office and tell him you want to see him, also General Phelps; I know you would like to have a word with him." General Phelps: "I should; but I have never met him."

Dr. Sharp (to stenographer): "Tell your brother that I would like him every morning after he got up to go right out into the open air, and inhale and exhale on an empty stomach, and to take a good drink of cold fresh water the first thing before he does anything else."

General Phelps: "How often should he inhale and exhale?"

Dr. Sharp: "Every morning before he eats a bite. As many times as he feels the lungs are filled with good air. Understand that, when he inhales, it goes from the bronchial tubes down to the stomach, and it passes through the bowels, liver, heart, by expanding the chest as much as he can a little every day; and he should keep that up all summer long."

General Phelps: "I suppose it gets through the blood."

"Dr. Sharp: It gives strength to the veins, muscles, and sinews of the body, and it gives the breathing tubes better action."

A conversation about whipping children and lynching ensued between General Phelps and Mrs. Wriedt.

W. T. Stead: How do you do; how do you do General?"

General Phelps: "I am fairly well. I am sorry I never met you in life."

W. T. Stead: I am delighted to meet you at Julia's Bureau." (To Mrs. Harper) "I am very sorry that times have changed and conditions have changed; but I want you to stand erect; carry out everything you can, and well, and there is no necessity for you to drop work at the Review office. Plenty to do for you if you carry it out as I did. Now, Trefauls, I want to talk to you in regard to Edith and the book. I want you to have that book done. I want it printed as cheap as you can print it. And I want you to help Edith to do it. I want you to speak to——. You know; who you were speaking to a fortnight ago."

E. T. H. (the stenographer): "Yes; I understand—the publishers."

W. T. Stead: "And I hope it will be done in my publishing house......I want you to see about it first thing—my publishing department, and I don't think——will interfere. He has no right to interfere if —— says she can have it done."

E. T. H.: If —— (mentioning a certain firm) do it, they will pay. I want Edith and Estelle to have the result. I want Edith to consult——." (Trumpet dropped)

Mrs Wriedt: "I want you to answer those questions. I got a letter from Rochester. Did you go to a medium there and tell him you wanted him to take the Bureau up and carry it out in America?"

W. T. Stead: "No I did not. It is a falsehood."

Mrs. Wriedt: I got a letter that you came to him through a medium, and also a medium in trance, and also an automatic writer, saying the same thing through each of them."

W, T. stead: "No, that is not true. Julia's Bureau remains where it is. It should not be transferred to any part of the globe with my consent."

Mrs. Wriedt: "If you were over there, why didn't you tell Austin I was here?"

W. T. Stead: "I had too much to do. I have stopped running round to mediums, for they don't get the message right, and I am not strong enough to use anyone's magnetism. But I didn't tell Mr. Austin any such thing; they are making it out of stained glass."

(General Phelps tells me that the mere reading of these notes gives no idea of the nature of his interview with Stead. The voice was raised after the first few words, until it literally bawled and was heard in the garden below,—W. U. M.)

Mrs. Phelps now manifested and spoke to her husband for several minutes about their children and grandchildren.

Charlie: "You are as bright as a young rooster."

General Phelps: "I don't feel so."

Charlie: "I hope you will live for fifteen years to settle the vaccination question."

General Phelps: "It will take fifteen years."

Charlie: "Yes, to get the ignorant people of the world to understand."

General Phelps: "They are afraid of the doctors. My great hope is that the doctors are gradually being penetrated with the feeling that they are wrong."

Charlie: "They cannot, because they fear losing money on it."

General Phelps: "At the same time they are losing credit. All they can do now is to swear there is going to be an epidemic."

Charlie: "It has not come, and for five years they have been predicting it. It is the dirty and filthy people that would cause it."

General Phelps: "How soon after you passed away did you recover consciousness?" Charlie: "Three days." General Phelps: "And your clarity of sense?" Charlie: First week or nine to ten days."

General Phelps: "Then your mind was clouded?"

Charlie: "No, no; it was just like a dream, as though you were in a slumber, dreaming; and then I really pulled myself together—I found I had gone into another sphere."

General Phelps: "You say you are in the fifth?"

Charlie: "My mother is in the sixth sphere, seventh realm. I am glad to see you so well and happy."

(Some conversation of a private character here took place.)

Charlie: "I am glad to see you this morning, and I came to you because I wanted to help you. I did not do anything for you on this earth, but I will now."

General Phelps: "Now what are you going to do for me?"

Charlie: Keep you well, and see that your boys are better than they are now. Goodbye."

Dr. Burnett announced himself.

General Phelps: "I wanted very much to bring your memory back to last year, when you told me something about my eyes, which I have stupidly forgotten. You said the lens was misplaced, and my sight prejudiced. There was a little weakness in the optic nerve, and that could be strengthened; and I said that I did not want to be treated by any other physician."

Dr. Burnett: Your blood is not sufficiently oxygenated to keep the nerves in proper time—tune. You are a little anaemic; the blood is a little impoverished. At the Generals age, reporter, it is hard to blow up the sparks. We can give him strength and we can give him health, but to put new vigour in him it is impossible. But to treat the eyes, bathe them in a weak solution of salt water—a mild solution!"

General Phelps: "Soft water too, you told me!"

Dr. Burnett: "Yes; strain it well two or three times, warm it, and put the salt in it—a mild temperature—and slap it up to your eyes. Don't pat the eyes; just throw the water up loosely, because if you pat the eyes you bruise them back into the sockets. The eyes must protrude a little round, and by manipulating the temple and back of the ears, it strengthens the nerve. Don't press on them (the nerves); rub them round— round the ear to the base of the brain. All these nerves are centred in the spine, and by manipulating the spine you get to the nerve which leads to the ball of the eye."

General Phelps: "And this basilar nerve; I feel that is connected with it."

Dr. Burnett: "I will tell you. It leads to right between the spine and the neck and the shoulders; it goes right through the base; it leads to the spine, and we find it near the base. Bow your head down till I show you. It is there" (touching).

General Phelps: "Yes, quite right. Has anything special to be done down there?"

Dr. Burnett: "If someone could manipulate the spine—if you could find someone. They call it the Keiro Practic—the manipulation of the spine."

General Phelps: "Is that a foreign practice?"

Dr. Burnett: "No; that is the name of it technically."

General Phelps: "I can find in England someone——."

Dr. Burnett: "Someone that understands how to locate the nerves. You have to manipulate them with the two middle fingers and the thumbs."

A Voice: "Father—my son!" General Phelps entered into a private conversation with his father, which ended thus:—

The Voice: "I wanted you to take a lesson from my experience. With your children you were the strict one; your wife was the loving one. The father has the mind, and the mother the heart. Every mother gives out the last drop of life for her child. And whatever you did, my son, you did it well. I have no regrets, only your poor health; that is the only regret I have. You are a valuable man; you are too valuable still to your nation. You have worked, and given strength to the land and the sea—and what more can a man do? You look at death as a natural consequence; you look at life as the true part of manhood, womanhood, girlhood, and childhood. You despise cruelty, you despise vaccination. You love the human race; you treat them alike, black and white. God spare you your health for years to come. There is a devotional thanks to God for giving me such a son. Goodbye."

Julia: "Good morning General."

General Phelps: "I hope your 'Bureau' will long continue."

Julia: (to E. T. H.): "Just a moment; I want you to tell Edith that I have never given a message, outside of her pen, to man, woman, or psychic; and, when I do, it will come from a source that she knows well. Please give her that personally. General Phelps, this 'Bureau' will last under the controlling influence of the hand that brought it to the light, and Edith K. Harper. Miss Harper brought this into public notice with Mr. Stead, and she scattered seeds of kindness throughout the universe. What I mean by that is, she wrote letters, and it belongs to her, the name 'Julia's Bureau.' No one has connected themselves with the religious right of this 'Bureau' like the private secretary to Mr. William T. Stead, of the Review of Reviews. Where he has dropped off she will take up, and she will weave the threads of kindness hither and thither. She will do the work that he has done. She will work up the political, physical, mental, and spiritual along the lines of spiritualism, and her name will be famous if her health permits, and if the people will stand by her. General, every man has his span of life, has his time to play. Mr. Stead has played his on the hilltops, and he will never see this 'Bureau' fall, and especially into the hands of the psychic research. It shall live under the same name, and Miss Harper must be supported, so as no one can rob her of the name 'Julia's Bureau.' There is only one founded on the banks of truth by your good man, Mr. Stead, and his helpmate in the work, Miss Harper. I want her to handle it as she has in the past. And I want you not to worry; time will bring good tidings of great joy. My dear General, remember what I want to say. I know every one of them will stick to Miss Harper in writing the life of W. T. Stead. I know they will take copies from her, and send them to others far and near. So tell her to write it—the sooner the better; for I don't want two stories about his life. I want Miss Harper to write his psychical life. She has begun it, and I am helping her; and I want you, General, to encourage her, that she may have light upon the subject, to strengthen her brain, and not give way. Now I will bid you good day till we meet again. Good day."

June 5, 1912. Present: Mrs. Wriedt, General Phelps, and the stenographer.

After greetings by John King. Mrs. Wriedt: "There is someone here by the name of C——gs."

General Phelps; "I knew a man in life named C——gs. Has he a dark complexion?" Mrs, Wriedt: "He looks to me as though he was very white." General Phelps: "Is he a clergyman?" A Voice: "Yes."

General Phelps: "I am afraid I have spoken rather disrespectfully of you."

A Voice: "Well that is no fault of yours. It was my ignorance that led me to say so."

General Phelps: "Were you the chaplain of A——?"

The Voice: "Yes."

General Phelps: "He used to send over to England for a fresh wife when his former wife died."

The Voice: "I was not alone in that course."

General Phelps: "I heard an amusing story about him. Between A—— and the neighbouring country there was a tunnel, and one day he was travelling with his wife in a pony carriage, and they met a train of camels, The pony shied and threw them out, and with great presence of mind Mr. C——gs groped in the dark and sat on the pony's head to keep it down. After he had sat there some time he heard a voice calling: 'It is not the pony you are sitting on, it's me!' And it turned out to be his wife."

The Voice: "It was not my wife. It was the pony I sat on, and I first put my coat over its head."

General Phelps: "I bought a cow from you."

The Voice: "I hope it served you better than I did."

General Phelps: "You never did me any harm."

The voice: "Well, Goodbye. Your mother told me you were here."

General Phelps: "I did not know that you knew her."

The Voice: I know her over here. A lot of people—thousands and millions gather together."

General Phelps: "Are you pretty busy now?" Voice: "Yes, I am in the fifth sphere."

[The mother of general Phelps now manifested, and a long conversation took place of a private character, ending by a discussion on the merits of vegetarianism.]

A Voice (Dr. Sharp: "Do you understand that such people never eat potatoes raw, and do you stop to think that when they are boiled the substance is boiled out of them?"

General Phelps: "A good many of the salts are boiled out."

Dr. Sharp: "When you boil vegetables in water you take out all the goodness. When you have meat the proper way is not to boil it. Put it in a pan with a drop of water, and put the lid on firmly, and season it well, and keep it tight, and you will have all the blood of the meat in the pan."

Mrs. Wriedt: "You mean to steam it?"

The Voice: "Yes, and the same thing with potatoes—the best way is to bake them."

General Phelps: I could not eat a baked potato in its skin. To me it is poison."

The Voice: "The acid of the liver and the stomach is not sufficiently vivacious to carry it off."

General Phelps: "Is not sufficiently what?" The voice: "Vivacious."

General Phelps: "There is a theory that the length of the alimentary canal of man shows that he is a vegetarian by nature."

The voice: "You understand that the animal is born under the same conditions as the human race. They are human in their race, the trees are human in theirs. There is the male flower and the female flower— the male tree and the female tree. There are always two—the male and female."

General Phelps: Sometimes the tree has both in one organism."

The voice: "Then it is comparatively very coarse—full of knots, and decays very quickly—remember that: I heard some remark about four dimensions the other day."

General Phelps: "The fourth and fifth." Dr. Sharp: "Did you know there was a fifth?" General Phelps: "Yes."

Dr. Sharp: "Well where is it? Rise up a minute. There is one dimension" (touching the General on the right side). "There is another" (feeling on the right shoulder and across the chest, then up and down).

General Phelps: "That is three—length, breadth, and depth—that feels my hand and left leg."

Dr. Sharp: "Now stretch up your arms, stretch out your arms, and from finger to finger that is the fifth."

General Phelps: "That is beyond my comprehension."

The Voice: "It has staggered a good many people. What you can reach, what you can feel, what you can see, what you can hear, and what you know—these are the five dimensions. Now what are the other five? Seeing, touching, smelling, tasting, and hearing."

General Phelps: "I am tapped on the head."

Dr. Sharp: "They are dimensions of sound. Feeling is a sound vibration on the heart. Anything that vibrates on the heart is sound, and smelling is a sound."

General Phelps: "I thought it was a vibration."

The Voice: "Where does it vibrate to?—the middle drum between. When you touch a pin, where does it sting?—it is a sound. When you hear, where does it sting? It sounds on the middle ear drum. Where that bell rings is a sounding plate for the whole entire system."

General Phelps mentioned the Creator.

Dr. Sharp: "May I ask you what you mean by the Creator? I mean the seed of life— the seed of life is the great Creator both of the heavens, the winds, and the seas, and the great romance that we are looking at today. The law of nature is the seed multiplied by millions of seeds. There is no personal God; there never was. The law of nature covers and rules all things, and it cannot be disputed. Ask yourself the question. The creed says men never made them; they were made by the law of nature—the seed of life. The vales and valleys on the side of the earth, where did they come from? The hand of nature. The very stones in the earth they grow, they have life. It is not from the law of God; it is the law of nature. God is the abbreviated word for good; Lord is the abbreviated word for Love."

General Phelps: "What I can see of it, you put the thing one step further by using the word 'Nature' for 'God'!"

The Voice: "Jesus of Nazareth, King of the Jews, was a medium, sir; he was a medium. We have mediums today who have done more than he."

General Phelps: "With the same difficulties?"

The Voice: "Yes. Many of them have been persecuted just like He. When Jesus of Nazareth, King of the Jews, was on earth, can you tell me where he was from birth until the age of thirty? At twelve years of age he disappeared. Where did he go to? They hunted for him, and could not find hem. He was concealed in his fathers chamber, sitting for the development of the sprit voices. He was with Joseph, His Father. Jesus of Nazareth, King of the Jews, was a son of Joseph, who was well pleased with Him. Mary would not divulge her secret: she was true to her word of honour; and he took her and his son because they were one; and when she was sought in the manger with the child they tried to......it, because that was the first child born in that mysterious way. Today the Roman Catholics put the wrong construction upon it. Who was it that formed Roman Catholicism? Constantine, one of the worst criminals on earth; and when you believe Constantine to be the founder of the true religion, you are drifting on through the wrong channel—the true religion is your conscience. Going back to Jesus when he sought men, why did he not go into the multitude of men? Why did he only go to the lowly men? He took the fishermen because they were mediums, and when he was materialised upon the waters they did not all see him—just a few saw him. We have that today; but, Mr. Reporter, remember that the people who saw him were mediums. The whole city of Judea, the whole Israelites, did not see him; He was seen by a handful of people, and his friends betrayed Him, and put him to death because, He was the mediator between the spiritual states—and you. Adam and Eve were the first man and woman. Now the wrong interpretation is placed upon that. Adam and Eve were the first man and woman seen in the beautiful garden committing adultery."

General Phelps: "They were man and wife!"

The Voice: It was before they were man and wife. They were driven out. They were not married, and never was; there was nothing of the kind in those days. There's where the story comes from, and that is the whole substance of it; It has been put into the book form by seventy or eighty men—into the Bible. Moses never wrote that......any more than he wrote the Pentateuch."

The voice went on to say that the Roman Catholics burnt the sixth and seventh books of Moses because they said it was damnation; there are little bits of it printed here and there, but they call it the "Black Art." There are little clippings of the seventh and eighth books of Moses.

Julia: "I am very glad to meet you. Tell Edith I will be here tonight, and tell her William is very pleased with the notes, and wants them read this evening at Edith's disposal." (To General Phelps): "I am afraid we have taken a great deal out of you this morning. Dear General, we will see you again; I will bid you good morning."

General Phelps; "I hope they won't infringe your patent, and carry off 'Julia's Bureau' to America."

Julia: "Miss Harper will see to that. I don't want my name flitting everywhere; it belongs to Mr. Stead, and nobody else."

June 8, 1912. Present: Mrs. Wriedt, General Phelps, and the stenographer. Water was sprinkled on the sitters. Cardinal Newman: "Good morning, gentlemen and Mrs. Wriedt, how do you do?" General Phelps: "I am fairly well, thank you."

Cardinal Newman: "In the name of all that is good and holy, may it pour forth its blessing down upon you; may you live in peace and happiness through all eternity."

General Phelps: "I would like to ask you about your project for the college at Oxford. Had you carried it through, I suppose by this time the number of Roman Catholics in England would have been——"

Cardinal Newman: "It seems to me that I put forth the wrong light, and it was quenched out as suddenly as I was quenched out. And, I had to be quenched out so that it would be quenched out. I was not allowed to live to promulgate the truth, to teach the doctrine of the Christian endeavour, and the truth of God and his holy crucifix. Because it is not understood, and we are on the side of religion with Roman Catholicism. The true religion is the Christian teaching of your own common sense, and we ought not to be separated—one great diocese here and there, not one religion fighting against the another. There is only one great universe, and we are all working for it. There is one new London in the world, and there are many ways of getting to it; there is one universal power, and there are many ways of getting to it; and let us look within, and we will see the truth printed upon the soul vibrations. Good morning."

General Phelps: "if he had succeeded in carrying out his project which was frustrated, I think, by Cardinal Manning, it would have put the Roman Catholic religion on a very different footing."

The Voice: "I did not look at religion in a right and proper way; I looked at it through a glass eye. I thought people were allowed to think too much for themselves, and there should be a halter, and we should all draw them in it."

Mr. Harper (stenographer): "What was that referring to?"

General Phelps: "I asked the reason of his conversion when he found things unbearable in the Church of England, where things were at a loose end, and nothing was fixed for them to believe."

A Voice: "CHARLES!"

General Phelps: "Well Charlie, how are you?"

Charles: "I am very well, how are you?"

General Phelps: "Fairly well."

Charles: "You are a little tired."

General Phelps: "Yes I knocked about a good deal yesterday."

Charles: "You were enjoying yourself, but this muggy weather makes you tired."

General Phelps: "It is partly that, and partly that I am worn out! How are you all on that side?"

Charles: "All happy and well and wish you were. I brought mother down to the house to see—and everything looks nice; I have no home. We do not have any home."

General Phelps: "You do not have any home when you have gone to the other side?" The Voice: "I am speaking about the material home."

General Phelps: "Your grandchildren had the home. I am reaching the same age as William, and I suppose we are constructed to last only so many years."

Charles: "Our lives are planned and fixed for us. There is no getting away from it. If it was for us to decide, we would live for ages and hundreds of years, so many of us hate to die, and want to live for what this world is."

General Phelps: "It would be dreadful if we became Struldbrugs like the people imagined by Dean Swift."

Charles: "That has been greatly exaggerated." General Phelps:" Do you have music on the other side?" Voice: "Yes everything from the Banjo to the bones." General Phelps: "Do you have your own Rojaon?"

Charles: "There is not a thing I had at home that I cannot have here. Some people have their horses and dogs, etc., etc."

General Phelps: "I believe animals survive just as well as human animals." Charles asked what was meant by a human animal,

General Phelps: "The human animal stands on its hind legs, and its brain develops upwards."

The Voice: There is no animal on the face of the earth that talks and shows its individuality excepting by force. Show me one that does. A dog will squirm and bark; but, if you don't pet it, it will slink away. If you take a dog which takes a fancy to one member of a family, it would rather be with that one than anybody. You say that we are human animals. No, we are not. Animals walk on four legs; that is an animal. A human being walks on two legs. A bird is a fowl because it walks on two legs and has no arms."

General Phelps: "That does not remove it from the category of animals. I disagree with you."

The Voice: "Take the Peacock." Charles went on to assert that the peacock was ashamed of its feet, and would never look at them. If he did, it was ashamed, and tried to get away from them.

General Phelps said "He considered the peacock was proud of its feet, and was most graceful when dancing."

Quite an argument took place with reference to this, and Charles told the General to study it up.

Here ensued a conversation of some length between the General and his wife in spirit life. Mrs Phelps was followed by Captain W. Phelps, who talked with his brother about the sale of his house and about his will

Mrs. Wriedt: "There is a man here named Paris, or Parras!" General Phelps: "How are you old chap?" The Voice: "Fine." General Phelps: "How is the violin?"

The Voice: "Going strong." (Whistled a tune to imitate the violin.) General Phelps: "Bravo."

(The general explained that he was a friend in India. And that he had gone to America and had overworked himself in selling his estate, and had died about three years ago. It was a great disappointment to the General, who had hoped to have him come and stay with him. It was delightful to hear he was still enjoying himself, and music.)

Mrs. Wriedt: "He came to talk to you, but you have done all the talking, and he has gone."

Mrs. Wriedt: got the names "Matilda" and "Eggleton." General Phelps: "I do not recognise either." A Voice: "How are you?" General Phelps: "Fairly well thank you. I cannot hear very plainly." Voice: "I am T—— (Nellie's Father)."

General Phelps: "Do you mean my father?" Voice: "No; you know where you were yesterday, and didn't you see my daughter?"

General Phelps: "I was at the Army and Navy Stores——(recollecting). Yes, of course, are you Mr. T——?"

Voice: "Yes."

General Phelps: I saw her, and she was looking very well indeed. It was the day before yesterday."

The Voice: "I cannot quite tell that; we have no clocks over here."

General Phelps: "I was reminding her of what I saw in your house in Madeira sixty years ago."

Voice: "The old Timepiece?"

General Phelps: "No, the birds nests."

Voice: "Do you remember the eggs?"

General Phelps: "I should think there were eggs in them; but they were fossilised. Your daughter seems very, very happy."

The Voice: "We will meet here, and will know each other better than we knew them there."

General Phelps: It is curious that your family should have petered out that way."

The Voice: "Planetary conditions rule our lives. We are born into an old planet; our lives drop out quickly. That is a law we don't understand on earth, and people don't seem to like the idea of it."

General Phelps: "There are some Haywards left." Voice: "Two or three." General Phelps: "I think they are in America—Julia's nephews and nieces." A Voice: "Well, dear, goodbye, God bless you." Julia: "Good morning, how do you do this morning?" General Phelps: "Fairly well."

Mrs. Wriedt: "Here is our pioneer, General Phelps."

Julia: "Mr. Stead wished to be kindly remembered to you. I want to draw your attention to the fact that, although he did not know you, he had heard of you, and he is glad to know that you are one who is taking up the threads and weaving them into the better light."

General Phelps: "My little chapter is the Vaccination business."

Julia: "It is a wonderful thing......and if the people would be clean, and could be clean, there is the whole centre of the disease—cleanliness comes next to Godliness, and without cleanliness we cannot be clean."

General Phelps: "Our bodies are......"

Julia: "Our bodies are a turmoil, but we can regulate it just as you can regulate the spokes of a wheel. We can make them limp or we can make them stiff, but we prefer them strong and firm, and we must keep the body straight."

General Phelps: "'Life's fitful fever' accurately describes it."

Julia: "If you could see yourselves as you are, you would be disgusted, for we are a mass of corruption when we pass into eternity."

General Phelps: "We are in eternity now!"

Julia: "In one sense, but not the real sense; we are only visitors on this mundane sphere. We are here top do our duty. We are here to probe the ministry of God. What is life and what is death......? We are only here for a short time at the longest, and then we see towards the end of our time that we have not done much. I have not done anything, but you have done your work, and done it well."

(General Phelps writes under date of September 24, 1912: "I think the most evidential fact of all my séances was the coming of Mr. T——. I had not seen him for sixty years, but I had called upon his married daughter two days before—a fact which was not in my consciousness at the time, and entirely unknown to anybody except the lady, her husband, and myself."

Note.—In the records of general Phelps séances I have included Dr. Sharp's sayings, though I must confess they read, in some cases, like pure nonsense. May it not be that they are genuine, if unsuccessful, efforts to explain phenomena with an inadequate vocabulary? I am not interested so much in the truth of what he says as in the vigour and power displayed by this energetic spirit. His voice is ever the same, deep and audible outside the room when the door is locked; every word is clear. The General associates himself with this note.

From Major-General Sir Alfred Turner, K.C.B.:—

November 25, 1912.
Carlyle House
Chelsea Embankment,
London.

My dear Admiral,—
        Herewith I send my experiences......

Very truly yours,
        Alfred E. Turner.

I have frequently been requested to relate my experiences in psychical matters, of which I have been a steady and serious investigator for many years. Up to a short time ago I always declined to do so, as the thick wall of unbelief appeared to be quite impenetrable, and it seemed of little use to impart information as to what I had seen and heard in spiritualism to people who would not, or could not, understand; and who, in their hearts, if not openly, would have derided my statements. Not that I should have been concerned because of their jeers, which would have had the same importance in my eyes as "the crackling of thorns under a pot"; but I thought that to attempt to bring conviction to the minds of such people was equivalent to so much valuable time wasted. As time goes on, however, the desire earnestly and Honestly to learn more of this all-important subject is rapidly growing, and I feel I should fail in my duty to me fellow creatures if I did not divulge what I had learnt from personal experience as to the state of existence in the land of the hereafter.

I have been urgently requested to communicate to Light some of my recent experiences as manifested at séances conducted by Mrs. Wriedt, a well – known American medium, who came over to England last spring through the agency of my deeply lamented friend W. T. Stead, who had intended to travel back to England with her. He, however, was fated never to return to his home on earth, as all that was mortal of him went down and perished in the awful calamity of the Titanic. About ten days after the foundering of the monster ship I held a small and carefully selected séance in my house. No professional medium was present, but Mr. Stead's private secretary and her mother (who lived at Cambridge House, Wimbledon) were among the sitters. We had hardly commenced when a voice, which came apparently from behind my right shoulder, exclaimed "I am so happy to be with you again!" The voice was unmistakably that of Stead, who immediately (though not visible to anyone) commenced to tell us of the events of the dire moments when the huge leviathan settled down to her doom, and slowly sank to her grave two miles below the surface of the sea. For himself he felt no fear whatever. He had a premonition of his physical ending, as we know, from *the last* letter written by him from Cherbourg a few days before the disaster, that he felt that the greatest event of his life was impending, but he knew not what it was. When the Titanic sank there was, as regards himself, a short, sharp struggle to gain his breath, and immediately afterwards he came to his senses in another state of existence. He was surrounded by hundreds of beings who, like himself, had passed over the bourne, but who were utterly dazed, and being, at all events for the most part, totally ignorant of the next stage of life to come, were groping about as in the dark, asking for light, and entirely unconscious that they were not still in the flesh. He set himself at once to do missionary work by enlightening these poor and unprepared creatures; and in such work, he told us, he was still employed, with the assistance of numerous spirit inhabitants of the next plane, whose task and bounden duty it is to help and enlighten those who pass over. I can well imagine the contemptuous sneers of many who sit in the seats of the scornful on reading the above, and whose extent of belief is limited to their powers of comprehension—not an excessive quantity, as a rule.

Stead had then a long conversation with his Secretary, during which he gave some instructions to her. Asked by me if he would show himself to us, he replied: "Not to- night; but if you go to Cambridge House on such and such a day, I will do so." The voice then died away.

On the day in question I went to Cambridge house, where I found a large and incongruous circle. As he had promised, Stead appeared twice in rapid succession. He was dressed in his usual attire, so familiar to all his friends, and looked supremely happy. He remained only a few moments in each case, and said nothing. Mrs. Wriedt was the medium. We had no further manifestation of any kind, at which I was not surprised. I went once more to Cambridge House, to sit with Mrs. Wriedt. There I found another large, incongruous circle, which sat for over an hour, without obtaining any results whatsoever. It is an indubitable fact that the manifestations which had taken place at séances depend more upon the nature, disposition, and state of mind of those present than on the psychical development of any medium; and that where incredulity, and especially scoffing, is felt the spirits will not, or cannot, manifest themselves or demonstrate.

After this Mrs. Wriedt sat twice in my house, as a friend, not as a paid medium. On the first occasion a small, but psychically very strong, circle was assembled, with the exception of one lady, who had had no experience in such matters. She had lately had a very terrible bereavement, and had begged me to let her attend a séance, in the hope of getting into communication with her lost one. A few minutes after we assembled several voices were distinguishable; and I, sitting next to the lady in question, made inquiries from their owners, who did not appear in person, about the passing over of the relative of the lady. There had been some doubts as to the circumstances of the death. The spirits, who were all controls well known to us, one after another assured us that it was purely accidental, and that there was not an atom of truth in the rumours that had been disseminated. A few minutes later the voice of the young man himself—unmistakable to his mother, for such the lady was—was heard; and son and mother had a long conversation, most of it heard by all of us, in the course of which he expressed his wishes as to the completion of a book which he had nearly finished, and about which no one present knew anything but his mother. All this time we heard, but saw nothing. The circumstances of the communication were beautiful and touching in the extreme, and I am sure there was not a dry eye in the room. The mother went away consoled and resigned, assured that her loved son was "not lost, but gone before," and that their reunion was only a matter of time. Let the scorners and scoffers contemplate this case, and even the hardest and most callous of them will not mock at the bereaved mother, and the peace of mind and comfort that her communion with the spirit of her son brought to her crushed spirit and wounded heart. We had many more communications, but none equal in interest or importance to the one I have related.

On the second occasion Mrs. Wriedt sat alone with me, and for over an hour we had incessant communications by voice, but no appearances. Many of those I have "lost awhile" spoke to me, and John King and others gave me some very strong advice, which cast serious reflections upon one I thoroughly believed in and trusted. They were most urgent and emphatic, which was all the more strange because up to then he had spoken in other terms of the person in question. What he impressed upon me at this séance has turned out to be absolutely true. Had I followed his councils, I should have been saved from infinite trouble and disillusion later.

Mrs. Wriedt is a most remarkable and powerful medium. I only saw two materialised figures with her, and those were both appearances of Stead; but the oral communications which come through her are extraordinary, different voices being heard by different members of the circle at the same time. No powers of ventriloquism could produce such a consummation, and all possibility of fraud was excluded, as it always is by me at séances. I can bear the strongest possible testimony to the mediumistic power, perfect honesty, and good faith of Mrs. Wriedt.

(signed)   Alfred E. Turner. November, 1912.

The following letter was received by me in July, 1912, from an Irish gentleman:—

Dear Sir,—The experience of my friend and myself at the séance at Cambridge House on the 29th ult. Was most satisfactory.

Quite unknown as we both were, to anyone else present, a very clear and distinctive communication came from a departed friend, with many characteristics of identity.

Mrs. Anker (whom we had had the pleasure of seeing when in Dublin), quite unknown to those in the circle, arrived downstairs while the séance was going on. A communication, however, informed us that she was below, which we found was the case on coming down.

Mrs. Anker's daughter was one of those who communicated, and in Norwegian.

My friend and I feel much gratified at having had the opportunity of sitting with Mrs. Wriedt, and hope the way may be open for us to see her again in Dublin.—

Yours Faithfully.   Thos. Hy. Webb.

A deputy-lieutenant of one of our Midland counties, in reply to some questions of mine, wrote to me in September, 1912, as follows:—

Dear Admiral,—Your letter received......Mrs. Wriedt is correct. Towards the end of the season I used to begin by trying for phenomena with her out of the room, and sat for a minute or two alone in the dark. usually with no result. I suppose I tried seven or eight times.

One day I heard "Good morning" distinctly said three times.

Mrs. Wriedt was, as a rule, if not always, further off than the bathroom, I thought; downstairs, or in the room beyond the bathroom.....97

The door was always carefully closed by me, and usually, if not always, locked as well. I think always.

During one sitting the loud voice of a man directed me to hold the medium's hands. I think the voice was that of John King, but I am not absolutely certain. I did as directed, and held Mrs. Wriedt's two hands with my two. A table, with a bowl of flowers on it, was brought from the far end of the room—i.e., from near the cabinet, right up to me. We were sitting about the middle of the room. It came with a loud clatter. Mrs. Wriedt turned on a light to see exactly what had happened. She then said she "wondered if it would be taken back again?"

We turned off the lights, and I held her hands. The table was taken back again, not quite, but almost as far as where it had come from.

I have been given flowers on numerous occasions under conditions which, to my mind, preclude the possibility of Mrs. Wriedt having had anything to do with it. On at least two occasions a flower has been placed, in the dark, in the small end of Mrs. Wriedt's trumpet—a difficult feat to perform at any time.

On one occasion I was literally deluged with a shower of flowers and water from a bowl which stood on a table to my left, Mrs. Wriedt meanwhile sitting on a chair opposite to me, from which she could not have moved without my knowing it.

On several occasions I have seen brilliant flashing lights, the room being almost lighted up by them.

I sat with Mrs. Wriedt once in a top room in this gentleman's house. The house was undergoing repair, and was reeking with paint and whitewash. Mrs. Wriedt went to the door to switch off the electric lights, and said to me: "Before I put the lights out, would you like to hold the trumpet to your ear?" The distance between us was eighteen feet. I placed the small end of the trumpet to my left ear, holding the trumpet at right angles to a line between myself and the psychic; and, while it was in this position, I obtained a clearly audible message from a spirit, of valuable import. The lights were then switched off, and I enjoyed a good sitting in the dark.

The following letter was sent to me in October, 1912, by a lady who lives in London:—

Dear Admiral Moore,—As you ask me for some of my experiences with Mrs. Wriedt, I will do my best to tell you what I can, though it is somewhat difficult, as one cannot mention names, and so much that took place was of a private nature. "I had a great many sittings, but was always alone with her; generally the moment we sat down the voices began, and the oftener I went the clearer they were, and the better I could hear. Sometimes we were in the light, generally in darkness; sometimes with the trumpet, sometimes without. I often saw lights and occasionally forms; the spirits always touched me, took my hands, and tapped my knees to attract my attention, and I almost always heard the sound of kissing before they left.

Mrs. Wriedt and I talked a great deal in between; I mean when one spirit left, and we were waiting for another to come, often the spirit voice would begin while we were talking. I have heard two or three voices at the same time.

A little incident which occurred was, to me, a great proof that those on the other side know much about our doings here. I have some relations at Munich—there are two young children in the family; the mother had written to ask me to buy and send some hats for them. This I did. One afternoon soon after, when I was sitting with Mrs. Wriedt, a spirit who came said: "The hats you sent are all right; they fit nicely." I said: "How do you know anything about them?" The reply was: "Oh, I have just been over there, and saw them."

On another occasion the mother wrote and told me that one of the children was ill, and that she feared that he had caught some fever.

Soon after, when with Mrs. Wriedt, the same spirit said: "You need not worry about the children; it is really nothing; it is only the change in the weather which has affected them." I said; "I only heard that one was ill; are you sure that both are laid up?" The spirit replied; "Yes, I am certain; I have been to see them"; and in the next letter I had from the mother the fact that they had both been ill was verified.

Another time I had motored to Wimbledon and had a new chauffeur—quite a small man. The spirit suddenly said: "How do you like the little chauffeur? I think he will do; I should keep him if I were you; he is a respectable looking man, and I believe he is honest. He is just as good as one of those big men. I think he will suit you; but he must get used to the car; you will see that, later on he will be better." Another day he mentioned the chauffeur again, and said: "Give the little chap a chance." I may say that this advice induced me to keep him, and I find that he is satisfactory.

Once I asked Mrs. Wriedt if I could come to one of the evening circles, thinking I might see something different to what occurred when I was alone with her. So one evening I arrived about 6.30 and found several people waiting; but directly I entered the room a feeling came over me that I must not stay. I battled against it, as I was curious to see what would take place. However, I felt so strongly that it was not for me that I left before the séance began. The next time I went to Mrs. Wriedt the spirit said: "I impressed you to go home the other evening; I did not wish you to stay. You would not have liked it." I heard afterwards that it was not a pleasant séance.

My husband is a good linguist, and can speak four languages, one just as well as the other. Thinking I might convince him if I could give him a message in Spanish (I can neither speak nor understand it myself). I asked a spirit to give me one. This he did, spelling it out word by word, I writing it down carefully in the dark. Next day I repeated it to him, although I did not know what it meant until my husband translated it to me. This test, alas, did not make him a believer in spiritualism. When I asked the same spirit to give another message in Spanish, he said; "No; better let him alone; he does not like it. Let him seek and find for himself. Don't force it on him, and don't keep harping on where you have been. Wait until he asks about it."

I may mention that numbers of my relations and friends came to me, gave their names, talked and laughed if there was anything amusing said; and one, who is very musical, sang a song. Nothing disagreeable ever happened during my many sittings. Once I had a blank. The first time I went afterwards a spirit said: "I was here last time, but could not get enough power to speak."

I am sure that much that the spirits and myself talked about could not possibly have been known by Mrs. Wriedt or by anyone else in London. I can never feel thankful enough to her for what she has done for me; I think it would be quite worth while to go to America to get a few sittings with her. I know now that our dear ones are not dead, and that "ever near us, though unseen the dear immortal spirits tread, for all the boundless universe is life—there are no dead." I must tell you that I used to take notes in the dark, and wrote down, as nearly as possible, what was said. One spirit told me, with a laugh, that I was quite a "reporter," and sometimes he would stop and say: "Have you got that down? You are quite an expert at writing in the dark."

I do not know if you will find anything here interesting enough for your notes......— Yours sincerely. Z.

The following letter was received by me from a lady at Bognor in December, 1912.

I said I would send you a narrative of my séances with Mrs. Wriedt, but I find it a little difficult, as I made no notes, and have only one report of Mr. Harper's [the stenographer], which does not help me much, as it gives a mixture of voices which came to me with others who spoke to the members of the circle. However, I send you on the report, as it may be of some little assistance to you.

To me, all was most convincing and consoling. At the first séance I certainly felt alarmed when the Indian, Grayfeather, gave his weird war cries to announce his coming, but that feeling disappeared when I heard the spirit visitors speak to their friends, and when I myself was spoken to. The desire for recognition of some who came seemed to me to be intense, and was hardly adequately met by the replies of the sitters addressed; but in each sitting I attended everyone present obtained much comfort from hearing the voices of their individual spirit friends.

The first to come to me was my son, who had passed into spirit life as a little child; his voice, though that of a young man, did not sound strange to me. I seemed to recognise tones in it which were familiar. He was able to assure me that all who are near and dear to me in spirit life were with him, and I heard their whispering voices, as if they were close to me, but wished him to do the talking. Other relatives came and spoke afterwards; as I was not thinking in any way about them, their manifestations were all the more remarkable. The medium could not possibly know anything of the various sitters with whom she is brought into contact, and therefore I do not understand how any doubts can creep in when such evidence was given to us all.

One quite remarkable piece of evidence was given by my brother in spirit life to my sister who accompanied me to the third séance. He asked her if she remembered a song he used to sing to her when she was a little girl, and then began to sing a most quaint old song in which she joined. I certainly never remember hearing it, but she knew it at once. My brother said he was quite well, and laughed just as we remember he used to do; he was also able to tell me who was with him, and gave me a message from an uncle who, many years ago, lost his life in Africa. I had brought with me a small leather cartridge wallet that this uncle used in his travels; my brother said he was there, with them all, and desired me to keep the wallet in remembrance of him.

Then an aunt spoke who had not long passed over. During her life she would never have listened to a word of spiritism, although she was very devout. We felt surprised that she should have come to speak, and when we asked her how she knew we were sitting she replied: "Your brother James told me you were here." She said she was very happy. E. Murray.

EVIDENCE FROM SCOTLAND

My friend Mr. James Robertson, of Glasgow, is a bicycle manufacturer. He is seventy years of age, a spiritist of some thirty- five years' standing, and author of Spiritualism: The Open Door to the Unseen Universe. Although he leaves it to my discretion to "cut and carve" as much as I like, I prefer to leave his narrative just as he wrote it. It reveals the man better than anything I can say of him. His letter is appended:—

5 Granby Terrace,
Glasgow, W.
November 11, 1912

Dear Admiral Moore,—I now send you some pages I have penned, and, though they may lack the direct point which your own articles have conveyed, still I hope you will be able to make some use of them. I cannot say that I am at all pleased with what is sent, and had some thoughts of beginning again, but have resolved to let them go as they are. The beginning you will think perhaps out of place. One of my daughters to whom I handed the pages for perusal said: "Cut all that out"; but I will leave you to cut and carve as much as you like, and if you should think of sending them back to me with any hints I will do what you may desire. With all kind regards and appreciation of your grand work.—

Yours most sincerely,
James Robertson.

Carlyle has said; "Men have lost their faith in the invisible, and believe and hope and work only in the Visible." The belief in another world, whose inhabitants could take cognisance of this sphere, has been a very vague and shadowy faith. Only the material, the immediately practical, has been of import to us. Of course we had traditions, which we thought we believed in; but no feeling of certainty came into our lives. The wisest and best of men, with the largest culture of the intellect, found nothing in their investigations of external nature which gave the slightest hint of this invisible world of which ancient books had somewhat feebly spoken. That the world could become possessed of such new phenomena, a new power and knowledge that could relate to us an invisible world, was thought to be the rudest conception that could be offered. Neither the men of accomplished minds nor the custodians of religious verities would admit for a long time that nature had such possibilities to unfold. It has to be admitted that this new phenomena, which claimed to relate us to this unseen universe, did not show their best face at first. It seemed crude and rude that a revelation of such transcendent importance as the opening of the gates of that other world should be ushered in by noises, which naturally clashed with our prepossessions regarding that hidden realm. It was an appeal only to our external senses. But, like every new thing, it gradually presented to the world a more varied programme; the same power which caused the rappings claimed to move the pen and lips of those who first paid attention to the matter, and soon there were great numbers who spoke out messages that bore evidence of being prompted by those whom we had talked about as dead. A light began to shine in the darkness; scientific and scholarly minds were attracted to the subject, and found that the messages poured out were neither unintelligible nor obscure, but bore the stamp of reason, of wisdom, and were in accord with the principles of nature. How the light spread at first over the continent of Europe, and eventually found a footing in England, it is not my province to dwell upon. That such men as D. D. Home raised the temperature of many thinking minds is undoubted. The phenomena which transpired in his presence dissipated much of the materialism which abounded, and gave an elevation of soul to many who were made to feel that religion might be a tangible thing after all. That such men as Crookes, Wallace, and Robert Chambers were attracted to this man evidences that there was a current of noble quality running through him. Thackeray was brave enough to admit into the columns of the Cornhill Magazine (then in its palmy days) an article which described the phenomena which transpired in Home's presence. Society invariably shows small favours to its guides and teachers, and so Home, with all his striking gifts, which brought consolation to weary hearts, had to run the gauntlet of fierce opposition. Many a poisoned arrow was aimed at him, but he left behind a record which is unassailable. It is quite thirty-six years since I was drawn into contact with this modern spiritual movement, at a time when I utterly disbelieved in the possibility of any light on the subject of a future life being possible. It is said that to become thoroughly acquainted with a truth we must first have disputed it. I held the idea in such contempt that I could not calmly listen to its claims; and yet, when I did open my mind and viewed the facts, these facts beat me, and I have never had cause to retrace my steps. I was illuminating throwing a light for me on every realm of thought. Vague yearnings were satisfied, dreamy fancies became realities. It became a fountain whose waters refreshed with gladness my whole being. It was crude phenomena, which the world would laugh at, that brought the conviction that unseen beings could act on matter, that they could see us, read our minds, and reveal an intelligence outside the knowledge of the sitters. It has been my privilege to come into close contact with nearly all the phenomenal mediums, whose powers make evident that they are but the servants of those who are wiser than themselves. Light has been shed through every form of mediumship. I have looked at faces I had known on earth; I have heard descriptions given by clairvoyants which were photographic of the person described; I have had messages hundreds of times which could only bear one interpretation—that is, they were the thoughts of those we called dead. I knew intimately for years the three brothers Duguid, who were most plastic in the hands of the spirit operators. I became intimate with their inspirers and helpers, and I have the conviction that these spirit workers were all they claimed to be—simple-minded Indians, or philosophers, or painters such as Jan Steen and Ruisdael. This other world has a mission to bring home to earth-dwellers that immortality is a natural fact, and that the real salvation of the world will be brought about when humanity realises its truth. I have had close acquaintanceship with the workers whose mental phenomena have produced a literature which cannot die away into insignificance and oblivion, for the writings of Davis and Tuttle are a perennial well from which the most useful knowledge comes forth. Years of friendly converse with the inspirers of Mr. J. J. Morse and Mr. E. W. Wallis have built up a conviction which nothing can destroy. It has been in my own home—perhaps sitting with my own family—that my inmost heart has been reached, and all doubt of the loving friendship of spirit people has been dissipated for ever.

I thought after thirty-five years close observation that I had been brought as close to the spirit people as ever I would likely get; but in this I have been mistaken. I had clear memories of Lottie Fowler's mediumship, which perhaps was the most striking of my experience. A fragile woman, yet one who forced conviction on you, your whole life and its circumstances being opened out. I have always thought of her as being the high-water mark of mediumistic development. It was a vision which could not be disputed, but it was fitful and erratic, becoming cloudy at intervals, the woman herself giving little idea of spiritual development. She was a machine through which spirit people found they could carry conviction of their presence and power. I have met with many who, through her gifts, have been brought from the depths of their grief to participate in a pure joy.

I had thought, as I have said, till the autumn of 1911 that the channel of communication had been opened as wide as it would ever be in my day. I had read Admiral Moore's clear-cut descriptions in Light and Reason of his experiences with Mrs. Wriedt of Detroit and had perhaps the feeling that the statements made were coloured, or that America gave conditions which were not available in this country. This doubt, however, had soon to be dissipated. My friend Councillor Appleyard, of Sheffield, wrote me that he had Mrs. Wriedt as a guest staying with him, that he proposed bringing her north on a holiday jaunt, and that she would be pleased to give me a sitting, with liberty to invite such friends as I desired. I spent the evening of her arrival at her hotel, and the next morning, with Mr. And Mrs. Appleyard, we went on an excursion to Loch Long and Loch Lomond. I had a whole day's converse with her, and found her clear, simple, and true, glittering with no lustre but that of common sense. At night there were gathered together in my library the friends and relatives whom I had invited—a company of fifteen persons in all. The place in which we sat had oft-times been used for such gatherings, while the group of persons assembled had all seen something of the subject except one man, a minister of the Church of Scotland. I had met this gentleman on board a steamer while on a trip to the Canary Islands a short time before; I had given him a promise that if, at any time, I had any satisfactory evidence to offer which would substantiate the truth of what we had spoken so much about, I would invite him to be present.

We sat in the darkness, the trumpet having before this been brought out of its case and handed round for inspection, being afterwards set on the floor in the middle of the room. I was not anxious for any tests of spirit identity personally; my wish being that the others who needed it more might get the full assurance that had been mine for so many years. My desires, however, did not rule. We had been conversing together for only a few minutes when a loud and clear voice was heard speaking, Mrs Wriedt informed us that this was Dr. Sharp, whose work it was to manage matters from his side of life. I heard voices speaking, faintly, close to me but could not well make out what was said. "Did I not know Harry Smith?" I was asked by the Doctor. "Yes," I said, and then Harry related his story, which was not of any deep import to me beyond the great fact it demonstrated that here was one I had known on earth who could still interest himself in me. Harry Smith was a mechanic who had been in my employment for many years. Of course he knew of my devotion to Spiritualism, and had heard me speak at our hall. Not only had he come, but he had brought with him several other old servants who were determined to speak, and would only resign the trumpet when they were fully recognised. I confess that, while this talk was going on, I was anxious it would end; I felt I was monopolising the power, while the stories of these old mechanics were not of the first importance to me. There they were, however, and left quite happy when I had admitted the truth of some trifling incident they brought to my memory. A most interesting feature in all this was the part played by Dr. Sharp. You felt here was a strong robust nature who was guiding a team, pulling up this one and letting some other go in front, determined that those he let come to the front should be understood; While Mrs. Wriedt came in now and again with a word to straighten out matters when they were apt to get confused. The form of mediumship I was now witnessing was quite new to me. I felt I was being brought closer than ever before to the dead; there was a sense of face-to-face conversation, a steady, continuous stream of speech, not fugitive and streaky, but robust and direct. The unseen friends seemed determined that I should be saturated with evidence, whether I desired it or not. My Son-in-law, who was accidentally killed in Italy some years ago, came and revealed a personality about which there could be no mistake. Evidently Dr. Sharp had no trouble in teaching him how to use the trumpet; he was a man of quick intelligence, scientific to the finger-tips. He spoke of the past so clearly, and of the present position of his wife and children, naming them without hesitation, and showing that he had the most complete knowledge of things as they were. It was among the finest bits of evidence I ever had that the veil which separated human hearts was a very thin one. Some things which were not detailed, but suggested, carried as much to my mind as his other narrative; the subtle hints were a revelation of character which could scarcely have been more complete. That the members of the family were deeply moved is only a prosaic expression; there was a stirring up of the whole nature, a confidence which no time can weaken; a knowledge which will warm life, and a light borne in which is real sunshine.

My dear old mother, who in the earth life had so many regrets that I had drifted to what she called "unbelief," came and expressed her gladness that I had followed the light that had come. Of her presence in our midst I had oft-times been made familiar, but here she was again, if not in the body at least in the heart. She spoke to my girls, who were present, as only she and no other would speak, calling them by the pet names she used while on earth, and which had been forgotten, made reference by name to other members of the family, and revealed an identity about which there could be no mistake.

The voice of my mother was the voice I was familiar with, the same broad Doric speech, as if she had never gone from us. The Scotch idioms were never departed from for a moment; if we did not see her in the habit in which she lived, we, at least, felt she was unchanged in manner; the girls present were still children to her, and her memory of the earth life and its people quite keen. She spoke to me as if we had but parted yesterday, called me "Jeems" as she had always done while in the body, and as she had often done since when influencing other mediums to speak to me. Here, it was speaking direct as it were without using another's voice. Mrs. Wriedt could not by any possibility have given a replica of the Scotch tones I heard, for while my mother was conversing with my daughters the medium was talking in her usual Yankee tones.

It was not my mother alone who spoke in true Scotch; each one of the spirit visitors who had been natives alike spoke in the vernacular in which they had been reared, without a tinge of anything foreign. My friend, Mr. Peter Galloway, a Glasgow merchant, held communication with his two sons, who had been drowned in the Atlantic, in the purest Scotch; and marvellous was the knowledge they seemed to have of their father's going-out and coming-in in his daily life. A clever imitator could not keep up the Scottish dialect beyond a few words; he could not deceive a native who had been used to our lowland Scotch. Dr. Sharp, the controlling intelligence, who claimed to have been a native of Glasgow, used many Scotch words, quite like one of ourselves, but he did not keep this up for long. Once, when he asked us to sing together an old Scotch song, which he named with a true accent, I asked him where he could have heard it; he at once said, "I learned it at my mother's knee."

All of this conversing with the so called dead, however regarded by those who have not come in touch with spiritual phenomena, had no relation to miracle, magic, or monkish legends, but was a plain, natural fact, proving that the world of spirit and the world of matter were no longer Twain, but looked into one. As Milton said long ago; "Man is one world, and hath another to attend him"; and here was the evidence.

Perhaps as striking as my own experiences were those of the clergyman who had not come close to the subject before. He had at one time had a charge in Canada, and quite a number of his old parishioners came and spoke to him. It was amusing to hear some of the quaint names, which the minister recognised at once, and the incidents which were recalled to his mind. "I don't remember that, Jerry," the minister would say; but Jerry would go on bringing out something more which had to be admitted. Incidents of his Canadian career were told out and accepted without difficulty. A brother also came to him and spoke about the members of his family. The minister evidently felt that what we were participating in was the common daily food with which spiritualists were regaled at their gatherings. He had no idea of the patient efforts by which many had drawn together the accumulated bits that had brought conviction. It is not often that anyone at once has the evidence of the unseen world brought home conclusively. But something of more importance was to follow. A personality of more importance now came upon the scene, a voice unlike all the others which preceded it—that of Andrew Jackson Davis. The great seer had been very close to me for years; while in the body our correspondence was frequent, and he unburdened himself to me about many things which were unknown to the world. After his death he gave me a message to send to his wife through the mediumship of Miss McCreadie and asked her to send me the skullcap he wore at home, which his wife, accepting the message as valid, at once did; so that it will be seen that there was a link formed between Davis and myself which would naturally bring me into my surroundings.

It was not to me, however so much as the clergyman to whom Davis spoke. He had evidently read his mind, and seen the wavering between the wish to believe and the ability to do so. With a lofty eloquence and clear, calm enthusiasm for truth, he gave a reading of the inner side of his nature, and urged him to follow the light that had come to him, at whatever cost. It was a magnificent piece of rhetoric, burning with the loftiest ideals. It was purely spiritual, the mundane being cast aside. Scarcely ever before have I listened to an address from the spirit side that conveyed so much, compressed into such a short space. It did not go beyond the senses' comprehension; there was nothing suffuse, but a simple sublimity that touched all. The seer who had given himself to the discovery of truth seemed bent on its diffusion. The minister said but little, he recognised that the person who spoke had read his heart, knew all his doubts and fears, and how his mind had been swaying to and fro. When he had returned to his parish he at once wrote me that, while he never doubted the reality of the unseen world, what had been given at that séance was most extraordinary. "It is cheering and assuring." He continued, "That the communication can be so clearly established. Andrew Jackson Davis's address to me will remain vivid and impressive, and I hope inspiring during my earth life." That some chord was struck and kept vibrating is evidenced from the fact that, a few weeks afterwards, I was surprised to hear from him that he had resigned his charge, where he was loved and respected. Davis had evidently given his mental struggles some power to come to a decision as to his attitude towards truth as it was now presented to him. I do not know that what he wrote me revealed to the full the influence the séance had upon him. He wrote: "Lest you attach any blame to yourself" (I had advised him to hold on to his work, as, situated as he was, his sympathy and tenderness would be an influence for good, more perhaps than in the open field), "I hasten to say that, perhaps for twelve years, I have thought as I now think, and have fought against the thought, compromised, and did as well as I could. I will confess, however, that Mr. Davis's words at the séance thrilled me." I need not add more on this point, but return to other incidents of the séance. Dr. Sharp explained the difficulty he had in teaching the crowd who were around us how to form the vocal chord, so that we might hear the voices clearly, One old friend of mine, who was present, is a lady who had waded through a sea of troubles, many of a very tragic nature, yet ever feeling strengthened through the blessed light of spirit communion. There are some persons who find no difficulty in their quest for light. I have met with those who, I was apt to think, were credulous, so readily did spiritual communications reach them; but I have learned to recognise that there is a receptivity in the nature of some which is not in others; that, while many have to wait outside the gates for long before conviction comes, there are others who in a moment recognise the reality of the spirit's presence. To this lady there came messages which touched and reached her inmost heart. All flowed to her so naturally, the messages from husband and family gone on. There was only one conviction that could be borne in— that a door was actually open through which the inhabitants of another world came and gave us glimpses of their continued affection, and of their active, earnest, natural life. I know that such gatherings as I am seeking to chronicle are rare. With us there was the most complete harmony—each was calm and confiding. With one accord and mind we sat in a room which had been oft-times magnetised with the spirit's presence, so that what might be called perfect conditions prevailed. If what transpired among us, the many bits of spirit identity, could only have been realised by the outside world, then the great question had been conclusively settled. Doubt could no more prevail; gloom and darkness would disappear, for we had the certainty that our dead (so-called) were alive. I have not given a garbled description of what transpired, yet I have left untold many bits of deep interest which concerned the several sitters, all of whom had some conclusive evidence. Wonderful was the playing on an unseen cornet and the melodious voices which sang at intervals. We sat for over two hours amid this ameliorating and uplifting influence. How much more of evidence regarding a future state must needs be given before the minds of men will be conquered? Will humanity continue to envelop themselves in the shadows of tradition while this real light is showing itself in their midst? Sir Oliver Lodge once said: We were so conservative in our temperament that it took three generations before a proved fact, if it was a novel one, could enter into the minds of the people, with the view of its being incorporated into the daily life. Three generations have now gone since the advent of modern spiritualism, so that the ripened period is at hand when across the doorway the greetings of the unseen will be gratefully accepted. Mrs. Wriedt, unlike others who have carried the torch of truth, makes no claim to be a superior person, but only an instrument who helps to reveal, in measure, the possibilities that belong to our human nature. It was admirable to see the calm, unaffected manner with which she sat through the proceedings—a spectator seemingly outside it all, nothing seemingly abnormal. There was no show of vanity or conceit, only a sense of gladness that so much consolation had come to those who had gathered together. All the marvels I had witnessed before were a prophesy of what had now come before me, and I saw in the future time a still further evolution of spiritual gifts springing forth which would remove the last tinge of doubt regarding an after death state. Never before was I so deeply affected by the great possibilities the future had in store. I saw the crust of prejudice being broken through and a new brighter colour given to human life through the certainty that death does not put an end to the co-operation which had existed. Other voices will be heard which will win their way to the world's recognition that there has been found a pathway to another world.

However doubtful be the welcome they may receive now, there is no cause for fear; they will stay in our midst till recognition has come. And it is certain that, even as the evidence has become more clear, and science has begun to give attention to the subject in our day, the doorway will open wider all the time. The volume of well- attested facts which Admiral Moore has brought together cannot be sneered at nor ignored; they are in line with what Crookes and Wallace had previously attested, and in harmony with the natural world in which we live.

During the summer of 1912 I have been privileged to be present at several other gatherings at which Mrs. Wriedt has been present. At all of these there have been similar revealments of the presence of my dead friends, and messages given in languages of which the medium could have no knowledge. I have realised more fully than ever that we do not need to wait till death before we can come into touch with the spirit world. As Gerald Massey has said: "Instead of the other world remaining dim and helplessly afar off—a possibility to some; a doubt to others; a perplexity to many, and an abstraction to most—it will be made a living verity, visible to many, audible to more, present with and operant through all."

By Mr. Thomson

An account of two sittings with Mrs. Wriedt, the American trumpet medium, held in the house of James Robertson, 5 Granby Terrace, Glasgow:—

For some months back I had been much interested in an account of séances held with the above medium by Vice-Admiral Usborne Moore; and one day, before going off to Fife for my holidays, I called on Mr. Robertson, when he told me that he had just got a letter from Councillor Appleyard, of Sheffield. It was to the effect that Mrs. Wriedt was staying with him as his guest, and that he intended to bring her to Scotland for a holiday, and would be delighted to give Mr. Robertson the opportunity of arranging for a sitting or two.

We arranged there and then that I would be present, and I was delighted to get the chance of studying this, to me, new phase of mediumship.

At the first sitting there were fifteen of us, and it was held in absolute darkness, the window-shutters being closed, and then covered over with heavy curtains. Mrs. Wriedt we found to be quite American in her style, with the usual smart, confident, and assertive manner of talking which is peculiar to the U.S.A.

Her visible stage property was an aluminium trumpet, which I think was in three sections, and could be drawn out in telescopic fashion to about two feet. She explained that, usually, the trumpet would touch the party who was to be spoken to.

The library table had been removed from the room, and we sat in the circle with the trumpet standing upright in the middle of the floor. After the light was switched off, it was not long before a number of friends and relations of Mr. Robertson's family spoke through the trumpet and gave to them satisfactory proof of identity.

One of the circle was a minister who got quite a number of messages. He had formerly been located in Canada, and one of his old members, who could not give him his name, tried hard to make him remember the gift of a turkey.

This evidently had been a frequent occurrence with our ministerial friend, for he had to express his regret at not being able to recall the particular incident. Others who spoke to him had not the same difficulty, and one who claimed to be his brother gave him the number of the members of his family—twelve, I think, in fact, he appeared to know more about them than the minister himself. At this point Dr. Sharp, the spirit control of Mrs. Wriedt, spoke through the trumpet in corroboration, and further explained that the brother wished him to say that two of them were in the seventh sphere and three or five in a lower sphere, either the third or the fifth.

All this time I had not been so much interested in what was spoken through the trumpet as in trying to grasp all the details. Mrs. Wriedt sometimes gave a description of the spirit who wanted to talk, also the name; and often she would be talking at the same time as the trumpet, so it was clearly evident all through the sittings that she never left her place. Once I very clearly saw a white shadowy form, but it was not fully enough developed to resemble the human body. At other times I could see a white or grey cloud which would move from the centre of the room to one of the sitters.

My study of phenomena was rudely interrupted by the trumpet striking me on the knees in quite a violent manner, and the spirit speaking gave the name of Campbell. He also wanted to know about "Grace." I could not settle my thoughts to consider who this could be, and, after fruitless questions for more information from him, he seemingly got quite annoyed, and said very forcibly: "Man, Thomson, you are very dense." I then got the name "Alexander," and my wife, who was sitting next to me, agreed with me that it was my (deceased) cousin, Grace's husband, who was speaking. I asked: "Is my grandmother there?" when I got the reply: "Which grandmother?" On explaining to him, he said: "All your friends are here tonight." He then addressed his remarks to my wife, who had quite a conversation with him, telling him that she, the month previously, had seen his daughter Grace and her husband, and that they had a nice little baby. He appeared to be deeply moved by this, as his voice broke somewhat, and the trumpet was laid down in front of the medium.

My face was then touched gently on the left cheek by the trumpet, and my father spoke to me, and said that my aunt, his sister Joan, was with him. His concluding words were: "God bless you."

The medium then said that someone giving the name of Annie wished to talk to my wife, but the voice was too faint to get any definite idea as to who was there.

SECOND NIGHT'S SITTING

During the first night's sitting Mrs. Wriedt said that someone giving the name of "House" wished to speak, and she thought it was intended for me. Before I could collect my thoughts our minister friend spoke out and said that he knew someone of the name "Hess," and that the message would probably be for him. He asked some questions, but nothing came of it, and I thought the incident was closed.

Tonight, however, I was struck smartly on the hand by the trumpet, and the name "House" was pronounces most distinctly, and, further, that he knew me, and wished to speak. I asked where he was from, when he replied "From across the water." I then asked: "Was he William H. House?", and he said, "Yes that's my name," in a loud and most emphatic tone, and then went on to talk of business matters which were known by no one in Scotland but myself. He also gave me some personal details without mentioning names, but which I fully understood, and I was surprised to find that he entertained a grudge against one who was known to me. I cannot, of course, go into this matter further, but it was clearly evident to me that his business life was still filling his mind to a great extent, and that he was fully aware of what had transpired at the time of his death.

This gentleman was the president of an American Buttonhole Manufacturing Company, for whom my firm had acted as representatives in Great Britain and Ireland. Unfortunately, his Company, unable to compete successfully with a wealthier opponent, came to grief, and Mr. House took to his bed, and passed over after a short illness.

Later on I heard a very faint whisper from the trumpet, and, after a little time, got the name Lizzie B——, a young lady who had died a few years previously. She was a gentle shy creature, and there was no doubt to me that the voice was hers. She said that she had tried to make herself known to my wife on the previous night, but could not speak distinctly enough. She asked me to tell her father, but I replied that I had already told him of the truth of spirit return, and that he did not believe it. She replied: "I know but he thinks a lot about it."

I then asked: "Is Mina H.—— with you?" "No," she said, "but I will go and get her to speak."

Poor Lassie, she forgot, and so did I, that others were as eager to talk as we were, and, the line of communication being broken, it could not be picked up again that night, at any rate.

After another interval I was again spoken to, this time by my mother, who said that she had also been at the séance on the previous night, but had stood back to give the others a chance to speak.

I think that the best test of all was the feeling expressed in the tones of the voices when speaking. They were true to the life, and I can vouch that everything I got fitted in most wonderfully and accurately with the characteristics of those whom they claimed to be.

Glasgow, January 15, 1913.

Dear Admiral Moore,—

I send you something further regarding last year's gathering which you may consider of value. The writer is a nephew of mine, a young man, twenty-six years of age. I wish he had detailed more fully the several questions he put to extract the answers. I felt I had made a mistake in inviting him, as he was so positive that I thought he would upset all conditions. He would be satisfied with nothing which was not particularly clear. In the talk with my son-in-law, Joe Crowther, there was a mass of detail about the photos he was shown, and it was some time before he got the nature of the prints which they had been looking over. Until the night of the séance I had never heard about the interview at all. When it came to his fathers visit he made me feel the proceedings would be spoilt. "If you are my father, you can give me your name," and, persisting, he brought it forth with a mass of other facts. His father was a spiritualist; a very clever man, whom Gerald Massey looked upon as having one of the keenest intellects he had met with. He instinctively grasped the writings on Egyptology, and wrote a series of articles in the old medium. The family have had so many deaths, and got so little of value regarding their survival, that they got sick of the subject of spiritualism; but now all are awake to its realities. I feel more and more that your accumulated facts will break down the barriers which keep the light from streaming through.

All kind regards.
Yours faithfully,
James Robertson.

It may be safely said, perhaps, that since the consciousness of existence dawned on the human race, no problem has been greater than the mysteries that surround both life and death. It is perhaps true, also, that the desire to fathom, if possible, these mysteries has grown steadily with the ages, until with the present generation there are no problems more poignant with vital interest. It cannot be said that the origin of life can be in any way understood, and we remain baffled by that great problem. That there is a continuence of life after death is the confident hope of all such ages; but the problems of such a spiritual existence is to most people only a mystifying one, and can only be grasped vaguely. The desire for more light, however, is an ever-increasing one to most of us, for, as the years pass on, we must all experience the loss of dear friends and intimates. Family ties become broken, the parents guidance and loving care cease, the brothers and sisters we grew up among and loved, and the dear friends we were so familiar with, pass into that great silence; and, just as we cherished and loved them in life, our thoughts follow them into that great beyond, and we never cease to ponder over the mystery of it all; and the greatest desire is to know that perhaps that magnetic sympathy that united us in this world may enable us to meet with them again in that spiritual state beyond the grave. From the time that I had reason to think of these matters I have been familiar with hearing of the extraordinary and varied manifestations of a spiritual existence gleaned through spiritualistic séances, etc.; and, although such manifestations had hitherto interested me greatly, yet I could not credit or understand such astounding phenomena as my more credulous (as I then imagined) friends experienced and detailed to me. That I was soon to have these doubts dispelled I could not then credit; but it had been my desire, if an opportunity presented itself, to investigate for myself such manifestations. My mother had been fortunate enough to be present at a séance held in the house of my uncle, Mr. James Robertson, the medium being Mrs. Wriedt, and she was so impressed by the messages that came to those at that meeting, as well as to herself, that I determined, should I be fortunate enough to be able to do so, to attend a sitting held by this wonderful medium. I was not altogether ignorant of the astounding messages that had been obtained through Mrs. Wriedt's mediumship, for a very appreciative article appeared in Nash's Magazine just about that time, and it was through the kindness of my uncle, James Robertson, that I was able to be present at one of these sittings. The facts are very vivid in my memory, and I shall now proceed to give an exact account of what transpired. It must be understood that I went to this meeting quite sceptical, and determined to accept nothing that did not, in my own mind, bear the stamp of truth. The sitting took place at my uncle's house at 5 Granby Terrace, and, with the exception of my uncle and two of my cousins, the remaining ten or twelve people were entire strangers to me. In a casual way I was introduced to the medium, Mrs. Wriedt, whose personality impressed me immediately. One felt instinctively that here indeed was a gentle, kindly woman, and this helped perhaps to convince me that by such a person no fraud could be capable of being perpetrated. At the same time, I determined to let nothing of this influence me. It must be understood that this was the first sitting of the kind I had attended, and I was therefore, naturally enough, sceptical and determined to put matters to the proof if an opportunity presented itself.

We were seated in a circle, my uncle being next to me (whose influence, perhaps, contributed greatly to the fact that I received such extraordinary messages); the medium sat exactly opposite me, a few yards distant; and the trumpet, a long cylindrical one, like a miniature megaphone, was placed in the centre of the circle. Almost immediately I observed what appeared like a small, white cloud floating about, and after a few seconds the trumpet was lifted from the floor, and a voice addressed us. To say that I was astonished would be to put it mildly, as the voice was strong and deep, and kept swinging right round the circle in a most extraordinary fashion. This, as it turned out, was the spirit of Dr. Sharp, Mrs. Wriedt's control, or guide; but, of course, I didn't know anything about that at the time. On the contrary, I was quite suspicious, and listened intently for any movement on the medium's part, etc. On the contrary, she immediately began speaking to the Doctor in the most matter-of-fact tone in the world. I shall not detail the conversation that transpired, or the good lecture we received from the Doctor on the question of health, etc.; but, on asking if there were many friends present, we were informed that there were thousands awaiting an opportunity of making their presence known. Truly, an extraordinary fact! After a little while the Doctor, who evidently acted as a sort of superintendent and general interpreter, so to speak, relinquished the trumpet to his spirit friends, and the manifestations commenced. The first spirit to speak was my cousin's late husband, Joe Crowther; and I must confess that I felt a little disappointed, for in no way could I recognise the voice, or any other particular characteristic. It was not long ere the voice approached, and held conversation with myself, which, of course, was what I desired. After the usual preliminaries, I asked this spirit if he remembered the last conversation he and I had had together; to which he answered: "Yes, perfectly." Q.; "If you remember that, can you tell me what it was about?" A.; "Do you mean to say you do not remember?" Q.; "I remember perfectly; but it would convince me much more that this was indeed you, Joe, if you could detail it to me." A.; "Well, Do you remember I was showing you some photographic mining prints I had taken, and explained the various strata?" (This was exactly what took place.) Q.; "Yes that is quite correct. And now can you tell me where we had that conversation, and if anyone else was present besides ourselves?" A.; "It took place in this house." Q.; "Yes but in which room?" A.; "In the library, and there was no other person present." I may say that nobody, to my knowledge, ever knew of that conversation besides Joe Crowther and myself. The talk we had interested me greatly; hence my desire to know if he recollected it. Immediately after this conversation the trumpet was transferred to another spirit friend, and manifestations proceeded forthwith. At the same time my friend Joe continued to speak to me quite clearly, without the trumpet. I distinctly heard his voice, the voice of the trumpet, and Mrs. Wriedt's voice (endeavouring to explain some message which the recipient could not quite grasp); that is to say, three distinct voices speaking at once. I could detail the messages that almost everyone there received, but I am more concerned in detailing the manifestations I myself received, and shall not, therefore, go into other detail. The fact remains, they were all astonishingly convincing. Perhaps an instance might be mentioned. The little daughter of a gentleman there, after the usual distressing preliminary recognition's, said: "You do not sing so much now, father. Do you think we might sing one of those songs we used to sing together?" On the father saying he would, there began surely on of the most extraordinary duets that was ever listened to. The Girl's voice was clear and perfectly musical, and the song "Annie Laurie," was rendered quite beautifully.

After a little while my uncle, John Hutchinson, who died a few months previously, spoke, and almost from the beginning I recognised him by a peculiar kind of laugh he had. The questions he answered were altogether satisfactory. I asked if my father was present, and, if so, I should like to speak to him. Shortly afterwards a voice spoke to me, and on requesting to know who it was that addressed me I was told it was my father. "If you are my father," I said, "Tell me your full name." The answer I received was not distinct, but I could practically grasp what was being said, and it was correct. The voice in this case, and at this stage, was not very strong and distinct, but gradually improved. I insisted on getting at least my father's initials, and the answer was "J. M. M." (John McGregor Munro). I then asked if any of the boys (meaning my brothers) were present, and I was told that the three of them were there; and the names, given me without hesitation, were correct and in their order of age, etc. I asked my father also if he could tell me when we had been speaking about him last (my father had been dead seventeen years), and he said, "Yes, this morning." And detailed the subject that my mother and I had been discussing at breakfast time that day, which certainly no one could possibly have known of. Moreover, he told me a fact in connection with this conversation which I did not know, but which I verified when I arrived home. I should have liked to ask many more personal questions, but at that point the control was broken and the opportunity was lost. I can only say that the facts stated in the foregoing prove to my entire satisfaction that no fraud of any kind could possibly have occurred, but I must confess to a feeling of sadness that these meeting engendered. That is perhaps because of the fact that death is always the nature of a tragedy to us all and we are apt to picture the return of the spirits of those we held so dear in that category, without at the time being able to see beyond all that.

What I should like to know is more about this spirit world, which must be peopled by countless spirits; what domestic and social life exists; how long does the influence of this world hold them, and what, as spirits, are their aspirations, etc,. etc. And I trust that some day, by patient study and observation, I may be able to understand these most important questions—more important now to me by far than manifestations that spirits do exist.   (Signed)   Alex. Munro.

In reply to some questions from me Mr. Munro writes:—

202 Langside Road, Crosshill, Glasgow
Jan. 20, 1913

Dear Sir,—I duly received your letter of the 16th inst., and quite appreciate your desire to investigate the various tests which I mentioned in my account of the sitting I had with Mrs. Wriedt......The sitting took place at my uncle's house on July 25 or 26 1912. With regard to your second inquiry, it is quite true that I did not recognise the voices of my father or Joe Crowther, but the characteristics of style and speech were strikingly like in each case. Of course as my father was Highland and my cousin's husband English, neither of them had a Scotch accent. I think allowance should be made also for the change in tone, which the speaking through a trumpet makes in all voices. My father's style of speech was extremely striking, and I could remember, as of old, he appeared rather irritated with me for not taking matters more for granted and grasping the reality of his presence and what he was saying more quickly. Perhaps I omitted to emphasise sufficiently that I did not accept, without repeated questions and tests, any manifestations I received. Although there was no Scotch accent in the case of my father or cousin, for reasons explained, yet the Scotch accent was quite distinct and decided in several other cases; and not only that, but the Glasgow accent as well; and as you are no doubt aware, this latter is distinctly a language of its own. I may say that no doubts exist in my mind as to the genuineness of the medium, Mrs. W. (witness, for example, the three voices speaking at once, as well as the personal tests I received). Such tests are beyond the realm of fraud or trickery, and if these phenomena I have detailed in my account of the sitting can be explained I shall only be too pleased to receive enlightenment. It must be understood that I am only a humble student of the subject; but, although I feel convinced that the tests were quite genuine, yet the whole matter in retrospect seems to me quite unreasonable and unreal, and certainly not comforting so far as a future state is concerned. However, I shall probably learn more hereafter, and meantime, if I can be of further service to you, I shall only be too glad to give you any information you may desire. It would please me greatly to receive your views on the subject.—Yours faithfully

ALEC. MUNRO.

THE TESTIMONY OF MR. GALLOWAY
A MASTER-TAILOR OF GLASGOW

At the first visit of Mrs. Wriedt to Mr. Robertson's home in Glasgow (1911) I had the joy of hearing my sons' voices, clear and direct in their natural Scotch tones, exhibiting a knowledge of my external life and my inward thoughts; but I was gratified at a later stage with something which added to the charm of hearing the objective realisation of their presence.

At one of the sittings with Mrs. Wriedt in the house of Mr. Coates (Rothesay) I recall the following manifestation with great pleasure.

The circle was comprised of fourteen sitters, and, the conditions being very good, we had a great deal of wonderful phenomena, which had a deep interest for others; but what appealed to me most was the appearance of my son.

We had not been sitting long when white vapoury clouds were seen floating about the room; then suddenly a face formed out of the clouds, which I at once recognised as that of my son Jack.

I involuntarily exclaimed; "Oh, Jack!" when the face assumed a pleased expression, and seemed to give me a nod of confirmation. I had not long to wait for further proof, for the trumpet was brought over to me, and a voice at once said: "What did you think of my face, father?" I replied: "It is first class, Jack; I knew you at once." He then added: "I wish my mother had been here."

Jack was the youngest of my twin sons who were drowned by the wreck of the steamship Hestia on their way out to Canada then (aged seventeen years). They have both given abundant proof of their continued existence, and I am satisfied that I still retain their love.

At a sitting held in the house of Mr. Robertson, with a large company—I think about twenty were present—a voice, as distinctly Scotch as my own, addressed me, thus:—

"How are you, Mr. Galloway?" I replied: "Who are you, friend?" When he said; "I am McGillivray." I said that I did not know him, but he insisted that he knew me, and, on asking where it was that he made my acquaintance, he said: "Do you no mind that I worked with you in Coatbridge?"

I could not recall this, and asked him if he used to live in Glasgow.

He then said: "Do you no mind working in Coatbridge when you were a young man? You had just left home, and did not know your trade very well, and I did that for you while you sewed for me."

I at once recognised him, and asked if he remembered what we made "colliers vests" of. He replied: "Moleskin." I said that I meant their Sunday vests, when he replied: "Silk Velvet," which was correct. Well then," I said "now tell me the price per yard of the velvet?" Answer: "Twenty-six shillings." (I was under the impression that it was twenty-five shillings, but I may be wrong.) "Now tell me what they paid for the vests?" Answer: "Forty-two shillings," which, I believe, was correct.

I remember it struck me then as being out of place for a miner to spend so much on a vest; but at that time there was a great boom in the coal trade, and that was one of the ways they spent some of their money. I was a young man then, and only worked along with Mr. McGillivray for ten weeks. After coming back to Glasgow he called once on me, and I never saw him since. That is now thirty-nine years ago, and he is one of the last men that I would have expected to come back; yet here he was still interested in my welfare. Of course, this was a glimpse of one old associate, but many others came close to me whose identity was as closely marked, if not more so, than that of my old fellow-worker McGillivray.

(Signed)   PETER GALLOWAY.

APPENDIX TO PART 1

I regret to say that on May 29 I left Cambridge House directly after the séance, and therefore cannot personally, give evidence on the remarkable phenomena which happened in the dining room. From what others have told me I believe that Miss Scatcherd's account is correct.

From Light, August 3, 1912.]

REMARKABLE PHENOMENA IN THE LIGHT AT CAMBRIDGE HOUSE WITH MRS.WRIEDT

By Felicia R. Scatcherd

No record of the phase of phenomena described below seems to have reached you, so I send the following extract from my notes, written immediately after the occurrence.

The phenomena were repeated a fortnight later, with slight variations.

May 29, 1912. "Julia's Bureau."—We had nearly finished supper. The electric light was full on. We were all talking. Mrs. Wriedt was telling us about her first meeting with Mr. W. T. Stead, when I saw Mr. Mallinson looking with startled eyes at the very large marguerite bush that has occupied Mr. Stead's chair at the head of the dining room table for the last month. Mrs. Wriedt sat on the right side of the table, I on the left, facing her. So the plant was between us. I followed Mr. Mallinson's gaze to the blossoms nearest Mrs. Wriedt. They were in agitated movement one after the other, then all together. The rest of the plant was quiet. But as I looked the topmost blossom moved alone; later others "Bowed," as one of the guests said.

"Well done! Now move the whole plant," I exclaimed. It turned, pot and all, towards me.

"Perhaps you can move the chair also." Almost immediately the chair was twisted from right angles to a position of forty-five degrees from the table, so that the left corner of the chair faced me. Then, still keeping that position with reference to the table, it was shifted six or eight inches nearer to where I was sitting.

We all felt the floor, walls, and windows vibrating. I have twice experienced earthquake shocks in the Ionian Islands. The sensation was similar.

Mrs. Harper cried: "That's right Chief! Keep your word." We were all sitting away from the table, to be sure no involuntary action had shaken the plant, after we first noticed its movements.

I suggested the lowering of the lights. The electric switch was turned off, leaving us in darkness, except for light from outside.

Three violent shocks caused the windows to rattle; the crockery clattered, and the walls and floor were shaken by a deep-seated vibratory movement, that I can only liken, as I have said, to my earthquake experiences. This movement was accompanied by the sound of heavy footfalls, as of someone stamping round the room. Then all was still. We turned on the lights.

There were one or two slight movements of blossoms afterwards, otherwise nothing more occurred. The chair is a heavy one. It had moved to the left some eight inches, having previously twisted on its right back leg through an arc of forty- five degrees.

"Mrs. Harper, why did you say 'That's right Chief! Keep your word'?"

The explanation was that, about a fortnight before leaving England, one Wednesday, at the "Bureau" supper, Mr. Stead was rather scornful of the "raps," which he could not hear too well. "When I come back I shall stamp around the room and shake the floor and windows. There will be no mistake about my being there," or words to that effect. I was in Greece at that time. The statement was confirmed by all present on the occasion.

PART 2

RECORDS OF 1913

In March, 1913, it was represented to me, by some people who had enjoyed sittings with Mrs. Etta Wriedt in the previous spring and early summer, that it was important she should be invited to England again; that, if I did not undertake the charge of her, she would probably fall into the hands of undesirable people, who would exploit her for their own advantage; and that I was the only person who could undertake the enterprise in a satisfactory manner. I hesitated for a week; I was averse to again going through the risk, the trouble, and the work of arranging and carrying out the details of her visit. It was easy for me to visit Detroit and attend séances at her own house. However, on reflection, I recognised that this would be a selfish course to adopt, and I reluctantly consented to repeat the experiment of 1912. I therefore wrote to Mrs. Wriedt inviting her to visit me in England, and stating certain terms which she might accept or reject as she thought fit; and followed this up by another letter requesting her to cable one of three messages: (1) "Accept"; (2) "Not"; or (3) "On own." The last was to mean she was coming on her own responsibility, and without any reference to my control or protection.

On April 4 I received a wire, "Accept—May 1"; the date as previously arranged, meant the date of arrival. Invitation circulars to expectant sitters were at once despatched, a guarantor fund was inaugurated, and Miss E. K. Harper was engaged by me as secretary and hostess. This lady, as everyone knows, was the late W. T. Stead's private secretary; she had planned the séances for him in 1911, and for me, after his lamentable death in the Titanic, in 1912. She kindly consented to postpone her literary work, and perform a duty which she was well aware would be onerous—in the belief that she was thereby gratifying her former chief by carrying out a work he had very much at heart. Incidentally, she was pleased at being able to assist in bringing her numerous friends and acquaintances into touch with their spirit friends. I desire here to publicly thank her for her decision, and to honestly confess that I could not have worked the details without her experience and diligent co-operation. The duties she undertook proved more difficult than I had anticipated, from causes upon which I will not here dilate. Sufficient to say that, in loyalty to me, she persevered to the end; but I am certain that she will never accept the same duties again; nor do I wish her to do so. Mrs. Wriedt now understands English laws and customs; on her future visits she will arrange her séances and all other particulars herself.

I appointed the séances and private sittings in such a way as allowed of the psychic having two days and three evenings in the week entirely to herself. It is due to her to state that these periods of diversion and rest were not utilised by her, this year, in giving séances on her own account.

The high level of Mrs. Wriedt's mediumship was maintained throughout the sixty days she was my guest. There were some blanks and some indifferent séances. All people who understand the conditions necessary for psychic investigation know that this is inevitable with first-class mediums; and some, including myself, believe it to be a sign of genuineness, for nobody is so annoyed on such occasions as Mrs. Wriedt herself. I was favoured with some advice from those who, obviously, considered that they could manage better than myself, specially on the subject of the psychic "sitting too often"; and was more than once reminded of Æsop's fable of the man, his son, and the donkey. My kind advisers were the disappointed sitters, and the advice reached me after the event. I noticed one curious fact. There were no criticisms from these experts during the previous year, when the medium sat for very many more people, and these particular guarantors were successful.

The visit was a success, and the last day was the best. I was by far the largest guarantor, and enjoyed to the full the benefit of Mrs. Wriedt's mysterious gift, for I did not experience any blank sittings, and only two or three below the average. One of these was wholly inexplicable, as the conditions, so far as my poor judgment could determine, were perfect; the others I could account for.

Bad séances are generally due to one of four causes. Either the medium is disturbed in her mind about some imaginary grievance; the sitter or sitters are in bad health or low spirits; the atmospheric conditions are bad; or the sitter or sitters are disbelievers in anything they cannot determine by means of their normal senses. The latter factor can hardly account for any blank or poor séances in 1913, for there were but few strangers to the psychic allowed to guarantee. Great care was observed about this. Occasionally the blank is not to be accounted for by any known cause; but I think it possible that phenomena may be withheld by the medium's controls with the object of teaching us that nothing mortals can do will ensure success: we must be content to take what we can get and be thankful.

Neither in 1912 nor 1913 nor on any occasion during the four and a-half years that I have known her, has Mrs. Wriedt been in any sort of trance. She talks volubly during the séances and private sittings , sometimes on indifferent subjects, such as the superiority of American customs or the cruel restrictions of Admiral Moore; but more frequently in giving names and clairvoyant descriptions to the sitters. She asserts that she sees names in the air, inverted, and very difficult to secure, as the first letter disappears before the last is properly formed. Not unfrequently the name of a spirit who wishes to be known is whispered into her right ear.

I brought Mrs. Wriedt to Cambridge House, Wimbledon, at 7.40 p.m. on May 2,1913. After supper, at her suggestion, we adjourned to the séance room and held a private sitting. After my two trumpets had been rinsed with water and the musical-box started, the lights were switched off, and phenomena at once commenced. Iola spoke first a few words of greeting; then Dr. Sharp, who brought with him another spirit: "Here is a lady who wishes to see you." (Aside): "What did you say, madam?......Oh, this is a maiden lady who says her name is Searle. She says she lived near you when in life, and thought you were much deceived. Now, she has come to see if there is anything in it." (Aside): "What is it?"......"Yes, yes; she also says that her niece is now doing her work, and doing it very well, but she does not wish you to tell her." (A Miss Searle used to keep a small shop and post-office three hundred yards from my house. She passed over in September 1912. Her niece, Miss Holmes, is now keeping the shop. I never spoke to Miss Searle on the subject of spiritism, but she was no doubt aware that I lectured once a year at the temple in the town.)

W. T. Stead then manifested, and expressed pleasure at having influenced his widow to let me rent the house. It was the same voice I had been accustomed to hear in 1912. He said: "Tell Edith [Miss Harper] I am helping her all I can." Black Hawk turned up, and Iola was present all the time. It was a cheery, delightful sitting, and lasted forty-five minutes.

As, from a public, critical standpoint, my testimony obviously weakens in value, in proportion to the number of times I have sat with Mrs. Wriedt, and it happens that I have enjoyed the benefit of her gift on over one hundred occasions, I do not propose recording more than two—one private sitting and one private circle séance. I sat alone with the medium twenty-five times while she was my guest, and engaged five private circles, to which I invited my friends. At my private sittings I received much information of an intimate character, all of it most convincing to me, but of no interest to others. The medium very rarely heard a single word spoken by Iola, nor did she usually see her. As far as I remember, my guide used the trumpet only once throughout the two months.

The private sitting I now describe is remarkable as a singularly good exhibition of the coarser type of physical phenomena. It took place on May 17, 10.55 to 11.40. I had my two trumpets in the room. One was marked with the letter "I" on all its sections; the other was marked "F." They weigh thirteen ounces and eleven ounces respectively. Mrs. Wriedt's trumpet was smaller than either, and weighs not more than eight or nine ounces; but she preferred, as a rule, using mine, made by Whitely.

On this occasion the trumpet "I" was telescoped and lying on the top shelf of a bookcase behind Mrs. Wriedt; "F" was standing between us; our chairs were five feet apart.

First, Dr. Sharp manifested immediately the lights were switched off, and spoke clearly, talking chiefly about the condition of Dr. Peebles (whom he called "Our Pilgrim"), then ill in London. Then there was a long silence, after which Iola spoke for five or six minutes, using my trumpet for part of the time. She was followed by Grayfeather, who, after a brief conversation, said: "I am going to show you something, Chief." Take Mrs. Wriedt's hands." We both leaned forward in our chairs and clasped hands, her right hand in my left and my right hand in her left. There was a small square table one foot to my left, upon which stood a vase full of narcissi and water, weighing about three pounds. The room was pitch dark, as usual.

Presently a noise was heard as if a trumpet had fallen to the floor behind Mrs. Wriedt, then again dead silence. In, say, five minutes I heard Grayfeather's voice from near the floor where the "F" trumpet had been standing between our extended arms: "Mrs. Wriedt, light up." We disengaged our hands, the medium rose from her chair and switched on the lights. This is what we found: The small table standing two feet to my right; The vase of narcissi on the floor almost touching my right foot; Mrs. Wriedt's trumpet standing on the floor to my left exactly underneath where we had last seen it in the light on the small table; my "F" trumpet telescoped and lying on the shelf of the bookcase near where I had last seen the "I" trumpet; and "I" trumpet, drawn out ready for use, standing on the floor where "F" ought to be, between our arms.

The Indian had betrayed his movements only when he took the "I" trumpet from the bookcase; the three sections were loose inside one another, and in drawing them out from the shelf he had let two of them fall to the floor. This it would be easy to do for anybody in full light. All his other movements were executed without my hearing the faintest sound. Mrs. Wriedt's two hands were firmly clasped in my two hands from the moment Grayfeather had directed us "to take hands" to the moment he said, "Mrs. Wriedt, light up."

This is the most complete instance of telekinesis in the dark which I ever remember having witnessed. The drawing out and placing of one aluminium trumpet and the collapsing of another without sound, is a marvellous feat; and the movement of the table, the vase, and the small trumpet is a hardly less striking phenomenon.

This ended the sitting.

The first private circle I held this year was on May 3, the day after the medium's arrival. It consisted of six people besides the psychic, and, though the atmospheric conditions were not good, it was successful. Clouds of highly attenuated matter, faintly illumined, could be seen floating about the room, and the voices for most of the sitting were high (always a good sign). The Canadian gentleman who wrote in light two years ago under the name of Paul was one of my guests, another was my nephew, Mr. W., a clerk in the Bank of England, who attended a séance for the first time. As often happens, it was to this novice the principle evidence was given. I am assisted by his notes. The séance lasted for one hour and three-quarters. (The Canadian gentleman is the author of a series of articles in light, 1911, entitled "Comforting Spiritual Communion." These interesting papers commenced in the issue of June 24, page 296, and continued for several months. They contain an account of his search for the spirit of a nun called Adela. We have been friends

147

for six or seven years. After the séance we sat together twice privately, with Mrs. Wriedt, and obtained very remarkable results.)

Iola was visible to me, and manifested three times to Paul, who talked to her in French and English. Dr. Sharp, Grayfeather, and Blossom were much in evidence. I now quote from my nephew's notes:—

At 7 p.m. we all entered the room, the musical-box was started and played "Come, all ye faithful" for two or three minutes. Mrs. Wriedt then began the Lord's Prayer, in which we all joined. During the prayer I distinctly heard a voice mingling with ours, and the lady next to me said she heard several voices, not those of the sitters, join in the "Amen."

We sat silently for a few moments in oppressive darkness. The first thing I noticed was a "cigar smoke" filmy light floating above the medium, which was followed by a strong white light at her feet; this seemed like a strong magnesium light. Almost immediately my head was brushed lightly by some flowers, and I felt a distinct pat on the head. Shortly after a bunch of flowers, which I found later to be a bunch of carnations, was pushed up from the ground close to my knee, and I found, by feeling down, that the stalks were sticking into the smaller end of one of the trumpets. I held the flowers in my left hand for the rest of the séance.

Just after this we heard a voice which I was told was Grayfeather's. After talking to my uncle for a few seconds, he was introduced to me. The voice was opposite to me, and about a yard away; I fancy he was drawing from me. A conversation something like this took place: Grayfeather? "Hullo! little chiefy!" W.: "How do you do Grayfeather? I have heard a lot about you, and am very glad to meet you." G.: "I see you the other day." W.: "Where did you see me?" G.: "I see you scratchem." W.: "Oh, where was I scratchem?" G.: "In big place." He then described the office in which I work at the bank fairly well, and said that it was two moons ago" that he saw me; he also asked me if I knew a name like De Lancy, De Vaney, or De Vine. I could not recall anyone of that name. I told him this, and he went on to talk about that "scratchem" [Writing]. G.: "Somewhere in your topknot you think you leave that scratchem. You no go!" W.: "You think, Grayfeather, that I ought to stay there. Why?" G.: "You no go on water; land much better for you. You stay in London; good place London. You be big chief some day." W.: "You think I shall get on?" G.: "Yes, you stay."

Grayfeather then talked to my uncle again, but returned suddenly to me: "You have bad head?" W.: "Yes." G.: "And bad eyes?" W.: "Yes, if there is connection between the two." G.: "Yes, eyes make head tired."

W.: "Do you think I ought to see an eye doctor?" G.: "No, you put on 'Modecamentum.' You put some on your little finger and rub it into corner of your eye, near nose." W.: "Thank you very much Grayfeather." He also told me that he had seen me with a "squaw; much good for me, nice squaw."

The next spirit to come was Iola, my uncle's guide, to whom I was introduced. She came over to me and called me "third cousin" (I am her first cousin once removed). She evidently drew strength from me, and I could hardly hear her voice unless she left me and went to my uncle who was sitting next but one to me. She said that my grandmother and grandfather were very well and happy, and sent their love to me. I asked her who gave me the flowers. She replied: "Granny." I asked her to thank her, and to say that I had put one in my buttonhole. My uncle was able to see Iola, but I could not.

Dr. Sharp came next, and sent love to my aunt Isabella; he said that he was glad she was better; that she had been very poorly during the winter. He also talked about "Modecamentum," and repeated what Grayfeather had said about it; he added that it was a German medicine and good for kidney trouble if taken on a lump of sugar. He then introduced a spirit called R——, who was shy at talking and could not speak for himself at first. Dr. Sharp urged him to talk: "Do your own talking. I'm not going to speak for you." He was soon identified as Sir G—— R——, the grandfather of my left hand neighbour and a distinguished naval officer under whom my uncle had served forty years ago; he spoke privately to both.

The guide of another sitter (Paul) came and talked to him in a very low voice for some time. Her name was Adela; my uncle was introduced to her. An ancestor also came to this gentleman and talked in broad Scotch.

At intervals between their voices I could clearly see spirit lights, which were floating about the room. The medium saw, at my knees, the form of a child, and another time an old lady called Margaret, in a cap. This latter might have been the wife of a cousin of mine. She also saw, in Roman figures, the number fifteen. At another time she saw a tall gentleman in gray clothes, age about twenty-three, clean shaven, who was trying to speak, and seemed to step towards me. I could not identify him.

A spirit now came who said he was "James." After a few seconds he settled in front of me, and tried to make me understand him. I could only hear "James." And nothing else. He groaned, went away for a minute, and then returned; he seemed very upset at not being able to make me hear him. J.: "James" (a blurred sound). W.: "Are you a relative of mine?" J.: "Yes." W.: "Are you a relative of my father?" J.: "He is my son." W.: "I am very glad to meet you, and hope you are happy. Can I give my father any message?" J.: "Tell him I am proud of him." W.: "Yes, I will tell him." J.: "Tell him I am proud of him and his wife and family. He has had a hard struggle, and you are having a hard struggle too. I had a hard struggle." W.: "Yes grandfather, I will tell him that too." J.: "Tell him that I am very glad of this move he is making. It is a good thing." W.: "Are you happy?" J.: "Yes, now, but God robbed me." W.: "Of what did he rob you?" J.: "Of life, I had to leave my wife and family" (the spirit was obviously distressed on this point, so I said no more). W.: "Can you give any message for my father, so that he will recognise you?" J.: "Ask him if he remembers a chain and watch, a silver chain and watch?" W.: "Yes I'll ask him." J.: "Tell him to come here." W.: "I don't think he will do that, but I will tell him what you say." J.: "Yes, tell him I am proud of him." W.: "Will you come to me again?" No answer. (Pause.) J.: "May I touch you? Goodbye." W.: "Yes, I'll hold out my hand." J.: "God bless you, my lad." The spirit then touched me softly on the back of my hand; the touch was quite human to feel.

The next spirit to visit us was "Blossom," who was known to my uncle. He said: "How old are you, Blossom?" She replied: "Two hundred years." She had a high- pitched voice and a quaint laugh; presently she came to me. B.: "Hulloa. Little chief." W.: "Hulloa Blossom." B.: Who gave you that pin?" W.: "Ah, I shall not tell you that." B.: "I know; plenty nice girl give it to you." W.: "Well if you know, what was her name?" B.: "Mary." W.: "No, quite wrong." B.: "Then it was Fanny." W.: "Wrong." B.: "It was Mary." W.: "It was not." B.: "It came in a little box, a blue box, from Regent Street." W.: "Yes." B.: "You no got box now." W.: "No, I do not think I have. What did I do with it?" B.: "You put it in bucket; no, in basket." W.: "Yes, I think I did. What was I doing when I threw it away?" B.: "You clean em house." W.: "Quite right. What else did I throw away?" B.: "Collars and two ties." W.: "What did I do with them?" B.: "You gave them to squaw." W.: "Quite right. What did she do with them?" B.: "She fix up good ones and threw bad ones away." W.: "Who is telling you all this?" B. (indignantly): "No one." W.: "Who dropped that water on my hand just now?" B.: "Iola. She arranging flowers. Goodbye." Some more followed of no import.

(My sister Isabella is known to Dr. Sharp, for she and Mrs. Wriedt spent a day together in 1911. My brother-in-law tells me his father, James W., died in 1866, aged fifty-eight years; that he always wore a silver watch, which was very unusual at that time. He was about to move from one house to another. Blossom's chatter about my nephew giving away an empty box and some old collars, during house-cleaning, to the servant (squaw) was very apt. Mr. W, suffers much in his eyes. Of the "plenty nice girl" we shall hear more later.)

On May 24. I invited Mr. W., who had never been to a séance before. It was a very good séance; but I am unable to record the whole of it, as two of my guests are opposed to any publicity about their spirit visitors. In the middle of the séance Blossom manifested, and addressed Mr. W.:—

"Hulloa Chiefy! I come to see my smash" (mash). (I now quote from Mr. W.'s notes.) "Who is that Blossom?" The voice then approached me, and laughed: "Ah hi!" W.; "Am I your mash?" B.; "Yep." W.: "Thank you Blossom." B.: "Plenty nice letter you had yesterday" (here she made some weird noises). W.: "Yes, very nice. You were not quite right last time I met you about that pin. It was not bought in Regent Street." B.: "Oxford Street, then." W.: "Yes, that's better." (Blossom then went on to my uncle, who chaffed her about a previous sitting, when she complained that he had "pinched her" the moment after he had touched the trumpet.) B.: "Goodbye all; goodbye, mash. Ah hi!"

Grayfeather came to my brother, and said: "How's stripes?" (an allusion to his uniform). A.U.W.; "Two, thanks very much." G.: "I see you with three soon." A.U.W..: "Oh, not just yet." G.: "Not so very long!" A.U.W.: "I've got to wait a long time yet."

Grayfeather talked to me for a short time about my eyes.

(The notes of my young relative are most correct. The "Weird noises" were soon explained; the brother told me they were osculatory attempts. I walked down to the station with Mr. W., and he told me that he had become engaged to be married the day before. The letter he had received contained the final acceptance. But the young lady objected to spiritism, so he could not again accept my invitation. Later on, I told Blossom the reason "her mash" could not attend, and she said: "Ah hi; tell him I love her all the same." Mrs. Wriedt knew nothing, and knows nothing to this moment, of these young men or their occupations. Grayfeather's knowledge of the distinctive marks of naval uniform was shown once last year.)

Before closing my own account, which I purposely make brief for reasons I have already given, it is necessary to relate a detail of a curious sitting I had alone with Mrs. Wriedt on Tuesday, May 20, 10.50 to 11.45 a.m. After the sitting, which was a very good one, had been going on for half-an-hour, a voice that I had never heard before spoke through the trumpet in clear, deliberate tones, without any hesitation: "Sidgwick:— Tell Barrett that the young man who spoke to him was (George?) Alexander's son, who died of blood poisoning." Question: "Why did you not come to Barrett?" Answer: "I did not know he was here." John King was present at this sitting. When it was over, Mrs. Wriedt and I differed about the Christian name of Alexander (the sitting had been one full of incident to me). After lunch Mrs. Jacob arrived for a private sitting, and I asked her, if she had the opportunity, to persuade John King (if present) to give her the name again, and all details that he could. John King did manifest, and she wrote down all that he told her. When she came into the light she copied the script for me. I have before me this paper, and also the original scribble in the dark. It runs thus:—

Harold B. Alexander, died of blood poisoning, 17 years old, 13 Carrag (or Carrack, or Carrac) Head, son of John Thomas Alexander, lived in Dublin, Leinster Road, Sir William Barrett.

When Mrs. Jacob sent me the original scribble on May 28, she wrote that John King was uncertain about the spelling of "Carrag"; he corrected her when she thought it was Sir William Barrett who lived in Dublin; and, that he spelt out "Leinster" letter by letter.

I reported the above message to Sir William Barrett at Kingtown, co. Dublin, who at once informed me that he had found in the directory the name of Dr. Thomas John Alexander, 149 Leinster Road, Dublin, and that he had approached him on the subject. His sittings had been unsuccessful, and he was not aware of any boy having manifested to him. Two days afterwards he sent me the following note, which he had received from Dr. Alexander:—

My boy, Harold Beresford, died at sea on April 18 last of blood poisoning. He was serving as "middy" on board the ss. Carrigan Head, and was on his way home from New Orleans. He was sixteen years of age in August last. His death was announced in the Irish Times about (I think) a week afterwards, and all the above particulars except his birth month were given in the notice.

(Signed)   T. J. Alexander

The following is the notice in the Irish Times of April 26, 1913:—

Alexander.—April 18. 1913, at sea, on board the ss. Carrigan Head, of blood poisoning, Harold Beresford, the fifth and dearly- loved son of Thomas John and Ellen Alexander, 149 Leinster Road, Dublin, aged sixteen years.

"He giveth His beloved sleep."

When the paper was published Mrs. Wriedt was on the high seas. I have all possible inquiries, and am satisfied that she could never have seen this announcement. Observe, there are three discrepancies: (1) John King gave the name John Thomas, and the Irish Times Thomas John; also Dr. Alexander signs T. J.; (2) the age in the Irish Times is given as sixteen, whereas the boy was sixteen years nine months; John King says seventeen years; (3) John King dictates to Mrs. Jacob, 13 Carrag Head; the real name being ss. Carrigan Head.

So far, this is a spirit phenomenon, indeed; but, as we know that experienced spirits can read newspapers or anything else they please, it is not a convincing test of spirit identity. John King might have misread the letters "ss." (printed small in the Irish Times) for "13"; moreover, he may have wished to compensate Sir William Barrett for his blank séances. But there is something else to follow. I went out of town for a few days, and did not sit with Mrs. Wriedt again until June 3, 1913. John King manifested, and I thanked him for the test he had given me in the "Alexander" case. Here is his reply:—

Well, the boy was very anxious to let his father know that he was alive, so he first went to some undeveloped medium in Dublin and could not get through. Professor Sidgwick was helping him, and told him to come on here; and he tried to make himself known to the professor's friend.

The reply followed my remark instantly. If John King got the whole thing up as a fraud upon Sir William Barrett, it is very unlike him. I have known him for nine years, and can assert that he takes special pleasure in assisting in cases where consolation is needed. Neither Mrs. Wriedt, Mrs. Jacob, Sir William Barrett, nor myself knew anything about the death of a midshipman on the steamship Carrigan Head. I did not know Professor Sidgwick, nor did I take any interest in him, or his works, in this life or the next. I leave it to Sir William Barrett and the bereaved father to make what they can of it.

I now proceed to give testimony of others.

The three friends whose account of their visit is given below are Mr. And Mrs. W. Hasler Browne, and a cousin of the latter, Mrs. Owen.

Cambridge House, Monday, June 9, 1913, 7.45 p.m.

After one or two voices had spoken, Mrs. Wriedt said: "Mrs. Owen, there is a little girl on the floor by you with her head resting on your lap. Do you recognise who it is?" The reply was, "Yes, it is my little daughter, who passed over as a baby."

The reason for this reply was that this little girl had been seen clairvoyantly near her mother on several occasions. She had also been permitted by her guardians to communicate by automatic writing, and the mother had been given to expect that she would manifest at Cambridge House.

After a short time a sweet child's voice was heard saying through the trumpet, "Mother, mother, I am here," and the following conversation ensued:—

Q.: "Is that you Ruby?"

A.: "Yes, mother dear." (Kisses were heard through the trumpet.) "And for father" (more kisses). "It is nice to see you, mother dear."

Q.: "My darling, I am so glad to know you are here. Father was sorry not to be able to come, too."

A.: "Yes, dear mother,. Thank father for the flowers. I do love flowers." (This reference was not understood.) "And tell him I touched him; will you, mother? I was with him."

Q.: "Where?" A.: "In the dining room. I touched him. Will you tell him so?" Q.: "Yes, I will, dear. Did you help me with writing once?" A.: "Yes, mother." Q.: "Is anyone here with you?" A.: "Yes, grandma is here with me." Q.: "Which grandma?" A.: "Grandma Owen." Q.: "Give her my love." A.: "Yes, mother, she will speak to you soon." Q.: ""That's right; I shall be glad."

A.: "Goodbye, mother darling. My love to father and brothers and sister" (kisses). (She has two brothers and a sister still in the earth life. Two of these were born subsequent to her passing.)

She then turned to Mrs. Browne and greeted her with kisses, and, "I know you auntie, and love you. Give my love to cousins (kisses). Goodbye auntie." Then turning to Mr. Browne, she continued, "And you, uncle (kisses), I love you." Returning to her mother, she said, "Goodbye, darling mother," and left. She had not known, nor heard of Mr. And Mrs. Browne in her brief earth life. She died at the age of fifteen months.)

Mrs. Browne felt two taps on her hat which she had placed upon her knees. Then a voice, evidently that of a young woman, addressed her by name, giving her own name as "Mary Hills."

Q.: "I cannot remember having known anyone of that name." A.: "You are Mrs. Browne, aren't you?"

Q.: "Yes. Will you kindly tell me of some circumstance by which I might remember you?"

A.: "I come to thank you for your great kindness to me when I was ill, and for writing to me when I was in the sanatorium."

(Mrs. Browne regards this as conclusive proof both of the genuineness of the voice phenomena and, so far as herself is concerned, of the identity of the communicating spirit. Mary Hills was not in her mind at that time. Indeed, she had forgotten the name. It was not until this reminder had been given that she remembered the speaker as a poor consumptive girl whom she had befriended some twelve years ago. Certainly telepathy would seem to be inadequate in explanation of this incident.)

Subsequently Mr. Browne's mother came and greeted the three friends with affection. She also sent a loving message to her daughter. Her brief conversation afforded quite satisfactory evidence of her identity, and also showed that she was well informed of the circumstances and doings of her family syill in the earth life.

Considered generally, the sitting was a complete success. Several voices, audible to all present, often spoke simultaneously, and sometimes Mrs. Wriedt was speaking at the same time. Thirty years ago Professor H. Sidgwick said: "We must drive the objector into the position of being forced either to admit the phenomena as inexplicable, at least by him; or to accuse the investigators either of lying or cheating, or a blindness or forgetfulness incompatible with any intellectual condition except absolute lunacy." To an impartial investigator it would seem that the object above specified has been accomplished.

The above is a true account of our experience at Cambridge House, June 9, 1913.

W. Hasler Browne.
A.M. Hasler Browne.
Rosa Owen.
August 6, 1913.

From the acting president of the London Spiritualist Alliance:—

Dear Admiral Usborne Moore,—It was my privilege to have three private séances with Mrs. Wriedt, and, as requested, I have the pleasure of sending you a copy of notes made immediately after each séance. I desire to say that I found, though in physical darkness, the conditions such as to impress me with a feeling of complete confidence in the integrity of the medium, and this the subsequent phenomena confirmed. Whether the voices heard belonged to those purporting to be speaking can never be definitely proved; but presumedly they were, and without doubt they give information unknown to the medium or to my wife, and certainly far from my thoughts at the time.—Yours faithfully,

Henry Withall.

Séances at Cambridge House, Wimbledon

May 10, 1913, at 1.30; in utter darkness. Present, wife and self only, with Mrs. Wriedt the medium.

Almost immediately we were touched on the face and hands; and then, while I held Mrs. Wriedt's two hands, a flower taken from a vase was given to my wife, and another to me.

The first voice heard through the trumpet purported to be that of Dr. John, who congratulated my wife on being sufficiently well to attend, and, referring to the difficulties of last year, said that her physical health was improved, and that her psychical development was progressing in spite of physical drawbacks.

Stainton Moses next spoke, saying how much he was with me, and assisting in the work of the Alliance. He offered his congratulations on the work so far accomplished this year; assured my wife that her mediumship, now of some use, would soon be of service to him and to others; and that we could always rely upon his help when we sought it.

The next speaker gave the name of James Withall, and said he had been brought by his nephew George, son of his brother William (this should have been his brother Charles, as William had no children); and that he wanted to be considered as belonging to the family, though he was now forgotten. (He lived more than a century ago.)

My sister Helen then said a few words, but with difficulty. She stated she had placed the flowers in our hands, and hoped she would be able to do more at another séance, adding that there was a large gathering of friends present who gave us loving greeting.

John King gave us greeting with perfect ease. Rose Rogers said a few words.

All the voices were more or less indistinct, and would have been better could they have been produced without a trumpet.

May 19; conditions as on May 10.

Within a few seconds from switching off the light, and before Mrs. Wriedt could resume her seat, a voice greeted us. It was that of John King, who told me he had been present at the Geneva Conference, and had heard a conversation between Mr. E. W. Wallis and a stout foreign lady, whom he thought was of Dutch nationality; and he asked me to tell Mr. Wallis that he was not to accept the statement made to him as gospel, for the lady was mistaken in her conclusions. Meeting Mr. Wallis next day, I ascertained he had conversed with such a lady in Geneva, who had told him of what, to her, was an unsatisfactory dark Séance, in which she imagined that the medium had helped out the phenomena. It was this incident to which John King probably referred, and, if so, the message had evidential value.

Later during the séance two spirits spoke together, the one claiming in a loud voice to be my father, and the other very softly calling out the name "Winnie." We had to ask that one should speak at a time, as hearing the two was too confusing. We tried to catch Winnie's surname, which she repeated several times, but we failed. We believed we knew who it was, as she assented to our knowing her mother and aunt. Strangely, however, she did not mention her sister, and we made no suggestion. (I have since heard that the sisters had little in common.)

Mrs. Wriedt saw clairvoyantly a lady who had suffered greatly from some throat trouble (and probably passed out through it), but could give no name. This we believe to be our friend Olive, who had passed on through cancer of the throat, and who, speaking through my wife eight days previously, had announced her intention to accompany us to the séance. John King then greeted us again, stating that he would take advantage of the opportunity to aid the development of my wife's mediumship. My wife was certainly much influenced, feeling the force as a series of galvanic shocks almost too powerful to endure. As no further manifestations occurred, the power was probably all used up in endeavouring to help her.

May 26; conditions as on May 19.

We were greeted in a loud voice by John King, and then by one who called himself Mat Davies, purporting to be my grandfather; and with him came his sister Jane.

My grandmother's uncle was Matthew Davies, and his sister was named Jane; so there was some confusion in the relationship. At a subsequent séance Matthew Davies volunteered the statement that I had misunderstood him. He knew his relationship to my grandmother, and had correctly stated it; they both wanted to be considered as belonging to the family.

Frank Rogers tried to speak, but was too indistinct to be understood.

Dr. John congratulated my wife on her mediumistic development, and said how pleased her spirit friends were with the immediate prospects, though there was still a little difficulty with the physical condition. At any moment she might, possibly, be clairvoyant, and be easily controlled. He spoke also of the many spirit friends present with us at our séance at Oakwood on the previous night, and confirmed their statements as to their identity, specially mentioning the names of Stainton Moses, W. T. Stead, and of another. The last-mentioned then spoke to us in French, promising her further help in our home séances, and saying how we should recognise her if seen. Stainton Moses spoke quite naturally in a loud, clear voice, gave every encouragement as to our Sunday sittings, and told me that, if he did not occupy the chair at our Alliance meetings, he was not very far off. He was pleased with the way things were going, and how Light was carried on. He spoke of his pleasant association now with Mr. Rogers, Mr. Hopps, and Mr. Glendinning. He further referred to the fact that a mutual friend was a little subject to fits of nervous excitement and depression, owing to his health condition, and advised us to do what we could to cheer him up, for he was a very good fellow.

W. T. Stead said he had tried to control my wife on the previous evening; he was glad that he was able then to get his name out, and hoped he would do better another time, for he felt that with her mental attitude he mediumship would prove a blessing later on. John King then spoke in a very friendly way, stating that he hoped to visit us next Sunday, after he had been to Husk's, and would help the other spirit friends in their development work; and he then proceeded to charge my wife with magnetism. He advised us not to talk about Mr. Stead coming, as so many were claiming him as a control, which such was not the case.

The séance then closed.

From a mining engineer who has many and varied interests in the north of England.

May 7, 1913. Private sittings in the afternoon with Mrs. Wriedt at Cambridge House.

No one in room except Mrs. Wriedt and myself. It is difficult to give a full report of these sittings, as the major part of the conversations referred to matters of a private nature. Throughout all my private sittings my brother Jim was predominant. This was the first sitting I had with Mrs. Wriedt this year, and I was uncertain as to what results I might get; But immediately the light was switched off my brother Jim greeted me, and we fell into a conversation such as two brothers would who had been devoted to one another when both on this plane together. He immediately spoke of business matters which were causing me anxiety at the time, and showed himself conversant with many of the details. Two gentlemen with whom I was closely associated in business were ill—one confined to his bed, and the other away travelling for the recovery of his health. After being satisfied that he had possessed himself of all the facts without my assistance, I ventured to ask my brother if he could give me an idea of what the future would bring forth concerning my two sick friends, when he said: "Wait a few minutes, and I will take Dr. Sharp, and he will see them and then tell you." In the interval a sister who had passed out as a child nearly forty years ago came and spoke to me, giving her name very clearly. She correctly told me the cause of her death, and also voluntarily reminded me of some little occurrences in our child life, and went away with the parting advice ""that I was not to break my neck, as that machine thing I had went far too quickly." (I am guilty of driving at speed on the long straight roads of the north.)

Jim and Dr. Sharp now returned; the latter described the cause of the ill health of my two friends in detail. The one in bed, he said, was hopeless, as he had a malignant disease which would prove fatal in a few weeks; the other suffered from nothing more or less than excessive cigar smoking (I knew he smoked heavily), and would be all right now for at least two years. I may say here that the first case ended fatally on the last day of June, and the second gentleman is now in his normal health.

Dr. Sharp also told me that he had paid a visit to my mother in passing, and described the cause of her ill health, which only slightly differed from the diagnosis of her medical man. This is practically all that I can relate of this sitting, so much being of a private nature, yet so convincing to me that there is no death, and that my own friends were talking to me. During the earlier part of the sitting I saw a luminous figure moving about near me, and on mentioning it to my brother he said it was he.

I stayed to the circle sitting the same night, as on all subsequent visits to Cambridge House, save the last. I mention this so that it may be understood without further explanation. Space would not allow me to give anything like a detailed account of these circle sittings, nor could I do so without the permission of many sitters whom I do not know. I will therefore confine myself to describing the striking features of the sitting. I find by my notes that this evening during the course of the sitting there was heard the heavy barking of a large dog, and as no one seemed to follow it up in any way, I asked Mrs. Wriedt to question Dr. Sharp as to what the reason of the barking was. Dr. Sharp said it was a large dog with a child who had come—a little boy with light curly hair. Presently the little boy spoke to his father, telling him he had come, and had brought the dog (naming it), and went on to speak of his little child-like effects which his mother had put away in a drawer.

"Blossom," the little Indian girl, came and chatted with and chaffed many sitters in her own quaint language. One gentleman she charged with being an inveterate loser of tie-pins and cuff-links. His wife, who was present, admitted after the sitting that he was guilty of these continued little slips. My brother came and assured me that all had gone well at the works in my absence, and that there had been a shower of rain there in the afternoon. (Correct.) Dr. Sharp, in answer to a question by a lady, said that a "saint" was a child that had never been born to see the light of day.

I may say that my notes were written within an hour or two of the sittings, and amplified the same night in the hours at my disposal during a long train journey to the north, whence I travelled in the morning.

May 14, 1913. Private sitting. A great deal of this sitting was taken up by my brother, who brought relatives whom I had never seen, and who were able to give me a detailed explanation of what had hitherto been family mysteries of seventy years ago. One of the principals expressed himself to me in a very testy manner because I had made efforts a few years ago to solve the riddle for myself by making personal search in a distant and little known country; but in the course of conversation he became more mollified, and completed the missing-link in the chain of history. This, to me, was what might be termed a most natural interview, and extremely convincing. At this sitting, also, came someone whistling in an absent-minded manner. I asked him who he was, but failed to get his name clearly. He then began to explain that he had been killed about a month ago. I immediately recognised him as one of my employés who was instantly killed at one of my works. He referred to matters concerning his home which he must have learned subsequent to his death, and which were correct. Later, another old man turned up, and said he had worked for me many years ago at a certain colliery in the north. I could not call his name to mind, so asked him if he, too, had been killed. "Oh, no," he said, "I died of old age and rheumatics," and he went on to ask me if I did not remember telling him that he was too old to work down a pit, and I gave him an easy job. I said I was very sorry, but I could not call him to mind from among the thousands who had passed through my employ. He showed intimate knowledge of the place he spoke of, and which was perfectly correct, especially in describing its one rare and striking peculiarity, which, for obvious reasons, I cannot particularise here.

At the circle sitting in the evening there was a great deal of conversation between voices and the sitters, some of it being in French and Dutch. A sailor made himself known to a sea officer present, and seemed to enjoy calling to memory his escapades and punishments. The officer recognised him. Blossom came again and spoke in her lively childish way. Some of the sitters said they could hear her, but wished they could also see her. Instantly she said, "Me go squeeze myself, then you see me." In a moment I saw a column of light in the form of a girl, but it soon disappeared. John King came and spoke to us all, and Mr. Stead, who, in answer to a question from Miss Harper, said that he was very busy and pulled about here and there, but he was very glad to see us all and bear testimony to the great return; that, although they might try to stamp out spiritualism, it would still keep bubbling up. Julia also made a charming little concluding speech.

May 21, 1913. Private sitting. Again, most of the sitting was taken up with my spirit relatives, speaking of private matters, which showed that they had been following the events of the week so far as they personally concerned me. The old gentleman who had expressed himself testily to me the week previous now came and apologised; he voluntarily told me much that was previously unknown to me, and made past mysteries perfectly clear. He advised me to profit by what he had told me, and avoid similar trouble. Someone came and spoke, but I failed to recognise him, when John King broke in and said, "Have you a housekeeper?" I said I had. "This man," he then said, "is her father, and he wants you to understand that she is perfectly honest." I then recognised the name he gave, and he himself, by his continued reiteration of the statement, evidently wished that there should be no shadow of doubt in my mind about his daughter's honesty; he only desisted when I expressed agreement with his belief. He asked me how she suited me, and further gave good evidence of his knowledge and personality by saying that she was not strong as she was so tall, etc. He begged me to say nothing to her of his visit to me, as it would only "scare her out of her wits," as she knew nothing of "this." It was some time after that it dawned upon me that I had reprimanded her the previous day for disposing of certain papers she had thought useless, but which I wanted to preserve. I may have said more than was necessary, and the old man had no doubt been listening. During this sitting I saw lights floating about very similar in appearance to the glowing end of a cigar in the dark. I also saw clouds of light over the flowers on a table in the room.

The evening circle was not productive of much voice phenomena that I am at liberty to write of. During the séance a very bright light made itself apparent on the ceiling. John King spoke, at length, about the influence of spirits. My brother and sister came and spoke to me alternately, while other voices were speaking on the other side of the room. They spoke in a low voice and close to me, so that I heard all that was said, in spite of the other conversation going on.

May 28, 1913. Private sitting. The moment Mrs. Wriedt switched of the light, and before she had got to her seat, my brother commenced talking to me. His conversation was on private family affairs, so also was that of other relatives who came, so much so that there was not a moment's break in the "voices" during the whole sitting. I had a very interesting conversation with John King, who told me of the trying times he had had in some of his adventures on the Spanish Main, part of which I had visited. He expressed a strong note of regret at his mode of life in the West Indies, and said that his time now was spent in trying to make amends. John King is a fine character, and commands one's respect. I had taken a Kodak into the séance-room, and put it on the table ready for exposure, merely as an experiment; and, on the light being switched off, exposed the film. It was some distance (about eight feet) from Mrs. Wriedt about a yard from myself, and during the sitting I saw many flashes of light near to, and in front of, the lens; indeed, so bright were they that I saw the camera and the flowers standing behind it quite plainly. My attempts at photography evidently attracted Mr. Boursnell, for at the close of the sitting he spoke, and told me to leave the camera in the room until night, and they would try to develop something in it—but could not promise—and to leave it exposed and the room in darkness. This I did. In leaving the room in the dark I upset the trumpet, but on Mrs. Wriedt's advice left it, and we both went out together, the door being locked. About half an hour before the evening circle I went up to the room with Mrs. Wriedt. I entered, and felt my way to the camera and closed it. Then Mrs. Wriedt switched up the light. The first thing I noticed was that the trumpet had been picked up, and I drew the lady's attention to it; but, instead of showing surprise, she merely remarked that they would do it after we left in the afternoon, as they would have plenty of power remaining. I know that that trumpet was not picked up by earthly hands. I may say that the film on development showed absolutely nothing; it was not even fogged.

The evening circle sitting was quite a success, but almost wholly consisted of private conversation between relatives. My brother told me of a meeting that had been held by some of my workpeople in my absence on matters concerning their labour, and that it was not a success, as there were only two men present who seemed to be against me. This proved to be correct.

June 4. 1913. Private sitting. This was exceedingly successful, all my friends speaking with me at length.

My brother urged me to cease, immediately, having business relations with a certain individual, and gave his reasons. I had good reason to be grateful to him at a very early date following. A spirit, giving the name of a certain schoolmaster, came to me, and said I was to inform a friend of mine, and a one-time pupil of his, that "If he and his wife heard some knocking in their room it was only he." Curiously enough, the first person I met the following morning (about three hundred miles from Cambridge House) was this particular friend, and the first thing he related was that he and his wife had been disturbed by unaccountable knockings during the night; I then gave him the message. Towards the end of the sitting I felt myself being touched and pushed, and spoke to Mrs. Wriedt, who answered me from a distance of at least two yards. I then told her that I was being touched and pushed. When I had done talking, someone spoke and gave his name. I failed to fix him for some time, until he described himself as being the builder, and once owner, of the house in which I now live. He said that he had been feeling me to make sure it was true what they told him—viz., that he could "come back." He said he was quite satisfied now. I asked him where he got the money to build the house; he said by betting, and assured me that he had never robbed anyone. I knew he had been a prosperous bookmaker at one time. I suspect that the great event at Epsom had attracted him south, it being Derby day.

The circle sitting in the evening was a great success: voices spoke to most of the sitters. Blossom again made herself heard, showing especial interest in Mr. Withall. A decided sneeze was heard in the trumpet. Blossom said that it was a man who had "Fitznoenza." Mr, Withall suggested "influenza." To which Blossom assented. This child then began to monopolise the conversation, and Mrs. Wriedt politely begged her to retire and give others a chance: this not having the desired effect, Mrs. Wriedt spoke sharply to her. I am sorry to relate that Blossom did not reply in very polite terms, and was then ordered away peremptorily; and even while going she threw remarks at Mrs. Wriedt which can be described only as childish impudence. I mention it because it was such convincing evidence of voice phenomena, the heat shown by both disputants being so genuine. The others who were present will bear me out in this. Towards the end of the sitting I felt touched on the right leg. I asked Miss Harper, who was sitting on my right, if she had touched me, but she had not. Even while I was asking the question I felt touched on the left leg, and on inquiry of the lady on my left proved that she had not moved. A moment later something seemed to come on my lap with a certain amount of noise—indeed, sufficient for Miss Harper to ask me the cause of the noise; but I could not explain, as I felt nothing tangible. Just then my brother came, and said "he had brought the little dog, and it was on my lap." I could not feel it there, but on putting my hand down near where I had felt my legs touched it came in contact with what might be the cold nose of a dog. I called it by name, and immediately it gave a peculiar little yelp similar to the noise it made in its earth life when pleased. This was repeated three times in all, in answer to my calling it by name. At the close, John King gave a discourse about the effects of thought and sound in the spirit world; how they were recognised and found their affinities by infinite shades of various colours.

My last sitting was a private one in the afternoon of June 27. Again I am sorry that the private nature of the conversation precludes me from reproducing it; but I may mention that I had written certain questions on a card which I did not produce until I was in the darkened séance room. When my brother came I asked him if he could read the questions. He said, "Yes, he could," and he must have done so, for he gave reasoned answers to them all. More than once, while he was speaking to me at length, Mrs. Wriedt broke in, saying that things were very quiet, and that he must have gone. I told her we were very busy talking. Her remark in answer was that it was very strange, for she could not hear anything. The voice was speaking right into my ear, apparently without the use of the trumpet. This, up to the present, closes my experiences of the Voice phenomena.

These researches have led one who, by his very calling, is compelled to be practical, to believe in the continuance of life after what we call death, and in the power of the still living spirit to communicate with us, if we do but to provide the conditions, chief among these being love and belief. This narrative is from one who started years ago to prove the reverse, with the sure and certain knowledge of the sceptic.

I find, on inquiry, that M. E. travelled in the aggregate 6,656 miles to be present at Mrs. Wriedt's séances in 1912 and 1913.

This narrative is by a Dutch lady, who contributed an account in 1912.

Having had the privilege to be present at several sittings with Mrs. Wriedt in 1913, I have much pleasure in relating some of my experiences with this remarkable medium. On May 14 I had my first sitting, with my sister and my son, in a general circle, when my daughter, father, and grandfather welcomed us. They spoke partly in Dutch and partly in English, and seemed quite as pleased to see us as we were to hear them. When in earth life, my father could not speak English; and when I asked him how he learned it, he replied: "Your daughter taught me." During a few moments' silence my son began to whistle a tune, which was repeated by a spirit, who, however, did not reveal his identity.

Mr. Stead spoke in a very husky voice, and said to my son: "You are the young man who came to my office in a very depressed state of mind." This was rather remarkable, as it was the only time he met my son.

On May 28 I induced my husband to come with me. He was greatly surprised to hear his daughter say; "Father, how nice to see you!" She was very much upset, and wept; but, returning half an hour later, she spoke in a clear voice. Her father asked her whether she felt lonely; but she replied in the negative, and added: "I can't sit any more on your knee, father; you would not feel me—I am so light now." My husband's brother Pat talked a long time with him, and was pleased I had succeeded in bringing him to the circle.

An Indian girl named Blossom spoke in a very clear shrieky voice, addressing the gentleman as "chief," and the ladies as "squaw." She nearly always came to our sittings, and we liked her very much.

My husband and my nephew came with me on June 2. As soon as the lights were extinguished my daughters voice was heard. She started in Dutch, but continued in English. When her father asked her if she could still speak her different languages, she replied: "Yes, I do; but here we all speak one language—the language of thought"; and, added a few words in French and Italian.

Pat spoke about family affairs; his voice was a little husky that evening, but generally it is very strong and clear.

While my neighbour was in conversation with his wife, we suddenly heard the loud barking of a dog, which, she said, was that of a dog who is with her in spirit land.

On June 11 my son and his uncle of eighty-two accompanied me. Several Dutch friends welcomed the old man, but unfortunately we could not follow everything that was said.

That same evening we heard Mr. Harper and Grayfeather, both speaking very distinctly.

My son and an elderly friend of his came with me on June 10. The latter had not had much experience of spirit communion, and seemed rather surprised when several friends welcomed him in German.

After my daughter welcomed us with a few words, Mrs. Wriedt remarked: "I see a name; it looks like 'Gody.' Does anyone recognise that name?" We answered her that we knew a Mr. Gody in Brussels, when a voice said: "Its me; how can this lady see my name?—she must be a witch!"

We asked him how he knew we were there; to which he replied: "Your daughter told me to come for the sake of an experience, as it is all new to me." Blossom spoke at the same time, and said to Gody:" "Shut up, Gody; I am talking!" John King gave us a long address on the non-existence of evil spirits.

At our private circle sitting on June 21, when my sister, both my sons, and their old uncle were present, we first saw beautiful lights moving within the circle. My youngest son exclaimed: "There is Yvonne, right in front of me; I see her distinctly!" "Yes, it was me," she said; "But you seemed rather scared." Turning to me, she asked if I would sing one of the songs with her we used to sing before she passed over; and when I told her I could not sing any more, she sang a German song by herself in a soft sweet voice. She spoke to her brothers about their work. Addressing her youngest brother, she asked if he remembered how he used to tease her and pull her hair. Before leaving, she told us she always speaks without the trumpet.

Several Dutch people spoke to my old brother, but we could grasp very little of what they said; we find it rather difficult to understand the spirits when they speak Dutch. (I think this can easily be explained, as the Dutch language is full of guttural sounds. One evening, when my son was with me, he took up the trumpet, at the end of the séance, and spoke through it to us, first in English, and then in Dutch; but this last language sounded very indistinct.)

Pat was very much concerned about his brother John, who was ill in Edinburgh at the time. When I asked him, "How is he today?" he replied; "I shall go and see him now, and will tell you later." Before the sitting was closed he came again, and said he found his brother very poorly.

Blossom greeted us all separately. As usual, she was very bright, and asked us several questions. Pointing to my sister, I asked her: "Blossom, do you know this lady?" On her replying in the negative, We heard Yvonne's voice say to Blossom: "She is my Tante" (Dutch for aunt").

My last sitting before Mrs. Wriedt went to Scotland was on June 28, my sister and four lady friends being present. As usual, Yvonne was one of the first to welcome us. She spoke of her uncle John, and said he was still very weak. Pat's voice was very strong that evening; after having talked to me about private matters, he spoke to the whole circle about the general situation in Great Britain. My sister's husband, who passed over nearly five years ago, addressed his wife in Dutch; his voice was very weak and unintelligible. Next came my mother, who spoke in English; neither my sister nor myself recognised her personality, and later on I heard from another medium that, as mother could not speak through the trumpet, she asked another spirit to speak for her. At the end of the sitting Yvonne said "Goodnight," and named all the sitters correctly, although she did not know any of them in her earth life.

Our private sitting on August 7 was very satisfactory. We were only three—my aunt from Holland, my son Vivian, and myself. Almost immediately after the music stopped, we saw a beautiful light near the medium, and soon after we heard Mr. Stead's voice: "How do you do? I am glad to welcome you all here!" His voice was much stronger and clearer than I ever heard him before. When I told him so, he replied: "I know more than most people about the laws of communication between the two worlds." He then had a long conversation with my son, and gave him good advice about his work. Dr. Sharp came next, and talked with Vivian about the Organisation

Society. Yvonne welcomed her aunt in Dutch, while to my son and me she spoke in English. Her voice and way of speaking are always identically the same as they were in earth life. She asked Vivian if he was going to join his brother in Cowes (this was all the more surprising, as none of us had told her that he was there). I asked her if she found it difficult to come and speak to us. "Not at all," was her reply; "it is lovely to come like this!" My son told her we are going to the sea. "Yes, I know it; I shall go too," she replied. My aunt was very pleased when her husband, who died twenty-one years ago, said to her in Dutch: "I am so glad to see you here." He went on talking about family affairs, but, finding it rather difficult to understand him, she asked if he would speak English; but his reply, in Dutch, was; "No; I prefer to speak Dutch," and continued talking in this language. His son, who passed over when he was six weeks old, was with him, and spoke very sweetly to his mother. When I asked him, "Do you know Yvonne?" he answered me: "Yes, I am often with her, although I am in a higher sphere."

Pat was very serious that evening, and gave me some advice about family matters. Next came my aunt's father, who has been twenty-six years in spirit life. He addressed her in Dutch; but his voice was very weak, as it was the first time he had spoken through the trumpet. Dr. Sharp came again, and discussed political affairs with my son. He said that great changes would occur in Europe before the year 1915. What struck us most was, that he was au courant of nearly everything that happens in our family. I asked Yvonne if her sister, who passed over twenty-eight years ago, two hours after she was born, would come and speak to me. Suddenly a sweet voice was heard: "Mother, I am Magnolia!" (this is her spirit name.) I told her how pleased I was to hear her talking. "Mother," she said, "I do love you so, and I know you love me. I am often with Yvonne—she is so sweet." "Darling, in which sphere are you?" I asked. "I am in the Celestial sphere, mother. Yvonne cannot come up to me, but I often go down to her." A few minutes later Yvonne came back to say "Goodnight."

Our last sitting in a general circle, on August 17, was one of the most interesting, we have had for a long time. Very few voices were heard, but we had a most convincing physical manifestation. My aunt, my nephew, and a lady friend, besides five strangers and myself, were present. At first several beautiful lights were seen by most of the sitters, and soon afterwards John King welcomed us. He said to me: "Mrs. Findlay Smith, how is your boy?" "All right!" I answered. Give him my love, God bless you." He discussed the Balkan politics with one of the ladies, and then I asked whether he knew if my brother-in-law in Scotland was better. He replied: "He may be better for the moment, but he still is a sick man." "Do you think it will be good for him to go back to China?" "Let him go anywhere," was his answer. A very soft but clear voice was heard next. At first we did not know for whom it was; but soon afterwards it proved to be my friend's son, who was stillborn about thirty years ago. He spoke very sweetly to his mother, who was delighted to hear him.

Next came a distinguished soldier of the Turkish government, speaking about actual events in Turkey and the Balkans.

After this my daughter's voice was heard. She only said a few words. She expressed her delight in saying to my nephew: "How do you do, Max? I am so glad you are here." I asked her an important question, in Dutch, of a private character. She answered me in the same language, and showed her approval of what I asked her by a hearty natural laugh; she then whispered a few sweet words to me, and disappeared, saying: "I will come again mother!"

A few minutes later a loud ringing of a bell was heard all over the house: and when it continued for some time Mrs. Wriedt said: "I cannot understand what it is." She quietly left the room, and went downstairs to inquire; but could not find out anything, except for seeing on the switchboard that a bell was being rung in one of the bedrooms. This was quite incomprehensible to her, as she knew that the bell in that special room was defective. When she entered the bedroom , she did not see anybody, while the ringing was going on all the time; nor was the bell being pressed. Coming back she told us all this, and after a few minutes the ringing stopped.

Suddenly my friend said to Mrs Wriedt; "I wonder if it was my son who did it, as he promised several times that he would let me hear bells as soon as he would have the opportunity." "It is quite possible," Mrs. Wriedt answered; and at the same time a soft voice whispered: "I rang the bells, mother!" A few minutes later my friend was controlled by her cousin James, who said: "Yes, it was Joyful [Her son's spirit name] who rang the bells; it was a promise he had made long ago to his mother; it is fulfilled at last." My friend told me, after the séance, that her father was a bellringer in church, in his earth life.

No more voices were heard after this wonderful manifestation, which did not surprise us, as so much power was evidently necessary to produce the ringing of the bell.

There is no need to mention how very grateful we are to Mrs. Wriedt for procuring us the opportunity to converse in the direct voice with our beloved spirit friends.

E. Findlay Smith.
Riverside House, Twickenham, August 18, 1913

The following account is by a lady residing in London:—

I was present at séances with Mrs. Wriedt in three years, 1911, 1912, 1913, and was each time much impressed with the results. The character of the séances was slightly different each year: in 1911 white forms of somewhat indistinct outline, but bearing a general resemblance to the human shape, were seen at the beginning of the séance moving in front of the cabinet; in 1912 I saw two very distinct and clear etherealisations, one being the head and shoulders of Mr. Stead, and the other being the head of a man with a clean-shaven, strong featured face, and grey hair, who was not identified by anyone present. This year (1913) the room was differently arranged, no cabinet was used, and no forms appeared when I was present. The voices were equally distinct in all three years.

I took every opportunity of talking with Mrs. Wriedt, and feel convinced of her earnestness and sincerity.

It is obvious that she is quite unacquainted with any foreign languages. Such knowledge is very rare in America, and is, indeed ignorant of their sound. On one occasion, when a voice was speaking rapidly in Italian, Mrs. Wriedt turned to me and asked if they were speaking French. I have myself heard German, Dutch, Norwegian, Welsh, and Hindustani spoken. On one occasion I was sitting next to the medium, and so close that my hand was in contact with her dress during the whole sitting; and I am absolutely certain that she neither moved from her chair, nor even stood up. At this séance (my second visit) a white form appeared near the cabinet, very unsubstantial and ill-defined, but apparently clothed in a dress embroidered all round the hem. A voice then addressed me and claimed to be that of a nurse who had been with my grandchildren for some years and had died after an operation in America. She gave details of her illness, spoke of her constant visits to the children, giving their number and other details correctly, and then said: "Do you not remember my pretty white dresses? I tried to show you one when I came out of the cabinet." It is a fact that she was extremely fond of her white, embroidered muslin dresses, which she wore on Sundays. I certainly was not thinking of her, nor expecting to hear of her when I went to the séance; and the same remark applies to the next voice which greeted my daughter with whistling snatches of popular songs and many characteristic remarks. It was that of an old soldier whom she had visited for some years in the infirmary. He had passed away a few months before, and no one at the sitting had even heard of his existence. The way in which he broke off a song and began whistling, his familiar jocular style, and his reference to what had occurred, were most convincing. He spoke of the last letter he had received, and of fruit I had sent him, and when I asked, "Can you tell us what you were when young?" instead of, as I expected, replying, "A soldier," he began to sing, "The curtain rolled up and the band began to play." I could not understand this, but I have since learnt that, as a young man, he was a scene- shifter in a theatre. When he was in the infirmary his great pleasure was a small gramophone, and some of the records were the same ones he whistled and sang.

My father-in-law, whom I never saw, has spoken to me in German on two occasions. He introduced himself as Grandfather S., so may have belonged to an earlier generation. The first time he spoke only in German, and said he would give me a tap as a sign of his presence. Directly afterwards I was tapped on the head by the trumpet. The second time was at a private sitting, when he spoke in English. I then said in German, "I suppose you have not forgotten your German?" The voice at once poured out a stream of German, so rapidly spoken as to be most difficult to follow. I may here say that I have several times heard two voices simultaneously, and also Mrs. Wriedt speaking during a communication.

One evening a lady was present who is a professional musician, and, as there was some delay, she consented, after considerable pressing, to sing. Hardly had she began the "Jewel Song" from Faust when a strong tenor voice came from the trumpet and sung the song with her, making a wonderful duet. She afterwards told us that it was her husband's voice, and that no one but herself knew that he used to sing this song with her. Later she sang again, and was this time accompanied first by the same voice and afterwards by a violincello; and she also conversed with her father and mother, both in Italian and French. The tenor voice was unmistakably of male timbre, and resounded through the room.

Welsh was spoken to a lady on one occasion, and Hindustani on another, by a native soldier who had passed away in the hospital at some eastern town Rangoon, if I remember right. The voice spoke to an officer, and said that he had seen the speaker in his visits to the hospital, and also gave his name. The officer, however, did not remember the man, but stated that it had been his duty to go round this place and to see the sick.

On several occasions my husband spoke to me, calling me by name, but nothing much was said of importance; the voice was weak and the communications were very short. This year the voice was very much stronger, and at a general circle in June, after a few remarks to me, he addressed himself chiefly to two officers who were present, and spoke for some minutes in a very clear voice on the state of England, condition of the people, and so on, in a very interesting way, the voice apparently travelling round the circle and being distinctly heard by everyone present. In life he was very much interested in such subjects; but I must honestly say that I did not feel altogether satisfied as to the personality, although the name was given.

The manner and voice were not familiar, and I am still not convinced that it was not a personation by someone else who wished to be heard; and I have since received a communication to that effect through another psychic.

It was very different on the last occasion, when I had a private sitting. No one was else was present, and when I asked to have the light left on Mrs. Wriedt readily consented. She sat opposite to me, and told me to take the trumpet and hold it to my ear myself. As soon as I did so my husband spoke through it in a low but perfectly distinct voice, which was quite audible to Mrs. Wriedt, who sat three or four feet away, and showed her interest by appropriate exclamations. I may add that the trumpet was held with the large end resting on the back of a small chair and pointing away from both of us. The communications, which were of a personal and private nature, were, to me, absolutely convincing. After a few minutes Mrs. Wriedt suggested turning down the light, as the voice would then be more powerful, which was certainly the case. The voice first spoke of our children, and mentioned that a son in Brazil had not been well, and found the climate trying, and gave some details about his work, but went on: "It interests me much more to talk about yourself; there is so much I want to say that I cannot say in public."

After the more personal communications were ended I said, "Do you often see my brother?" "Oh, Yes, I often see Willy; what a splendid fellow he is! He is here today, and will speak to you himself," was the reply. Accordingly the next voice was that of my brother, who gave very good proof of his identity. When I asked about his son, he replied: "You mean Will, Will, getting on so well, saw him this morning in——." Then followed something which I could not catch, in spite of several repetitions. I made several suggestions, such as "London," "In a train," "An hotel," but the answers were always, "Absurd," "Nothing of the kind," "Of course not," and an eager repetition of the word, which at last came clear and distinct, "In his cabin." This was correct, but I was quite unaware that my nephew had sailed the day before on a new battleship, so was actually at sea.

I also asked if his little girl was with him, and he replied; "Yes, but now she is no longer a child; she is a beautiful young woman." (She passed over as a child of singular beauty a good many years ago.) He also asked after two of my sons, using their Christian names correctly. After this the German voice spoke, followed by a few words from John King. I have endeavoured only to give details which may be regarded as evidential, but must add that at the private sitting I felt absolutely in touch with the real personality who was manifesting, and am convinced of the genuine character of the phenomena. The fact that some sittings are complete failures is surely an additional proof of this, if such is needed.

On one occasion in 1912, directly the light was turned down and John King was speaking, one of the sitters unfortunately said: "Can you show us how you manage to get inside the trumpet?" It was at once dashed on the floor in apparent wrath and with much noise, and a dead silence followed, which nothing could induce the voices to break, and after long waiting the sitting had to be abandoned. People had come from a distance, and Mrs. Wriedt was obviously very anxious that it should be a success, but she was helpless in the matter.

It is interesting that the voices seldom speak to her; but one evening, when I was present, her sister Sarah spoke to her, to her evident surprise, and carried on a conversation with her for some minutes.

The real difficulty, to my mind, is to explain why some of these personalities come at all. They are often people in whom we are not and never were much interested, and they have, apparently, nothing to tell us. I have alluded to the Hindu soldier, and may add that a friend of mine went to a sitting, without giving her name, and was at once spoken to by two former servants, who gave their full names and other convincing details. One name was a most peculiar and unusual one, which I never heard before, so their could be no mistake; but she had never been especially interested in these two people, and had no wish to hear of them, nor did they tell her anything of value.

Perhaps some day an explanation may be forthcoming.

M. S. Schwabe

This narrative is by Mr. G. F. Oldham, M.R.C.S., L.R.C.P., A physician practising in the south of England:—

The tale I have to tell is that of the search of two sorrowing parents—Whether by any means they could pierce the veil that hid from them their much-loved youngest child, who, more than three years ago, passed away after a few day's illness and left them desolate.

My wife and I had two sittings in 1912 with Mrs. Wriedt; but we failed in the essential object of our search, though we heard sufficient to stimulate our desire for further sittings; and we gladly availed ourselves of the opportunity to have one general and two private sittings this year [1913].

The first was a general circle of about ten persons, and the first voice for us was that of an acquaintance, whose name we could only partially elucidate; his identity was clearly revealed when Dr. Sharp, the control, said that he had passed over from cancer of the throat, and I got from the voice the Christian named of his wife and her brother. Following him came for me a woman's voice, and again I failed to get it clearly. Once more Dr. Sharp came to the rescue, and said; "This is a lady here who wishes to speak to you; she passed over as a child." In reply to my questions, she said it was about fifty years ago, and that she died from bronchitis or some trouble in the throat. I gave my only sisters name, and it was accepted (she died forty-seven years ago from scarlet fever, which always affects the throat). I asked her, as I had previously asked Dr. Sharp, to get my little one to come. After this several people had visitors, including a most amazing interview between a gentleman in the circle and an Indian girl called "Blossom." Last of all Dr. Sharp said: "There is a little boy here with a little yellow dog"; and then after a pause we heard a whispering voice say: "Mother dear." I endeavoured to make sure of his identity by various questions. I called him "Billy," a pet name, and asked him what was his real name, to which he replied correctly: "Denis; but you always called me 'Billy.'" "What is the name of the dog we have now?" "Don" (correct). "Is he the same as the dog you have with you?" "No, he is not the same dog; but the same in the body" (I have now a yellow collie, and his predecessor was one of the same breed). "What do you call the dog?" "I call him 'Scottie'" (I called my previous collie "Sko," short for "Skolan," the name of a legendary Irish wolf-hound). "What is over the washstand in our bedroom?" To my surprise he said "A little prayer." Then I recollected that inserted into the frame of a photographic enlargement of him is an illuminated text with the words, "Jesus called a little child unto him," this same inscription also being on his tombstone; it seemed a typically childish confusion between a text and a prayer. "Whose picture is there?" "Billy's." The picture was placed where it is after we lost him, and I feel this little incident very illuminating, the confusion between text and prayer showing the child and excluding the common explanation of telepathy and mind reading. In reply to other questions he told me correctly how long it was since he left us, said our parrot was dove-coloured (if telepathy had been at work it would have been "Grey" in my mind), called our present collie tan (I should say "Yellow"), and said his mother had his clothes carefully put away in a drawer. What more confirmatory tests should I ask for? The whole interview was most moving, and greatly impressed the listeners.

About a fortnight after the above happened, we had our first private séance, and our little one came first. We had a little chat with him full of nothings, impossible to put down in pen and ink, but very real in the impression it left. My wife's mother came, giving correctly her Christian name and that of her husband, and expressing great joy at having her grandchildren with her, and she knew of and questioned me on an indisposition I had felt a few days before. Following her came one of her old servants, who gave the name of Ellen Burke, and whose Irish brogue was unmistakable; as she must have been in service over fifty years ago, I cannot verify her statement. Then an uncle who persistently spoke of his son as "the Colonel," though at the time of the séance he had become Brigadier-General. As my first cousin, I called him, when we met, by his Christian name; but when I asked the "Voice" for that name I got the reply "'the Colonel,' of course"; it struck me as somewhat strange.

The next incident was, to me one of the most striking in the whole three sittings, and tending to prove an unexpected possibility. In 1912 almost the first voice we had was one announcing to my wife; "You are my mother." Now this was an adult male voice, and, as I did not know at the time of the possibility of stillborn children surviving into the next life, it never occurred to me it might be my own prematurely-born child of seventeen or eighteen years ago. The voice said "Bernard," "Bertie," and something else I could not make out. I replied that Bertie was alive, and got "No!, No!, No!" meaning evidently that I did not comprehend what the voice was driving at. I must confess I felt somewhat hostile in mind to it, regarding it as an impersonator, and the trumpet dropped to the floor with a bang. During the following month it dawned on me that this voice was possibly as I have stated, and when the same statement came this year I at once took it up and asked: "Was it the voice of last year?" The voice replied: "Yes." "Are you then called Bernard, for you said that name last year?" "No, my name is George William." Something more was said which I could not catch, and John King came to explain that what he said was that he and his little brother's initials rhymed G. W. O. and D. W. O. Now to me this is very remarkable. George and William are my first and third names, and I have completely dropped the William on the score of superfluity; and D. W. O. are the initials of my youngest child. Here is a case of a child telling his father how he is named, and pointing out the rhyming initials a few seconds after the father had learnt the name of that child. Where does mind-reading come in here?

The weather was close on our last visit, and we somewhat feared a poor result; however, John King greeted us in a loud voice the instant the lights were extinguished, slightly startling both the medium and ourselves. After a little conversation with John King, we heard the longed-for "Mother dear." After a little talk, I suddenly, in pitch darkness, held forward the locket on my watch chain, exclaiming: "Can you tell me what this is?" There were some indistinct words uttered, then a loud wailing sound. "He is crying," exclaimed Mrs. Wriedt. We soothed him, and in a minute he spoke clearly again, saying it was his picture; then he called me "Dear Daddie." I heard the sounds of kissing, and the trumpet touched me on the cheek. It was quite clear to me that the crying was caused by his realising what sorrow on my part the locket typified, for it was attached to the chain after his death, and the touch of the trumpet was his nearest attempt to an earthly caress. It was all very spontaneous, and moved me greatly. We asked him to come again before the sitting was over, which he promised to do. Various relatives came and identified themselves to us; one stranger came whom I could not mentally locate or understand, till the ever- obliging John King announced that he was a relative of John Redmond, the politician, and bore the same name; and apparently, came from curiosity, as he wanted to see "how this performance was worked." Then came a long pause; the power was evidently failing, and our little one had promised to come again. At Mrs. Wriedt's suggestion my wife held the trumpet to her ear; the wide end was near my knees, and Mrs. Wriedt's voice sounded several feet away. We heard a feeble "Good-bye, mother." The promise was redeemed, but he evidently could do no more than say "Farewell."

Dr. Oldham writes again on August 21, 1913:—

Dear Admiral Moore,
We had a sitting on August 7. I send an account of it, in case you can make use of it.
I hope to see you some time this fall, when convenient to us both; there are so many things that puzzle me, and your larger experience can, I hope, throw light upon them.—Yours Sincerely,
G. F. Oldham.

So gratified were we with our three successful sittings that we gladly availed ourselves of the opportunity to have one more on Mrs. Wriedt's return to London. Our little one came a few minutes after the light was extinguished, and, after greeting him, we asked him various questions as tests. In the darkness he recognised a needle case he was to have given his mother for Christmas, had he lived; and knew that it should contain needles. In reply to "What had lately happened at home," he correctly said our old collie (alluded to at previous sittings) was dead, and that he was in the care of "Charlie," a teacher in the animal king-dom, who would train him before his little master had him. Asked if his brother was with him, he said that he was better now, and that he had been to his brother on earth in Canada where it was "Hot, hot. Do you hear, hot!", shouting it the last time. This statement, and the ex-traordinary emphasis on "hot," has puzzled me; I cannot understand a spirit complaining of heat. I showed him a pencil I had in my hand; he did not know the name of it, but it was to "make marks with." Asked if he remembered what he did at the sink in my dispensary (I used to give him two colourless liquids which, on mixing turned red), he said he used to make pink medicine. I tried, again, to get a little rhyme about the sun from him, but failed, instead getting another of which the only word I could catch was "sunrise." I said to him: "I am afraid you have forgotten a good deal." I shall never forget his reply: "But I have not forgotten you, daddie." Asked by his mother for a rhyme he said at breakfast table, he said his evening prayer of four lines beginning, "I lay my body down to sleep"; asked what was the other one he said in the morning beginning "A little lamb," he repeated "Mary had a little lamb," etc. We said that was wrong, and he could not repeat it. Now the evening rhyme, repeated correctly, he had learned and said for a longer time than the one he failed in. It seemed clear to us that no amount of detective work could have discovered a child's prayer said four years ago; coincidence will not explain the pat way it was repeated; telepathy from us would surely have given both rhymes; and so would personation on the other side, if sufficiently skilled, or else nothing at all, unless something incorrect.

There was a pause, and then an extraordinary alternation of a child's and a man's voice, not understandable and more or less overlapping each other, till we heard in indignant tones, "I want to speak to my daddie;" then a few seconds pause and a man's voice said, "John." I could not identify this John, and I must confess I had no great desire to; he soon dropped the trumpet. There was again a pause, during which I heard a strange rustling sound, faintly followed by three taps. I remarked on it to Mrs. Wriedt, and immediately heard: "That's my bunny, daddie." At my request Mrs. Wriedt turned on the red light, and I heard John King speak very faintly: but unfortunately, this exhausted the power, and we only got a faint "Goodbye."

The following account is given by the same sitters who recorded their experiences in 1912.

By the continued kindness of Vice-Admiral Usborne Moore, we were again permitted to sit with the famous American medium, Mrs. Wriedt, in two general and one private séance at Cambridge House, Wimbledon (the residence of the late W. T. Stead).

The following is a record of some of the remarkable phenomena witnessed by nine sitters and the medium:—

First general sitting, May 12, 1913.
We assembled in that memorable room, known by many as "Julia's Bureau," at 7 p.m.

The first spirit to manifest was Grayfeather, who announced his presence by saying, "Me here!" He then asked Mrs. Maybank: "How you do, Squaw Maybank? How you do, Chief Maybank? How you do,

Churchie?" (This last remark was directed to a gentleman in clerical attire.)

I then said that I was very glad that he had come to us. He replied that "He had helped us 'heap much' during the winter." I may say that this is quite true; for, contrary to all our expectations, Grayfeather (with many other "dear ones") is continually manifesting to, and helping, us in many and various ways.

I then asked him where the "Spirit world" was. He tapped upon the floor with the trumpet, and exclaimed: "All here!" He then said: "Good night: me go to Chief Moore from across big pond." We asked: "Where is Chief Moore?" He replied: "In his wigwam." [Correct. I was at Southsea.—W. U. M.]

Our dear son Harold was the next to follow our old and proved friend Grayfeather. We fully recognised his voice; it was the same as we had heard last year. He exclaimed: "Hullo mother! I am so glad that you are here; how are you dear? Hullo father" How are you?" We replied that we were well, and very pleased to hear him again. He answered: "I have brought a friend with me." We asked: "Who?" He replied: "Charlie Brown." (This young man had been a fellow apprentice in Chatham Dockyard.)

Several times during this sitting we sang different hymns, especially that remarkable one, "Nearer my God to Thee," when we heard as an accompaniment some very grand music, principally a cornet, played with such marvellous expression and power that we could but feel profoundly astonished at the fact that we were listening to such an outburst of harmony rendered by an invisible player on the spirit side of life.

Private sitting, May 13, from 1.30 to 2.40 p.m. Present—myself, Mrs. Maybank, and the medium.

Our dear son was the first spirit to greet us. He said: "Hullo mother! Hullo father! I am glad that you are here; I'll come again."

Then, very abruptly the voice of Dr. Sharp was heard to say: "I'm glad to see you Mr. and Mrs. Maybank. Now, Mr. Maybank, I want to talk to you about your wife's health." Then followed a long conversation of questions and answers.

Of course, it would be readily understood that this communication was of a very private, medical character, and would be of little evidential value to an outsider.

Our dear friend Grayfeather was the next to manifest by voice. He gave us the usual greeting—viz., "How you do Squaw Maybank? How you do Chief Maybank?" I said: "Grayfeather, you know my friend, P. Humphrey." He replied: "Yes, me know him."

I asked him about this friend's eye (for he had been blind in his right eye about twenty years), "as to whether he thought that the optic nerve was destroyed." He replied: "That is a chronic case, but me help him." I then asked about this friends daughter Clarice; whether "he could get me a message from her to give to her mother." He said: "That little squaw will come to her mothers home, and give her a message there."

Mrs. Wriedt asked: "What's that coming towards you, Mr. Maybank?"

We could see what appeared like a small cloud of vapour, about eighteen inches long, and there seemed to be as if a struggle were going on within this cloud, which finally resolved into the head and face of Mr. W. T. Stead. This was but a momentary appearance. Mrs. Maybank exclaimed: "Oh! This is Mr. Stead." Mr. W. T. Stead then replied: "I am glad to see you, for this will prove a great blessing to you." We thanked him and said that we felt much honoured by his coming to us.

Mrs Wriedt said; "Oh! Mr. Stead, this is good of you." He replied: "Tell Edith" (Miss Harper).

(Mr. Stead had promised at a séance, some miles away from Wimbledon, a few days previous, that he would show his face to us at his old home in the presence of Mrs. Wriedt, if possible; and by this manifestation had redeemed his promise.)

Our dear son again manifested, and had a long conversation with us. My wife's sister Flossie appeared, and conversed about family matters of a private nature. Then Mrs. Maybank's aunt, who had only passed over last Easter, said "I am very happy, and am with my son Isaac, and I do wish that you would cease to worry, as your dear son is quite safe and happy; I am frequently with him, and I will meet you with joy when you come over." Mrs. Maybank's Grandmother and grandfather came, and said they were glad to see us, and spoke of their sons and daughter, sending messages of love to them. My wife asked her grandmother to touch her with the trumpet. She was touched on the hand, and I was touched on the face.

My brother Arthur came next, and thanked me for going to his funeral. (There had been some slight estrangement between us previously to his death.) He had passed over as recently as last January.

Again our dear son manifested. There appeared a misty form passing round the room; it was scintillant, with a peculiar yellowish light that ultimately resolved itself into a definite face and hand, the hand throwing kisses; the form of this hand was an exact representation of that which had been so well known to us in earth life. The dear one asked the question: "Mother, dear, did you see me?" She replied: "Yes, dear."

To our wonder and surprise a voice said: "I am Dr. Templeton."

Dr. Templeton had performed an operation on my wife only as recently as last September, in the presence of Dr. A. Wallace.

(We had noticed reports in some of the daily papers, and in a weekly paper Light, of the death of Dr. Templeton on April 3. It had taken place in Norway, where he, with some friends, had been caught in a blizzard; he, and a friend, Mr. Warren, had strayed away from the rest of the party, and were found some time afterwards in the snow, dead.) He spoke of the nursing-home and of some of the staff where the operation had been performed, and remarked that these places were not the best of places to be in at any time. He then made inquiries, and gave information respecting the present condition of his patient, my wife.

I then asked if he was quite happy. He replied: "Yes, perfectly: but I should have liked to have remained on the earth a little longer, as I loved my work; and yet I find that we all have to go from one plane of life to another at the right moment." My wife said: "But you did not believe in spiritualism, did you, doctor?" He replied: "No; but I am now compelled to believe it."

May 14. Second general circle. 7.p.m.

We think that there were ten in number at this circle.

John King was the first to manifest, with his stentorian "Good evening, God bless you." He greeted each sitter in a similar way.

The next to speak was an Indian girl named Blossom. She was very interesting, and no doubt those to whom she addressed her remarks will give a report of the same.

Our dear son appeared and said much of a private and personal nature, and asked questions of local significance. He said that we had been having a general experience among the different churches in our search for the good and the true, and at last had found that which would give to us satisfaction and enjoyment.

One of my old shipmates, T. Mahone, then spoke, introducing himself in a very familiar manner—viz., by whistling. At my request he sang "Annie Laurie," and he asked the company to help him, and they responded by joining in the singing. He shouted out "Sing up." I replied: "You sing up, Tommy." He said: "You come over here and have a try; you will find it not so easy as you think." Mrs. Wriedt said: "I guess that you have found your match there Mr. Maybank."

At the same time that a spirit was speaking to one of the circle on the other side of the room I heard a noise like a little bird chirp in my ear. Mrs. Maybank said: "Is that Flossie?" Flossie replied: "Yes dear sister." Then followed a conversation of a general family character.

I asked Mrs. Wriedt how it happened that two spirit voices could be heard at the same time when there was only one trumpet. She explained that Flossie was speaking without the trumpet.

An Indian spirit was the next to manifest named Eagle. He spoke to the circle in a general way.

Mr. W. T. Stead was the next to greet us. He addressed each in turn, and then entered into a long conversation with Miss Harper.

Finally, that dear and gentle spirit Julia, the one who had acted as the guide and counsellor of the late W. T. Stead, spoke to the company by greeting each sitter by name, after which she requested us to rise and sing the Doxology, and the séance closed.

Truly it is written: "I have led you by a way that ye knew not."

The voices are many and various, each expressive of some needed note, in order to infil and fulfil, and thereby realise a grander outburst of harmony than the human embodied mentality of our outer consciousness of life had ever hoped to reach.

"Voices of the dead," do we hear someone say? Nay, there are no dead; life is always victorious, and we are but just beginning to learn this joyous truth from the many dear spirits that are ever ready to respond to the pure desire of our hearts to listen to their oft-repeated invitation, "To follow on to know."

J. Maybank.

This young lady wrote an interesting account to Lady Hill in 1912:—

Miss Norah Hill's Account, 1913

Mother, Vesey, and myself sat down with Mrs. Wriedt, and very shortly afterwards Mrs. Wriedt said she saw a young girl, who had died of consumption, of the name of Gertie. At first we could not place her at all; then the same thing happened in the case of an elderly man, who had died of paralysis; neither of these spirits spoke. Then uncle Tom came and spoke to us; he was followed by Colonel Cardew, who, you know, was father's great friend. He told us that he and the others had been specially sent by father to convince us that this was not "thought reading." His voice was wonderfully distinct. He said to Vesey, "What a fine fellow you have grown." (Vesey and I were not grown up when he died.) We talked to him for some minutes. The next communication we had was from a young fellow in the army Vesey met in Guernsey, whom he had almost forgotten. This voice was so indistinct that we could not catch his name, but he recalled himself to Vesey's remembrance by mentioning George Groves, and saying he was killed in the Boer War; then Stevie came to speak to us, and confirmed what Colonel Cardew had said. He seemed so bright and happy. Then father came. Mother asked him if he often saw her father and mother; he said: "Very seldom, as they have progressed, and are now on the seventh sphere"; then mother asked father, "Where are you?" He said, "I am on the sixth sphere"; Then mother said, ""Why are you not on the seventh sphere?" He said, "Because I am waiting for you." Lastly, Alice came and spoke. Vesey asked her if he could communicate with Willie Reeks. There was a silence, and Vesey said, "Oh, Alice, don't go yet": and presently she answered, "I only went to inquire; Willie has so lately passed over that he has not learnt to manifest yet." This brought the séance to a close. Later we remembered the first two spirits who came—the young girl, we knew at Penzance twenty-eight years ago; and the man, mother knew before she was married. It was perfectly right what Mrs. Wriedt said about them.

This narrative is by a hotel proprietor from Poole, Dorset. He sat last year at Cambridge House:—

Poole, July 14, 1913.

Dear Admiral Moore,

I enclose a rough outline of the notes I made as soon as possible after my sitting with Mrs. Wriedt. I believe it to be a fairly complete report of what passed, but, having a bad memory, no doubt some things escaped me.

Is there anything in the notes you would like to make use of? If so, I shall be glad for you to do so and to give you any explanation or assistance I can; for, having received so much comfort through being able to speak to my loved ones, I am anxious that others should receive comfort too.

To me the sitting was deeply interesting, and the evidence most conclusive.—Very truly yours,

Jas. Osman.

Private sitting with Mrs. Wriedt at Cambridge House, Wimbledon, June 4, 1913.

My son Reg came first, and expressed his pleasure at being able to speak to me again, and heartily thanked me for giving him the opportunity. He said he was now extremely happy and that everything was "all right." He told me that mater and Marie were there, and several others who were anxious to speak to me; after a few more remarks he wished me goodbye, to make room for the others.

Some man then spoke to me, but as his voice was thick I could not make out his name, but I could hear him say several times, "I am your old friend." He was so disappointed at my not recognising him, and so was I. He said, "I will come again."

Then my beloved wife came, and was, oh, so pleased to speak to me once more, and so grateful to me for coming from Poole for the purpose. She was almost too delighted, and begged me "to thank the Admiral for the kind invitation he sent me." We had quite a long talk together about various matters, and about our sons in Cape Town and Canada, and about auntie and her face affection. She expressed her pleasure at the way the hotel was being managed, and remarked how nice it looked. She told me what a happy party they were, and what companions Reg and Marie and she were.

I asked her various questions, to which she replied. I then said, "Do you know that friend Damon has passed over? Have you seen him?" She replied: "Why, I brought him here to meet you, and it was him you could not recognise just now; but he will speak to you again." She told me that she was often with Mrs. Barnes, Mrs. Keirle, and Mrs. Williams, and that the latter was there then, and would like to speak to me. After some loving remarks and kisses she bade me goodbye.

Friend Damon then spoke, and said what a privilege it was to be able to speak to me, and how thankful he was to my wife for bringing him there and satisfying me that it was really he. He referred to my visiting his wife on the previous Sunday evening, and said he was present at the time; he wished me to see her again and thank her for him for all her kindness and attention when in his illness, and for putting his old body away so nicely; also to tell her that he was well and happy. He also begged me to tell her how deeply he regretted the mistake he made in the legal document which had caused her so much anxiety, and that he was doing and would do all he could to help her through. He reffered to the mistake again, and called it his negligence; he hoped his wife would believe it was he that had spoken, but I feel sure that he was somewhat doubtful of it. He wished me goodbye.

Darling Marie then spoke to me in her usual loving manner, and, after she had wished me goodbye, Mrs. Williams spoke most clearly. She was very pleased to see and speak to me; she made a few remarks about their happy party, said a few kind things about myself, and wished me goodbye.

Mrs. Williams seemed remarkably bright and cheery. At the evening circle only Reg came to me of all my family, and said that he and mater went to London with me in the afternoon, and he noticed that I put away a very good tea; after which they went to Poole and found that everything was going on all right at the hotel. He wished me goodbye.

A man came to me and said he used to live at the hotel before me (when it was a private house), but I did not know him, and I do not know why he came.

Jas. Osman.

In reply to some inquiries Mr. Osman wrote:—

Dear Admiral Moore,

Replying to yours of the 16th inst., from Rothesay, I am glad you think my notes of some value.

My friend's name was Damon, and we were close friends for some thirty years.

I have not seen Mrs. Damon since, for various reasons, though I had hoped to do so. About ten days ago I sent her a copy of my notes, and she intended coming over from Bournemouth to see me.

On receipt of your letter I wrote to her, asking whether what was said at Wimbledon was relevant, but have not yet received her reply, but I know that Mrs. Damon had serious trouble about a deed (executed by her husband) in consequence of some word or words not being sufficiently definite (they were vague).

Mrs. Barnes, Mrs. Keirle, and Mrs. Williams were three of my wife's closest friends; the former passed over before my wife, and the two latter since.

Mrs. Williams passed over Christmas Eve, 1909, six months after my wife. On December 23, 1909, I was with Mr. Vango, and he told me my wife was spending her time partly with me and partly with Mrs. Williams, and that the latter would not see Christmas. A remarkable corroboration of this was given by Mrs. Williams the same evening; she called Mr. Williams and told him that my wife had just been to her.— Yours Very Truly,

Jas. Osman.

Dear Admiral Moore,

I did not reply to your last sooner, as I was hoping to see Mrs. Damon, and this I have done today, and had a little talk with her. She tells me that what her husband said to me was perfectly true and relevant, and that the document referred to was a deed poll, as her husband said.

I am very pleased to be able to send you this most satisfactory piece of information. So glad to hear of the success at Rothesay.—

Sincerely Yours,

Jas. Osman.

The attached narrative is sent to me by Rev. Charles L. Tweedale, author of Man's Survival after Death.

This year (1913) it was my good fortune to secure three sittings with Mrs. Wriedt at Cambridge House, Wimbledon—two circle sittings and one private. On each occasion I was accompanied by my wife. Last year I had not been able to get a private sitting, and was in high hopes that the one this year would be very evidential. Strange to say, with the exception of a short talk with John King, we had no communication.

Our two circle sittings, compared with last year's wonderful experiences, were also disappointing; but it must be said in mitigation of this, that the evidence given both to ourselves and our friend last year was of a particularly astounding nature. It must not be concluded, however, from this statement that this year we got nothing at all. On the contrary, we had two very interesting and evidential experiences, which I will discuss as briefly as possible. At our first circle sitting on June 16 a personality manifested for my wife, and the following conversation ensued:—

Voice: "It's grannie."
Wife: "Grannie Tweedale?"
Voice: "No." Wife: "Grannie Mc Leod?"
Voice (impatiently): "No, no."
Wife: "Who then?"

186

Voice: "Grannie Burnett."

Wife: (greatly affected and surprised): "What, father's mother?"

Voice: "Yes, yes."

Wife: "Have you ever been to Weston?"

Voice: "Yes, once." Wife: "Will you come again?"

Voice: "I don't like to come because of......" (Here a sentence relating to strictly private matter was spoken which absolutely staggered us, though unintelligible to the circle. It brought instant conviction to us both, that the personality manifesting had knowledge of certain affairs known only to ourselves, on which it is not possible to enlarge here.)

Wife: "Have you a message for us?"

Voice: "Yes, Mary is with me."

Wife: "Mary! Who is Mary?" (Here wife suggested several Marys whose names occurred to her.)

Voice (impatiently): "No! no! no!"

Wife: "Grannie, can you tell us what was your Christian name?"

The Voice made no reply, but a few seconds later Mrs. Wriedt said: "She says it is Catherine." This was correct. I had no knowledge of these details, and they were quite beyond Mrs. Wriedt's reach. My wife afterwards informed me that Grannie Burnett "Died" when she was a little girl and it was some time later in the evening before my wife remembered that her grandmother had adopted a girl named "Mary" under peculiar circumstances, and that this Mary had passed over about three years ago.

These details and experiences may seem trivial to outsiders, but the knowledge shown of a private event in our home life only known to ourselves, and also of particulars of my wife's family, which even she herself had forgotten and only recalled with difficulty, was most evidential to us.

During this first circle sitting on June 16, Mrs. Wriedt, who gave a number of clairvoyant delineations, said that she saw a little girl with very light hair in the circle, elevated a distance from the floor, and that she came for us. My wife, who is both clairvoyant and clairaudient at times, could not see her, nor could I.

At the second circle sitting, on June 18, one of the sitters (who was not present at our first sitting, and who was an entire stranger to us) sat next to my wife in the circle. She suddenly turned to her and said: "There is a beautiful little girl with very fair hair standing close to your knee. Do you see her?" My wife did not, nor did I, nor was the figure noticed by Mrs. Wriedt on this occasion.

We returned north on Friday, June 20. During our journey, when passing from the lower or tube station at King's Cross to the upper station in the open air, while in the long underground passage my wife suddenly cried: "See the girl?" The little fair- haired girl appeared to her, walking just behind the porter who was carrying our baggage, and, after accompanying us for about fifty yards, vanished when at the top of the steps and about a couple of yards out in the sunshine. On Saturday, June 21, I was reading my newspaper in the breakfast room, alone, and with the door shut. Suddenly I caught a glimpse of someone close to me stooping quickly down behind my paper. It was so realistic that it made me start violently. I thought it was one of my children. I at once rose from my seat, and looked under the table for the child. Finding no one there, I searched the small room; but, save myself, there was no other material person in it. During this search the door was shut, and I did not speak. I was just about to settle down to the paper again, under the impression that I had been mistaken, when the door opened, and my wife took a step forward into the room. Before I could utter a single word she suddenly exclaimed: "Oh, Charles! See the little girl." She saw her distinctly standing near me, the vision lasting for several minutes, during which the little one exhibited several symbolical figures of great interest, and which my wife described. I now told my wife of my experience a few minutes previously, and she questioned the little girl as to whether I had seen her. The reply (heard by my wife clairaudiently) was in the affirmative; the little one adding that she had allowed me just to catch a glimpse of her. On looking up my records, I find that the same little girl has been seen by our servant on March 29, 1912, and also a few days after that by my wife in broad daylight: also by my daughter Marjorie on March 19 of this year, again in broad daylight. My daughter took notice of the flaxen hair, remarking that it was almost white, so light was its colour. No details of these early appearances had previously been published, and they were known only to my family and, possibly, to one official of the S. P. R. All of those who have seen this apparition describe it as that of a beautiful little girl, apparently about six years of age.

From the above account it will be seen that this figure, seen and described by Mrs. Wriedt at her evening séance on June 16, has been observed by at least five other persons, including myself, under circumstances precluding all possibility of hallucination or fraud.

Charles L. Tweedale,
Vicar of Weston.
Weston Vicarage, Otley,
Yorks.
August 5, 1913.

These accounts are from neighbours of mine at Southsea. The lady furnished me with a statement last year:—

June 3, 1913. Present at a private sitting at Cambridge House, Wimbledon, with my wife and Mrs. Wriedt only, in the room called "Julia's Bureau." A few minutes after sitting down my great-grandfather, General Buchanan, speaking loudly through the trumpet, addressed me as his "Dear grandson," speaking of me as "a chip of the old block," and with praise and approval. He said that I inherited my love of beautiful and rare things from my grand-mother, his wife; that for fifteen years he had been looking after me, and would continue to do so; and would always assist me. He told me that I should not eat too much at a time, should not smoke so much, as nicotine got at my heart from too much smoking. He told me that he very much regretted formerly having been angry with my father regarding the profession he selected; but now rejoiced that he had followed his own choice, and that he loved and respected him for it. (The General was my father's guardian, and intended him for his own profession, purchasing him a commission in the Inniskilling Dragoons; but my father refused, and said he preferred to follow God, and chose the Church.) This is quite true, as I had often heard my father relate this story, and that the General never forgave him for not joining his old regiment.

The General then informed me that my father would speak to us next, and, assuring me that he would always assist me, departed.

A minute or two afterwards I was much moved to hear a voice speaking through the trumpet addressing me as "My dear son." He gave us a beautiful discourse interrupted with prayer, one passage of which I can call to mind, that "the Lord would lead me through green pastures," etc. He also spoke to my wife; I was so overcome with emotion at the time that I fail to remember his words, but they were very beautiful, and deeply touched both my wife and myself; then he blessed us both and departed.

(My father, the late Canon Hamilton, was a great preacher in his day. Fearless, and regardless of self-interest, he had only one object in his life—that of serving God.)

Next came a voice through the trumpet asking "where his leg was." I asked who was speaking; the answer was: "I am your uncle, Tom Parke." Then I knew what he meant, for I have in my house, Yarborough Lodge, Southsea, my uncle, Tom Parke's artificial leg, which was sent to me a few years ago by my mother, his sister. I told him I had the leg quite safe in my possession. He said: "Burn it; it is badly made, and I have no further use for it." I told him I had promised it to my cousin, Captain Parke, his nephew. He then said: "Let him have it." (My uncle, Tom Parke, passed over before I was born; he lost his leg through an accident in the hunting field.)

Next came my brother, Rev. William Hamilton, who died of consumption while yet a young man. Unlike the former speakers, who spoke loudly, my brother spoke in a hoarse but clear whisper, as of one suffering from tuberculosis of the throat. I told him I was very sorry that I was at sea when he died, and deeply grieved that he was taken from us just as he was getting on so well in the Church. To my inquiry he said he was very happy. He told us he had a small dog with him. My wife immediately exclaimed: "Is it little Willie Bone?" Hardly had she said this when she felt as if the dog was jumping on her dress. I said: "Is that little Willie Bone?" and we heard three loud barks, such as he used to give in life. I then said: "Kiss me Bone" which I often said to him when he was alive, and I felt as if a cold nose pressed my forehead; my wife experienced the same touch.

(Willie Bone was a little Yorkshire terrier who died on March 19 last, beloved by my wife, and myself, and all who knew him.)

Next came John King, who said he was glad to see us, and told us he would come to Southsea and help us. Here ended this marvellous and successful sitting.

P.S.—The General, when speaking to me, touched me twice on the head.

June 10. Present at a private sitting at Cambridge House, Wimbledon, with my wife and Mrs Wriedt only, in the room called "Julia's Bureau." Mrs. Wriedt turned on the musical instrument, my wife sitting beside me, the trumpet in front of me and the room darkened. In a few minutes the voice of General Buchanan was heard calling through "my dear Charles" (he spoke in his usual clear and commanding voice). He told me he was always assisting me, and had done so for fifteen years. He told me that his wife has helped me to arrange my curios in Yarborough Lodge. He said he had a favour to ask me, and hoped that I would grant it willingly. "He remarked," he said "That I was often too impetuous and hasty in manner and temper, and that I should not be so, that I should look calmly at things as if through rose-coloured glasses, and always be calm."" (I had brought some questions on a paper directed to the General and my father, which I had placed on the table beside me at the beginning of the sitting.) He desired me to ask them. I said

"One of them is, If I have a paper and pencil in a certain place at Yarborough Lodge, would he write something on it, so as to assure me he was present there?" He said he could not do it, but that he would come to Southsea and assist me to form a circle there.

Twice he touched me on the head, as if with his hand, and twice gently knocked my shoulder with the trumpet; he left us promising to always assist us, and said he was coming to Yarborough Lodge. In a few moments I saw a luminous object approaching us. Telling my wife a spirit was coming to us, we heard the General's voice again, this time not through the trumpet, but above us; he said he had brought his wife to us, and then we heard a lady's voice, sweet and gentle (and such a contrast to the General's), addressing me as her dear grandson, telling me (as the General had formerly told me) that I had inherited the love of beautiful things from her, that she loved me; and she also spoke in a flattering manner to my wife, and said she was much pleased with her. She asked me what had become of the General's two silver candlesticks, snuffers, and box of silver spoons that he had given my father? (When a boy I remember seeing all these things at home.) I told her that I believed these things were lost or stolen as time went on; that my mother was careless and extravagant like her own family. Then she said: "We are not"; but she added: "She is a good woman." She next informed me that she used to ask the "Major" (which was her pet name for her husband) to bring her home something rare and curious when he went anywhere, and when he came back he would say: "Wife, I have got something for you in my pocket," and he would place them before her, to her great delight. I asked her if there was any picture or painting of herself or the General anywhere I could procure. She said there were none.

Next an extraordinary thing happened. A low voice through the trumpet gave a name I did not understand. The spirit seemed hurt. "Why," he said, "You were at my funeral; I died recently. I am an old messmate of yours." Mrs. Wriedt then said: "I hear something like 'Evans.'" I said: "Then it must be Evan Nepean." "Yes," he said, "Evan Nepean," repeating it. I told him I met him a day or two before he died, and he said I was the last person he met out of doors. I asked him if he would like to come back again; he replied: "No, his body was painful." I told him that I missed him very much in Southsea, and said I hoped he would come to Yarborough Lodge, and to the room downstairs where I last entertained him. He replied that he knew the room well and that he would come. He asked me how his wife was. I told him that she had gone into a smaller house, and she said she had done right. He spoke also to my wife, and answered several questions she asked. She asked what he died of, and he said "an infection of the heart." (Fleet-Surgeon Evan Nepean was an old and valued friend of mine. I was the last to see him in the street before he died; I attended his funeral; he passed over as recently as March last [1913], which may account for his ignorance concerning his wife's movements.)

Next came my brother-in-law, Ley Brooks (who, as a child, was gifted with the most wonderful psychic powers), addressing me as "Charlie." He was most communicative and instructive; He told us he was now on the sixth plane, having progressed. I asked him what happened when we died; he said: "Having passed over, you wake up in three days and find you have left your body, which was just like throwing off an old coat you had no further use for." We heard him chuckling, which my wife recognised as being his habit in life. He promised to come and assist us to form a circle in Southsea, the number of which should be three or five. He said our little dog was sitting between my legs, and when we called his name "Willie Bone" we heard a low bark; then a loud one, as of a big dog, which might have come from a collie my wife once owned. We both asked Willie Bone to kiss us, and we each felt a cold touch as if of a dog's nose touching our faces. My brother-in-law informed me, without my asking, that the sad and grotesque faces, which had been my custom to see nightly in bed, and which, in my ignorance, I conceived to be evil or condemned spirits, were not so, but the faces of those who had died a violent death such as drowning, etc., and had returned to the earth to be recognised if possible. He further said that there were no evil spirits. Next came my wife's guide "Abdul," an Indian, who assured her he was always looking after her, but that in a few years he would have to leave her. He informed me that he would also look after me, as being of the family.

In my interview with General Buchanan I inquired of him regarding a Chinese stone, with a dog embossed on it, which I wear. I asked him: "Should I continue to do so"; he said: "Yes, do so until I tell you on whose arm to put it"; and, Finally telling me that he was looking after me, and that my father was fully engaged in looking after my mother, said: "Charles Buchanan-Hamilton, my grandson, I am proud of you." Here endeth the second séance I have had the privilege of attending at Cambridge House, Wimbledon.

Signed

Charles William Buchanan-Hamilton,
Deputy Inspector-General,

R.N. Yarborough Lodge,
Southsea, June 13, 1913.

Mrs. Buchanan-Hamilton writes:—

I had five private séances last June (1913) with Mrs. Wriedt—two alone, two with my husband, and one with two women friends.

I will now try and describe what happened at the two private séances when alone with the medium, and also the one séance with the medium and the two friends. At the first séance My father, mother, brother, and my guide (who twice came to me), and several of my husband's relations, all manifested themselves, speaking clearly and powerfully for some minutes at a time, each discussing family matters, especially my husband's relations, who gave me many tests and messages for him, each expressing a wish that he might come to a séance. This, I told them, I had already arranged and that he would be present the following day, when I had my second private séance, this time with my husband, whose narrative gives a description of our joint experiences.

The third séance I had was with the medium alone. At this séance many interesting events occurred, my first visitor being my mother, who wrote her Christian name on arrival; this was seen by the medium in the air, and communicated to me. She was much distressed and worried by the illness of a relative, so much that she broke down from emotion, dropping the trumpet at the time. My father then came; we discussed for a short time the illness of this relative, and I asked him what he could suggest, when all of a sudden he said to me: "Do you know Compton Burnett?" I answered: "No, never in my life have I heard that name before." "Well," he said, "I will go and fetch him." With this he departed, and a minute, not more, a strong powerful voice through the trumpet said; "Madam, I am Dr. Compton Burnett. What can I do for you?" I said that I was anxious about a relative, and what was the best treatment for her. He then said: "Give me her name and age, and I will go and see her and let you know." This I did. He then left, returning in about two minutes' time with the information that he had seen her; and he gave me a diagnosis of her case, which I afterwards found out to be a correct one; he then bid me farewell and departed. My father then returned, and stayed about five minutes, chatting on various subjects, among them giving descriptions of his beautiful garden with geraniums growing taller than himself; he also played me a bar on the flute (in answer to my question, "Do you still play the flute?"), an instrument in which he excelled when on earth.

My brother then came, giving me many messages, and discussing the pros and cons of the sick relative. In answer to my question, "Where was my little dog Willie?" he said: "He is sitting by your side now, trying vainly to sit on your skirt" (a habit he dearly loved when in earth life), "But your frock is so short he can't get on it. On your lap is sitting little Eny" (fox terrier). He further said: "I have brought seven dogs with me, all our pets at various times." I may add that my brother was a great lover of animals, and was, when on earth, a powerful medium.

Several of my husbands relatives came after this, giving me special messages for him; he was to sit with me at my next séance, the description of which is contained in his own narrative.

My fifth and last séance I had with the two friends referred to—Mrs. R. and Mrs. M., the medium, and myself. We were hardly seated when we were all much sprinkled with water, a spirit coming at once, saying, "I am Captain Stanley," and addressing himself to Mrs. R. This gentleman had only just passed over, and his voice was very quavering and troubled; he appeared to be not quite sure where he was, or what had happened to him. He addressed me by my full name, and asked after my husband. Then followed several spirit friends, relations, and otherwise of Mrs. R.'s, all coming and speaking wonderfully with very strong voices. My brother again came, telling Mrs. R., whom he addressed by her full name, that she had seen him in her home; this I afterwards found to be true. He further said: "I will help you in your mediumship, and you must do what I tell you," explaining to her what he wished to be done.

Dr. Compton Burnett again came, giving us information about the death of his wife, and answering questions about the health of one of my friends present; also telling me more about the treatment of my relative. Then a very qurious thing happened—a spirit coming laughing, which laughter continued increasing in force until it ended in a shriek, when the trumpet was dropped suddenly. Mrs. Wriedt, the medium, said that the spirit came for me, and I was impressed that it was my mother, and that the laughter was emotional, which prevented her manifesting. My little dog Willie again barked, and I was touched at the same time. This happened when a spirit friend was talking very earnestly with one of my friends present, and I was at the same time speaking to the medium. What I noticed as so remarkable at this séance was that my friend's spirit friends and my own always addressed each of us by our full names; for instance, I was called Mrs. Buchanan-Hamilton. The sitting I consider an excellent one, the spirits talking almost continuously for nearly three-quarters of an hour, most of them with great vigour.

(Signed)   Helen M. Buchanan-Hamilton.

Mrs. Richards contributed some of her experiences of 1912 in Part 1.

She writes from Thorverton: "July 14, 1913. My dear Admiral, I enclose what may be interesting. I have heaps of tests, but they are of such a private nature I cannot give them......"

Friday, June 20. Mrs. Mansell and self sitting.

We had most brilliant phenomena of lights. My sister, who passed over in 1909, etherealised full length in a most striking manner; the whole form appeared in a white garment, with a scarf or hood of the same colour over her hair. She raised her arm above her head. After the form disappeared she spoke through the trumpet, giving her name and asking if we had seen her. Then another spirit took the trumpet, and gave the name Johan Clementi quite clearly. He then spoke in what I understood to be Italian. As I only know a few words of that language, I said: "Can you speak French?"

He replied that he had only had a few words of French, but announced in that language that he was my grandfather, and that he played the harp. He then sung a beautiful air in Italian. (He did play the harp.) He told us, in halting French, that a great vein of music ran through my family, and especially mentioned my sister, Mrs. Jacob, as possessing this gift. (Correct.)

The impression we got was that he was being prompted in the French phrases from the other side, as he appeared to be listening to someone and repeating what they said. John King then manifested, and said he had been helping him with the language. He also said: "I want to tell you Mrs. Richards, God bless you, that this spirit is your grandfather on your mother's side." I said: "Great-grandfather, Johan?" "Ah, well, there's no great over here , he's your grandfather and he was an Italian, and can only speak a very little French, God bless you."

(I found out afterwards in Grove's Musical Dictionary that my great- great- grandfather's name was Johan—a fact I did not know at the séance, when the spirit spoke to me. On my mothers side I am the great-grandniece of Muzio Clementi, son of Johan.)

At another séance with Mrs. Wriedt, my daughter and I again sitting alone, my sailor brother, who passed over in August, 1910, manifested. He was very fond of shooting, and used to go out at night, near Sydney, after curlew. My other brother used to imitate the call of the curlew to tease him. At this séance he began to whistle like a curlew, and I repeated the call. He said: "No, that's not right, it goes like this," and then he gave the true curlew whistle.

Then an ancestor of ours came and showed his hand, with a particular ring he used to wear on his finger.

At one sitting with Mrs. Wriedt alone, the room was lighted up so clearly that I could see the other trumpet, belonging to Admiral Moore, standing on the musical disc box. I could also see the chairs in the room. Mrs. Wriedt spoke to me at the same time. She was sitting opposite to me, near the oval table.

Tuesday, June 24. Sitters: Mrs. Buchanan-Hamilton, Mrs. Richards, and [her daughter] Mrs. Mansell.

When we first sat down we were freely sprinkled with water, and we heard a voice say: "How do you do, Mrs. Richards?"

Q.: "I am very well—but who are you?"

A.: "Stanley."

Q.: "What, Captain Stanley?"

A.: "Yes, how is the Admiral?"

Q.: "This is Doone [her daughter]. Do you remember her?"

A.: "Yes."

Q.: "And this is my friend, Mrs. Hamilton."

A.: "Yes." (To her): "How is the Doctor?"

Mrs. Hamilton answered: "He is very well; did you know him?"

A.: "I have heard about him."

Q.: "Did you know about this subject before you passed over?"

A.: "I had read about it. Tell George all is well with me, goodbye."

[George is the husband of Mrs. Richards.—W. U. M.]

I said "we are pleased you came to us, I hope you will be happy."

(Signed) E. R. Richards.

Note.—Captain George Stanley, C.B., R.N., a friend of Mrs. Richards and mine, died on the night of Thursday, June 19, 1913.—W. U. M.

August 15, 1913: Sitters: Mrs Jacob, Mrs. Richards, and the medium.

A spirit manifested, giving the name Muzio Clementi, and saying he was a great- grandfather. (This spirit, in earth life, was a very celebrated musician and composer.)

He was very particular to impress on us the movement and time of one of his sonatas. He sang it through, showing how he wished it to be played and the way he interpreted it. This particular sonata is one which I have often tried to play. I said to him: "I am afraid you laugh at my feeble attempts at rendering it." He made no reply, probably to spare my feelings.

My sister, Mrs. Jacob, asked him if he was interested in her son, who is very musical. A.: "Yes."

Q.: "Could you help him?"

A.: "Yes, but he does not practice."

It was explained that he had so little time. The spirit asked: "How can I help him then?"

He now recited three verses in a beautiful voice. We could not remember them exactly after the séance was over, but they dealt with his life and musical success. He seemed very gratified that his ability had been recognised by the country, and, on leaving, promised to lead us to the marble slab where the inscription was given, "not far from here."

Muzio Clementi's grave is in the south cloister of Westminster Abbey. The inscription calls him "the father of the pianoforte," and states that he was born in Rome, 1752, and died at Evesham, 1832.

There is an interesting letter from this lady in Part 1.

Thorverton, July 27, 1913.

Dear Admiral Moore,

I have been staying here with my sister, and it has been so restful. I am sorry not to have written before, and regret I am only able to send you the enclosed, which may not be of interest. Of course, my sittings have been joy, and more than good; and I have learnt much from my spirit relatives, but of too private a nature to speak of.

Yours sincerely,
M. Jacob.

Sitting with Mrs. Wriedt on May 24, 1913.

Being "Empire day," I wore flowers of red and white and blue. When I first sat down, and the lights were turned off (the medium and I sat alone; almost at once bright white lights appeared about the room and over the medium; a voice spoke which was that of my great-grandfather, and he touched with the trumpet the flowers that I wore. I then asked him if he knew the meaning of the colours. He answered: "This is Decoration Day, but every day with us here is a Commemoration Day." After he left, the medium and I again saw lovely moving lights and a wave of light illuminating the whole side of the room; also, distinctly, three heads and faces of Indians. Over each head was a half circle of light like a halo. The forms appeared to be dancing and gliding—all movement. While this was going on a relative spoke and greeted me; I asked him what the figures were doing and what the beautiful lights were. He replied: "The Indians are dancing." He then said: "I will try and show myself." The voice ceased, and the lights and figures commenced again, closer this time, and I could see the chair near me showing the wooden back of it entirely visible by the brilliant light and the whole side of the room. On the seat of the chair was a smaller light, which my relative said was he, and which he then placed close under my face, and afterwards upon my lap. He said: "I have sat upon the chair." It was a most beautiful phenomenon, and lasted some time. John King came afterwards, and told me the "Indians had taken the floor," and that my power was strong that day.

M. Jacob.

The attached notes have been sent to me by a resident of one of our Midland Counties. I can vouch for his accuracy.

I have been asked by Vice-Admiral Moore to write an account of my experiences with Mrs. Wriedt, so I propose to give some details of my sittings with her.

My first acquaintance with Mrs. Wriedt was in the year 1911, but I did not write down any detailed particulars of my experiences with her until May 1912. On almost all the occasions I mention I sat alone with Mrs. Wriedt. Generally we sat in the dark, though on one or two occasions we kept the light turned up.

One of the phenomena I experienced in the sittings most evidential to me as to the presence of unseen spirits was the receiving of flowers; these were taken from the bowls in the room in which we sat. They were given me in almost every instance by my late wife, whom I shall designate by the letter F.

Another frequent phenomenon was the touching by unseen hands, which I felt from time to time; this was so evident and distinct that I could have no doubt about it.

As regards Mrs. Wriedt, she invariably sat in a chair at some distance from me, but not so far off but that I should have heard any movement that she made. I was in the habit of having by me an electric hand lamp, frequently two lamps, so that I was able to turn on a light at any moment, and this I frequently did.

I have been absolutely convinced that Mrs. Wriedt never in any way assisted in the production of any of the phenomena by any movement she made, and that the only way in which she did assist them was by her innate psychic powers.

As regards the voices, as will be seen later on, I had the experience of hearing them on several occasions when alone under conditions that absolutely prevented any mortal assistance from Mrs. Wriedt or any other person. Even had I had any doubts before as to the genuineness of the "voices," they would have disappeared with that experience. The voices of F. and other spirits who spoke sometimes came through the trumpet and sometimes not. When they spoke to me Mrs. Wriedt sometimes heard them and sometimes did not; similarly, when they spoke to Mrs. Wriedt I sometimes heard them and sometimes did not. The numerous conversations I had with spirits were as connected, clear, and continuous as if they were in earth-life.

I will now relate some particulars as to the sittings. I may first mention one sitting that I had with Mrs. Wriedt at Cambridge House during the year 1911. On June 20 of that year a late relative of mine spoke and said: "We will meet beyond the river, where the surges cease to roll."

Passing on to May 8, 1912, I went on that day to Cambridge House, Wimbledon, to see Mrs. Wriedt. Mr. Stead spoke to me, and said that he was glad to see me at Julia's Bureau. In reply to an inquiry I made, he said that he came out of his cabin before the Titanic went down. I had never actually met Mr. Stead, though I had corresponded with him. I may mention that Mrs. Wriedt has an aluminium telescopic trumpet, through which the voices most frequently speak.

F. gave me two flowers together at the same time—a pink flower that I had noticed in a bowl of flowers when I entered the room and a white flower, and later on she gave me a lily of the valley. She touched me, and sprinkled some water on my face.

On Thursday, May 9, I again went to Cambridge House. I bought some flowers on the way. While with Mrs. Wriedt I saw in the air appearances like Easter Lilies; they were luminous. Mrs. Wriedt first saw the light, then I did so. Later on I saw the light again when she did not.

F. handed me three flowers at different times—an Easter Lily, a purple iris (this flower Mrs. Wriedt called a flag), and a rose. Mrs. Wriedt said she saw the head of a dog.

Friday, May 10. F. gave me on this day two tulips. F.'s face was materialised twice, though I was unable to actually identify it.

May 11. F. pressed the stalk of a flower against my cheek until I took it from her.

Wednesday, May 15. I saw lights almost at the commencement of the sitting. Looking sideways at them they were bright, but in front they were quite faint. F. gave me two Easter lilies at two different times during this sitting. On the second occasion there was first a cold pressure on the point of my chin, then another touch on my face, after which she gave me the flower.

Friday, May 17. A light appeared waving towards the flowers on the table. A light was also seen waving up and down

John King spoke twice. He is a frequent control at the sittings with Mrs. Wriedt, and almost always speaks in a clear, distinct voice; indeed, sometimes so loudly that it amounts to shouting. (He was on earth Sir Henry Morgan, a celebrated buccaneer, knighted by Charles II, and made deputy Governor of Jamaica.)

Two relations of mine spoke, both of whom died many years ago.

Saturday, May 18. F. gave me a flower. Nothing more happened, and no voice spoke.

Monday, May 20. I had brought with me a psychic photograph that I wished to show Mrs. Wriedt. This was in a cardboard tube. F. placed a rose in the tube. F. said that, as she had mentioned before, lavender was now her colour, though pink had been while she was on earth. John King spoke.

Tuesday, May 21. John King spoke, and said, as I gathered, that F. was looking after a newcomer into spirit life. The newcomer was, I think, a relation of mine, whose funeral I attended the next day.

Thursday, May 23. A table with a bowl of flowers on it was on my left, at some little distance off. I wondered whether F. would give me a flower from it. She did so, for suddenly a deluge of flowers came, hitting the trumpet.

Saturday, May 25. F. gave me two roses; the first was held to my nose till I took it. I had with me a heavy electric hand-light in a leather case, and had it placed on a table to my right. This was now put into my hand and pulled at as I took it.

The trumpet was laid in my lap. A bowl of Easter lilies that was on a table to my left was lifted off and placed on the floor at my feet, a little to my left.

John King told me to be careful about my feet—I did not know why at the time—and he told me to turn on my light.

I thought that he said "to turn to my right." So I moved on my chair to the right, when he corrected me. I turned on the light, and found that a bowl of Easter lilies, that was on a table to my left, had been lifted off and placed on the floor at my feet, a little to my left.

Wednesday, May 29. I tried sitting alone first, to see if there would be any result. A voice said, "Good morning," and there was some tapping. Afterwards, with Mrs. Wriedt in the room, strong lights appeared waving up and down.

Thursday, May 30. With Mrs. Wriedt out of the room there was a faint voice and tapping. No other result this day.

Friday, May 31. With Mrs. Wriedt out of the room there was a faint voice from John King, and there was tapping. John King said later that he had tried to speak; as a fact, he did so.

With Mrs. Wriedt in the room there were various lights, and among them a waving light.

F. gave me a red rose. At first I felt a touch on my forehead as of a wet flower—the rose was on the floor. Later on I was given another red rose, one with a shorter stalk. I was told it was from F.'s sister.

Saturday, June 1. With Mrs Wriedt out of the room John King spoke faintly. With Mrs. Wriedt in the room, there appeared before my eyes etherealisations; first of Mr. Stead; and then of an ancestor of mine, as I was told. The etherealisations were like large cabinet-sized photographs, of a light brown colour; they were luminous. John King explained that they were made from oxygen and the flowers.

Wednesday, June 5. John King moved the table with the bowl of flowers on it till the table, or the vase on it, banged against the trumpet that I was holding out to the left. He also moved a chair. The chair I was sitting on was shaken twice.

I felt a wind sweep over me, and I was touched on my face.

June 6. The trumpet was lifted up and touched my head; and the big electric hand- light was moved by John King.

I was touched on the forehead, apparently by a flower.

I remarked that no flower had been given to me. A chair was pushed forward, and, on my stretching out my hand, I found that a flower was on the chair, and a heavy vase full of water and flowers was placed on it also. The single flower on the chair was a red rose.

Monday, June 10. Waving lights appeared.

Saturday, June 15. Flowers (two red roses and leaves) touched my face, and were held there till I took them. Spirit lights, like Glow-worms, appeared near the cabinet. John King spoke.

Friday, June 21. Many lights appeared—not continuous, but coming and going.

Saturday, June 22. A quantity of roses, white and red, were given to me. The trumpet had, apparently been removed, and when we turned on the light we found that a flower had been placed in the small end of the trumpet; standing up nearly alongside it was a big, electric hand-light, taken from the table on my right. Early in the sitting I was sprinkled with water (I suppose when the flowers were taken out of the vase).

Wednesday, June 26. I missed the big electric hand-lamp from the table on my right when I felt for it, and also the trumpet, which I had placed near me on my left. We turned on the electric light in the room and found the trumpet a little way off, with a red rose in the small end, and the big electric hand- light standing up alongside it.

John King, I think it was, in a loud voice, told me to take Mrs. Wriedt's hands in mine. I did so—her two in my two hands. The small table near the cabinet (on which was a bowl of flowers) was dragged forward till it came close to us. We heard it being dragged along the floor. Mrs. Wriedt suggested that the spirit should replace it, and the table was dragged back a considerable distance, though perhaps not quite as far as the point from which it had been taken. F. gave me another rose.

Friday, June 28. Two roses—one pink, the other red—were given to me by F., and were placed in the small end of the trumpet.

Brilliant waving lights appeared, and near by one single light, also numerous lights, in the direction of the cabinet and the trumpet.

Saturday, June 29. No result whatever. Wednesday, July 3. F. spoke of Mrs. Wriedt.

Thursday, July 4. A relation of mine spoke and said that he was helping others, and that where he was it was very much the same as here, but more beautiful.

Friday, July 5. Bright lights appeared, and something like an eye. A flower was placed in the small end of the trumpet, with a flower vase standing up on the floor alongside it. The trumpet was dropped on the floor.

Wednesday, July 10, 1912. At an hotel in London, with Mrs. Wriedt, F. spoke and there was also another voice. These voices spoke in broad daylight. We did not attempt to darken the room, and sat in the afternoon.

May 26, 1913. At Cambridge House. Very brilliant lights appeared, flashing and dancing about.

Tuesday, May 27. I began by sitting alone. I locked the door. John King spoke distinctly and gave his name. I went to the door, unlocked it quickly, and called Mrs. Wriedt. She was downstairs.

Wednesday, June 4. I first sat alone. John King spoke somewhat faintly a few words. Nothing else happened. It had been raining.

Friday, June 6. F. showed beautiful, small, pink rings in the air in front of us. We both saw the rings; they were somewhat elongated. We spoke of the colours and how beautiful they were. F. spoke and said something like this: "That colour cannot be duplicated—it is a spiritual colour."

Saturday, June 7. I asked F. if she had been at a wedding the day before. F. suggested that it was the day previous to that. She was quite right in this; I had made a mistake.

Wednesday, June 11. F. gave me two roses, first stroking my face twice with what was, apparently, a flower. Of the two flowers one had a long stalk, the other none. That with the stalk we found, on turning on the light, had been placed in the small end of the trumpet. The stalkless rose was lying on the table to my left.

Friday, June 13. Brilliant lights appeared. F. showed me a pink light close to me.

Saturday, June 14. F. lifted the trumpet more than once. F. handed me a red rose.

Monday, June 16. A pink rose appeared in the air. Etherealised figures danced.

Monday, June 23. I saw circles and dots of light. The trumpet was lifted till it touched my head, and it was placed on my knee.

Friday, June 27. When alone at first, F. tapped and spoke. A favourite dog of F.'s, who had died during her lifetime, barked several times.

Saturday, June 28. F. spoke. John King spoke long and loudly.

Monday, June 30. F. spoke, and remarked that they have a counterpart there of all that we have on earth, but richer and more beautiful.

Tuesday, July 1. My face was touched, apparently by a flower. A rose was handed to me. The trumpet fell with a crash. John King spoke.

Miss Mile's Testimony to the mediumship of Mrs Wriedt

I first heard of Mrs. Wriedt in the summer of 1911, when Vice-Admiral Usborne Moore told me of his discovery of this wonderful American medium, and by the Admiral's invitation I accompanied him on the evening of July 14, 1911, to Cambridge House, Wimbledon, where Mrs. Wriedt was then staying as the guest of Mr. Stead on her first visit to "Julia's Bureau." It was the first dark séance with a professional medium I had ever attended in my life; and I went with an absolutely open mind, because it was all so new and strange.

On this occasion I received no personal messages, nor anything evidential, so far as I was concerned. But I had direct evidence of the genuineness of Mrs. Wriedt's mediumship in the remarkable tests received by other sitters, notably the "O. B." incident recorded elsewhere. And I shall never forget the impression made on my mind by the sound of the spirit voices speaking from the unseen. It was an episode quite unique in a lifetime of great psychic experience.

The following year, 1912, and again in 1913, I had several sittings with Mrs. Wriedt, both private and in general circles. I possess the shorthand notes taken for me at the time by Mr. Trefaulx Harper, therefore I am not merely writing from memory. On these occasions I had direct messages giving names and incidents in my own life, absolutely unknown to the medium or anyone else present, which clearly proved that the communicating intelligences were the persons they represented themselves to be. Messages were also given to me for friends in my surroundings, bearing directly upon what was going on at the time, and proving that the cognisance of the spirit world is around us in our daily lives, and that the veil between the physical and the spiritual is gradually being drawn aside.

I also, at different times, saw etherealised forms moving about the room, and likewise have seen many brilliant lights hovering above the sitters. These lights were many coloured, and often took the form of circles and crosses.

I have heard as many as three different voices speaking at the same time, one loudly declaiming through the trumpet in the middle of the circle, the other two simultaneously speaking in an undertone to different sitters.

At the same time I wish to say that I do not accept the authenticity of any spirit communication unless accompanied by such tests and proofs of identity as to leave no doubt whatever in my mind that they are those whom they represent themselves to be.

(Signed)   Clarissa Miles.

The following letter to Light, published in the issue of July 22, 1911, will explain the reference to the "O. B." incident:—

Sir.—Kindly permit me to testify to the really wonderful mediumship of Mrs. Wriedt, of Detroit U.S.A., in whose public circle I sat last week. A cousin [Surname given] spoke to me in the direct voice on a purely private matter. Later came my grandfather, calling me by name, and asking after my father, by name also. He reminded me of a most unusual domestic incident that occurred over thirty years ago. Finally came an uncle, asking after his daughter (by name), announcing himself as "O. B." He was never called anything else by his intimates. I went as a complete stranger, and in no case did I take the initiative. All the sitters were more than satisfied with their individual results......

W. Cooper Lissenden.

The "O. B." incident is one of the best tests I have ever heard at a general circle.—W. U. M.

From Colonel E. R. Johnson. His experiences in 1912 are described in part I.

During May and June of 1913 I attended twelve séances by Mrs. Wriedt at Wimbledon. They were all held in complete darkness, and the voices usually, but not always, appeared to come through hollow aluminium trumpets, which were provided in order to increase their power and resonance. At some séances I sat alone with the psychic, at others with a circle of nine or ten other sitters. The private séances were all very successful; one of the others was entirely without phenomena, and another was almost so. I afterwards asked the "Control" the reason of this failure, and was told that it was not due to hostility on the part of any of the sitters, but "the magnetism" was absorbed like a sponge as fast as it was given out.

I had sustained conversations with four of my relatives, some of these lasting for over half an hour at single sittings. The total number of these amounted to sixteen. Twelve people, nearly all intimate friends, also spoke with me, and I have noted the names of twenty others who spoke. I heard many others speaking while they addressed other sitters, and whose voices were therefore more or less indistinct. It was also quite evident that there were many others anxious to speak, but were not permitted to do so.

Sometimes two voices were heard at the same time. On one occasion the voices of two communicators, that of the control and of the psychic, were practically, if not actually, speaking at the same moment.

The voices varied much in character. Those speaking for the first time were often difficult to hear. Their own names, the names of other people, and the names of places seemed to be especially troublesome to remember and pronounce. One of my communicators told me this difficulty was due to want of practice, "names not being used among us"; other voices were quite strong and clear, as well as characteristic of the persons they represented. The voices of old people, Men, Women, and children were recognisable at once, and they all improved after the first or second visit very much. They were often affected by various motions, and a dramatic tone was not uncommon, especially at first, but it usually wore off in a short time.

English was generally used, sometimes with a provincial accent. I also heard French, Italian, Dutch, German, Servian, and Croatian. I only recognised three of these six languages; the other three are given on the authority of foreigners who were sitting with me. There was a marked difference in the ability of the sitters to see phenomena. For my own part, though my vision is excellent, I might put myself in the lowest class. On two occasions I saw circular blue discs of light moving rapidly before me, and intermittent in character, like the light of a firefly. At another time I saw a similar light of a bright red colour. I was told by a relative who spoke to me immediately afterwards that there was also a green light, but this I did not see. Many of the sitters could see lights and faint forms when I could see nothing, and the psychic said she could see the forms, features, and dresses of people. She also often saw a hand writing names, which she then called out. If the name was known to the sitter near whom it appeared, the visitor was generally allowed by the control to speak. This system seems to have been devised to keep out visitors coming to the séance from idleness or curiosity, for it was apparent that they came as the ghosts appeared to Odysseus in Hades at first one by one, then in an awe inspiring swarm.

The other physical phenomena, not being vocal, were the movements of the trumpets, with which people were touched, and which were sometimes shaken or upset; sitters were at times sprinkled with water, or felt a cool breeze of air. At one séance I had a hand placed on my knee by a friend who wished me goodbye. Three dogs of mine, which died some thirty years ago, came on three or four occasions. They all barked, and one small lap-dog was placed for a short time on my knees. It was also held up so that its cold nose touched my cheek, and I think this was also done to two of the other sitters who were near me. One of the dogs was said to be running about within the circle, and it apparently touched one of the trumpets which rocked to and fro on the floor with a vibrating sound. The entity known as Blossom, supposed to be an Indian child, came several times. She generally entered the circle with a loud, high-pitched cry, something between a scream and a chuckle, but at the same time musical and childlike. As I had heard her last year, and she was known to be an expert in identifying articles, I had brought in my pocket a small shell with a peculiar toothed mouth, which I took out and held in my hand, asking her what it was. She said at first it was a bone, but when told this was not quite correct, said "a shell." At a request for further particulars, said it had five teeth in its mouth. I had not then counted them myself, but the number was quite right. At another séance I gave her an even more difficult test. While walking round the garden at Wimbledon, where the séances were held, I found embedded in the garden pathway a very perfect paleolithic flint, evidently a harpoon head, with one barb, and I supposed it was intended for catching seals or fish. It was, of course, a good many thousand years old, and as no one saw me find it, and I was careful not to show it to anyone, I could not imagine a better test object. Blossom at once said in a contemptuous tone, "Pooh! Fishing thing!", and then began to name jewellery and ornaments held out by other sitters, which seemed more worthy of interest than a rough flint. These she named correctly without hesitation. She, however, made a mistake about the number of gold coins I had in my pocket, saying that there were six when I only had five. When this was pointed out she at once retorted, "Look in the other pocket"; but even this did not save her, for, though there was silver in the other pocket, there was no sixth gold coin.

I heard her telling a naval officer, who was present, that his plans had been much upset, and that he had been very disappointed by a change that had been made in the date of the séance. She also told him the number of telegrams ("scratchums" she called them) that he had been obliged to send in connection with this alteration of dates. He said she was quite correct.

I was told by one relative at a séance that "everyone has a guide." I was at once interested, and thought that to get further information on the subject was to make inquiries as to my own case. Little scraps of information were given me at successive séances, with the result that my "guide" was said to be an Italian artist, who was born early in the sixteenth century. I found his name in a dictionary of painters, and the particulars given there agree essentially with those told to me. He was said to have two friends, contemporary artists of the same nationality, but much more celebrated than he was, and that they were all three occasional visitors at my studio.

I have always been interested in drawing and painting, and I do not know if "my guide" concerned himself in any of my other pursuits, but he evidently knows a good deal of this part of my life. At one séance he was announced, and said he had come down from the celestial sphere to the first sphere to speak to me. The proof he gave of his identity was remarkable. He said he had helped me to make three sketches some twenty-five years ago, which he named. I had almost forgotten them, though I have since found two in an old portfolio, and the third I now remember perfectly. He said one was a sketch of an old man, with a red turban. To which I replied: "Do you mean the old man sitting on the drum?" "Yes," he said, "that is the sketch I mean, but he was not sitting on the drum. The drum was by his side, and why did you not finish this sketch?" On examining the sketch afterwards I found that the man was sitting on a box, with the drum beside him, and the background had been left uncompleted. It is curious that two out of these three sketches won prizes at a provincial exhibition, and it is evident that they are considerably better in technique than any others in the portfolio, which were all done about the same time.

I made inquiries and asked many questions as to the environment, occupations, duties, beliefs, mode of life, etc., of relatives and friends who have preceded me, and I will not waste time by giving the questions I put, as the replies alone will be sufficient in most cases. I have tried to write these, from notes made immediately after each séance, as far as possible in the actual words given to me. They are probably not verbally accurate, as it was impossible to make any notes in a pitch dark room, but they are substantially correct, for I wish only to record facts and not support theories.

A Relative: "There are no churches, bishops, or priests."

A Relative: "We have a universal kind of religion, not founded by one man, but by the community in general."

A Relative: "Religion with us is one great universal one of love and beauty."

A Relative: "There is no set service, but we meet for singing among beautiful scenery. We have no personal deity, but our religion is right thought and action, following the dictates of conscience."

A Military Chaplain (with whom I had arguments regarding dogmas):"I was quite wrong, but you never know what is in a mans head till you irritate his heart. Without strife the truth will not be arrived at. There are Catholics, Protestants, Methodists, and Presbyterians. They are all on the bias, but God is here, and as there are a thousand roads in London so there are a thousand ways to reach the beyond."

A Relative (with reference to the last paragraph): "He then had settled opinions, but now found everything very different. He was ashamed of his dogmatism, and his talks about something he knew nothing about."

A Questioner: "When will the day of judgment be?" Answer: "Every day."

A Relative: "There are no such beings as angels or other non-human inhabitants known to us."

A Relative: I was originally a materialist, and could not believe what the Church taught, as the clergy did not practise what they preached. Some of Darwin's inferences are correct, others not so."

A Friend: Theosophy is not true in every sense, and there is no reincarnation." A Spiritualist: "Things are very much what I expected and taught."

A Schoolfellow, afterwards a naval officer: "There is no reincarnation. When I rowed my boat over the river I did not leave my oars crossed."

A Relative: "There are seven spheres, the highest being number seven."

A Relative: "Getting beyond the third, into the forth sphere, is like crossing the water into a new country."

A Relative: "The idea that the lower spheres are uncomfortable is all nonsense. On arrival at the forth sphere you will be welcomed by a crowd of friends. The whole journey will take about five minutes."

A Relative on the seventh sphere, second realm: "The terms 'sphere' and 'realm' may be understood by supposing the sphere to be a kind of mansion, though not a mansion of stone and brick. You enter at the front door into a large hall, in which are other doors leading into separate rooms. These rooms might indicate the different realms."

Another relative, on the sixth sphere: "The realms are departments of the spheres. I myself do not belong to any realm. You may imagine a person living in a certain house, corresponding to a sphere, who might or might not belong to a club, corresponding to a realm, which was only visited at times."

A Relative: "When I passed over I had the choice of going to higher spheres or of remaining among earth conditions. I chose the latter, as I wished to stop among familiar scenery. I stayed there till I was quite tired out, and then elected to join my father, who was on the sixth sphere." When asked if he regretted the first choice he had made he replied: "When anyone has a good suit of clothes on he will hesitate to cast them off if he does not know what the next suit will be like."

A Relative: The sphere called 'Mercury' is a very hot place, and we do not speak of it."

A Relative: "First arrival on the other side is not disagreeable. I was astonished and surprised at the interesting surroundings in which I found myself, but soon discovered that I was obliged to make my chief happiness in helping others. Everyone could do this if he wished, in either world."

A Relative: "The colours of the seventh sphere are: three greens, five mauves, five browns, five blues, three whites, three yellows, slate colour, shot colour, drab and dove colour. (Total, twenty-eight.)"

A Relative: "The colours of the celestial sphere are white (pure snow-white)' scarlet (like the setting sun), indigo, purple, cinnamon, brown, golden brown, and, greatest of all, orange and blue (the colours of Jesus of Nazareth). There are no half colours or half tones, no mauves or greens. (Total, seven, excluding white.)"

A Relative: "Mars (the planet) is inhabited by a short, dark people, resembling the people here. They have no houses, only huts."

A Voice: "Voices here are produced by the materialisation of the vocal chords, only, in the trumpets, and not by the materialisation of the throat and mouth."

A General Officer: "I am quite astonished at being able to talk with you. I never imagined such a thing was possible till I was told just now. I hope you will let me know whenever there is an opportunity again, for I enjoy having a crack."

A Relative: "No one can be a guide till he has reached the celestial sphere."

A Relative: "Various pets are kept by us, the men having horses, others dogs, birds, lambs, and other animals."

A Relative: "Chinese, Indian, and other foreign people have separate communities, and there is very little intercourse between them."

A Soldier who won the Victoria Cross: "I am very happy, and as straight as a string."

A Relative: "I help in the kindergarten school, teach singing and amuse the children by talking to them of flowers and showing them my dogs. There are many hundred children."

A Relative: "We can sleep if we like. Time is the same as with you, also the summer and winter, but we do not feel the cold."

A Relative: "Later on a catastrophe will happen to the world. The date is not known, but it will depend upon the planetary influence of Mars and Venus. Something will fall upon it—rocks, and water, and heat. Some people will perhaps be left alive, but it will come like a thief in the night."

A Friend (who had visited Egypt): "If you go to Egypt, don't bring back a mummy case, or anything at all, not even a cat. Leave it alone. I don't wish to speak of it."

A Relative: "There has lately been a great increase in the number of people on the earth. A thousand years ago the world had only one quarter of the number of its inhabitants."

The last part of a farewell address by a control:—

"......When the veil will be torn away, and beyond the river an angel will call. At that time there will be no police or judges, no persons or churches, but every man, woman, and child will be guided by a good conscience."

A Relative: "I felt sinking and sinking, till at last something broke— the thread of life. I was then able to see what passed, and saw my own body. I came back again in the evening; and on the day of the funeral, where I was an unseen guest."

The Same: "I am not there, only my body, which is no more than a cast off garment."

The Same: "I was given charge, after my death, by higher and wiser people, of a kindergarten. This gave me a great insight into the new world."

The Same: "Children from the age of three to six are assigned to the sixth sphere. In the fifth sphere the children are from seven to nine.

Younger children are in the higher spheres. Children who have had no earth life are called 'saints' and go at once to the 'celestial'." [N.B.—It may be assumed from the above that children from one to three years of age would go to the seventh sphere.]

A Celebrated painter, who died in the seventeenth century: "Put down your impressions. There is a perfect and an imperfect side to everything—i.e., imperfect to the eye. If you take a stream, one side is interesting and the other not so, and on this dull side put in a figure, an animal, or a rock, to fill it out."

A Relative: "We use our eyes as you do, though somewhat differently. Reading a closed book is possible, though not easily done. Still, we are able to penetrate through objects to some extent—for instance, to sense the condition in a stone."

A Brother Officer, who had been beheaded on active service: "My end was fore- ordained and planned ahead. It was arranged according to the position of the planets."

The Same: "I woke up on the third day, like all the others, and saw my own body."

A Brother Officer: "I regretted my attempt to settle in a new colony, for there I lost the position I had in India. People going out there expect too much. It is a great mistake to go out, as I did, beyond middle age."

Another Officer: "I am on the fifth sphere. It is good enough for me. If I had had a home as good as this is while on earth, I should never have wanted to leave it."

A Relative: "My work is in a children's school, where I teach painting and the science of colours."

A Relative: "My coming to a séance is not in any way prejudicial to my advancement, and does not make bad conditions."

A Relative: "There are no societies or churches with us. If information on any subject is wanted, it can be got from the higher teachers. Instruction is given by actual demonstration, and people are made to see everything for themselves."

A Relative: "The atoms themselves could be seen, though their vibrations are too rapid for observation."

A Relative: "Robert Ingersoll had not been able to find anyone through whose aura his work could be continued."

A Control: "I have been doing my present work for a great many years. I am quite happy and satisfied so long as I can help and give comfort to others. I may be employed in the same way for another thirty years."

A Relative: "The higher spheres have a more rapid vibration than the lower. They are also more like a home among friends."

I have already said that I do not wish to support theories, but I am tempted to finish this account with a quotation from the work of one of the most eminent astronomical writers of the present day. The book is so technical that perhaps a good many would not care to read it, but the quotation shows how nearly physical science is approaching the region which some of us are now trying to investigate and understand.

"The ether is assuredly the seat of intense activities which lie at the root, most likely, of all the processes of nature. Cosmic influences can be exerted only through its aid: unfelt it is the source of solidity, unseen it is the vehicle of light; itself non- phenomenal, it is the indispensable originator of phenomena. A contradiction in terms, it points the perennial moral that what eludes the senses is likely to be more permanently and intensely actual than what strikes them" (*Modern cosmogonies*, by Agnes M. Clerke, Hon. Member R. A. S., etc., pp. 191,198).

E. R. Johnson.
26 Aubrey Walk,
Kensington, W.,
August 11, 1913

This narrative is written by the same practical lady who penned the account of her experiences in 1912.

I have again been asked by Admiral Moore to write some of my experiences with the wonderful medium, Mrs. Wriedt, with whom I sat this summer seven times. I had five private sittings (two of which were blanks) and two circle sittings. I am extremely sorry I am still unable to publish my name and address, as I feel very strongly that these reports carry far more weight when the writers name is given; but my friends on the other side will not permit me to do so, as they say my relatives here would not understand in their present state, and would only say I was "queer." As most of the conversation at my private sittings would not either interest or convince the public. I propose to deal chiefly with incidents which took place at the two circle sittings; and only to give one or two conversations which I had at private ones. At the private sittings I had several good tests of spirit identity; but, I must add, I absolutely failed to get any of the tests I asked for. This seems to be often the case, and is quite unaccountable.

The two public circles I attended on June 11 and 16 were, to my mind, most convincing and interesting. We sat about twelve people, none of whom I had met before excepting Miss Harper and the medium. Everyone present had, I think, some message, and I heard a great deal of the other people's conversations, though at times their spirit friends spoke too low and so very near them that I missed some. The chief thing that impressed me at the first circle was the easy way a spirit came and talked to some Dutch people next to me, first in English and then in Dutch; they appeared very satisfied and pleased with all they got. Another spirit who came to a naval officer and his wife called herself Mabel, and she had great difficulty in explaining why she had come, as they could not locate a Mabel. Dr. Sharp came and helped her out, and said, "This little spirit Mabel has come to tell that lady and gentleman that she was the influence in their house some time ago when they sat with a lady medium, and got some incorrect messages through about Mrs. Wriedt. This little spirit has never before had the opportunity to clear herself and tell them that the medium was not a reliable one, and it has been a great worry to her." This information much startled the people to whom it came, and they said it was perfectly true that in 1911 they had received, through a medium in their house, some messages about Mrs. Wriedt, which afterwards they found to be absolutely untrue; but, at the time, they had believed them, and it had prevented their taking sittings with Mrs. Wriedt in 1911. They, however, sat with her in 1912, and were quite satisfied that there was no truth in the things which had come through that medium.

A voice came to me saying, "I am (blurr) father." I said I could not hear, and it turned out to be "your husband's father." He gave a short message, and kissed me through the trumpet, touching me gently in the middle of my cheek. At this séance the spirit lights were lovely, and several people exclaimed at the same moment that they were being sprinkled with water.

The second circle I attended on June 16, at 7 o'clock. Among the sitters I found a well-known clergyman and his wife. He first repeated, at the mediums request, the Lord's prayer, and afterwards sang "Lead kindly Light," in which several spirit voices joined, one being very deep, and I think it must have been John King's voice. After this, Cardinal Newman spoke at great length, and particularly addressed the clergyman present, congratulating him on his advanced views, and giving quite a little sermon on "Spirits in Prison," much of which I lost owing to the voice dropping at times to almost a whisper; but those who heard it said it was very beautiful. A lady in the circle was slightly deaf, and her spirit friends could not make her hear, and at last tried giving her symbols instead of talking, which proved quite satisfactory to the lady. One spirit who came showed the medium his thumb, with a covering over the whole arm, and also gave the medium his name (I think written in the air); anyhow, he was recognised then at once, and I thought this a splendid test. John King came in and told the lady she was very sceptical, and that was the reason her spirit friends found it so difficult to talk to her.

After this a voice spoke to me and said "I am Uncle E——." "But," I said, "There must be a mistake, for I had no uncle of that name." The reply came immediately, "Yes, you had." I then asked: "On which side of the family?" Reply: "On your father's side." It then flashed across my mind that I had a great uncle on my father's side of the name mentioned, but I had never known him; he died before I was born. I then asked: "Are you a great uncle?" Reply: "Yes, I am your great uncle. Your father sent me to speak to you," he went on. "Well the boy has not come then." I said: "What boy?" Reply: "Your husband."

I then said: "No, he could not come; some business kept him; it was not that he did not wish to come." He added a few words and left. (My husband had intended sitting that evening in place of me, but was prevented doing so.) Julia came soon after this and wished us all Goodnight, and I had a conversation on psychic development with her.

At one of my private sittings my father, who came, replied as follows to questions:— Question: "Who dined with me last night?"

Answer: "Merl," it sounded like.

Question: "I cannot understand that; will you say it more clearly, please?"

Answer: "Your sister." (correct.) He could not get the name out, so I gave him her nick-name, to which he replied:

"That is not her real name, only her child name." He then gave her real name.

He left me, and Mrs. Wriedt saw the name "Home." The name, however, was given by the spirit soon after, and proved to be a friend who passed over, when quite young, a few years ago. I asked: "Where are you L——?"

Reply: "I am with my mother."

Question: "And do you see your father?"

Answer: "Yes, but I am more with my mother."

This I think, is very likely to be the case, as her father died long after her mother, and I feel sure would not, in any case, be in as high a sphere as either his wife or daughter. When she left me she gave me her old laugh (quite a typical one) into the trumpet, and said: "Good-bye, old girl." This she said in life, and it was a good proof, I consider, of her identity.

At another private sitting I asked my father what some of his sons were doing: they are mostly abroad. I named one who has lately taken to good works, and changed all his religious ideas.

I said: "What is G—— doing?"

Answer: "He is a proselyte."

This is a true description, but proselyte was not a word I should ever have used in connection with him. *I am still much in the* dark as to understanding this philosophy, but of one thing I am sure, there is much yet for us all to learn, and that to those who attend séances in the right spirit much will yet be given.

On June 5 Mr. F. F. Cook, of Brooklyn, U. S. A., the author of *Whence, Why, and Whither*, was my guest at a private circle with Mrs. Wriedt. The conditions were very good, but, for some inexplicable reason, it was not a very successful séance. He was not in the least disconcerted, and while going back in the train we both prophesied that he was not to leave England without better proof of Mrs. Wriedt's gift. His second and last séance with her took place on June 9. The following day he wrote to me as follows:—

Authors' Club, 2 Whitehall Court,
S.W., June 10, 1913.

Dear Admiral,

As we rather anticipated, the séance was a wonderful success from the start, for more than two hours of almost continuous demonstration. Not only did the supernal visitors join in singing, but someone added what appeared to be a cornet performance. I was particularly favoured. My wife came with many demonstrations of affection, and was pleased to see me in good health and enjoying myself so well. Later an old spiritualist friend (Mr. Newton), who died about fifteen years ago, announced himself, and we had a jolly chat, and he reported himself in "apple-pie order"—very characteristic of him. He said my wife had brought him, and when I remarked he had a rather sudden exit, he replied: "Yes, the cars broke my neck." That is true; the accident happened at the Fiat-iron Building crossing, in New York, and led to greater protection for others. John King was in immense form, and spoke for fifteen minutes or so, in a voice that would have filled Albert Hall. He announced to me that Margaret Kane was present. "Who?" I inquired. "Why, Margaret Fox Kane, and she wants to thank you for what you did for her." This was a wonderful test. When in her aberration she pretended to "expose" her raps, and was deserted by spiritualists generally; I looked her up, and it was at the house of Mr. Newton that I met her. I then cared for her for a year or two, with the help of others whom I interested in her, until her death, about fifteen years ago. At first I wondered why Newton should come; but you see the connection, which did not occur to me until after the séance. It was very wonderful indeed, yet the "conditions" were exceedingly bad; the weather was heavy and threatening, it rained later during the night; and there were eight women to three men......

> —Always sincerely yours,
> Frederick F. Cook.

From a lady friend who lives at Twickenham:— August 20, 1913.

I have been very interested in spiritualism for many years, and have been in many séances, but never got any convincing personal evidence till my last séance with Mrs. Wriedt, on August 20 of this year. My husband and I sat alone with her, and we had hardly taken our seats when we heard the trumpet move and a faint voice talking. Mrs. Wriedt called out: "Do you know anyone called Nugent, for he is here and wants to speak with you?" I said I had a brother of that name, and at once the voice got stronger, and we had a long conversation. He addressed my husband by his surname, as he always did in life, and asked after our "Boys, especially the baby, who is a darling." I said: "He is no baby, but a Captain," and he said: "I know, he is a splendid fellow, and you may well be proud of him." After more conversation, too private to be of general interest, he was followed by another brother, who opened the conversation by saying, with a laugh: "This is a new kind of thing, isn't it?" He also said: "We are all young here; I'm not an old man." He was about forty-seven when he passed over. The next manifestation was very startling. Mrs. Wriedt said: "I see the head of a man with white whiskers, and he is bowing to you." A minute or less later we saw what looked like the head of an old man bowing towards us, and soon after heard a voice calling "William," My husbands name. This was his father, who seemed delighted to see him, and made some most gratifying remarks to us both of praise and affection. He seemed distressed to think my husband was not well, and when he said he was ill, he said: "No, he is weakly, but was never one to complain"—very characteristic of him. He was followed by an aunt of my husband's, who said his mother was going to speak to him, which she soon afterwards did. She also addressed him by name, and, like his father, thanked me for all the care and kind nursing I had given him. I said: "Then you must know of his bad illness," and she replied: "Of course, we were all there." She then asked me, "How were the children?" and when I said I was very anxious about one, who had constant bad luck, she said: "Don't fret about him. His Horoscope will change in 1915, and things will go better with him." This, coming from an Evangelical Protestant, who, in life knew nothing of astrology, or any strange 'ologies, was very remarkable. I then asked her how she knew we were there, and she answered: "Why, the boys told me." I said: "What boys? Do you mean my brothers?" She said: "Yes, they are so good to me, more like my own sons; I am very fond of them." As she never knew them in life, this also seems interesting and strange. After taking a touching farewell of us, saying she was "waiting for us in the sweet beyond," the most wonderful manifestation of the sitting happened. We saw a globe of light forming on a vase of flowers, and Mrs. Wriedt called out: "Do you know any gentleman who has had two fingers shot off, as I see a maimed hand?" I thought at once of a cousin, a Colonel W——, who had such a hand, and then we saw floating in front of us a ball of light, with two fingers reflected fluttering on it. My husband said: "You must be John W——," and he said: "Of course I am. Didn't you see my hand? I have my five fingers again, though, now." He then addressed my husband as "General," and with a laugh said, "You have beaten me, General," meaning that he had lived longer. (Mrs. Wriedt later apologised for not having given my husband his title, not being aware of it.) I asked him if he had any message for his widow, who has married again, and he said: "Give her my love. I am so glad she is happy and contented again, as she was very lonely." I then said: "Do you often see her?" He said: "Every day"; and on my asking him if he knew everything that went on here, he said: "I am not infallible, and only God is that, who knows everything," and much more in a serious strain, very remarkable, coming from one who, on this side, was very jocular and light-hearted. He also told us, as did my brothers, that he was quite happy.

People often ask what is the use of spiritualism, even if it is true, as the communications are often so trivial. They have not been so in our case, and we returned from this séance not only convinced, but happy, faith in human survival having turned to knowledge of the same; and, for the rest, "content to wait."

(Signed)   Barbara Gillespie.

My husband wishes to confirm the above, and to add his satisfaction with the convincing manifestations he both saw and heard.

(Signed)   B. Gillespie.

The following, from Miss Estelle Stead, gives an abridged account of a few of her sittings at Cambridge House:—

On May 6, 1912. I went down to Cambridge House full of grief, sorrow, and bewilderment, wondering and hoping. I was not alone at the sitting; several others were present. The scent of flowers filled the room, and there was a feeling of awe and expectancy in the air. The lights were turned off, and for a few moments we sat in darkness; then came a bright light, followed by the etherealisation of one I admire and love, who passed over into spirit life some years ago; this passed, and in its place I saw my fathers face. For a few seconds I gazed, hardly able to realise that he had indeed passed over and was not physically among us in the circle as of old. Then the etherealisation faded, and in a few seconds his voice rang through the room. He spoke to me, and for a little time our emotion overcame us, and then he bade me not to grieve. But he himself was full of grief at having to go when there was still so much to be done—"if only he could come back for an hour"—and I found myself comforting him. It was a meeting full of anguish, mingled with joy. He talked of home matters, of people, of arrangements, etc., all unknown to Mrs. Wriedt or the other sitters.

On June 3, 1912, my brother and I had a private sitting. Mrs. Wriedt put out the lights, and started the musical-box. Presently we saw a light in the cabinet, and in a few minutes we saw father's face etherealised. He came right out of the cabinet over us. It was not quite so clear an etherealisation as the first time I saw him, but it was unmistakably father. He seemed to be holding his hand to his face. He disappeared, and presently we saw him again; this time he did not move from the cabinet, and the etherealisation was clearer. He turned to my brother and to me and smiled. My brother said he saw his tie and collar and front quite plainly. Again it disappeared; then once more we saw him, and this time he came right over to us. He disappeared, and we waited a few minutes; then Will spoke. He greeted us both, and said father would speak in a few minutes, and we soon heard father's strong voice, full of emotion, as he greeted us both, and we talked for some time about our life and work etc. He spoke of the strikes going on in England at the time, etc., and how he would wield his pen still, but was unable. He could go to the office, but no one saw him, or heard him.

On Monday June 7, 1912, we had another sitting, and it was at this sitting that father gave us the signal light with which he had invariably signalled his approach at our sittings since.

This year (1913) I have had four sittings, three with splendid results. At the second sitting, directly the lights were out, we saw round the musical-box a cloud of light; this faded, and fathers signal followed. He then greeted us, his voice as strong as ever; but he had no sooner done this than the trumpet was put down, and, although we started the musical-box and sat for some time, we got nothing more. The following day I had a sitting, and Will explained the reason for the sudden breaking off. It was of a private nature, and enabled one to realise more than ever the delicacy and difficulty of communion.

At the three other sittings the lights were hardly out before father gave his signal, and commenced talking at once. At times he would tell us he was tired, and put down the trumpet, and my brother Will or some friend on the other side would carry on the conversation while he rested. We spoke of the past, my work at present, and discussed many things; but I must admit very little of what his life and surroundings are at present. He is still keenly interested in affairs here on here on this earth, and very busy helping and impressing from where he is; but he says he is realising more and more the wonder of the life

To which he has gone; he would not come back, although at times he longs to wield his pen again.

Added to my notes I find the following:—

"There always seems so much to say, and so little time do they have power, that I had no time to ask about his life or impressions," etc. etc.

Many will agree to feeling thus; but all who have had the privilege of sitting with Mrs. Wriedt must love and revere her for that subtle power which she so generously allows to be used to enable us to talk with our loved ones, and to know without a doubt that communication is possible.

E. W. Stead.

The following narrative is from Lieutenant Basil W. R. Hall, R. N., Inspector of Lifeboats. The lady he alludes to as "C." wrote an account last year:—

A few years ago no one could have been more sceptical of the possibility of a life after death than I was. I have always been deeply interested in the discoveries of modern physical science, and steeped myself at one time in the literature of the materialistic school of the latter half of the nineteenth century—Spencer, Huxley, and the rationalists.

It appeared to me then that these discoveries not only cast a doubt on the idealistic philosophy, but absolutely disproved it; so that I came, like Huxley, to adopt the belief that there was not any life after death, as an article of philosophic faith.

This somewhat positive attitude was shaken first by Wallace's Miracles and Modern Spiritualism, and later on by other books on the subject, notably that by Admiral Usborne Moore, *Glimpses of the next state*, which appealed to me as the work of one whose training and reading had led him to look on life in much the same way as myself. Finally, the first séance my wife attended, when I was unable to be present, did much to convince me.

The first séance I went to myself was on May 5, 1913; it was an absolute blank from beginning to end—not a shimmer of light or sound took place. The next was on May 7, which was very interesting; but, except for Blossom's remarkable knowledge of certain trifling events in my past life, did not affect me personally to any great degree. The third and last, is described in the following notes, in which it will be seen that the episodes related, although very trivial, are nearly all of a "test" nature. They allude, for the most part, to very trifling matters, of but little moment even to myself; but the very triviality of the statements and the method of their communication may serve to afford a calmer and more dispassionate test of the genuineness of the phenomena than if they had purported to be solemn messages from anyone who had been very near and dear in life. In this connection may I add that I went to these séances without either the expectation or, indeed, the desire to communicate with any special individual, but merely as an interested inquirer; and this very difference from the majority of those who attended the séances may possibly add a value of its own to the experiences related.

What these experiences prove I am far from having made sufficient study of psychical research to feel certain about my own mind; but they have convinced me, once for all, of the existence of phenomena in Nature wholly ignored by the physicists; and it must be confessed that the simplest explanation of these phenomena is that they are what they profess to be—namely, that the minds of those who have died on this earth continue to exist in another phase, and find means of communication with the minds of those still on earth. Any other solution of the problem would appear to land one in greater difficulties.

The following does not profess to contain a verbatim account of the conversations, but gives the gist of them truthfully:—

Notes of the séance held at Cambridge House, Wimbledon, on Tuesday, July 1, 1913. 7 to 8.30 p.m., in the presence of Mrs. Wriedt, the medium, and twelve others.

The séance began in the usual way by shutting off all light and setting the musical- box going. After the music stopped we sat more or less silent for a while; several people said they saw lights here and there, others that they saw figures, etc. During the whole séance, which lasted for nearly an hour and a half, I personally never saw anything whatever except the faint glimmer of the outside daylight at the window, which it had evidently been impossible to block out entirely.

After waiting some time a hymn was started, then another, and "Auld Lang Syne," during which a deep bass voice was heard in the trumpet joining in the singing; when it ceased, it was ascertained that this was John King. I pass over what he said, as he did not address himself particularly to me, and I propose in these notes to limit myself (with some exceptions) to my own experiences, as others are more competent than myself to deal with the more general aspect of what passed.

John King I may say, appeared to be present during the whole sitting, and occasionally interpolated remarks, sometimes commenting on or explaining those of the other voices.

Shortly afterwards the shrill, girlish voice of Blossom was heard in the trumpet, punctuated by ripples of laughter, as of one in the highest possible spirits. After "compliments," she began by stating what various people held in their hands, and apparently always correctly; but when C. asked her: "Blossom, what have I got in my hand?" she replied: "Pansies." "Oh no!" Said C. "Yes, it is pansies," said the voice, emphatically, and again, "pansies." So C. gave it up, murmuring something about her having made a bad shot this time.

(Note by C. My recollection of her first reply was: "Only a pansy blossom," and I thought she was unable to say what the article was, and was joking.—C. H.)

Next day C. held up to me the little mauve bag in which she carries her handkerchief, money, etc., etc., and remarked: "Funny that Blossom should have said 'pansies.' I don't know what she meant." "But they are pansies," I said at once, observing, for the first time with any care the little flowers embroidered over the bag. She showed the bag to a third person, who knew nothing of this conversation or the cause of it, and asked him what he thought the embroidered flowers were supposed to represent. "Pansies, I should say," he replied.

The only other episode of this nature was so remarkable that, although I did not occur to me personally, I cannot help referring to it. In reply to Colonel Johnson's query as to what he held in his hand, Blossom said: "A fishing thing."

(After the séance the Colonel showed me a small stone, and asked me what I thought it was. "A flint arrow-head ," I replied; but on closer inspection I saw that it was not an arrow-head, having only one side to the head, which was barbed, something like a harpoon. It was this, which he had picked up in the garden before the séance, that the Colonel had in his hand.)

Blossom then turned to me (I use this expression figuratively, of course; the voice appeared to be that of a person who was turning to address me), and said: "Well Hauley, how are you?" and added: "You have kept me running about a lot all last week—six different places......and such a lot of scratchums, scratchums, scratchums all the time......"

(As a matter of fact, I had had an unusually busy week, and had inspected a different lifeboat station every day, and had actually slept in six different places during the immediately preceding eight days, a fact which I verified by my diary afterwards; it was not in my head at the time. This extra work involved a correspondingly unusual amount of writing—reports, letters, demands for stores, etc.)

"......What do you mean?" I said, referring to the expression "Scratchums." "She means scratching on paper," put in C., in a low voice. "Yes," said Blossom at once. "Oh," I said, "that's true; I have had a lot of reports and letters to write." "Yes, and telegrams too," said she; "Three on Sunday because you were disappointed."

(As a matter of fact, I had sent precisely this number of telegrams on the Friday—not Sunday—and for the reason given. On account of the alteration in the date of the séance I had to give up a visit to Scotland, and in telegraphing to the friends with whom I should have stayed I used the word "disappointed"; the other two telegrams were sent for the same cause.)

"Yes," added Blossom. "And two today." "No, only one today," I replied. "No two." "No," I repeated; "I got one, and I sent one." "Well, that makes two," with a gleeful little shriek. Then, turning to C.: "You know, squaw, I was watching when you sent that telegram changing the place of meeting today, and when you came along the road to meet Hauley, and he walked, so tired...... You were so tired weren't you?" turning to me.

(C. had sent a reply paid telegram to me that morning, changing the place where she would meet me for tea, previous to the séance. She had come part of the way along the road to meet me. I, being late, had bicycled up Putney Hill rather faster than was good for me, and I was feeling rather tired and exhausted. Not a soul could have known anything of this trivial series of episodes but we two, and, presumably, the telephonist concerned.)

After many voices had spoken to various sitters, sometimes two at the same time, came one purporting to be that of C.'s mother, who, after greeting C., turned to me, saying; "Well, my son"; then, after some other conversation, she said: "You will like the new port." "What do you mean?" I said (my first thought was that she was alluding to a brand of wine!). "The new port," she repeated, "the new work in the south." Then I realised that she was alluding to the fact that I am transferring to the southern district in November. So I said: "Why shall I like it?" "Because," she replied; you will get into a new class, a new environment, and you will have a more contented mind. C., too, will be happier......"

Then the voice of C.'s sister, speaking to her, and afterwards to me, saying, among other things: "You will be happier and things will go better in October." "You mean November, I suppose," I said. No, October; you will be better in October." Presently, the voice of John King explaining that every seven years a man's mind and body are renewed and changes take place in him. Then I remembered that my birthday is in October, and that I then enter a new septennial period. It was this and not the new district I go to in November that was alluded to, I suppose.

(One word as to C.'s mother's use of the word "port." It is incredible that such a word to describe a new life-boat district could have occurred, by any remote possibility, to C. or myself, either consciously or sub-consciously. But thinking it over, I see that it is quite the sort of word that a woman might use who only knew me as a naval officer, and who would not necessarily be very accurate or careful in choice of the mot juste in technical matters, and both C. and I laughingly agreed that it is just such a phrase as her mother would have used.)

Among other remarks which passed between C.'s sister and myself was a question on my part; "Can you see me?" at the same time leaning forward, with elbow on knee, to catch her rather low-voiced reply: "Yes," she said, "I saw you lean forward then.)

(Signed)   Basil Hall.

The following notes are from a lady living in Oxford. Blossom is the little Indian spirit referred to:—

My daughter and I sat with Mrs. Wriedt at Cambridge House on May 19, at 2.30 p.m., and on June 21, at 1.30. On the first occasion the spirits of several relatives communicated with us, and one or two good tests were given. In one case inquiries were made about someone whose name I took to be "Alice," but the spirit who was talking immediately corrected me and gave the name "Ellis," recalling to my memory a relation of hers, a girl who bore this rather unusual name, and whom I had known slightly. In another a curious pet name was given quite clearly. These incidents struck me as noteworthy, because, on the whole, it was difficult to get names distinctly. This was especially noticeable at the second sitting, and consequently, though a succession of spirits spoke with us, identification was not always satisfactory. In some instances I am still in doubt whether our visitors were really the persons they purported to be. At the end of the sitting, however, a little Indian girl disclosed her presence by pulling a hairpin out of my hair and dropping it on the floor. In a voice much clearer than the others she remarked, laughingly, that "She had done that for fun." Then something touched my daughters knee, and the voice said: "I was sitting on your knee." She then commented on a white dress, "with a bit cut out off the neck," which she said she had seen her wearing "one day when it was hot." The following quaint colloquy then took place:—

"What was I doing when you saw me?"

"You don't mostly do anything."

"Really? I thought I was rather a busy person."

"No, you not. You only thinking; that's lazy business. You do all your busy thinking sitting still."

She went on: "Who gave you that picture on your bureau?" She described the picture as representing a man in a "boosting" suit—a man with a smooth face. We could not understand this, and she seemed rather annoyed, whereupon John King came in, very loud, to explain. He said: "Did you ever have a picture of your brother in a canoeing suit?" My daughter replied: "There was a photograph of him in his college boating suit over my writing table." "Yes, that is it. In her country they call it canoeing or 'boosting,' They do it with one oar, what you call paddling."

It was curious that all the Indian girl's remarks were applicable only to my daughters life at Oxford. The picture referred to hung, and still hangs, in the study there, where she worked until last October.

The séances of Mrs. S., of Bournemouth, in 1913 at Cambridge House, Wimbledon.

The first circle on May 8 was composed of Mrs. S.; her son, Mr. W. S., a civil engineer; her daughter and son-in-law, Commander and Mrs. V. U.; Mrs. Endicott, the Devonshire medium; and Admiral Usborne Moore.

The same people (with the exception of Mrs. Endicott) sat together on May 11, 1912.

Notes were taken by Mr. W. S. , and it is upon these I principally depend for the following account. I can vouch for their accuracy:—

Dr. Sharp first spoke to W. S.:

"How is my namesake?" He then told Mrs. S. to take her hand from her face, as he would not hurt her (a little joke).

He then spoke to V. U.: "The goose hangs high."

When asked to explain his meaning he said: "The saying is a Scotch one, meaning that all is going on well with you."

M.: "How are the conditions tonight doctor?"

Answer: "Splendid."

Mrs. S.: "Are we sitting right?"

Answer: "Yes, a good number." (Dr. Sharp has been heard several times to say that he prefers the circle to consist of seven people.)

M.: "We will remember this in future." After one or two further remarks Dr. Sharp said: "Au revoir."

Mrs. Wriedt sees initials C. A. R. (the middle initial is wrong), and soon a voice is heard:

"What are you doing here?"

M. explains.

The Voice: "Is that what you are doing?" M.: "It is Cecil Rhodes." Mr. Rhodes greets M.: and said he met him three years ago. (It was two years.) M.: "Do you see much of Stead?" C. R.: "Oh, yes, we are better friends than we were. I let my head run away with my heart, but Stead let his heart run away with his head." He went on to say that he was glad he had not left Stead his money, for certain reasons.

C. R.: "What do you think of this scandalous business in the East?" M.: "Are you not ashamed of this Montenegro business?" C. R.: "It's rascality; the Powers are a lot of savages. If I was here, I would fight; I would give it them hot, I bet. Give everyone a chance of earning bread and butter." W. S.: "Shall we not all be fighting soon?" C. R.: "Yes, it will be an universal and religious war." Mrs. V. U. "Why religious?" C. R. (in a hesitating way); "Because there is so much humbug in some religious people. I must be off; I am just passing through."

Annie S., a sister-in-law of Mrs. S., now manifested. She had passed over about a month before. She said in a very low and gentle voice: "Here I am." Two or three of the sitters exclaimed: "Are you Julia?" but Mrs. S. said: "Are you Annie?" Annie S.: "Yes, yes. How do you do?" (kisses in the trumpet). "We can talk freely here." Addressing herself to Mrs. V. U.: "How are you getting on with your music? I love to hear you. Do you still play the 'cello? I like it so much." Mrs. V. U.: "I did not know that you had ever heard me." Annie S.: "Oh, yes, I have" (Mrs. V. U. plays the violoncello); then, turning to Mrs. S.: "Well, dear, I am very happy to come; I am not at all sick. It is a great pleasure to see you all here. Goodbye." The spirit returned shortly after and said to Mr. V. U.: "I have a message for you; I am your Aunt Annie." (Mrs. V. U. was doubting her identity, which probably explains her coming back.)

Grayfeather burst in and spoke to M.: "You gettee scratchum from hitch-up" (meaning wife). M.: "There is some mistake." G.: "No, no mistake. She no sickee, but what you call 'cough'" (by "cough" he evidently meant pain). G. to Commander V. U.: "You stickee to me, I stickee to you." V. U.: "Why?" Grayfeather then reminded him that at a sitting last year he had indicated three rings for him (promotion), and had told him they would come "in cherry time". V. U. asked him if he would go to Halifax, as he had predicted last year? G.: "Yes, later on. You stickee to big red man. You know what red man tellee you? Big chief, he go to sleep, you take his place. Heap much die. When you go away it will be very suddenly." Here Grayfeather made the noise of a steamer passing through the water; it was most distinct and very well done.

The spirit of Mr. Richard Kelly, Mrs. S.'s brother, now came in, and spoke in a very gentle voice: "My sister is here; it is wonderful. I am so glad to see you." Mrs. S. asked him how he was getting on, and if he was happier; she added that she thought of him oftener than she used to. R. K.: "I am very happy, oh yes." He seemed to be with all his relations. Mrs. S. asked if her brother Fred could come as well; he said he would, but this promise was not fulfilled. R. K. to W. S.: "I see you: it is wonderful how very much you are like me as I was when a young man, in size, colouring, and movements." W. S.: "In disposition as well?" R. K.: "No, not at all. You are a much better man than I ever was. You are a very good man, a very good man. All family very well." Mrs. S.: "Talking is difficult when we meet like this." R. K.: "Not difficult, but charming."

Iola manifested, and spoke to M. and a few other sitters. She said she would not stay, as she wished to make room for others.

Grayfeather, again, speaking to W. S., made some remarks about his doing "scratchums" (i.e.., taking notes). He said it would not do much good. He then went on: "I like your little room very much." W. S.: "Which one, the one I sleep in, or the one I work in?" G.: ""The one you work in; heap much good influence." M. asked him to imitate a rocket. He first imitated the noise of a squib, then said he would send a great big rocket to Southsea. This he simulated exceedingly well. Iola's mother now came, and talked with M. and others in the circle. M. asked her if she was more reconciled to Grayfeather and his ways. She replied that, "when he came, she liked to go." This lady is distantly related to V. U., but passed over twenty-five years before he was born. She told him that his father was very well, and said: "My blessed boy, how are you?" adding that she was very glad to see him, his dear little wife, and his charming mother-in-law. (probably the surname of V. U., which is the same as her own, attracted her to the circle. It is often thus.)

Mrs. Wriedt described a rather short old lady standing close to M., of name Jane. She was also seen near Mrs. Endicott, and then walked outside the circle to V. U., and talked for some time with him and his wife. This lady turned out to be the wife of a veteran admiral, John M., and an aunt of V. U. She had been in spirit life over twenty years. She said, when speaking of her husband: "He will not be long here. I am waiting for him." V. U.: "What are you doing?" Answer: "Helping John." "What do you think of L.?" (one of her daughters, who had recently married a second husband). Her reply indicated that she thought if the couple were happy it was all right, and that the main thing is to live in comfort in this world. She also mentioned G. (another daughter), whom she said was very happy. She said: "It would not do to invite her husband to a séance." (This I can affirm to be true.)

The father of Mrs. S., Mr. Kelly, now manifested. He said that, during his earth life, he was much opposed to spiritualism, but he knew more now. "It is true, and everything that is true is worth investigating. What will not bear investigating is rot. It does no harm. A free-thinker thinks for himself: the man who thinks for someone else is a fool. The next generation has much more brains. They are wiser than I was, but we did good in other ways." The voice turned to Mrs. S.: "How do you do my little girl?" In conversation he talked quite easily of V. U. by his Christian name. M. asked him how this was. Mr. K. replied: "Of course, I know the name well; it is the name of my grandson-in-law. I hear it forty times a day; I hear my grandson-in-law's wife and my daughter say it, and my grandson." V. U.: "Do you often see us?" Mr. K.: "Oh, yes; I often look in at your table and elsewhere."

A voice tried to make itself understand by V. U., but it was very difficult to understand; the only clear word was "Admiral." Dr. Sharp asked the sitters not to talk so much, as he should hear more clearly if they talked less, and added: "The Admiral said: 'Hulloa, Captain! Hulloa U.!'" He then described the spirit as a man with white hair, white moustache—" whiter and of bigger build than M." (Admiral Usborne Moore). It was suggested that it might be Admiral Foley, and Dr. Sharp said "Yes, that is right."

The Admiral now came again. Asked if he was Admiral Foley, he answered: "Yes; Well! Well!" He talked to V. U. about a commission they had served together. V. U.: "I am sorry that you passed over." The spirit: "I wasn't well; I suffered internally. I should have given up before." Turning to M., the voice said: "How are you Admiral Moore?" M. conversed with the spirit for a minute or two about his father, under whom M. had served in H. M. S. Revenge just fifty years ago.

During the séance Commander and Mrs. V. U. were touched several times with the trumpet. Occasionally two voices were heard simultaneously. Mrs. Endicott saw phantoms, and was often touched by the trumpet. She once saw two babies together. Mrs. Wriedt saw a few symbolical pictures, also a black-edged letter being presented to her. At the end of the sitting a very small voice was heard in the trumpet saying: "Goodnight, mother." Mrs. Endicott thought it was probably her baby daughter, who comes very often to wish her "Goodnight."

On May 18, 1913. Mrs. S. invited her family circle again. This time there were present Mrs. S., Commander and Mrs. V. U., Mr. W. S. and Mrs. Scratcherd. I was not present, but I again depend upon the careful notes of W. S. I understand that Mrs. V. U. expressed a wish, audibly, for the exhibition of the commoner sort of physical phenomena. Her wish was complied with. Trumpets were moved and put into ridiculous positions; flowers were handed about; a small table was moved about, and fell down several times. The most important phenomenon was the following:—

The small table, with a vase of flowers standing upon it, was outside the circle. Mrs. Wriedt and the other five sitters were holding hands, Mrs. Wriedt's left hand holding the right hand of W. S., and her right hand holding the left of V. U. The table, with vase upon it, moved in to the circle, between Mrs. Wriedt and V. U. In order that the vase should not be upset by their joined hands, Mrs. Wriedt relinquished the hand of V. U., still holding the hand of W. S. The table proceeded on, clattering along the floor, and upset sideways in the centre of the circle, close to the feet of V. U.: vase, water, and flowers forming a mess on the linoleum.

Nothing occurred which afforded evidence of the proximity of spirit friends of the sitters. The lights were lit now and then to see what particular phenomenon had been performed. In comparison with Mrs. S.'s séance of May 8, this sitting may be called a failure.

This communication is from a lady at Hove, who sat at Cambridge House with a friend, Mrs. C——:——

We attended five séances at Cambridge House. The first was a blank. The second was very interesting; upon singing "Lead kindly Light." A voice was heard joining in through the trumpet: Then Dr. Sharp's loud and distinct Scotch tones greeted us. I understand he is one of the medium's controls, and he talked a good deal at this sitting. A lady present asked him if the doctrine of reincarnation were true, and he answered that he had never heard anything about it on that side. Voices came one after the other, sometimes through both trumpets simultaneously. We were struck by the prattling tones of a little child talking to and answering the questions of his parents. Just after, we heard a bark of a large dog.

Then I heard my name whispered quite close—"C."; then again with my surname. I said; "Who is it?" The voice whispered "Mother." I said: "I cannot recognise the voice or hear very well." It replied: "I have never been to an affair of this kind before." I said: "Try to tell me something that I may know it is you, mother." The voice: "Aunt E—— was very ill this winter." This fact is correct, and was only known to myself and husband (who was not present), so I fekt assured my beloved parent, recently passed away, was trying to speak. My friend's first name. "I——." Was said. She answered the voice, which seemed to be her husband; he said a relation had helped him to come, and he spoke of his children; but my friend could not get their names from him, though he referred to the confirmation of the one.

Séance No. 3 was a failure—no voices, but when the light was switched on, one trumpet was balanced on the top of the other.

Séance No. 4. A number of voices spoke—an Indian girl Blossom, a man Grayfeather, who sang by request in his language. Several relatives spoke to my friend; an old lady in Hebrew; also her brother and uncle appeared to speak. My friend was startled by the touch of a cold hand on her face; she cried out: "Who touched me?" Voice: "I did, dear; your sister." The trumpet then touched us both on the knees, and I touched the metal with my hand.

Séance No. 5. A private one, and most satisfactory. Mrs. C——'s husband talked some little while with her about their sons' future, giving his views very decidedly about sport, and saying he did not wish them to enter a certain profession, etc.; also he asked to be presented to me. "Introduce me to your friend," were the words—a good test, as I never saw him.

Then a very old lady's voice spoke, saying she was Mother or Grandmother C——. She said; "When S—— first came he was distracted at leaving you and the children; he wondered how you would get on." A voice came to me, giving three names. My husband's father; he wished his son were present too, and sent a message to his own wife. Tell her I am with her morning, noon, and night." Another voice claimed to be my husband's brother. "Have you forgotten Ted?" "No; very glad to hear you; have you seen your father?" "The guv'nor; why, he has just been." This very jovial spirit touched me on the head and face with the trumpet very gently. Then mother's voice lovingly spoke of family matters; and, turning to Mrs. C——, I am so pleased to see you." My friend replied: Dear Mrs.——, do you really show yourself to H.?" (A mutual friend who is clairvoyant.) "Yes, dear, I do; I do." I could not restrain my tears, and said: "I only wish I could see you too; I miss you dreadfully." She replied: "Don't cry, darling; I had to go; it was God's will; I am so happy; try and be happy"; and we heard her sob too. I said: "Does it trouble you to come?" Reply: "Oh, no! I am so glad." "Are you ever with dad, and H——, and Grannie?" "With them all, and H—— is here now." She made the sound of kissing and left.

H—— then came, and made a joke about his surname, which I could not understand. John King (Mrs. Wriedt called him) came for a moment, and explained ti. H—— then reappeared, and talked to us. I said: "How long have you been in spirit life? Tell me, if you remember." He answered: "Over twenty years." (Correct, twenty-two.) "I found work to do directly I came till now." I wish I had asked what work; here he was a lawyer. He said one or two private things, speaking very affectionately to me. I asked: "Can my father speak to me?" Reply: "I will go and see if I can find the old gentleman." However, that was the end; no other voices came.

My friend and I have talked it over carefully, and we came to the conclusion that we could not recognise one of the voices, because it is like hearing them afar off through a telephone. Occasionally there was a difficulty in getting names; but the manner and way of speaking were just like my mother, kind and sweet, and her husband, slow and deliberate. Further, the private matters referred to were only known to ourselves; and in the case of my mother she spoke first of an incident which I should not have even mentioned before others. To sum up, we believe our dear ones must have communicated with us. Who else could?

The following notes have been sent to me by a friend, a military man upon whose accuracy I can implicitly rely:—

The following is an account of several private sittings with Mrs. Wriedt during May and June 1913. Names and places are suppressed, and fictitious initials given, for obvious reasons. Much was of such a private nature that it could not be published. It will be observed that at one or two sittings practically no results were obtained. The sitters sat in a circle, the trumpet on the floor in the centre, and the room was in complete darkness during all the phenomena, with the exception of the time when the trumpet rose up as described, when the red light was turned on and everything clearly visible in the room.

First sitting: May 10. Eight sitters.

John King spoke loudly through the trumpet, and came repeatedly during the sitting to explain what the other voices could not make intelligible. He told us his name had been Henry Morgan when on this sphere; that he had been at one time Governor of Jamaica, and that he could speak more clearly than other spirits because he had been practising for two hundred years. A voice came to one of the sitters, a lady, and held a long conversation in fluent Italian, and appeared to send kisses into the trumpet. The lady said she recognised the spirit as a Monseigneur whom she had known very well in Rome. He was over seventy then, and he used to kiss her. He spoke of political and private events, and gave the name of a Cardinal whom he said would be elected Pope after the death of the present one. Another voice spoke to another sitter, advised him on business matters, and warned him against investing money in a proposition lately received. The sitter said the advice was quite to the point, and he was glad to have it. A voice came to a lady saying, "I am your Uncle B——, and I am known to your husband but not to you." He asked after the health of her husband, calling him by his full Christian name, which was never used by his family. The lady did not, at the time, recognise this spirit, but told us afterwards that she had found out that all was correct, and that he alone used to call her husband by his full name. Grayfeather came and said he had not been sent by Admiral Moore as he had been last year, but came now of his own accord to see how we were getting on. He told us the Admiral was in his wigwam. This was correct, as he had just gone to Southsea.

Voices joined in singing, and a cornet was played. Several sitters were tapped on the head. A voice called the Christian name of one of the sitters, which was recognised by another sitter (a relative also) as his father's voice, and said, "How are you darling A——?" to his granddaughter, who was in the circle. He asked after his grandson, and said he disliked being so far away, and that he could do as good work nearer home. The grandson is now in East Africa. As a test he gave us his daughters name correctly, which is a most uncommon one. He spoke of private matters correctly, and had the same abrupt manner which he had in his lifetime.

A voice spoke a long time to another sitter, saying he had known him in South Africa, that he was in the —— Regiment, and had been killed at Spion Kop when with his regiment. This spirit was not recognised, and the regiment he mentioned was not in Natal during the war.

Second sitting: May 15. The same sitting with the exception of one lady.

After a long wait the trumpet was taken up, and a voice, at first feeble then stronger, said he was Arch-deacon Colley, that he knew we all sympathised with him, and that he was perfectly happy now. Several sitters were touched on the face and head outside the circle. One was tapped on the shoulder by the trumpet, and one of the sitters felt a cold hand laid on her face. The trumpet was held by one sitter to his ear, and he heard a faint whisper "I can't."

Third sitting May 20. Same circle as in number one.

One of the sitters brought a large gramophone horn, which was placed in the centre by the trumpet, on a small table. Directly the lights were put out one of the sitters felt the horn put on his knee, and nearly all the sitters were touched by the horn. A long Latin prayer was said through it. John King spoke through the horn in stentorian tones, saying he liked it. A spirit stating that she was Marie Antoinette spoke for a long time in French to a French lady present. The horn was then placed over the head of one of the sitters, the lights were turned on, and it was seen in this position. The lights were put out again, and the circle joined hands. The sensitive's hands were held by two

gentlemen present. When the lights were turned on againit was found that the table had been turned over, and the trumpet was inside the horn, which had been inverted. No sound was heard.

Forth sitting: May 29. Same circle as number one, with two ladies extra.

Voice to a sitter: "I am Z——." Q.: "Do you mean Z——? It is a long time since we met, is it not?" A.: "Yes, a very long time."

Q.: "Do you remember the crammer we were at together?" A.: "Yes." Q.: "Can you give me his name?" After many unintelligible attempts the name was given nearly correctly. Q.: "can you remember the names of any others there?"

Two names were given which were not correct. John King said afterwards that this spirit had passed over at a certain place, which was correct. Another voice: "I am Y—— ——."

Q.: "Are you the Y—— who was in my regiment, and who came to see us last year here?"

A.: "Yes Major K——, I am."

Question by another sitter who was in the same regiment: "Why do you call him Major K—— so formally?"

A.: "Oh, it is all right M——" (laughing and using a nickname by which he is known in his regiment). "I used to call him N——." (Correct.)

Q.: "Can you give us your own nickname?" This was given correctly. Q.: "Do you see your daughter now?" A.: "Yes, she is here now, and tried to speak to you last week, but could not." Q.: "Can you give me her name?"

A great many ineffectual attempts were made, but at last the name was given correctly.

The questioner was the only one present who knew the name and recognised from the beginning that the spirit was trying to give the correct name, but would not help him, as he wished the name to be heard and given by the other sitters who did not know it, which was eventually done. The spirit mentioned the name correctly of another brother officer with whom he had stayed when he was ill.

After an interval one of the sitters gave a slight scream, and said that the pins had nearly been pulled out of her hat, which was pushed to one side; the sitter next to her said he had been thrust aside, and something had burst out of the circle. One lady had very satisfactory and comforting communication from her relatives of a private nature, two voices being heard distinctly simultaneously. One of the sitters saw light clouds of vapour so bright that he could see his hand and sleeve in them.

Fifth sitting: June 12. Present—same as number four.

On the lights being put out, a table which was outside the circle with vases full of flowers on it was moved almost noiselessly into the circle, the flowers brushing the hand of one of the sitters, who was holding the sensitive's hand. The lights were turned on, as it was feared the vases might get knocked off the table. While the lights were on, the trumpet, which was in the centre of the circle, rose from the floor and hurled itself over the shoulder of one of the sitters, and fell with a crash outside the circle. Two or three of the sitters absolutely saw the trumpet leave the floor. After the lights were put out again flowers were taken out of the vases and put into the hands and on the laps of the sitters. No voices were heard at all.

Sixth sitting: June 13. Two of the original circle and five new sitters.

A voice spoke in what sounded like Hindustani; but, though two of the sitters understood that language, they could only make out a few words. The trumpet again flew out of the circle. An extraordinary noise like an exaggerated syren motor-horn was heard close to the heads of two sitters. No other phenomena. One of the sitters heard the same noise repeated when she was in bed the same night.

Seventh sitting: June 14. Five of the original sitters and two others.

John King came immediately. One of the sitters complained of hay fever, and was recommended the following remedy by him. Put a teaspoonful of spirits of camphor in a small bottle of water and some paper over the top of the bottle with a hole in it, and sniff it up first one nostril, then the other. He asked a sitter about a man who had come to see him on business, which he described, and told him to beware of him. He volunteered the following statement to one of the sitters: "I know you want to know why I did not come to you in your last two sittings. I was not there at the last; but at the one before I was there, but the power was so great—it was stronger than ours— and we could not talk. It was I who threw the trumpet; to show what great physical power there was." The child of one of the sitters came, giving his name correctly. He said he was now grown up, though he had passed over as an infant; that he knew and loved his brother who had passed over long after: but that he was not with him very much, as he was more advanced and on a higher plane. A lady came to a sitter and talked in unintelligible French, and could not be recognised. Two or three voices came, but were not recognised, one exclaiming impatiently; "Good heavens, can't anyone understand?" The father of one of the sitters came for the second time, and said his wife was with him: on being asked if he ever saw his sister-in-law (the mother of one of the sitters), he said: "Oh, yes." On being asked her name he gave her second Christian name, which was never used. The sensitive said she saw the name K——, and asked if anyone recognised it. A sitter did so, and immediately the trumpet was taken to him.

Q.: "Are you K——, whom I knew at the Club?"

A.: "Yes, of course; and I used to go with you to the Chapter."

Q.: "Can you give the sign?"

A.: Oh, yes; but I cannot give away all our secrets" (laughing).

The other sitters assured him they would not listen, a private conversation followed, and correct signs were given by rapping.

Q.: "Did you know I was at your last rites?"

A.: "Yes, I knew you were; and several of the others."

The spirit tapped the sitter with the trumpet, and asked him to go down to his old house, and that he would try to be there. A voice came to one of the sitters, Mr. J——, saying: "I am L——."

Q.: "Do you mean Dr. L—— from V——?" A.: "Yes." Q.: I am very glad to meet you, but I did not know you very well." A.: "No; but I often saw you on the cricket field." (correct) Q.: Surely, Dr. L——, you remember Mr. And Mrs. P.? who are here now?" A.: "Oh, yes: of course I do. How do you do Mrs. P.? I am very glad to see you."

After a little conversation he said to Mr. J——: "I see several silver threads among the gold now." (Correct.) "Oh, Mrs. P., Do you remember that song which you used to sing so often?"

Mrs. P.: "Oh yes; but I don't sing it now." Dr. L.: "Oh, do sing it now slowly, and I will sing it with you."

Mrs. P. sang the song "Silver Threads among the Gold," and the voice joined, singing the words actually ahead of her, clearly and distinctly.

Dr. L.: "So you remember another song you used to sing?"

Mrs. P.: "Do you mean 'Dem Golden Slippers'?"

Dr. L.: "Yes; sing it."

Mrs. P. sang it, and again the voice joined with her quite clearly.

Dr. L.: "Do you remember the song something about a cottage by the wood?" This was not recognised.

Mr. J.: "Do you remember, Dr. L., your old friends the M.'s, whom you knew so well at V——?"

A.: "Oh, yes; but Mr. M. has gone." Mr. J.: "Oh, no, he is still on this sphere."

Dr. L.: "Yes I know that; but I mean he has left V—— a long time, and he used to sing this song."

Dr. L—— then sang by himself a verse of a song that Mr. M—— used to constantly sing.

This is one of the most wonderful tests at our sittings, as we never connected Mr. M—— with any song, and never thought of this one until reminded of it by Dr. L——.

Mrs. P.: "Shall we tell Mr. M—— about this?" A.: "You must use your own discretion."

Dr. L—— spoke of his son and said: "Poor fellow; how he has suffered." (Correct.) He spoke of life as being on different platforms, and seemed rather a fatalist.

The following narrative is written by Miss Edith K. Harper, the late Mr. W. T. Stead's private secretary. She has probably sat with Mrs. Wriedt oftener than any human being. As both she and her mother are psychics, it will be understood that some of the phenomena here related are clairvoyant experiences.

The manifestations in the dining-room of Cambridge House, Wimbledon, on May 29, 1912, are also described in the Appendix to Part 1:—

After considering a record of about two hundred sittings with Mrs. Etta Wriedt during her three visits to England, of which the notes of the general circles alone would fill a huge volume, were they written in extenso, I will try to relate, in brief, a few of the most striking experiences my mother and I were provoleged to have through Mrs. Wriedt's mediumship.

Looking over my notes of her first visit, in 1911, the following details stand out as among the principal features of the séances:—

(1) Mrs.Wriedt was never entranced, but conversed freely with the sitters, and we have heard her talking to, even arguing with, some spirit person with whose opinions she did not agree. I remember once Mr. Stead shaking with laughter on hearing Mrs. Wriedt suddenly reprimand the late editor of the Progressive Thinker for his attitude towards mediums, and the evident confusion of Mr. Francis, who, after an attempted explanation, dropped the trumpet, and apparently retired perplexed.

(2) Two, three and even four spirit voices talking simultaneously to different sitters.

(3) Messages given in Foreign languages—French, German, Italian, Spanish, Norwegian, Dutch, Arabic, and others— with which the medium was quite unacquainted. A Norwegian lady, well known in the world of literature and politics, was addressed in Norwegian by a man's voice, claiming to be her brother, and giving the name P——. She conversed with him, and seemed overcome with joy at the correct proofs he gave her of his identity, and of his conscious life and continued work in the world of "many mansions." Another time a voice spoke in voluble Spanish, addressing itself definitely to a lady in the circle whom none of the sitters knew to be acquainted with that language; The lady

thereupon entered into a fluent conversation in Spanish with the spirit, to the evident satisfaction of the latter.

(4) Flowers taken from the vases and placed in the hands of sitters in different parts of the room, once or twice a vase containing flowers being placed in someone's hand. (All this in the dark.)

(5) Sitters touched by invisible fingers (hair stroked, hands or face patted), and very frequently rapped by the trumpet, as though to recall wandering attention or to urge a hesitating person to answer promptly when spoken to.

(6) The appearance in our midst of luminous, "etherealised" forms, objective, because visible to everyone, which glided rather than walked, and often waved or bowed a greeting to members of the circle by whom they were recognised, or for whom they came Of these forms the faces were seldom clearly visible to everyone, though clairvoyants were usually able to describe minutely the features, hair, and general aspect, even to the design of the embroidery or lace on the beautiful white draperies. The forms were, of course, not solid to our physical touch, but after their appearance and disappearance the voice of Dr. Sharp or of John King would often announce the name of the spirit visitor, or say for which member of the circle the friend had come. It is impossible adequately to describe the effect of those radiant beings, who seemed to bring with them something of the *diviner air* in which they dwell. We often saw children's forms. On one occasion when a little child appeared, Mrs. Harper distinctly saw an indication of light, silky hair and the outlines of small, baby heels. The child gazed wonderingly around it, and then ran hurriedly back into the cabinet.

Mrs. Wriedt never sat in the cabinet, which was not at all necessary for her form of mediumship, though probably it served as a focus for the *psychic force*. It was Mr. Stead's property, and formed part of the furniture of Julia's sanctuary.—E. K. H.

Another interesting manifestation was the frequent singing through *the trumpet*, sometimes a voice alone, sometimes in unison with the circle, again, at times, singing with some particular sitter.

For example, a lady, an operatic singer, was present one evening. Feeling impressed to sing, she began, in Italian, the opening bars of the duet "Home to our mountains," from Il Trovatore, and was instantly joined, also in Italian, by an unmistakable tenor voice through the trumpet. The air, she assured us, was rendered absolutely note for note as her husband had sung it with her during his earth life, even to certain characteristic phrasings and modulations peculiarly his own. This lady's husband had only recently passed over, and, naturally, she was much affected by this evidence of his presence.

Another frequent manifestation was a luminous disc like the full moon, and quite as brilliant, which would move round inside the circle, pausing for a second or two before one or another of the sitters. Often the sitters were lightly sprinkled with drops of water, and very often a current of cool air would play over the circle; heavy objects were often moved from place to place in the room, such as books, chairs, vases, pictures from the walls, and so on. It was a common occurrence to hear two spirit voices talking together, the urbane and sonorous utterance of Dr. Sharp and the familiar, deep-toned voice of John King being more than once distinctly audible discussing the pros and cons of some suggested manifestation.

One evening my violin was taken out of its case, at the far end of the séance-room, and brought over the heads of the sitters. We could hear the strings being twanged as the violin was carried across the room, and Dr. Sharp's voice anxiously saying: "Be careful, John King, be careful!" To which the latter replied laconically: "It's all right!" Next moment the violin was placed on my knee, the bow put into my hand, and I was told to "'play." Then the violin-case, a heavy, old-fashioned, wooden one, was placed wide-open on the floor at my feet. Before the sitting it was firmly fastened, as usual, by two strong brass clasps. Then my fathers voice spoke to me, saying: "I asked John King to bring the violin, to remind you to practice!"

With regard to the possibility of hearing the voices in the light, my mother and I have several times talked with friends and relatives in the drawing-room, during the afternoon, in broad daylight. Mrs. Wriedt, sitting sewing, at a distance of several yards, occasionally took part in the conversation. Once I remember being in an adjoining room and hearing the unmistakable tones of John King's voice booming from the drawing-room, and Mrs. Wriedt's exclamation, "Sake's alive!" On that occasion my mother and the sensitive were alone.

Frequently, at the end of a séance, and while Mrs. Wriedt was at the door in the act of switching on the electric lights, one or both trumpets (we sometimes had two in use) would be flung lightly across the room. Sometimes they dropped from above. Once or twice one was laid on my mother's arm, sometimes on mine. In the expectation of trumpets dropping from aloft, we began to keep a watchful eye on the ceiling when *Mrs. Wriedt, after remarking, "Well, I guess were through!" put her hand* out to turn on the lights. On several occasions we saw one of the trumpets lying on the middle of the ceiling, whence it dropped with a clatter the moment the light flashed on it. The best phenomenon of this kind was when, one night, we actually saw both trumpets lying side by side horizontally on the ceiling near the central light bracket. They remained thus for a second or two, then dropped lightly, one on the head of a sitter, the other on the floor near him. It is remarkable that they never fell with such force as to hurt anyone. Gentleness was a marked characteristic of the sittings held in Julia's sanctuary.

On the eve of Mrs. Wriedt's second visit (1912) occurred the dreadful event by which Mr. Stead himself was called suddenly into that "other world" whose mysteries he had so long and so patiently sought to unravel. In the early days of April, just before he sailed, he discussed with me the final arrangements with regard to Mrs. Wriedt. "I shall probably wire to her to join me in New York," he said, "and bring her back with me to England."

But when Mrs. Wriedt arrived in England, for the second time, on May 5, she came alone. Mr. Stead's body was beneath the Atlantic waves; but his spirit voice had already spoken to her in New York, at the house of a friend; and Mrs. Wriedt had at once cabled to me the brief but eloquent words, "Here to meet Stead, but he has gone!" which swept away our last remaining straw of hope.

It is our firm and unshakeable belief that during the two months following we constantly saw and conversed with Mr. Stead, both in circles and in private sittings. He gave me many tests of identity, and made use of familiar phrases and expressions absolutely unknown to the medium. He gave us minute particulars of his passing over, saying that he was struck on the head, and never actually felt the sensation of drowning. The first occasion on which he spoke to me through the trumpet he took up the thread of a conversation we had had a few days before he sailed, in which he expressed his wish that I should write his "psychic life"; that is, the aspect of his manifold career dealing more particularly with his psychic investigations and experiences, in which I had the unforgettable privilege of being so closely associated with him.

Not only did we frequently see his "etherealised" face, head, and shoulders, but, on our calling out to him in greeting, he would bow his head and smile in recognition. Near the end of Mrs. Wriedt's visit, my mother and I had a private sitting with her one Sunday evening, and I shall never forget the variety of the manifestations. Balls of light, white, or sometimes tinted red or gold, floated about the room. They came behind us, and moved up and down in front of us, over our heads, sometimes one, sometimes two or three at a time, in different parts of the room, and again in the cabinet, where they seemed to rain down like oval-shaped meteors. A large pearly light appeared in front of the cabinet, from which spread a beautiful radiance, covering the cabinet and rising far above it. Then the two trumpets on the floor were suddenly illuminated, and became clearly visible in the darkness, standing side by side. At the same time another globe of light floated towards us from the right-hand side of the room. Sometimes two lights appeared, large and brilliant, travelling together slowly up the cabinet curtains. Suddenly a large wooden cross and Calvary, which stood on the top of the cabinet, were brightly illuminated, as though silhouetted in light. Above the cross hovered a brilliant ball of light, like a small moon, and while we looked at this a radiance began to spread from the arms of the cross, gradually assuming the shape and appearance of outspread wings, which extended more than a foot on each side of the cross. This light was not brilliant like the other, but looked soft and "feathery," and was the purest white. I well understood this symbol, for it had a very sacred significance for me. The phenomenon just described lasted for several seconds, then the light spread out in every direction and rose up to the ceiling.

Suddenly Mrs. Wriedt exclaimed: "There is a light among the flowers!" Looking round, we saw a small disc of light travelling across the room and apparently from the direction of the masses of flowers on a table, which stood at some distance behind. As the light came nearer to us it grew larger, and simultaneously we all three exclaimed: "It is Mr. Stead!" And so, indeed, it was. He came forward and bent over my chair, and, looking up, I saw his face smiling down upon me. It was, perhaps, the most perfect of the many etherealisations that I have seen. His attitude and movements were singularly natural and unconstrained. He then became invisible, and immediately his voice spoke to me through the trumpet. We were afterwards addressed by John King and Dr. Sharp, and several other etherealised forms appeared, one of which, a woman's was stated by John King to be that of his daughter Katie. My father and other relatives and friends also spoke to us. Mrs. Wriedt has frequently referred to that sitting as one she will never forget, and certainly we, the other two sitters, can never forget it.

Mrs. Harper obtained some interesting results in spirit photography during the séances of 1912, and had frequent advice from Mr. Boursnell through the trumpet. Unfortunately the very best of the negatives, on which the face of Mr. Stead was clearly recognised by all who saw it, was afterwards damaged when sent away for an enlargement.

I shall conclude this very brief and inadequate summary of our experiences of last year by quoting from my notes the account of a remarkable manifestation which took place in the presence of Julia's private circle on the evening of May 29, 1912.

At supper in the dining room after the sitting there present Mrs. Wriedt, Mr. And Mrs. Mallinson, Miss Scatcherd, Mrs. Anker, Miss Stead, and Mrs. And Miss Harper. Admiral Moore, Mr. J——, and Mr. E. T. Harper had left just before supper; Mr. R. King and Mr. Skeels were also absent. In Mr. Stead's place at the head of the table was his chair, on which stood a heavy plant pot and stand, containing a very large marguerite plant in full flower. This plant measured about one and a-half feet in diameter, and four feet in circumference at the widest parts. The chair faced the table in the ordinary way, as though our Chief were sitting there. The pot of margarites, Mrs. Wriedt's gift, had been placed thus on the chair at each weekly meeting of Julia's circle. But, though the flowers were a silent yet eloquent witness to Mr. Steads bodily absence, nothing unusual had happened in connection with them till the night in question. We had just finished supper, and everyone was talking with animation, when Mr. Mallinson exclaimed: "Do you see that leaf moving?" We all looked in the direction of the plant, but continued talking. Mrs. Wriedt was speaking of Mr. Stead. All at once several of the topmost flowers began to move rhythmically to and fro, the very tallest flower at the top of the plant bowing forward as though greeting us. Conversation ceased, and Mrs. Wriedt said: "Let us all join hands." This we did, forming a chain, but not touching the table. Mrs. Wriedt then resumed her remarks about Mr. Stead, and mentioned the name of Julia's "bureau." At that moment the plant was lifted as by invisible hands and turned partly round upon the chair. Our attention was rivetted. Conversation was resumed, but all eyes were fixed upon the plant, which was again turned further round towards the right. We still talked, and Mrs. Wriedt called out "Mr. Stead, Mr. Stead, is that you?" Three raps followed, and a chorus of joyous greetings rose from the circle. Next moment not only plant and plant-pot, but this time the heavy oak dining chair also, were again rapidly turned till the chair and its contents formed an angle with the table. Then the floor began to vibrate under our feet. Miss Scratcherd suggested turning out the lights in order to assist the manifestations. Up till then three powerful electric burners had been alight above the table. These were now switched off, leaving the room in deep twilight, but not in complete darkness. The floor continued to vibrate with increased force, and the table was so violently agitated that the cups, saucers, plates, and dishes rattled loudly. Then the sound of heavy footsteps reverbrated through the room, stamping round the table. Mrs. Harper called out:

"That's right Chief! Keep your word!"

This brought to our minds a remark Mr. Stead had made at the supper-table, after Julia's circle sitting, about a fortnight before he sailed. "When I get to the other side," he declared, ápropos of "raps" and "Knocks," "I'll not only rap, I'll stamp my feet like this, and shake the whole floor!" And he accompanied his remark by stamping his feet heavily. We recalled the episode then as we listened to the violent shaking of the floor and the sound of heavy footfalls. Not one of us was but convinced that Mr. Stead had kept his word.

A special feature of Mrs. Wriedt's mediumship was her clairvoyant reading of names. "written up," as she phrased it, in the darkness. When a name was recognised by a sitter, almost immediately a voice would be heard speaking through the trumpet, and a conversation followed. It was as though the spirit-visitors had decided to announce themselves and obtain recognition before attempting to give a name through the trumpet. I remember once at a circle-sitting Mrs. Wriedt announced a name which was not recognised. Whereupon John King's voice broke the silence, exclaiming, with brusque good humour, to the invisible owner of the name: "You had better clear out, my friend, nobody knows you!"

At a private séance this year (1913), at which my mother and I were sitters, Mrs. Wriedt said: I see the name Hub—Hubbard, or Hubback, written up...... it is in connection with an old man." We recognised the name Hubback. Immediately a voice spoke through the trumpet, greeting us in the unmistakable Yorkshire dialect and in an old man's quavering tones. He said it made him very happy to speak to us again, and that my father had told him to come. Also that he thought we must have left "the old place," as when he went there sometimes to have a look round he never saw us walking about "like you used to." He said that he was very happy, and free from pain now, and thanked us for our "kindness in the past." This was all quite evidential, the old man having been a groom, whose daughter was a servant in our family many years ago, in a village on the borders of the North Riding of Yorkshire, where we lived. He died of a long and painful illness. We had never spoken of him to Mrs. Wriedt—indeed, he was one of the last persons in the world of whom we were thinking. The reference to our having left "the old place" was interesting, as we left the neighbourhood some time after his death. His voice and manner of speaking through the trumpet were extremely characteristic, especially the exclamation "Ay, ay," with which he interspersed his remarks.

Another time, at one of our private sittings, Mrs. Wriedt saw a very unusual name, beginning with the letter I. This was at once recognised by my mother as being the name of a great-aunt of her own, who died when my mother was a young girl. They were greatly devoted to each other. Mrs. Wriedt most certainly had never heard of this relative's existence. A very soft, sweet, and clear voice then addressed Mrs. Harper by name. "My dear, I have come from my home in the seventh sphere to speak to you. Do you hear me?"......She went on to make some remarks of a very evidential nature, of family interest only, but proving her identity beyond all doubt. Mrs. Harper then asked: "Have you seen my sister?" The reply was a curious one. "Yes, she understands it all now. She knows what the wild waves are saying." This at once brought back to my mother's mind a duet that she and her sister frequently sang together as children, when this little sister, like Paul in Dombey and Son, used also to wonder and ask, "What did the waves say?" Another interesting feature of the communication was the intense anxiety evinced by this spirit as to my mother's religious beliefs, the great-aunt in question having been brought up in the strictest tenets of the Scottish "Kirk."

At our private sitting on Whit-Monday, 1913, no fewer than thirteen different voices spoke to us, all being identified. Mrs. Wriedt said that such a number was very unusual at a private séance, especially in conjunction with the "etherealisations" and the lights that we saw. At this sitting Mr. Stead etherealised. He was first clairvoyantly seen by my mother, and, as she remarked this, he became visible also to Mrs. Wriedt and myself. My mother saw the change take place from clairvoyance to etherealisation, the form of Mr. Stead appearing in precisely the same place as she had seen him clairvoyantly a second or two before, at her right hand. His face, head, and shoulders were clearly visible, first to my mother and Mrs. Wriedt, then to me. I was sitting at my mother's left hand; Mrs. Wriedt was sitting facing us, but rather nearer my mother. Following his appearance he talked at great length, referring to events which had happened during the interval since his passing over, and giving me such wise council, as in old days. Also at this sitting a luminous form, draped like a woman's, crossed the room and stood by Mrs. Wriedt, then moved forward to us, and what looked like a ball of light appeared on my mother's knee. At the same time Mrs. Wriedt looked as though covered completely with a luminous, white mist. As soon as this manifestation ceased Julia's voice spoke to us.

At this sitting also John King manifested most wonderfully, blowing some beautiful bugle calls for us through the trumpet, saying that was how he used to call his men together, in the old buccaneering days, one most terrific blast illustrating his signal to fight. John King manifested at all our sittings, and gave us many particulars in regard to his earth life, in Jamaica.

The voices did not always resemble the physical voices of the persons speaking, any more than voices heard through a telephone are always recognisable. Yet they never altered in individual character—that is, whatever tone of voice a spirit first used, that spirit spoke in the same tone of voice on every subsequent occasion. Mr. Stead's manner was always characteristic. His voice sounded much as it did when he spoke in a great hurry through a long-distance telephone, as I have heard it so often, when, for instance, he telephoned to his office in Mowbray House, Norfolk Street, Strand, from Hayling Island, seventy miles away. He several times spoke in what Mrs. Wriedt called the "independent voice"—that is, without using the trumpet. He frequently expressed his great interest in the affairs of the Near East, and said that he was much in the Balkans, at the seat of war, working for peace.

Personally, I did not need the voices to convince me of the reality of "life after death," having been, for as long as I can remember, conscious of communion with the world invisible. But had I needed such assurance I have certainly received, through Mrs. Wriedt's mediumship, proofs in abundance that our dear ones are with us continually, sharing our joys and sorrows, and watching over us with constant tenderness and solicitude, not as super-human beings far removed from earthly interests, but as fellow-travellers along the path of spiritual evolution, separated from us only by the physical senses, and rejoicing whenever opportunity is given them to break through the barriers we ourselves, often unconsciously, create.

Edith K. Harper. Wimbledon, July 27, 1913. I beg to confirm my daughter's narrative

S. A. A. Harper. The lady who wrote the account below recorded some of her experiences on page 38, et seq:—

Being a member of Julia's circle, I had the privilege of attending the weekly meetings, with Mrs. Wriedt as medium, during the summers of 1911 and 1912. I also had some private séances with her in 1913, and was most fortunate in my experiences of wonderful phenomena.

I heard the voices of many loved ones on the other side, and was most anxious to see an etherealisation of my son. During a séance he spoke to me for some minutes, and I begged him to let me see his face. A streak of light appeared; then, a flickering oval. I recognised the shape of his head, but his features were blurred. It was as though a stone were thrown at the reflection of the moon in a pool. I expressed my disappointment, and he said: "I am showing you this etherealisation through your own aura, which is vibrating with great intensity; this makes it impossible for me to succeed."

A luminous appearance flashed before me, so real and vivid that we (four members of my family) involuntarily called out my father's name. It flashed here and there in the intense darkness, coming close to us and retreating. It was slightly on the slant, and seemed to me to be a reflection from another dimension (if such an expression be permissible). I have seen nothing earthly like it. The colour was silver and gold; the eyes opened and shut. For those who suggest fraud I must say that my father's face was not as I last saw it, with white hair and beard, but as a man of about thirty-five, with thick dark hair and moustache. The very striking and only portrait of him thus was destroyed twenty-five years ago. I also noticed that his hair was wavy. In life he had straight hair, and often said he wished for curly hair.

An etherealisation of an elderly lady appeared, with close white cap double frilled about the face and chin. On asking the name, my son's voice told me it was my maternal great-grandmother. I had imagined she died at about thirty years of age, but, on inquiry, I found my mother remembered her death; also recollected the cap I have described.

During one séance Mrs. Wriedt's guide, Dr. Sharp, gave me a prescription and advice, and I am very grateful to him for curing me.

I was constantly touched by materialised hands. They would come from a mass of white mist, and I thing were formed as far as the wrist. They patted me quickly on the cheek or hand, then left me. I felt they did not want me to grab, and, on mentally promising not to do so, they gained confidence and stayed with me the whole séance, sometimes coming from the wall behind me, or above, resting on my head, and bringing me flowers from the other side of the room. Mrs. Wriedt sat about eight feet away from me, and talked constantly.

These hands never groped, but often touched my eyelids in the intense darkness. They were not abnormal in any way, but strong, firm, and dry.

Through three summers, weekly I have heard these beings speak through Mrs. Wriedt's mediumship; the tone and characteristics of speech never varied. I shall never forget the cultured and refined tone of Iola's voice, the sweet yet determined voice of Julia, the clear, curt, yet kind speech of Dr. Sharp, the powerful bass of John King, and my own son's voice, differing indeed from his earthly voice, yet with all his memories and characteristics as of old.

I am sorry when I constantly read of the "puerilities of spirit utterance." I wish such writers could have shared my experience, for every scientific, medical, or religious question was fully answered, and I learned a great deal that was of the deepest interest to me.

I may add that I did not put any difficulty in the way of those on the other side, who are working so earnestly to pierce the veil. I made the conditions as perfect as possible. Each séance, I felt, was a communion service, and tests were not needed, for I had innumerable and convincing proofs given unasked. My husband and myself liked the medium very much, and found her straightforward, unselfish, and generous; and this liking may have helped us a little.

One test given unasked was an etherealisation of Mr. Stead, who spoke and referred to a conversation known only to him and myself; I still have his dated letter referring to this subject. This conversation happened at a circle séance. During this, the third summer of my experience with Mrs. Wriedt, I had not so many physical phenomena, but had several prophecies; some of these have already been fulfilled, and, were most unexpected happenings. I cannot give particulars publicly, as other persons names are involved, but would do so privately if called upon. During one séance, my husband, myself, and Mrs. Wriedt being present, a very large, soft, violet cloud appeared. I exclaimed loudly; a deep and beautiful voice said, "Be still and speak softly; we are about to show you the spirit light of W. Stead." A golden star appeared, and a smaller one about a foot behind it. These stars whirled about with tremendous rapidity for a few seconds. These lights were not misty, and were not seen clairvoyantly by us. They were like actual pieces of fire. I asked for my son's spirit light, and a pink star appeared with the same tiny star behind, and this also revolved in the same way. A large silver crescent floated about and settled on Mrs. Wriedt's lap; it rather startled her; also a pure red star appeared. The medium told us she had seen nothing like this form of phenomena, and she thought it might be something to do with our home séances. We, indeed, have the large violet cloud, but do not get further. Between each light the room seemed full of commotion; a white mist gathered, which turned to deep violet, about the size of a man, and the star appeared revolving rapidly about a circle two feet in circumference.

M.M.

From a lady who lives at Horsham:—

I went to a private séance with Mrs. Wriedt in June, 1913, only herself and myself being present.

Two or three minutes after the light was put out I felt a touch. I said: "Something touched me"; and Mrs. Wriedt said: "Is anyone there?" and a voice replied: "Yes; Will." I said: "Is it Will W.?" (mentioning an uncle who was dead). The voice replied: "No, no; Will L——" (Mentioning a great friend of mine who died some years ago in South Africa).

I then said: "Do you want to speak to me, Will?" The voice replied: "Yes, you understand; and my dear ones do not; tell E. (his wife) that I am quite happy, and can see her all the time." The voice then ceased.

But I forgot to say that, before I heard a voice, Mrs. Wriedt said: "I see a figure coming towards you, holding his hand over his heart. He died from an operation, or something wrong with his heart."

Will L——, whose voice I heard, had, as a matter of fact, died in an instant from an aneurism of the heart. The figure which Mrs. Wriedt saw coming towards me, she described, and it corresponded in every way with Will L——.

Other voices were heard, but the messages I received are too private for publication.

When I commenced Part II, I had no intention of again obtruding my own experiences on the public, for the reason that I have sat so often with Mrs. Wriedt, and am so compromised on the point of her genuineness as a medium, that my evidence is, to some extent, vitiated in the eyes of those who are earnestly seeking for the best testimony; but I find in my notes that I have two unique items of evidence in August which ought not to be omitted.

Mrs. Wriedt, as I have recorded, left me for Scotland on July 1, 1913. After holding many successful sittings in that country, she rented Cambridge House, Wimbledon, and gave sittings to her friends throughout the month of August. I sat with her, during this period, six times; each séance was perfectly successful. In five she sat with me alone in the room; on the sixth (and 1st) two American friends were also present. One of my private sittings I am now about to describe.

Cambridge House. Monday, August 25. 4.3 to 4.40 p.m. Within one minute of the lights being switched off, and while the musical-box was still playing, John King spoke with hearty greetings; he remained a couple of minutes. Then Iola came for some few minutes, after which there was a short pause and dead silence. Presently appeared a bright etherealisation of a woman in snow white; the features were not visible, but the figure and height were those of Iola. The white robe was in constant movement, as if there was some action of the arms disturbing the robe. Mrs. Wriedt, who was sitting eight feet from me, exclaimed excitedly: "Oh, Admiral, it's the baby," and shortly after: "Cannot you see it? This is the most wonderful thing that ever happened here." After a great deal of movement in the white robe, a separate form appeared, standing beside Iola. It was snow white, and obviously the etherealisation of a child a little over two feet high. Mrs. Wriedt said: "I must come over to you, Admiral, and see if you make out what I see." She left her chair (unwisely, I think), and came over to me and grasped my right hand with her left. We were thus placed while the taller figure faded away and the baby stood alone. Its features could not be seen, but it was plain that it had on its little head a cap of some sort pointed on top; apparently, it was standing on the floor about two feet from me. It remained in view about two minutes and then disappeared, when Mrs. Wriedt returned to her seat.

Iola was then heard speaking to baby: "Speak to grandpapa, dear." The voice of a very young child said: "Grand-papa." Q.: "Yes dear?" A.: "It's me." Q.: "Have you anything I can tell daddy?" A.: ""Hug for daddee; hug for mother (sic)." Then (as if speaking to Iola): "Fotchie, Fotchie (a corruption of the name of her great-aunt); again: "Grand-pa-pa." Q.: "Yes, dear?" "It's me" (more whispering to the child). "Grand-pa-pa, goodbye" (then kisses). (The clear "goodbye" impressed me very much.)

Iola to me: "Did you see her kiss her hand to you?" I replied that I could not. Shortly after a light appeared in the air at a level slightly higher than my head. It waved up and down about six times; the diameter was about two inches. I could not distinguish it as a hand.

Then I heard the trumpet being rolled about the floor. Iola whispered to me: "It is baby playing with the trumpet." Finally the trumpet was thrown against my left leg. Iola went on talking to me about various subjects but off none that would interest the reader.

At the commencement of the sitting, directly John King departed, a large illuminated disc, apparently four inches in diameter, was waved to and fro in front of my face. Mrs. Wriedt neither saw his, nor the light representing baby's hand.

The séance ended with a discussion between Iola and myself about cremation, Iola declaring it was a good way to dispose of the body, but that it should not be carried out till the third day after death, as time was thus given for the spirit to leave its earthly habiliment. Her final words were: "It does not really make much difference, but it is better so."

(I had the misfortune to lose a granddaughter through an accident in April, 1911, aged five months. I have frequently heard of it since. (See *Glimpses of the Next State.*) This is the first time that I have seen it clearly as an etherealisation, or heard it say more than one or two words; it has frequently been seen clairvoyantly. On a subsequent occasion, Iola told me that the child did not use the trumpet, but spoke without its aid. She also said that she had brought the baby in her arms and put it on the floor, where she supported it by holding its arms behind for a few moments. Even now it cannot pronounce the names of its sisters, but calls them "the neighbours.")

Cambridge House, Friday, August 29, 1913. Present: Mrs. Wriedt, Mr. And Mrs. Z. (of Toledo, Ohio, U.S.A.), and myself. For a short time after the lights were switched off the musical-box continued playing the Russian National Hymn. Directly it stopped Edna, the nun, manifested by throwing a little water into our faces. She gave Mrs. X. a rose, and touched each of us on the face with the small end of the trumpet. It occurred to Mrs. Wriedt to suggest that the spirit should be asked: "What colour is the rose?" Answer: "Hold it against your dress (addressing Mrs. Z.);......it is pink and cream." Question: "You mean pink and white?" Answer: "No I do not; pink and cream." (At the end of the séance, when the lights were turned on, we found that the prettiest rose out of a bowl, close behind my right elbow, had been taken out; it was pink shading off to cream. I had not heard any movement among the flowers.) Edna was seen by Mr. And Mrs. Z., and talked for two or three minutes with them.

Dr. Sharp now came with a few words of hearty greeting; he was followed by Iola, who welcomed Mr. and Mrs. Z., and said she had manifested to them in America, and would do so again. She gave a rough description of what she had said to them, which was not quite correct. Then we were visited by Mr. Samuel Jones, late mayor of Toledo. A very clear conversation ensued about his widow and other relatives. He told

Mr. Z., in a confident manner, that he would come to England again. I said: "He tells me he will never come." Answer: "Don't believe a word he says." (laughter.) Then he repeated his assurance. And added that his widow and another lady would accompany the Z.'s on the next occasion on which they crossed the water.

Grayfeather made himself known with his usual shout, "Me here!" and talked to us about his medium, J. B. Jonson, and other matters.

The advent of the spirit of George Z. was the great event of the séance. He had, apparently, accompanied his brother and sister-in-law during their travels in Germany and Holland. (They had arrived eight hours before from Holland.) He said: "I saw you at the Hague." Q. by Mrs. Z.: "Did you see any of the notables about us at the Peace Palace?" A.: "You mean the Princess?" Q.: "That was the queen?" A.: "I did not see any queen; I thought she was a Holland duchess." Then the spirit said: "I saw Will give you that amethyst necklace. When I saw it, I said right away, that is for you; I'm glad you've got it; the amethyst is my favourite stone." (Quite correct. Mr. Z. had given Mrs. Z. an amethyst necklace at Zurich; she was wearing it at the séance.) Shortly after our visitor said: "Who did you get those beads for?" Mrs. Z.: "For Frances" (her grand-daughter). "Oh!" (The beads were at the Cecil Hotel at the moment; they were purchased at Amsterdam.)

Again George Z. showed his knowledge of his relatives' movements by asking: "Where did you get your comb?" For two minutes Mrs. Z. was puzzled, and could not think what her brother-in-law meant. Q.; "I did not get any comb, George." A.: "Yes, you did; I saw it; the one with stones in it." Mrs. Z. (suddenly recollecting); "Oh" do you mean the tortoiseshell barrette, for the hair?" A.: "It looked to me like a comb." (I have a barrette on the table in front of me as I write. To me, a mere man, it looks like a comb, and I am sure that if I had been the spirit I should have expressed myself as he did. Mrs. Z. had bought one at Cologne, which she showed me; it had no stones in it.)

But the quaintest evidence was to come. George Z. said: "What did you say—'Did you ever see such a funny car' for?" If I had been in the flesh, I should have roared" (laughter in the trumpet). "Oh, yes, I should have roared." (The Z.'s landed for the first time in England on July 4, 1913, at Liverpool. They tell me that when they were shown into the ordinary first-class carriage, which was to take them to Chester, it was so different to the carriages in the United States that Mrs. Z. exclaimed: "Did you ever see such a funny car?") This spirit also asserted that the Z.'s would make another visit to England.

Silvermoon now came in with a loud war-whoop, which he repeated. He showed his moon, a large disc, to Mr. and Mrs. Z.: but I could not see it, any more than I could see Edna at the beginning of the sitting. He shouted a few unintelligible words.

We now had a visit from W. T. Stead, which was very evidential. He spoke loud, and welcomed my friends to "his temple"; the manner was much as it always is in the séance room. He said to Mr. Z.: "Will you tell Mr. Thomson how sorry I was not to be able to visit him to pay him a visit at Toledo?" Mrs. Wriedt corrected: "You mean Mr. Jonson, Mr. Stead?" "Yes, yes, Jonson." (Short pause.) "Now, sir, will you give Mr. Thomson my regards, and tell him I am sorry that I did not see him?" (Mark this! Just before sailing in the Titanic Mr. Stead was exercised in his mind about inviting the Jonsons to England. It is well known to his private secretary and others that he seriously intended to send them an invitation to come to Cambridge House. Observe also his knowledge of where Mr. and Mrs. Z. live, though their real names are not given in my accounts of sittings with them in *Glimpses of the Next State*, his only earthly source of information.) He chatted for some few minutes, speaking two or three times to me and once to Mrs. Wriedt. I had not had a chance of talking to him since May 2.

Iola came again for a short chat. I saw her three or four times during the séance, but she did not make herself visible to my friends. I remarked: "Well, these pleasant meetings are over; this is our last talk." A.: "No, it is not; I shall speak to you." Here Dr. Sharp came to wind up the séance. I said: "Dr. Sharp, what does Iola mean? She says that I shall speak to her again." Dr. Sharp (aside); "What did you tell him?" I heard Iola talking eagerly to him, but could not catch the words. Then Sharp said: "Well Admiral, I may not see you again, so I will now say 'Goodbye' and thank you for all your kindness to my medium." He continued thus for a minute or two speaking in a very appreciative and warm manner, wished the Z.'s a pleasant voyage home, and departed. This ended one of the most evidential sittings I have ever experienced.

(I refer those readers who may be interested in my séances with the Z.'s at Toledo, Ohio; and Detroit, Michigan, to the accounts given in Glimpses of the Next State. As to Iola's premonition of our talking together again, it is not impossible, as Mrs. Wriedt has not yet returned to the States (September 10), but it seems to me highly improbable. Should it come true, I will record a note before this book is completed. Mrs. Wriedt is in Holland.)

The following narrative is from Mrs. Alleyne, who has sat with Mr. Cecil Husk, The blind medium, over two hundred times. It has been a disputed question among some spiritists whether John King, the control of Husk, is the same entity who has been so active at the séances of Mrs. Wriedt. I have never doubted that he is, having sat over thirty times with Husk myself:—

On Sunday evening, August 24, 1913, I went to Wimbledon, accompanied by a friend (the widow of a clergyman), to attend a séance given by the American medium Mrs. Wriedt. As I am an old spiritualist, I think that my experiences at it may perhaps be of interest to some.

The first thing that occurred was a sign, given to me by my husband (who passed to the other side of life nearly sixteen years ago), of his nearness to me; he was, in fact, standing close by me the whole evening, but he did not use the trumpet, giving up the power he might have used to the husband of my friend, as he (my husband) and I have daily opportunities of communicating, I being clairaudient.

Then my old friend, John King, spoke to me in his powerful voice, reminding me that again we were meeting at a Sunday séance, after many months. Sunday is the day on which, for years past, I usually attended a séance at Mr. Husk's, the well known blind medium, who has been ill for more than five months, and whose chief control is John King. I asked John King if Joey (another control of Mr. Husk's) was present, and he answered: "Yes, my dear Mrs. Alleyne, he is sitting at your feet."

Then my father talked to me, calling me by my name, and my mother followed him; my father said a few words also to my friend, who was sitting next to me, and whom he had frequently seen with me at Mr. Husk's séances. A voice then came through the trumpet that at first I did not recognise, and I asked who was speaking; the reply came: "I am Mrs. Massey, Mrs. Alleyne dear. I was so sorry to have to leave you so suddenly, and that I did not see you before you went away" (Mrs. Massey passed after an illness of a few hours only, while I was in Switzerland last spring), "but I am so happy." Then followed a message to Mr. Husk, finishing up with, "and tell him that all that John King told me is true." She spoke in an old emphatic manner I remembered so well. After Mrs. Massey had ceased speaking to me, another voice said: "Mrs. Alleyne, Mrs. Alleyne," and I again asked who was addressing me; the voice replied: "Mrs. Husk," whom I knew some years ago, and who also passed with great suddenness. She thanked me gratefully for kindness shown to her husband during his two long illnesses, and sent a lengthy message to him.

Just before John King spoke to me, at the beginning of the séance, a large globular- shaped light formed in front of my friend and me, afterwards passing round the circle of about twelve sitters. Uncle (yet another control of Mr. Husk's) spoke to my friend and me in precisely the same curious voice we are so familiar with at Mr. Husk's séances, and Joey whistled an air he is fond of singing at the same séances. Other spirits were talking to their various friends in the circle, and I once heard two conversations going on simultaneously.

Dr. Sharp, Mrs. Wriedt's control, then gave us a beautiful little address, and the sitting was brought to a close with the singing of the Doxology.

Thus ended a very interesting sitting, and one which proved to me, beyond the shadow of a doubt, that John King, uncle, and Joey, the controls of Mr. husk, had been present with me that evening at Mrs. Wriedt's séance.

On our return journey to town my friend and I had the carriage to ourselves, and at once I perceived a particular spirit-perfume my husband is in the habit of bringing to me, which was followed, two or three minutes afterwards, by a well known perfume, often wafted over us by uncle at the séances at Peckham, and in other places, notably when we are travelling back to our respective homes after a sitting.

E. A. K. Alleyen.

From Mrs. W——, the widow of a clergyman:—

I accompanied Mrs. Alleyne to a séance at Mrs. Wriedt's on August 24. After Mrs. Alleyne's father had finished speaking to his daughter, he greeted me by name, saying he knew me well, having seen me so often at Mr. Husk's séances.

Presently I heard "Edith" (my name) called, and felt a sharp tap from the trumpet on my knee; a voice said: "I am Minnie." This was a cousin, whose father and brothers have materialised many times to me at Peckham, sometimes telling me Minnie was with them. One of the cousins materialised before I heard the news of his death. Minnie and I had a short conversation, and then another voice called "Edie," and said he was my husband, giving his name. No one else ever abbreviated his name. He spoke out very clearly, no doubt because he is accustomed to speaking at Mr. Husk's, and at the same time another spirit voice was holding a conversation with a friend across the circle.

Uncle, a control of Mr. Husk's, spoke to me, calling me by my name, in exactly the same voice we have always heard; and Joey, another control (who declined to use the trumpet, so John King said), whistled a song he often sings at Peckham, "Down by the Swanee River."

I heard John King mention many of the sitters names in greeting, but I did not catch mine, so I asked: "Have you noticed me John?" He answered: "I am always noticing you, dear Mrs. ——."

I have had many proofs that this is true, and that some members of his band, as well as my relations and friends, know what I am doing, and that they compass me round with kindness, sympathy, and the help that is in their power to give.

As Mrs. Alleyne and I were going home in the train (no one else in the carriage) a gust of spirit-perfume was puffed in our faces, which we recognised as that made by uncle, and brought by him as a kindly greeting. This is his custom when we are leaving Peckham after a séance with Mr. Husk.

The following are the experiences of Mr. R. B——. M.A. Cantab., F.C.S., M.I.A.E., a gentleman of independent means, engaged in private research of various kinds; with Mrs. Wriedt, at Cambridge House, Wimbledon, during May and June, 1913:—

Having been requested to give an account of the personal experiences of my wife and self at these sittings, I have endeavoured to do so, as far as a lack of practice in verbal reporting permits. Notes were in every case taken at the time, and usually written out the same evening; and, while there are occasional omissions of portions of a conversation, the substance of it is correctly given, The voices and replies are given in inverted commas. On each occasion our personal communications occupied a very few minutes of a sitting of nearly two hours, during the rest of which we were listening to the most varied and diverse conversations of the spirit friends of other sitters. I have heard French, German, Italian, Gaelic, and Dutch spoken, also Servian; though, being ignorant of the latter tongue, I cannot testify personally to it.

We had attended one of Admiral Moore's sittings in 1912, which, as regards voices, was a blank one; otherwise we had no personal acquaintance with Mrs. Wriedt, nor with any of the sitters except Admiral Moore. A later acquaintance with this gifted medium enables us to thoroughly endorse the opinions of her other friends regarding her integrity and sincerity.

May 22, 1913, Admiral Moore's circle, 7 p.m.

On the lights being turned out, water was sprinkle in our faces, and I twice felt a touch on the forehead, followed by a faint voice, giving the name, "George B——," and identifying itself as that of an uncle of mine, who had passed over many (I think over twenty) years ago. The voice was weak and difficult to hear, but finally stated that my mother, and two other relatives, were present, and that she would try and speak later on. (This prediction was not fulfilled till July 20, at Rothesay.) Then the loud voice of Grayfeather was heard, during which another voice was talking to Admiral Moore, and George B. was trying to make himself audible to me, but soon gave it up; there was, however, no doubt of the three conversations proceeding simultaneously—a fact commented on by some of the other sitters.

Towards the end of the sitting the trumpet was placed in my wife's hand, and a voice tried to speak; but, on Mrs. Wriedt asking her to put it down, she did so, and no further phenomena occurred.

May 28, 1913, general circle, 7 p.m.

Dr. Sharp spoke as soon as we had sat down, and was introduced to the sitters. After various communications to them, during which I heard French, Dutch, and Italian spoken, a voice addressed my wife, saying: "Sister." Q.: "Who is it?" Indistinct reply; then, still indistinctly: "Gertie" (name not clearly heard). Then much more clearly: "Iris's godmother. How is Iris?" John King's voice interrupted loudly: "Surely you remember Gertrude?" (My sister-in-law, who was my daughter's godmother, had passed over some years ago.)

A short conversation ensued between her and my wife, in which she gave a personal and significant message to her mother, and the names of her brother and sister (both on the other side).

June 2, general circle, 7 p.m.

Dr. Sharp spoke, also Grayfeather—an unusual circumstance when Admiral Moore was not present. After other messages, including two for a Servian gentleman who was present, a voice came for my wife: "Sister, Katie." (This was a sister who had passed over in childhood.) "I am much happier here; there is no worrying to please everybody." She then gave a significant but private message for her mother.

After an interval of communications for other sitters, the loud voice of Grayfeather called: "Someone for Mr. B——" (giving a comic perversion of my name).

Then a low voice in the trumpet to me: "My son."

Q.: "Is that father?" A. "Yes, and Bob is here." (This was another uncle of mine.) The voice was faint, and, though a short further conversation ensued, I could not record it on that account. In later sittings matters much improved.

June 7, 1913, Admiral Moore's circle 7 p.m.

(Prior to the sitting I had placed a photograph of a family group, and a watch of peculiar pattern, that had belonged to my father, in my pocket, without, of course, mentioning the fact to anyone.)

After some physical phenomena and voices for other sitters, my father spoke: "My son, how are you?"

Q.: "Do you know what I have brought?" A.: "A picture." Q.: "What else?"

204

A,: "watch."

Q.: "What kind of watch?"

A.: "Cleaned face."

(The watch had had a tarnished silver face, and I had recently cleaned it.)

Q.: "What is the back like?"

A.: "Engraved. I don't see the other watch, the closed one."

(I have of recent years habitually carried a hunting watch, but neither my father or I used one in his lifetime.)

My father then addressed my wife: "Your sisters are here." Q. (by my wife: "Which ones?" A.: "You ought to know; there are only t——" (last word indistinct). Q.: "Two?" A.: "No three." (correct.) Q.: "Will you come again?" A.: "I come every day." Q.: "Who is with you?" A.: "Mary is here. It is a great privilege to be able to talk to you like this." Q.: "Did you send a message through H——?" A.: "Yes, but that was a long time ago."

(Some seven or eight years previously H——, a relative, had told me of a message received from my father, at a private circle, and this was the only instance of a personal communication that concerned me that I had ever heard of up to the present year.)

Then a very loud and clear voice spoke: "Mary, your aunt. How delightful to be able to talk like this. I am so glad to see you." (some further conversation not recorded.)

Q.: "Is uncle Robert there?"

A.: "Oh Bob is here."

Other voices, including Blossom, an Indian girl, then concluded the sitting.

June 16, 1913, general circle, 7 p.m.

After a long series of communications for other sitters, a voice came for my wife, giving the name, "Sophy B——."

Q.: "Shall I give any message to your brother?" 205

A.: "Yes, but do not write."

Then my father spoke: "How is baby?" My wife said: "You never knew her." (This was a grandchild, born three years after he passed over.) "I see her every day. Mother and I are together. How is E——?" (This was my son.) My father continued: "He is not very well." I replied: "He is going to Cambridge in a year or two." A.: "It will do him good."

This concluded our sittings, for the time, at Wimbledon. It will be noticed that we made little attempt to get prescribed tests fulfilled, preferring to wait until evidence offered itself, even at the cost of more prolonged observation. Our further experiences at the Rothesay sittings justified this attitude: names, in particular, suddenly asked for, were sometimes given with difficulty or not at all: but, unasked, they were given constantly and in every case correctly. The difficulty in recalling a perfectly familiar name, when suddenly asked for it, is not without parallel in everyday experience.

Sept. 13, 1913

Dear Admiral Moore,

I send my accounts of Rothesay and Cambridge House sittings herewith; the latter have had to be boiled down considerably, as so much of the details referred to matters which you will understand I do not wish to publish, as they relate to inventions not completely protected; while of the rest a good deal was of as little outside importance as everyday conversation, and only evidential to ourselves so far as it indicated complete familiarity with family affairs. To make this clear would entail verbose and uninteresting explanations. Altogether eleven relatives and four friends communicated at one time or another; while in only one case was a name given which I did not recognise, and this was afterwards said to be a friend of my uncle.—

Yours sincerely,

R.B.

By the kindness of Mr. Coates, to whom we were then personally unknown, we were enabled to have further sittings with Mrs. Wriedt at Rothesay during the latter part of July, 1913. These ten in number, were in each case in general circles at Mr. Coates's' house, sixteen to eighteen persons being usually present. While this did not allow of very prolonged conversation for any individual sitter, the enormous number of identifications and tests that we witnessed was ample compensation from an evidential point of view—names, relationships, and family facts being given correctly to the various sitters; while the contrast between the broad scotch of the many spirits with the English speech of the spirit friends of the less numerous Southrons was remarkable.

I might here mention that, as regards ourselves, all the spirit friends who have communicated, with two exceptions, passed from this life more than twelve years ago; my surviving relatives are few, and both my wife's family and my own were entirely unknown either to the medium or to any of the other sitters.

We arrived in Rothesay on July 12, and had our first sitting at Glenbeg House the following evening. The conditions seemed excellent, and voices came almost without intermission for nearly two hours; a voice spoke at some length in German to a sitter next to us. I had a brief conversation with my father, which, except for the mention of the name of a hitherto unmentioned relative, had nothing of evidential value for publication.

The following evening (Monday) Dr. Sharp, Mrs. Wriedt's control, made some references in his usual opening address to the proposed spiritualist temple to be built in Glasgow. He quoted parts of a sermon preached by a sitter elsewhere the previous day with correctness.

We were sprinkled with water: and Dr. Sharp, who intervened to explain, or clear up misunderstandings, more frequently than at Cambridge House, stated that a spirit child was pulling a flower out of a vase on the mantelpiece.

My father again spoke, and told my wife that her mother was much better, and much interested in our experiences. We were aware of the latter; but certainly no one else knew that my mother-in-law had been very unwell, was undergoing a cure at a health resort, and that we were awaiting news of its result, which was as stated. He also gave some advice as to our sittings for spiritual communication at home.

On July 15 we sat at 2 p.m., and waited some time before any voices came. After several others had communicated, a voice came for me, giving a surname E——? I asked: "What E——? I know some people of that name, but they are living." Reply: "Edmund E——, Your father told me you were here. I thought I should like a little talk with you." This was an old friend who had passed over many years before; no connection of the people of the same name I was thinking of. I inquired about his daughter, as I remembered one had passed over. "You know I had three daughters." (Correct.) "I went away to [name of place inaudible], but it did me no good." (Correct. I knew what the name of place should have been.) "I am much better now." In reply to some further remarks: "You know my wife is here and one daughter." This I know to be correct as far as it goes. I have not heard of the family for some years.

July 16. Sitting at 2 p.m. My father came early in the sitting, and spoke to me. I remarked that Mr. E—— had come. A.: "I told him you were here, and thought he would like a little chat. We are in the sixth sphere together." This was the first mention of "spheres." I had never inquired about them. We talked about the beautiful situation of Mr. E——'s old home, and he said: "He has a beautiful spot here. Mother is here and will speak to you." (This did not take place till the 20th.) "Were you satisfied about the way things were left? I have rather worried about it." (We replied we were perfectly satisfied.) "We were afraid you might have thought us selfish." This was intelligible to us, and characteristic, though the suggestion was quite unfounded. At the end of the séance Dr. Sharp said to another sitter; "We want people like yourself who are bold enough to come out and tell people how they stand. You've got to give the bird a grain before you give it a loaf. Twenty years hence you will be surprised, and a hundred years hence you don't know where you'll be. You won't live to see it, but your children will." He concluded by making a forecast of the rise of Jewish influence.

Thursday, July 17. 2 p.m. A very wet and muggy day. At the beginning of the sitting a luminous figure of a tall woman appeared at the opposite end of the room, visible to us all, and beckoned to one of the sitters. Dr. Sharp spoke, telling us who the figure was, and then had a conversation with Mr. Coates. When he had concluded nothing happened for some time, and the lights were turned up, when the three pieces of the jointed horn were found, stood up on end, in front of us. On the lights being turned down again, heavy footsteps were heard; the horn was moved about, and Mr. Coates complained of being hit by it on the nose. My wife said; "I wish they would hit me." Soon after the horn hit my wife and myself in the face gently, and she grasped it. No other voices were heard on this occasion, and the sitting concluded: the only partially blank one that occurred.

On the evening of the same day we sat again. After various voices for others, my wife was addressed by her sister: "K——. Sister." She replied: "I want to bring some of the others here" i.e., to Mrs. Wriedt's sittings). Voice: "Poor mother couldn't come to anything like this; she's too nervous." My wife repeated that she wished to introduce it to her sisters. Voice: "Don't try and force it on them; they don't understand." (Very pertinent statement.) My wife continued to talk to K——, who was trying to speak to me, and replied: "I don't want to speak to R——." My wife: "But you don't know him." Voice, loudly and emphatically: "I do know him. I want to speak to R——. Your mother is here." I asked: "Will she speak?" "Yes: but she was not one for pushing." (true.) "Is my father here?" A. "Yes." (I had never known K—— in life, and had first met her at Cambridge House.)

Friday, July 18. 8 p.m. We had an excellent sitting. Another sister of my wife's communicated, and my father came: mentioned my wife's spirit relatives by name, gave some further hints regarding home sittings, and reassured my wife regarding affairs at home during her absence, about which she was usually prone to worry. A voice came for another sitter in a strange language, which no one seemed to comprehend. She tried French with it, to no purpose. I caught a few words of Italian, and addressed it in that language. An excited reply followed in what appeared to be Italian patois. I could not make much of it, except that the speaker had been in Florence. Dr. Sharp then spoke, and explained that he had been born in Sicily, and had been a violinist in Florence, and had met the sitter or friends of hers abroad.

Sunday, July 20. 8 p.m. Dr. Sharp spoke as usual, and we saw lights. Mrs. Coates and Mrs. Wriedt both saw Stead's face. I have noticed various degrees of luminous appearances; at times, as on the 17th, their nature has been conspicuous to those, like myself, who have no pretensions to clairvoyant vision; at other times what was merely a luminous appearance to me seemed to possess detail for other sitters.

After other voices, my mother came, saying; My dear, I'm so pleased to see you." I said: "I am so glad you have come at last." Voice: "Yes dear. Here is the professor at Cambridge. You remember him." I inquired: "Which professor?" Voice: "The professor that stuttered. He wishes to speak to you." I replied: "Oh, professor S——. You will come again, and we shall have further opportunities to talk?" Voice: "Yes. Goodbye, dear."

A clear and rather deep voice then addressed me by name: "R—— B——, I am S——." I said: "I never thought when I last heard you speak that I should hear you like this." Voice, in an amused tone: "Through the horn!" Then, after a pause: "B——. You remember the letter that was to be read. They have found out the whole thing now."

Other voices prevented the further pursuit of the subject. Mr. Coates, as well as myself, recognised the allusion to Myers's posthumous letter; but I never had the honour of any intimate acquaintance with professor S——, though I had known him at Cambridge, and both my wife and myself had frequently heard him speak at the S. P. R. meetings. I had a more intimate acquaintance with Mr. Myers; but to professor S—— I could only have been known as one of a fairly numerous group of undergraduates more or less interested in psychical research. Certainly no one present could have been aware of his ever having known me. My mother passed over before I went to Cambridge, and had not known him in life.

A sister of my wife's then spoke for a short time; then another voice, which was very faint, and which we could not identify; but, at the moment, at least two other voices were speaking to other sitters.

July 21, 8 p.m. At this sitting my wife's brother came, giving his name clearly; referred by name to the sisters who were with him, and gave a message for his wife.

Shortly after, Mrs. Wriedt described a spirit as present carrying a roll of music, and supposed he was a musician. Dr. Sharp intervened to explain he was not a musician, but a paperhanger—giving his name—and that the roll was not music, but wallpaper. He was duly recognised by a sitter.

My father came and spoke for a short time; his voice and manner were very characteristic of him, the former being clear, deliberate, and distinct. Mr. Coated remarked subsequently on its being "The voice of a cultured English gentleman," and on its contrast with the Scotch of so many of the other communicators.

July 22, 2 p.m. After the usual singing (which is alleged to produce conditions conducive to the phenomena), lights became visible and a form appeared, vaguer, however, to me than that on July 7. Dr. Sharp spoke; among other things he gave us some recommendations regarding private sittings: "Do not force mediumship. Sit at a table; put a glass of water and a pencil and paper on it."

Some spirits came and spoke in Gaelic, recognised by some of the sitters. I have no personal acquaintance with the language, which was familiar to many present. There was a sound of stamping and dancing accompanying the strange language.

We had had news that morning regarding a friend's marriage. On my sister-in-law making her presence known, my wife said: Have you heard the news about H——?" Voice: "You mean about the lady? I do like the little lady, and I am so delighted." Q.: "Any message?" A.: "Tell him I wish him much joy and happiness." There was nothing in the form of the question that could have indicated the nature of the news, which was in the highest degree unexpected; and the communicator had been on the other side for over a quarter of a century.

My father then came and had a short talk; reassured my wife about matters at home, regarding which she was apt to be anxious when away. Then an uncle of mine came, giving his name and speaking with remarkable loudness and clearness, which, as it was his first communication, was particularly striking. His conversation was chiefly on the significance of these phenomena, and his surprise at their being possible: "If a man die, shall he live again? I will help you to make this truth known through your efforts." We had quite a long conversation on the subject which I could not record. At its conclusion I inquired about his daughter, whom I had not heard of for some years. He replied, in a surprised tone: "She is with you" (meaning in earth life). I said: "I know that she is here, but have not heard of her lately." To which he answered: "She was abroad for a time. I will try and bring you to meet."

This concluded the series of sittings we had at Rothesay. Being unused to note-taking of the kind necessary, my records lacked completeness; but the accuracy of any passages reported verbatim has been maintained to the best of my ability, and checked by independent notes taken by my wife. It would, however, be wasting valuable space to give conversations even as fully as reported, except where evidential tests are involved: and this is even more the case in the following series of sittings at Cambridge House in August, at three of which only myself and my wife were present with the medium. Under these circumstances our spirit friends conversed on each occasion for about an hour.

Cambridge House, Wimbledon. On August 19, at 7 p.m. About six other sitters were present. One of my sisters-in-law spoke, and then my father. He alluded to my being busy, and asked: "How is it at the works?" This puzzled me, as I am not concerned with any works, and it seemed the sort of thing that might be incorrectly inferred concerning me. I inquired: "What works?" He replied that he meant an invention in which I was interested, naming it. No one present but myself and my wife could possibly have known of it or of my connection with it, still less that I occasionally visited the X—— factory, where some work in relation to it was occasionally done. He proceeded to show a complete knowledge of what was being done in regard to it, and expressed strong opinions about what ought to be done, which seemed on the whole very well founded. I asked if he knew what I did the previous day. He replied: "Do you mean about the doctor?" (This was the case: I had been relating some of these experiences to a medical man who was much interested in the subject, and who had known my father.)

I assented, and he replied: "I am much more interested in the invention at present," and talked about it for some time longer. My sister-in-law, K——, spoke and stated that the lady referred to on July 22 was not English. (This we have not yet been able to verify: it is quite probable.) Voices for most of the other sitters were also heard. Mrs. Wriedt commented on the word "tomfoolery" used by one of them as being quite new to her.

August 15, 2 p.m. My wife and myself alone were present with Mrs. Wriedt. John King spoke, and a luminous hand became visible overhead. Then my father spoke, but soon said: "I want someone else to talk to you."

A voice then came for my wife: "Uncle ——" (name not audible), in answer to her inquiry, "On father's side?" After some blurred sounds, the name was given, "Uncle Henry." My wife: "Give me time; I can't quite remember. I don't know you." Voice: "No; but I know you at S——" (our home). "I come to you at the table." Q.: "What table?" A.: "Your little table. I will come to you when you sit." Another sister-in-law then spoke, and, in reply to an inquiry as to who the uncle was, said that he was uncle Henry, that my wife's father never knew him, that he (the uncle) was born before him.

(All this was quite unknown to my wife; subsequent inquiry from her mother, however, elicited the information that there had been such a relative, who had died in childhood before his brother's birth: and, to the best of her recollection, his name— his second name, she thought—was Henry.)

The next voice was that of my mother, with whom we had a long conversation on personal matters. Lastly, my uncle George B—— (who had been the first relative to communicate, on May 22), spoke, and, after some talk on other matters, alluded to the invention mentioned in our sitting of August 10, saying he had been discussing it with my father. I much regret that, for obvious reasons, I cannot publish the conversation, and can only say that he showed an astounding familiarity with it, and with difficulties we had to meet. Alluding to the people concerned, he said: "There are five of you." I thought this was a mistake, and said: "No, four." A.: "He (i.e., my father) said 'there were five,'"

I then recollected that another man had been just added to the number—the mistake was mine. A long conversation on the same subject followed.

Dr. Sharp then came, and gave further advice about sitting at home; then began to talk to my wife about our daughters studies, with much good council regarding them, which concluded the sitting.

August 18, 12 noon. Sitting at Cambridge House; conditions as on last occasion. The first speaker was John King; then my sister-in-law K——, who was followed by my father. He again discussed the matter of the invention. I asked him if he remembered Z——, naming an old fellow pupil of mine. He replied, "Yes."" This was all that passed about Z——; the mere mention of his name. My father them, after mentioning that my "guide" was an inventor, proceeded to describe another invention which he wished me to bring out. Again I regret the impossibility of publishing the details; but for probably ten minutes or more we were engaged in a technical conversation regarding it. Objections of mine to certain points were met and discussed in a scientific manner; for instance, the amount to be allowed for expansion due to temperature changes in a certain part was stated, and, as I believe, correctly. The surprise of Mrs. Wriedt and my wife during this conversation, the subject of which was of course unfamiliar to them, was quite amusing.

At its close another sister-in-law spoke to my wife for some minutes, and then a voice addressed me, using a nickname and then a variant of it, by which I had been known at a private tutor's five and twenty years before. I had not even heard it for twenty years. This was Z——. If he had given his name, it would have had little force, as I had previously mentioned it, without any allusion to who he was, or even to whether he was a man or a woman: as it happened, the mere name did not clearly show this.

But the mention of this long-forgotten nickname was a distinct "test." A conversation on old times showed further memory of the period when we were together.

My wife then had a conversation with her father on family matters. To an inquiry regarding "Uncle Henry" he replied: "He's my brother, and I asked him to come and see you. I am glad you were able to give your mother bona-fide evidence." The sitting concluded with some conversation with Dr. Sharp.

August 23; sitting at 4 p.m.; conditions as last time. We found some acquaintances there who had just had an absolutely blank sitting, so doubted if we should get anything. However, no sooner had we sat down than water was sprinkled in our faces, and John King's deep voice said "God bless you!" He gave further advice about sitting at home, saying: "You're only children in this cause. You may sit four years, or you may sit a year, before you can get something satisfactory to yourselves." An aunt of mine then spoke, and was followed by my father, who alluded to a meeting I had attended shortly before, and showed knowledge of what had passed there. He talked at length about the inventions, going into all kinds of mechanical details. He then asked if we had seen a light when sitting at home the previous night. As a matter of fact, we had been sitting in the dark, and my wife told me at the time that she saw a luminous appearance; but no mention of this had been made during the sitting. My father resumed; "it was one of your sisters." Much further conversation on family matters followed, and continued when my mother's voice succeeded my father's.

My wife then had a long talk on private matters with her sister, and then asked if she remembered a favourite song of hers, beginning to sing it. My sister-in-law's voice then joined in and continued the song. Her father then communicated, and, after much talk on family affairs, said, in reply to a question, that he was in the sixth sphere: and after a few further words about the spheres said emphatically, "In this house are many mansions"; and went on to quote the context from the fourteenth chapter of St. John. This had to be his favourite chapter in life.

Dr. Sharp concluded the sitting as usual, giving us further advice about sitting, and about practising mental control and quietude.

On Tuesday, August 26, we were present at a farewell gathering of friends at Cambridge House, following which we had a remarkable sitting. Everyone present had a communication from some relative; while my sister- in- law was speaking I heard two voices simultaneously—one conversing with another sitter. My father spoke again about the "inventions," and said "that, on consideration, he thought I should postpone dealing with one, and give my attention to the other. I don't want you to have too many irons in the fire." This was significant to us. I have too many interests to devote sufficient time to any of them.

Remarkable addresses from Stead and from "Julia" formed not the least interesting part of the séance, which none of those who were present will soon forget.

In concluding this account of our experiences, necessarily much abbreviated, I find it difficult to define the exact point at which the evidence that we were in actual touch with our departed friends amounted to conviction. It is not easy—perhaps it is impossible—to obtain mathematical proof of identity; but the amount of evidence needful to lead to a correct conclusion as to identity has been shown by professor Hyslop in what is, as far as I know, the only series of practical experiments in the matter, to be far smaller, and more trivial, than we should have supposed— infinitesimal, in fact, compared with the mass of correct names, correct statements, and exhibitions of personal characteristics which occurred to the hundreds in the course of these sittings. I have been familiar with the possibilities and pitfalls of psychical investigation for upwards of twenty years, and entered on the investigation a spirit of the most cautious scepticism. In the result I am compelled to admit inability to maintain this attitude without assuming a distrust of all physical perceptions that would reduce their ordinary employment to absurdity.

R.B.

EVIDENCE FROM SCOTLAND

In answer to my request that he would give me his opinion as to the nature of the voices which spoke in the séances of Mrs. Wriedt when she was in Scotland, Mr. James Robertson wrote as follows on August 7, 1913:—

One of the most striking things associated with the mediumship of Mrs. Wriedt is not only that the voices tell out their tale clearly, but in the dialect or language that the spirit used when and earth-dweller; particularly is this the case with the lowland Scotch with which I am so familiar. Again and again there were dropped words conveying so much—words of old Scotch which today are getting obsolete. Dr. Sharp, the wise manager or control of what is transmitted, is one who is undoubtedly familiar with the Scotch of Robert Burns; it is not a case of imitation, but the idioms of one who had been saturated with the Scotch language or dialect. He is a native, and to the manner born, and calls forth the words which, though strange and harsh to the English ear, speak so much of the Scottish heart. According to his story, he was removed from Glasgow at an early age; but the words he so often used would be those which were used in his homestead in America. Like all educated Scotch, he speaks good English; but in conversation with a Scot like myself he seemed to take delight in falling into the words of his childhood days. I was face to face with a countryman, and when he would say "Ye'd better bide a wee," or "You would be better to wait for a little time." I did not think it strange; I had lost sight of the fact that I was speaking to a spirit for the moment, and was face to face with an inhabitant of my own country. It was not a role which he assumed once; but at every sitting which I have attended in Glasgow and Rothesay there was given the revelation of Scotch character which could not be imitated so as to deceive an old Scotsman like myself. There was not the slightest trace of anything foreign in it all; he was as familiar with all the common words used in conversation as I was. "Thank you for spiering," he would say; that is, for asking or inquiring. "Twa three were there"—that is, a few were present. The other visitors speaking to their friends lisped the old familiar words in their old tones: "Don't greet"; that is "Don't cry" would be heard; "dinna" do this or that, "do not"; the "braes" or slope of a hill, in reminiscences of the old life were referred to; "braw chiel," a handsome man, was spoken of. My mother, who came repeatedly to me, spoke just as she had done in the body. She was as familiar with my life now as she had ever been; and she addressed me in her broad Doric: "My laddie, we were baith together then." She ca'd, that is "named" me as she did when I was a boy. My family were "weans"; each she spoke of, and their traits, in the vernacular; but why repeat a catalogue of Scotch words? She was present with me, giving forth her thoughts and feelings and expressing her delight that I had followed the spiritual revealment so faithfully. I cannot feel she is ever far away from me, and my joy is great that these voices have seemingly brought me closer to her than before. It is a great mystery how the vocal chords are formed which enable friends to come so near. Mrs. Wriedt is evidently a block of magnetism out of which the spirits hew some of the material they use. In most of the mediumistic controls some part of the instrument shows through; here there was not the slightest tone that brought Mrs. Wriedt into view; she was but an interested spectator. How this mediumship has unfolded year by year. Once identity was a somewhat rare occurrence; now troops of spiritual beings reveal themselves, and make their presence clear without a doubt. Wonderful and brilliant as is the light which has shone on us, will this light become brighter as the years roll on? I think so! What a march outwards since the "Raps" at Hydesville in 1848! With similar growth in the development of phenomena, the time must come when such a thing as doubt regarding the future life will not be possible. The early pioneers caught hold of the truth that there was a door open between the two worlds, and they realised that the subject was capable of uplifting and ennobling; few of them could have foreseen the possibilities which this mediumship of Mrs. Wriedt has brought to view; but

> This is true—that you can never
> Seek to know, and fail in finding;
> Seek to end, and it will ever
> Grow more near and be less blinding

> Oakley,
> Prestwick,
> Ayrshire.

The following narrative is written by Mr. John Duncan, T.C., Deacon Convenor of Trades, Edinburgh:—

A few notes of a séance held by Mrs. Etta Wriedt at the house of John Duncan, Dunearn, Granton Road, Edinburgh, on the evening of Sunday, July 27, 1913, at 7.30.

There were only five present, our object being to have it as private and select as possible.

I had asked to meet Mrs. Wriedt, along with my wife, daughter, and self, Mrs. Sharpe, who had accompanied us to Rothesay, and was present at a few of Mrs. Wriedt's séances held there, and Mr. Morrison, who was also at Rothesay, both of whom I knew to be sincere and zealous spiritualists. The séance was opened as usual by repeating the Lord's Prayer, after which a verse of a hymn was sung. We had not long to wait before our daughter Lizzie came, who passed over a babe, thirteen months old, over thirty years ago. She is now well known, both here and in Rothesay, at the séances we have sat in; at times she has spoken to her mother and I for twenty and often thirty minutes at a time; this time she came in her usual mild and endearing manner, and said Bob, her brother, was with her, and a great many others. Next my grandfather Veitch came; he passed away at the age of ninety-five, about fifty-six years ago. This is but the second time he has come to me and made himself known. Although going back such a number of years, I well remember his tall, erect figure; he was a typical Scot of the old Calvinistic times, ultra orthodox, and belonged to a religious body in

Scotland then known as "Cameronians," who would not pray for or acknowledge any crowned heads. He asked for my son John, and how he was getting on (in business I suppose).

Then my son Bob came; he has been in spirit life thirty-three years, and passed away a boy of about six years of age. There are few of our relatives and friends now in spirit life but what Bob has been the means of bringing back to us; he is known on the other side as a great worker and missionary. On coming to us on this night he seemed overjoyed at meeting his sister Teenie (Christena), as she is called. She will not be styled a spiritualist. She left home a few years ago and learned the occupation of a nurse; he expressed pleasure at her now being at home helping her mother, told her nursing was too heavy work for her; how he would make things smooth, and do all he could to help her, and in parting said she was his favourite sister. Then my dear old grannie Veitch came; she has been in spirit life fifty years, and was nearly ninety years of age when she passed over. She was also a typical Scotswoman of her day, but quite a contrast to her husband (my grandfather). She had a winning character during her earth life, loved by all for her kind, gentle manner; truly it could be said of her: ""he went about doing good."" In talking with us tonight, how she enjoyed herself, and laughed heartily about me falling off a gate when she lived six miles from Edinburgh. I was on a visit to her with my mother, and would not be more than four or five years of age at the time to which she referred.

An old friend came, who had been with us in spirit at Rothesay— Mr. Taylor, who was at one time stationmaster at Galashiels. I used to do part business there, and was intimate with Taylor. He was noted for being a great joker, and always carrying out his fun in a practical way. I asked him if anyone had brought him tonight; he said he was now able to come himself. (It is only about three weeks since he passed over.) My wife asked him if he remembered when he came last to us what he promised. (This had reference to a private sitting with Mrs. Wriedt at Rothesay.) Evidently at first he forgot; but immediately said: "Oh! yes; my snuff-box," and at once we heard the lid clink, which was to be the signal to us when he was present. He told me Robertson and he were not together in spirit life. Taylor and Robertson were well known to each other during their earth lives.

A nephew came next, Mackenzie by name; he was known to all of us during his earth life as "Mac"; he passed away fully a year ago, after a painful and lingering illness. His conversation was mainly directed to my daughter, and at first was rather indistinct. He was most persistent about his wife (Teenie he always called her); said she was thinking about making a change; how it would be better for her not to do so; but if she did, he would do all in his power to help her; told my daughter to give her this message, but only if she cared to do so. This he repeated more than once; his idea, no doubt, being that, as my daughter was not a spiritualist, he did not insist on her giving the message. I put in a word once or twice during the conversation; but he replied rather sharply; "It was Teenie (my daughter) he was speaking to. "It was apparent he wished to talk with her. She was to give his love to his wife Teenie and his son. He then asked me how John was getting on, meaning my youngest son. I asked him if he remembered my other son's name. He replied at once "Bill," which was correct.

Mrs. Sharpe, who was present with us, got very striking tests. The first to come to her was her daughter Anne, who passed over nearly three years ago. We could all hear her saying "I am Annie." She then asked how her mother was keeping; then something was said that Mrs. Sharpe did not quite catch, at which Annie said to her mother: "You are not deaf." She then asked for her sister Jenny, who is called by Mrs. Sharpe and the other members of her family "Jessie," but always called in earth life by Annie "Jennie," and that is the name by which she still remembers her—a very striking proof to Mrs. Sharpe and her family as to Annie's identity. I may here state that Mrs. Sharpe got the same test at Rothesay. Annie then told her mother that Jennie's health was a little run down, and she was needing a change very much. Then Mrs. Sharpe asked if she knew where they were going next day for their holiday. Annie replied: "A lonely place, and they were going by sea." Sure enough a lonely place, their holiday being on the island of Iona, three hours sail from Oban! Mrs. Sharpe then spoke a few words in German to Annie, in which language she was an adept during her earth life. No better proof could we have wished for than to listen to mother and daughter talking in German, and which was also known to Mr. Morrison. Then a Mr. Scott came to Mrs. Sharpe; He had been a schoolmaster at Granton, three miles from Edinburgh. He thanked Mrs. Sharpe for delivering the message he gave her at Rothesay to his wife, and said he was far happier where he was than on the earth plane. Mrs. Sharpe asked him how he knew she was here. He replied: Annie sent me." Mrs. Sharpe's mother-in-law next came, and gave unmistakable proof of her identity. She was so pleased at being able to come back; said grandfather was with her and Mrs. Sharpe's husband. She asked for Mrs. Sharpe's son David, giving his name, and, on leaving, promised to come back before long.

Mr. Morrison I had known now for some time as a genuine spiritualist; he makes a sympathetic and harmonious sitter. The proofs he got this night I consider really wonderful and convincing. The first to come to him was an uncle, who had been killed in a coal mine, and he spoke to his brother, who had passed over in the same way. The uncle spoke so kindly and made special reference to Mr. Morrison's daughter Kitty who has been seriously ill for nine months; how he knew all about her, and said she was making a favourable recovery. (None of us that knew her thought at one time she would pull through; but, thanks to those on the other side, who have been tending and watching over her, she is now making what her doctor calls "a miraculous recovery." Mr. Morrison asked his uncle if he had seen his father; he replied: "He is here and will speak to you." After many kind inquiries as to friends on the earth plane, he left, wishing us "Goodbye."

Mr. Morrison's father came next; we all heard him crying, "My dear son," twice, "How glad I am to be able to come and speak to you again." As a test, Mr. Morrison at once asked him where he had last spoken to him, and without the least hesitation he answered: "Rothesay." This was so, he having spoken to Mr. Morrison at one of Mrs. Wriedt's séances there.

Mr. Morrison had some hesitation in introducing his brother Willie's name, as he and his father had been somewhat estranged in earth life, and could not get on together. Mr. Morrison's father at once seemed to realise the position, and said: "That's all right now, my son; there is no bitterness here. Where you are there are bitters and sweets; but in spirit life we entertain no bitterness, and have only the sweets." Speaking of his son Willie, he said he was now in Canada; to let him remain there, as he was doing far better there than he could ever do at home. Morrison then spoke to his father about his sister Mary; to which he only replied: "Poor Mary! Poor Mary! She has been in a poor state of health for some time." (Truly there is little passing here but what our spirit friends know about and feel interested in!) Mr. Morrison next spoke to his father about his mother; she is seventy years of age, and hale and hearty. The spirit told him to give her his love and his blessing. Mr. Morrison then asked about his children in spirit life. He said his little girl "Sang like a nightingale"; this he was most emphatic about. He next asked his father if he knew where his brother Jim was at present, and, with a laugh he answered: "He is here in Edinburgh with you." (His brother Jim was through from Glasgow to Edinburgh, spending the week-end with his brother and family.) Then there was a conversation between father and son of a somewhat private nature about one of the family named "Gilbert." Mr. Morrison assured me after the séance that his father, in speaking of his brother Gilbert, had told of past events in his life that no other one could have done. Mr. Morrison" father, in parting spoke with some emotion, and again referred to his children, specially naming Kitty, whose life so recently had been despaired of. In concluding, I must say I have sat at many séances, but never at one where such convincing proofs were given to everyone present.

At my request, Mr. James Coates, Glenbeg House, Rothesay, Author and well known student of the occult, has consented to furnish for this work some notes of proceedings in Scotland, especially séances held with Mrs. Wriedt. I had the pleasure of being at some of these, and I can accept with confidence the reports which follow, as I recognise in Mr. Coates a patient and cautious investigator, and one whose accuracy of statement may be fully relied on:—

THE PSYCHOPHONE IN SCOTLAND

By James Coates

Author of *Self-Reliance* and other works

Rothesay, September 8, 1913.

Dear Admiral Moore,

In sending you the following notes on psychophone and allied psycho-physical phenomena, in which Mrs. Wriedt was the centre round whom they took place, I wish to say that either the notes are written by persons the accuracy of whose statements are verified by my short-hand notes, or they have been taken down during interviews by myself. As desired, they are specially contributed to your book.

Concerning the medium Mrs. Wriedt I have nothing to say, as neither her personality nor her mediumship depends on my opinions, being adequately testified to by your works and others which have been given to the public. Personally, I think she is the finest medium of her kind, and in her the late Mr. Stead found the most valuable and reliable instrument for psychophone communication with his family and the world. A brief account of some of these communications are given in Has W. T. Stead returned? and to the press. Remarkable as this has been, it falls far short of the evidences presented—in her presence—of the knowledge possessed by departed friends to those on earth, whom they were able, over the psychophone, to address. If it be impossible to multiply the evidences by giving demonstrations in all centres of the movement, we must rejoice in having such a rare instrument as Mrs. Wriedt with whom to experiment. The manifestations in Mrs. Wriedt's presence are analogous to telephonic messages—hence my use of the name psychophone. While many of the voices heard were characterless in expression, muffled in sound, as if inadequately transmitted by telephone, the majority became definitely clear, individualised characteristic of the voice of the departed in life, towards the end, when the "distant" speaker and the person receiving the message got into freer communication. The voice identification was—in addition to the humanly identifiable nature of the communications—most evidential. If it be objected that the messages were in some instances short, although the names and incidents were correct, or the voice of the supposed speaker was not recognised, my answer is "These are not sound objections, and would not be advanced by an experienced psychic investigator. The latter would esteem the shortest voice communication of value. It is neither the length or brevity of the message which matters, but the contents." The voice being transmitted in this way may be feeble, muffled, or clear; yet, however valuable the clear voice, that in itself is not so important as the import and aptness of that which is said. As a Naval officer you will appreciate as an illustration the hailing of ships at sea: a few flags hoisted and pulled down during the day; some lights flashed at night, or if near enough—in the old days—a hail or two from the quarterdeck, and you obtain all the information you wanted, the name of the vessel, destination, number of passengers, cargo, and bon voyage. It was not much, but was sufficient. So has it been in the séance room. If the messages were in some instances brief, they were sufficient; identification was complete, and kindly greetings were exchanged. In these days of scientific discovery great advances have been made, and the intelligences in the invisible are evidently keeping up to date. In advance, indeed, for long before telephonic communication was deemed possible on earth, voice phenomenon was reported in séance-rooms. As a rule, a telephone message is only heard by the user; but not so with the psychophonic messages. They are not only heard by the person most interested, but are heard by all privileged to be present.

In the Rothesay circle it is the rule not to admit any person for the first time, unless introduced by one whose bonâ-fides are acceptable to me. When we have a professional medium like Mrs. Wriedt, the same rule holds good. Although there are expenses, no one is admitted either because of demand or ability to pay. A well- meaning friend, being thoroughly convinced himself and anxious to make the facts known, wanted to invite some persons—clergymen, magistrates, and so on—thinking, if they were convinced, great good would be accomplished; he was willing to pay all expenses. I objected; but, to save his feelings, consulted "Dr. Sharp." Who stoutly refused, saying, "When people are ready and have a longing in their hearts for communication with their loved ones, the way will be found for them, but not for these outsiders. Bring a minister in, and ten to one, if he is convinced, he will not have the courage or honesty to speak the truth; if he is not, he will be the first to proclaim from the pulpit what he is pleased to call 'a fake.' Magistrates—rubbish; invite no one because of their position and influence. Yes; there is room for sincere men and women; but we have no time for these persons, the bulk of whom would never put to good use what they got. Christ warned his disciples not to throw pearls before swine, but some people wanted to throw pearls into them. No! no! tell your friend we will have none of these folk."

Dr. Sharp has experience, and he is right. Honest scepticism in the open-minded has never hindered phenomena, but it is a fatuous proceeding to introduce the unfit and the unready into the séance-rooms in order to convince them

Another good friend who received valuable evidence last year here was anxious to give a few friends a sitting, and so arranged for a private séance. What came was very good, but his friends were neither ready nor anxious for these messages, and one oof them afterwards attributed "the voices" to ventriloquism—a double error, arising from ignorance of the range and scope of ventriloquism and the possibilities of psycho- physics.

To those who admit phenomena, but object to them on the ground that they proceed from evil spirits personating our departed friends. I have nothing to say, contenting myself with stating the objections. Having said so much, I will present a few cases and let them tell their own tale.

THE TESTIMONY OF MR. WILLIAM JEFFREY

No. 1.—Mr. William Jeffrey, 15 India Street, Glasgow, keen observation and of recognised business ability, is the sole partner in one of the largest timber and sawmill businesses in that city. He had several séances with Mrs. Wriedt. In an interview with him I took the following notes:—

"I became very much interested in Mrs. Wriedt's mediumship, through reading in Light lately your account of the séances held in Rothesay in 1912, and determined to have some séances with her as soon as convenient. I met Mrs. Wriedt shortly after her arrival in Glasgow from London, and our first séance was held July 2, in my own house, 15 India Street, Glasgow. In addition to my people, I phoned a few others and made up the circle. There were seventeen present, all of whom I knew to be genuine people. As you wish, I will not touch upon what took place as far as the other sitters were concerned, but only with that which appealed to me personally.

"The first voice we heard was that of my wife, who welcomed to her house all there, addressing several by name, including Mr. Galloway, Mrs. Birrell, and a visitor from London, whom (in life) she did not know. Her voice, which was quite clear, said, 'O, Willie, I'm awfu' glad to be here, an' speak in my home to you and these friends.' My wife (who usually spoke good English, could, and often did, lapse into old Scotch ways of speaking when either very pleased or talking to intimates) addressed us in her earnest, homely, and rapid way, 'I trust you will have a pleasant evening.' Then she went round and spoke to each member of the family. The voice never erred when it addressed 'Bella' or 'Sally' in a loving way, or prefixed 'Mr.' or 'Mrs.' To persons whom my wife would have addressed in that way in life.

"A voice which we recognised at once came close to me: 'Bill, Bill, how are ye?' 'Who are you friend?' I asked. 'Neil, Neil; I'm Neil, man!' followed by a hearty laugh. Neil McQuarrie was a relative by marriage, and had been for many years our cashier. He had a peculiar way of speaking, and at times was ' verra braid an hamely,' and his laugh was not like anyone I knew. For a little while he spoke to his wife, about his children, each by name. There was no mistaking his references, and his kindly expressions, designed to cheer, conveyed a world of meaning. Mrs. White, who sat next to me, whispered, 'Do you think he'll know me?' and immediately the answer came, 'Dae ye no think A ken ye, Annie White? Hoo are ye a' in London?' The voice then addressed my son-in-law, Mr. Kerr. 'Charlie, hoo are ye keeping? But a'm surprised to see ye here. Ye'renae sae lang-headed as Bill (myself), whom ye thocht was a wee bit off; but ye'll get something tae-night that'll convince ye.'

This was so like Neil, and he followed this outburst with a genial laugh. It was his laugh at this point which made the recognition unmistakable. The voice came to me and thanked me for certain things I had done for him in life, and for his wife and children since. I'll not forget it, and ye'll never lose by it." To my daughter (Mrs. Kerr) he said, "" hae tae thank ye for lookin' a'ter ma boys." Mrs. Kerr: "o you think I have been too severe in chastising them?" 'Weel, no; they're a bit self-willed an thro' 'ither; but that is because they've nae faither to gie them bit guidin'; min' that. Ye're doin' quite right; bit lead them whiles.' Then he bid us all good night.

My daughter Isa came next, and we all had a nice little talk; and she left sending out love and kisses to us all.

Another voice came saying 'Jeffrey!' 'Who are you?' 'I'm Captain George Miller's father.' I said, 'I did not know you.' 'Well, man, I ken ye fine, an' wis wi' ye an 'Captain George when ye wis on yer holidays in Orkney an' Shetland last month.' This was pretty much to the point. I asked, 'What did you think of them?' The voice, 'It wisna much of a holiday for weather, but it pit a lot o' backbone in ye.' I hoped so, and said I would tell Captain George that he had been. 'Man ye needn't fash. Ye might as well tell a log, for he will no believe ye.'

"Fifteen of the seventeen visitors present received messages. I think they were satisfied, and many were delighted. Owing to my wife being able to manifest so fully through Mrs. Coates some months previously, I had looked for her to make herself known—according to her promise—on this occasion. Yet what took place was beyond my most sanguine anticipations. It was simply marvellous. The medium, Mrs. Wriedt, was a stranger, whom I met for the first time that morning. The séance was hurriedly convened by wire and 'phone, and took place in a room hastily arranged for the purpose. If the results are not evidence for spirit return, then I am at a loss to know what could be more valuable or important.

"The next séance we had was on Thursday, July 3, and was held in one of the rooms of the Glasgow Association of Spiritualists, Berkley Street Hall. I got a 'phone asking me to come and bring a few others, as they were short of sitters. I 'phoned Mrs. McMaster, and she came by putting off an engagement—so that, as a visitor, her presence was wholly unexpected. This lady had never been to a séance before. The very first voice which came was that of her husband, who had passed out nine months before. He came saying, 'Nellie, Nellie!' Mrs. McMaster replied, feeling it was him. 'Is that you pa?' 'Yes dear,' was the response.

I said I thought the voice was like his, and suggested that she speak freely to it. 'Yes, dear,' giving kisses. 'I am so pleased to come and talk to you. You were a good lass to me. I'm so glad to see you getting on so well. Give my love to Jeffrey.' Mrs. McMaster; 'You can give your love to Mr. Jeffrey yourself, for he is sitting next to me.' The voice emphatically: ' No, no; I want you to give my love to my little boy, Jeffrey McMaster.' The whole of this conversation, and the circumstances under which it took place, were most telling. Before McMaster left, he said 'It was Bella' (meaning my wife in the spirit world) 'brought me here'; and concluded giving his love to his wife and messages to his family.

"Mrs. Jeffrey came in her pleasant way and had a homely chat, and this was followed by a word or two from my daughter Isa. There was one feature at this séance which impressed us—namely, the free sprinkling of water upon us all. I mention this, too, as there was no water in the room. I did not see any, and Mr. Galloway, who had the preparation of the room, said there was none. Apart from this phenomenon, the meaning of the sprinkling is, I am told, 'blessing and purification.'

We had another sitting in the same place, Friday evening, July 4. There were present my daughter Mrs. Kerr, niece, and myself. My wife came and spoke for a little while to all of us. I asked, 'Bella, did you like the service I had at your funeral?' 'Oh, it was very nice indeed, but,' with a laugh, 'the minister said far more about me than he knew.' (We did not think so, as my wife in her lifetime was a good friend to anyone in sickness and distress.) She thanked me 'for the nice way you laid me to rest,' and said she was 'pleased to see all the folk had come to it.' She finished with a little talk to us all about our affairs in a general way and some kindly counsel to myself. To my daughter, niece, and myself, what the voice said was conclusive.

"The Séance on July 5 was attended by my daughter, son-in-law, and niece. I mention these to indicate that I am not assuming nor imagining what took place, but give their evidence. Here again my wife appeared and spoke to her daughter and Mr. Kerr. This sitting was brought to a close by the presence of a sitter asking impertinent questions about tramways and flying machines over there. The trumpet was put down with a bang, and there was no more voices that evening.

Monday, July 7, Berkley Street Hall. Mrs. Kerr and I attended. I had been thinking about Bella, my wife; but the first to address me was a very old friend named Sterling, who had departed this life some twenty years ago. I asked him who brought him here. He said, 'Mrs. Jeffrey; she is helping a lot of people to come.' As he had only given his name,

I said, 'Are you the Mr. Sterling I knew long ago?' 'Yes,' was the reply. 'Well do you remember what was the matter with you before you died?' I asked. He answered, 'I was totally blind for five years.' This was correct and a strong bit of evidence to us. Mrs. Kerr: 'Have you seen Mrs. Sterling?' 'Oh yes, dear; we are very happy here.' I need not detail what was said; all was correct.

"Mrs. Wriedt said there was a spirit present who had shot himself. He was for Mr. Robertson of Helensburgh. 'Did he know a man like that?' Mr. Robertson: 'Yes; he was thought to have committed suicide by shooting himself.' Afterwards the voice addressed Mr. Robertson, and he, satisfied to the identity, asked, 'Did the gun go off accidentally or intentionally?' The voice assured him it was an accident. 'Man, I had nae need to do it' (commit suicide). Everyone seemed to think he had, but Mr. Robertson was always of the opinion it was an accident, and what the spirit said accorded with this belief. The man had been with him a night or so before his death, and told him, among other things, who nicely everything was going on in business and other matters; he was in a cheery mood. The voice insisted that the story of his suicide was not true. 'Man, I'd nae need tae destroy masel.' Although the incident is not exactly personal, it so struck me, I thought I would mention it.

My last sitting with Mrs. Wriedt in Glasgow was on Thursday, July 24. There were eighteen present, including the medium, my daughter, son-in-law, niece, cousin, and a friend. The first to speak was my wife, and, after a kindly word and inquiry to each, said she was sorry that these meetings were coming to an end, and of the great comfort they had given her. I was to understand she was always with me. I asked her how it was she had spoken to me in all the sittings but one. (I had several sittings in Rothesay between July 7 and 24.) She said it was because other relations wanted to speak to me, and 'I did not wish to be selfish and monopolise the time and prevent others speaking to their friends.' (She had brought many to the sittings.) She finished by bidding us 'Adieu till we meet again.'

"A voice purporting to be Mr. Kerr's mother spoke to us and to him. My daughter then spoke to the spirit, calling attention to the differences which had taken place between them owing to her engagement to her son. They had always been on most pleasant terms till within a short time of the marriage. The spirit answered in a clear and trembling voice, 'Let bygones be bygones, dear. We will not talk about that, but you must allow for a mothers feelings when she loses her only son.' All very natural and very true.

"Another voice spoke, that of the late Mr. Kerr—my son-in-law's father. He had been in spirit life some years. He gave us 'his crack' freely. Addressing his son 'Charlie,' said he was 'verra pleased tae see th' business progress he was makin' in life. Many thanks tae yer faither-in-law fer what he's done for ye. Ye hae had a better startin' in life by faur than ever A had.' Then addressing me, the voice said: 'Thank ye Jeffery, for what ye hae done for me laddie, an' ther's ae thing A'll sae fer him, he'll ne'er gie ye a red face.' After some friendly and kindly counsel he left.

A voice saying, 'Colin!' 'What Colin?' 'Colin Buchanan,' and shortly afterwards addressing Mrs. McQuarrie already referred to, touching upon some sad and private matters, which I knew were unknown to anyone in that room—never spoken of by me to my daughter or to the nearest friend. It went back into old history of forty years standing. This was a revelation indeed. The facts unfolded were of a character which cannot with propriety be given to others. I regret that this should be the case, for it is evidence of this kind which is so convincing. To say that we were all deeply affected is the least that can be said.

"Mr. Bothwell had a friend who had been drowned, who came and spoke to him. He entered into details about the fact of his passing out, which no one knew anything about. This gentleman was much surprised at what he heard, as he had not believed such communications were possible. In addition to the foregoing another voice may be mentioned, which spoke to Mrs. McMaster. It was that of her daughter 'Serina,' who came giving this name, by which she was called in life. She sent her love to all her friends, naming them one by one. She spoke particularly about her only sister, sending her a very pertinent and thoughtful message. She then came to me, and spoke to the rest of her friends present, addressing each by their Christian name. There was no getting away from these facts, which came out in the presence of eighteen sitters. Everyone had a communication in that sitting, and some several. Not one of the voices that spoke that night blundered or was in error."

Mr. Reid is an artist, living at The Terrace, Ardbeg. His statements referring to phenomena taking place in the presence of fifteen to eighteen persons, including myself, and verified by my shorthand notes, can be taken as correct—except in this, they lack from brevity—and under-state rather than over-state what took place. I have suppressed much of a private character, but there is enough left to give an interesting and coherent account.—J. C.

The Testimony of Mr. Peter Reid

Tuesday, July 8. I was present at this, the opening séance. There were sixteen present, including Mrs. Wriedt, the trumpet medium. I came to these sittings with all the more confidence, as I had the privilege of being present when similar séances were held here last year. While tempted to deal with all that I saw and heard, I will confine myself to what appealed to me personally. The first to come to me was my father, who said; "How are you my boy?" His voice was very distinct for a little, but while he was talking a childish voice broke in. I was informed this was little Blossom, an Indian child. Although we had the phenomena of two voices speaking at once, my father, failing to make himself understood, withdrew. My father, a Perthshire man, spoke excellent English, with sufficient of the Caledonian burr with his "r's" to make his nationality distinctive enough to our English visitors. During the little conversation we had I asked my father; "What work are you engaged in?" He replied he was engaged in mission work. A statement like this from him was significant because the year before I got the same answer through Mrs. Coates. The voice made reference to my mother, and said she would be able to speak for herself, and to other relatives. There was enough in this brief psychophone conversation to establish his identity. Neither Mrs. Coates nor Mrs. Wriedt knew that my father in earth life, in addition to his usual occupations, had a deep interest in church mission and Sunday- school work. It is quite conceivable that he should be working on similar beneficial lines in the life beyond.

The next one to come was a young friend named Gertie. In her natural, impulsive way, she asked me twice if I had seen her. There was an etherealised firm which came towards me from the cabinet; but I did not recognise that to be her. That same day, before leaving for the meeting, I put her photograph and lock of hair, which had been in my possession since her death, in my pocket book.

I asked her what I had of hers in my pocket. She immediately answered; "My picture and the lock of my hair"; then made pathetic references to our attachment and other matters which she alone could speak about, and with "adieu" left.

Dr. Sharp came with some friendly counsel and said; "There is no love like the first love." Although not prepared to accept all he said, I was much struck by the aptness of his remarks. Gertie was a young girl of sixteen and a-half, when she passed over, twelve years ago. As young people we were much attached to each other. This was the first time she had been able to manifest by the direct voice which was it-self clearly identifiable.

Wednesday, July 9, 1913, at 8 p.m. This was an excellent evening. I heard a voice saying "Booth, Booth," and was surprised to learn it was General Booth, who delivered a characteristic address. Another and different voice shouted: "Joun King, God bless you." I do not know him. Dr. Sharp said: "Mr. Reid, have you a sister in the spirit world?" I replied I had not. He said; "Here is one who says she is your sister, at any rate." Dr. Sharp said to her: "He has no sister." The voice answered: "I'm his sweetheart." "Why did you say you are his sister?" "Because I thought I would not get in." This produced a laugh. I said: "Come away, Gertie; glad to hear you again." The voice came laughing, just as she would do when in a merry mood in life, and said "she did this to get in." She then reminded me she really was my sister, as I had act-ed a brothers part to her family and to herself: "So it is all right after all," once more with a laugh. She talked of things private to ourselves, greeted my wife, and concluded by giving me directions what to do with her picture and lock of hair. Dr. Sharp came with a laugh, saying: "I got diddled that time."

This sitting was most evidential, knowing as I did the complete ig-norance of Mrs. Wriedt of the names, voices, and mannerisms of my personal friends.

Thursday, July 10, at 2 p.m. At this I was present with my mother-in-law Mrs. Wyllie. Although neither received personal evidence, we were both deeply interested in what was given to others. This was Mrs. Wyl-lie's first experience. Archdeacon Colley manifested to Mr. and Mrs. Coates; Mr. Edward Wyllie, at one time a psychic photographer, had a conversation with his brother-in-law, Canon Dawson, and with Mrs. Wriedt the medium and Mr. and Mrs Coates. At the evening sitting Mrs. Wyllie got some interesting personal particulars, which I have not yet received and have no authority to furnish you.

Sunday, July 13, 8 p.m. This, too, was a most interesting meeting, full of startling incidents and personal evidence to those present. Mrs. Wriedt described a dark person wearing a jewelled turban and yel-low robes. Immediately a voice with a foreign accent said, "Raja, Raja," and then "Wood-Sims" "(Mrs. Wood-Sims is a friend of ours, and her chief control is a Hindu called "Rajah"). I asked the voice: "Are you Rajah?" The answer, "Yes, yes!" came with eagerness, followed with an address in what purported to be Hindustani. We could make noth-ing of it. We had, however, sufficient in broken English to understand who it was. I promised the speaker to let Mrs. Wood-Sims know that he had come.

Mrs. Wriedt said: "I see the name 'Tetlow'; does anyone recognise that?" No one answering, I said: "I suppose you mean 'Tetley'?" She said that was correct. It appears she gets the name presented in mirror fashion reversed, and the first part disappears before the whole is completed. While I awaited further particulars Mrs. Wriedt asked if anyone recognised the name of "Pearson." As no one responded, I said: "I know that name." Later on a voice said to me: "I am Mr. Tetley......I wish to thank you for your kindness in the past to my family." Mr. Tetley, who was the father of Gertie, died abroad about two years before her. This was the first time he manifested by the direct voice. After reference to his family, and again thanking me, he left. Another voice greeted me, saying; "I am Pearson." I asked: "Are you Mrs. Wyllie's brother?" "Yes." (I did not know his Christian name. There were four brothers in spirit life and two in the body.) The voice assured me he was "James Pearson." I asked him had he any message for those at home. He said: "Give them my best respects." Not much this, but I sent it to Mrs. Wyllie. In her reply, dated July 17 (22 Clarendon Street, Glasgow), she says; "My dear son-in-law,—Thanks for the little bit you put in......It is, in my view, very conclusive proof. My brother James always sent his best respects to everyone. The last time he was in Glasgow 'A' refused to speak to him, but Jim said: 'Never mind; we'll likely meet in heaven.' And in this station he said: 'Be sure and give 'A' my best respects.' I am glad that he came, for he was kind to me from childhood. I am also glad that Annie (Mrs. Reid) saw the wonderful sight she tells me of. Be sure to keep note of them all, so that I may be told everything......"

Sunday, July 20, at 8 p.m. On this evening there were many striking manifestations. My young friend Gertie came again. As she was a fine singer on earth, I asked her if she would sing to me one of her songs. She said she would sing one of her Scotch songs (Gertie was English), and offered to sing me 'Annie Laurie." She wanted me to sing with her. I could not manage this; but Mrs. Coates, who sat next to me, sang with her. Gertie sang sweetly. It was a very affecting manifestation. Just as the séance was about to close, my father broke in, and said he wanted to speak to "his boy" (he always spoke of me as "his boy" or "my boy"), and in his hearty greeting referred to matters specially apropos to my life and himself.

Wednesday, July 23. My father came again, and for the first time mother spoke to me by the direct voice. My mother had often come to me through the mediumship of Mrs. Coates. Mrs. Wriedt was ignorant of this. Mother spoke to me, among other things, about my brother, who is in the United States, and gave me what I believe was suitable advice. I fully understood and appreciated all she said.

If I had detailed all that had taken place, my narrative might be more interesting—or wearisome. The evidence to me was most convincing. My father's voice (his Perthshire English), my mother's "braid Scots" and affectionate impulsiveness, Gertie's winning manner and convincing statements, were to me most valuable; more so than the etherealisations, though the latter were remarkable. As evidence for survival in some unseen state, these direct-voice messages are priceless.

Mr. Coates notes:—

"It would be impossible to give one tithe of what took place in the Rothesay séance room during the forty odd séances held with Mrs. Wriedt there. While I have to suppress some very telling evidence, as the relation of them would give pain to the living, I venture to supply in this and other cases striking evidence of spirit persistence in manifestation. I have sat in a few séances in my time, but seldom came across a case where the sitters—honest, sincere souls—failed so often to grasp what was said, and the determination of the spirit friends to give the facts was more apparent. The visitors were Mr. and Mrs. Raw and their son, Mr. John Edwin Raw , of 14 Car Hall Road, Nelson. In a conversation I had with Mr. Raw subsequently to the séances, he said: 'I was puzzled, and didn't know what to say, and, being a little deaf, I didn't catch what was said; but I am now satisfied the whole thing is too wonderful for words.'

"Now for the account. Mr. J. E. Raw—who, by the by, did not give me his Christian name or those of his parents—wrote intimating that his father, mother, and he would like to visit Rothesay on their holiday, and have a sitting with Mrs. Wriedt, if possible. Being satisfied with their bonâ-fides, I agreed, but warned them it was a great risk to come so far for one sitting."

Mr. J. E. Raw says:—

The testimony of Mr. J. E. Raw

These séances (held July 12 and 13, at 2 p.m.) were conducted in such informal manner, with every facility for inspection of appointments, as to give assurance that their object was the dissemination of knowledge and experience of psychic phenomena. Both séances were crowded with incident, practically everyone present receiving verbal communication from arisen relatives and friends; while beautiful spirit- lights floating round at intervals denoted the highly spiritual conditions prevailing, culminating in the etherealisation of a beautiful form (a guide) enveloped in a golden halo.

The clear, concise, and pertinent remarks of the principal manifesting spirit, Dr. Sharp, were a source of much interest, his loud voice proving a thorough knowledge of what was to us a hitherto unfamiliar power, and in striking contrast to the laborious efforts of other spirits. He afforded a splendid test by instantly rapping the trumpet upon father's hand when requested to do so—a suggestive action in a dark room where it was impossible to see one's neighbours.

Our personal visitants were quite unexpected, though both gave convincing evidence of their identity.

(Mr. J. E. Raw gives a correct summary of their experiences; but to illustrate the point of spirit persistence forcing recognition of identity, in spite of difficulties in apprehension, I fall back upon my own notes to give a more detailed account.) Mr. Raw concludes with: "It is very fitting that by affording so generously such exceptional facilities for the demonstration of psychic phenomena your efforts should result in the comprehensive and conclusive manner they have done, as attested by a wide and rapidly extending circle of adherents, all so fortunate in making acquaintance with Mrs. Wriedt and her wonderful gifts. My mother, Mrs. Eva Raw, and my father, Mr. George Raw, join me in good wishes and appreciation of the good work in which you are engaged...... Although our Christian names were unknown to you, the spirit friends who addressed us gave correctly their own and our names......

J. E. Raw."

Mr. Coates continues:—

As to the more detailed account of what took place, it is to be noticed that none of the "voices" were from persons expected. In addition to what has already been given, that which follows is most evidential. Again and again this has occurred in these séances. Now, to illustrate what I mean. The first voice which came was not grasped by Mr. Raw, senior, and it was only by repeated urging we could get him to speak. The spirit voice was wasting energy trying to give its name; "Heckle," "Sexton," were understood to be given. When they were suggested the "voice" declined them with a weary "No, no, no." "After other attempts, the spirit voice said: "Are you deaf? I am William." "What William?" "Your brother." "I had no brother, no brother William." After considerable effort and persistence the voice gave the name of William Theckston, Mr. Raw's brother-in-law, following the name by many statements of a private nature and intimate application to prove the identity beyond doubt. "So, it's William!" joyfully exclaimed Mrs. Raw. It was remarkable the way the voice rejected all help, would have none of the names suggested, and never stopped till recognition was obtained. I could give interesting addresses, and, indeed, more readable matter; but to my mind "William Theckston"—in spirit—addressing "George" in the flesh as "brother" was evidence of the most valuable kind.

Another voice addressed Mrs. Raw shortly after the foregoing. It seemed a difficult matter to make out what it said at first. Mrs. Raw, although she could make nothing of it and denied all knowledge of knowing a man who used to come about her father's place, was readier in her address, and encouraged the voice to speak. Failing to get the name, she invited the spirit to tell her something which she would know him by. It was evidently the voice of a man—an Irishman we thought—whose attempts to give his name sounded like "Macguire." The voice: "Dae ye remember the place where ye was a little girl?—Dae ye mind the man that had the horses?—Dae ye mind the bay wan?" Mrs. Raw did remember where she lived as a girl. It was somewhat like as described by the voice. Of course there were horses, and a gate by the road-side, but she could not place this man. "Well," said the voice, "Dae ye mind me puttin' ye on the bay horse, an' teachin' ye to ride?" "Yes." "Well I'm the man, Dae ye forget the about the penny I gave you?" "No." "That's good. I believe it was the first penny ye ever got in your life. Now, do you remember me?" "Yes," said Mrs. Raw delighted, "I do," at which the voice laughed. Then the story came out bit by bit, and this old-time neighbour Swire, not Macguire, established his identity by the human touch of reminding her that her father never got paid for the horse he took away. As Mr. J. E. Raw puts it: "These trifling though distinctive details and characteristics were synonymous with the old-time neighbour and horsedealer named 'Swire,' and to us convincing proof of the genuineness of the phenomena witnessed at Mrs. Wriedt's séances.

This gentleman is a pharmaceutical chemist, doing business at 96 Craven Park Road, Harlesden, London, N. W. I have selected his case owing to the evidential factors, and to the persistence of his late wife in proving her identity. Another reason for my choice is, that he was a stranger who appealed to me. He attended three sittings on July 13 and 14. Neither Mrs. Wriedt nor anyone in the circles knew his name. Even if they did, that would not account for the following revelations:—

The Testimony of J. C. Berry, M.P.S.

Dear Mr. Coates,
Harlesden, August 16, 1913.

I was very much impressed from the first by the brightness and cheerfulness of all the friends gathered together, as well as by the spiritual atmosphere. One felt quite at home from the beginning. At the first meeting (July 13, 2 p.m.), when we had been sitting a little while, a voice came near to me calling "John, John!" But, although I spoke, I could get no reply. There was another voice speaking at the other end of the room. A little later the voice came again with "John, John!" I said, "Who are you?" The answer was not clear, but in what followed I knew who it was. The voice: "Yes; have you come all this long way from London to see me?"—"Yes, dear." The voice: "Forgive me, John, for being so irritable with you; I could not help it, the pain was so great." I told her not to worry, as I quite understood. She said she was quite happy now. I told her I had been wearying to speak to her, and she said, "I did not think I could use the horn." In conversation, she said she came morning and evening to our home and kissed the children. I do not give all we talked about. After my wife had gone, Dr. Sharp said to us: "This manifestation was an example of what a person could do who was less than six months passed over." (Quite true, J.B.) So determined was she to get in touch with her husband and children that she was able to speak without the use of the horn. Her voice was quite clear.

In the evening sitting, 8 p.m., my wife came again saying, "John, John! I have come back again. My throat is better now. I have no tube in my mouth." I asked her if she knew what was wrong, and she said: "Yes, dear, I knew it for months, but did not wish to worry you by telling you." (I did not know she knew, but she did and kept it to herself; this was fully in keeping with her disposition.) I was upset when she asked me: "Why were our days together so short? What harm had I done that I should be taken away so early? I tried to do my best......" I sympathised as best I could. I really did not know what to say. I suppose she had taken on something of the earth conditions.

I decided at the next sitting, if the voice called I would test it. A was perfectly satisfied, but my friends would be sceptical. At the third sitting, July 14, 8 p.m., when the voice called "John, John!" I said, "Who are you?" The voice said "Oh I am Katie." As before, the name was not very clear. One man said it was Lizzie, and asked if she was for him.

The voice: "No; I want my husband John Berry." This was said clearly and emphatically. That there might be no mistake about for whom the voice came, it gave me certain directions about my children, the articles I was to keep for them, and so on. The voice told me she (the mother) "Had been up at grandma's (where I had taken them) seeing the little ones, and they were very happy." I was told not to worry about the past, as everything had been done for her that could be thought of. In bidding me "Goodbye" she said she was coming home with me, and would try and speak to me in Harlesden.

What took place in the séance-room was beyond all possible anticipation. I was not the only one who obtained messages by direct voice. But to me the most wonderful thing was the foregoing. No one in that room—not even you—knew anything about my wife, children, or myself. None knew my wife died of cancer; that she had a tube in her throat. Yet here all was given, and that by the only person who could tell it— my wife. What is the benefit of all this? It has brought home to me, more than anything else, the fact that THERE IS NO DEATH; that the passing out is only to a life more abundant. I realise more than ever my duties to my neighbours, and will seek to live more in harmony with all.

I am, etc.,   John C. Berry.

Do Animals Survive Death?

Mr. Coates adds:— I would like to follow up the testimony of Mr. John C. Berry, with a incident which occurred at his last sitting. I offer no explanation, merely recording what took place, and that because of the evidence it presents of supernormal knowledge manifested. Mrs. Wriedt suddenly said, "O dear me; I do believe I see a dog." From the description I concluded it was a fox terrier. Further, "It is running about the room. It is frisking about and jumping on you sir" (Mr. Berry). Presently we all heard repeated several times a terrier's yelp. Leaving aside Dr. Sharp's explanation about the "animal kingdom" in the spirit world and the survival of dogs etc., the facts are as stated. Dr. Sharp told the chemist this was one of the many dogs that had been put to death in the discharge of his many duties. Mr. Berry admitted that Dr. Sharp was correct. Dogs had to be destroyed for many reasons; but he, however, would never undertake anything in that way, leaving the matter to the authorities and the lethal chamber. Whether animals survive in the Other World Order or not, I do not know; but, as a matter of evidence, no one in that room knew Mr. Berry was a chemist until after the dog yelped and Mr. Berry made his explanation.

Mr. Wright holds a responsible position in railway affairs, and has had valuable evidence through Mrs. Wriedt's phenomenal mediumship. I asked him for the report of his manifestations of a niece at the Rothesay circle. I now give his report without curtailment. To hear that sweet, pleasant, and naturally unaffected Irish voice was a treat. The facts, however, are of greater importance.—J. C.

The testimony of Mr. David Wright

16 Mannering Road, Shawlands, Glasgow.

September 10, 1913.

Dear Mr. Coates,

I am in receipt of your letter of 8th inst., and have much pleasure in complying with your request for a short report for publication in Admiral Moore's book of the séances held in your house, in so far as they affect myself or family. Admiral Moore, who was present at our third séance, was much impressed; and, indeed, the sitters were moved almost to tears during the time my wife's niece, Mary Ellen Gibson (a bright and lovely Irish girl of eighteen years who passed to the higher life two years ago), spoke to her aunt through the trumpet. This happy spirit spoke at all the sittings we attended, and I cannot do better than confine myself to a résumé of the conversations we had with her. I was not present at the séance on Saturday afternoon, July 19, having made way for my son, who was anxious to be present, and I append his report.

At the sitting on the evening of the same day my wife and I were present, and the meeting had not been in progress for more than ten minutes when a voice, addressing Mrs. Wright, said: "Auntie, it's me, Mary Ellen."

We gave no thought to grammatical exactitudes; the significance of the name "Ellen" meant very much to us. At the first séance the name was given formally as "Mary Gibson"; but now, when speaking directly to her aunt, she used the full Christian names "Mary Ellen."

To those acquainted with the people of the rural districts of County Down the importance attached to the full name will be appreciated.

"I am Mary Ellen auntie." Mrs. Wright speaking: "Well, Mary, what can you tell me now?" A.: "Not much, auntie; but I am glad to speak to you." Q.: "You have got your little niece over beside you now, Mary." A.: "Yes, little Lala is here: but she can't talk much to me yet, she is such a child. I was sorry that she had to come." Q.: "Mary, were you with me at my home crying, the night before I got the telegram stating she had passed away?" A.: "I was indeed!" Q.: " Mary, your uncle is here; would you like to speak to him?" A.: "Sure, I would; how are ye uncle?" Q.: "Very well, Mary dear; how are you?" A.: "Oh, I am all right, uncle, and happy." Q.: "Do you remember the happy time we had in Ireland three years ago, Mary?" A.: "Deed, I do. Oh, we had a fine time, playing and singing." (She was passionately fond of music.) Q.: "You are much missed at home, Mary." A.: "Well, I'm sure I can't help it. My poor father and mother! Tell them it won't be long till I see them again. Goodbye, auntie and uncle; a great many are waiting to speak to their friends. I will come back again. Goodbye. Love and kisses to everybody." Kisses through the trumpet, and she had gone.

At the third séance Mary again addressed my wife, saying: "I am here, auntie." "Yes Mary, how are you?" (How bald and inconsequent it seems when put upon paper; but words cannot portray the deep feelings aroused by the voices from the other side, and it must be acknowledged that difficulty is ofttimes experienced in carrying out a conversation. One has so much one could say or ask; but when reviewed the communion is found to be very commonplace indeed.)

Mrs. Wright continued: "Mary, I want you to do something for me." "I will if I can," was the answer. "You remember how you used to play and sing, and your uncle played the violin? Well dear, try and sing to me the song you sang then." After a short pause Mary replied: "I cannot just remember it; I sang so many songs." "The song about the soldier," Mrs. Wright said.

The spirit made several attempts to sing, but unsuccessfully, and I asked Mrs. Stevenson (one of the sitters) if she would kindly begin the song, "I like a Soldier fell"; she did so, and Mary joined in and sang the first verse in a sprightly fashion. She continued, addressing myself: "I liked that song, it was lovely; then there was another about 'the sea,'" and she sang in a sad and mournful way something about the sea which we could not quite follow.

Again she spoke: "I am very happy, uncle, and we shall all meet again. Goodbye, goodbye: don't forget to tell mother.

At the fourth sitting Mary came again with the usual salutation: "It's me auntie; I see uncle is here too. Uncle, do you remember I sang to you about your grey hairs?" I replied: "Yes, Mary; could you sing it to me again?" and she began at once and sang the first verse of the old song, "Darling I am growing old, silver threads among the gold."

Turning in the direction of my wife, the voice said: "Isn't it lovely, auntie?" "Yes Mary; is there any message you wish to send to your mother, so that she would really know you had been speaking to me?" She seemed to pause a little, and then said: "Tell mother I was awfully pleased the way she laid me out." My wife could not understand this, and said: "In what way, Mary?" "When I died," was the answer, "everyone was so kind; I was covered with beautiful flowers." "Yes," I said "all the people in the village were very sad when you were taken away." "Yes, indeed, uncle, I knew everyone loved Mary Ellen. Now I'll have to go. Goodbye, auntie and uncle dear, and give them all my best love and kisses"; and then she sang the following extemporised couplet:

Goodbye, ladies all, I am going away;
Goodbye, ladies all, I can no longer stay";

And many kisses through the trumpet, with the parting words "to everyone." I may add that at a later séance (July 24), in the house of Mr. William Jeffrey, India Street, Glasgow, Mary again manifested, and spoke of incidents unknown to anyone save ourselves.

Yours sincerely   David Wright.

Statement of Mr. David Wright, Jnr., in Confirmation of the foregoing.

Accompanied by my mother, I attended the séance held on Saturday afternoon, July 19. After the opening prayer all present sang the hymn "Nearer, my God, to Thee," and at the last verse we were joined by a loud voice, recognised by some of the sitters as Dr. Sharp. After wishing us a good afternoon, and giving some advice regarding the conduct of the sitting, the Doctor, with whose strong, masculine voice I was much impressed, left us. Another hymn was sung, after which there was a short silence. Suddenly I heard a voice saying: "Mary Gibson, Mary Gibson." This is the name of a cousin who passed away in County Down, Ireland, two years ago, and to whom we were all very much attached. The suddenness of her presence seemed to strike us dumb, and we allowed the name to be repeated several times without acknowledging it. Mrs. Wriedt broke in with: "There is a young girl here named Mary Gibson, who is asking for her aunt. Does anyone know the spirit?" My mother said: "Oh, yes, I know Mary Gibson." Immediately the trumpet seemed to swing right round to where we were sitting, and the voice cried: "Auntie! Auntie!" "Yes, Mary, I'm here!" "Oh, Auntie, How pleased I am to be able to come and speak to you!" The spirit conversed with us for a few minutes, and then departed with the assurance she would come back at the evening sitting. In the evening she gave her uncle and aunt some very good proofs, to which I can add my testimony. In earth life she had such an endearing insinuating Irish way with her, she was always first in anything she undertook, and this characteristic she still appears to retain in spirit life, viewed by her prominence at all the séances.   David Wright, Jnr.

It would be wholly impossible to touch on all the incidents which took place during the course of these séances; but I thought it well that some statements should be made about them by others rather than myself. Mr. William Jeffrey had a friend—a journalist—who knew nothing of spiritualism, and asked permission to bring him. Knowing the journalist, I consented on the following conditions: first, that nothing should be communicated to the press; and, second, that he was to give me an unbiassed report of any manifestations which had a personal interest to himself. Mr. Gavin Fleming (referred to by Admiral Moore in his report as "Mr. F.," and by Iola as "the Newspaper man") agreed, and was admitted.

The Testimony of Mr. Gavin Fleming

J. C.

Bute Mansions, Rothesay, August 15, 1913.

Dear Mr. Coates,

The following is a brief account of the séances which I attended with Mr. Jeffrey on the evening of Tuesday, July 22:—

At the outset I should remark that the subject of spiritualism has previously been often discussed between Mr. Jeffrey and myself, and for some time I had a strong desire to attend a séance. I attended the séance with a perfectly open mind, and I am certain that this accounts for the experience which befell me, and which was remarkable in the extreme.

It will perhaps add to the clarity of my narrative if, at the outset, I confine myself simply to my own personal communications. The séance had not been long in progress when a remarkably clear voice was heard, saying: "Fleming, Fleming." No one recognised it. Mr. Jeffrey, who was sitting beside me, suggested that it might be that of my father (who passed out about eleven years ago), and that I should address it. This I did, with some qualms, for it must be kept in mind that this was my first séance. I asked: "Who are you friend?" The answer came: "I am your father, Fleming." I was urged to converse, and I asked: "Is my mother with you and Jimmy" (my son, who passed over eight years ago); and he replied: "Yes, we are all here together." He then asked: "How is Jeanie?" (My daughter): and, in the course of further conversation, said: "I am always with you." Shortly afterwards a boyish voice said, two or three times, "Pa," very clearly. It was suggested that this boy's voice was for me. I said that my boy never called me "Pa" on earth: but Dr. Sharp explained that he had picked up this expression from other children in the spirit world. He evidently heard me, for he addressed me afterwards as "Father." Rather oddly, one of his first questions was, "How is Jeanie?" Just as my father asked. He afterwards said, "How is mother?" and followed with asking, "Why is she not here?" On my answering him, he said, "Tell her I was here: tell her I love her," and ended up with three kisses, heard most distinctly. During the course of the séance a spirit form was clearly seen by all present on the right hand side of the cabinet. To my sense it appeared to be full length: others commented on its height. Subsequently Mrs. Wriedt said, when the spirit form returned: "Mr. Fleming's sister." I said I had no sister. Mrs. Wriedt could not get away from the impression, and then I recollected being told that a baby sister died before I was born. I was asked how long ago that was, and said it must have been over forty-five years ago. A spirit voice who had been talking to Admiral Moore, whom I was told was Iola, said: "Tell the newspaper man that was his sister who was showing herself to him, and that she is taking care of his son." Dr. Sharp, who speaks with a loud, clear voice, said there was development on the other side, in consequence of which she was now a spirit woman, and teacher of spirit children: also that when my boy passed over she had met him. This concludes all that refers to communications between myself and departed relatives at this séance.

The spirit, Dr. Sharp, was much in evidence during the evening, and honoured me with a considerable amount of attention. I was doing my best in the darkness to take a few shorthand notes, and he saluted me as the "man with the papers round about him," and said there were schools in the spirit-world where they taught children. Speaking on the general subject of spiritualism, the Doctor said that it was "the first religion on earth; it was recognised by the Apostles, taught by Jesus Christ, and would last to all eternity." On the question of séances being conducted in darkness Dr. Sharp spoke as follows: "Everything that grows on the face of the earth comes out of the darkness, and everything that is good comes out of the darkness. There is not a thing on the face of the earth that has not been developed out of the dark. Nothing grows in the sun, whatever it may be; it grows at night. You hear people say that the dew falls. It does not fall, it rises; and the leaves of the trees are wet from the bottom. The moisture from the mother earth nurses the flowers at night." Addressing me, he said: "You can report that if you like, Mr. Journalist; it is for the benefit of those who ask why these sittings are held in the dark." Near the close of the séance the Doctor thanked Mr. Auld for the comfort he had in the room. Then suddenly he said: "Poor Mr. Stead, he is doing his work in Turkey, fighting like all the rest of them. He said the Turks will get back their place, and they will get it." (Certainly, since above was given, to the surprise of the Embassies of the great powers, the Turks have baffled their enemies in Thrace, the diplomacy of Europe, and are once more in possession of Adrianople.—J. C.)

I am afraid my notes of the séance are rather long. I cannot, however, close without giving a portion of the conversation between Mr. Jeffrey and (the spirit of) his wife, as I was brought into it. At a sitting earlier in the day Mr. Jeffrey had (the spirit of) a Mr. Campbell address him, who used to keep a tobacconist's shop in Rothesay, but with whom Mr. Jeffrey was unacquainted. At the evening sitting he mentioned this to Mr. Jeffrey, whereupon she said right off: "Well dear, if you did not know him, Mr. Fleming did." "Yes, Mrs. Jeffrey," I replied, "I knew him well; he was Tarry Campbell's father." "Yes," said she laughing; "he was Tarry Campbell's father." This, I may mention, was a nickname we had at school for young Campbell. I may add that, While the voices of my father and my son were quite recognisable, that of Mrs. Jeffrey was absolutely life-like, and my short conversation with her was in some respects the most remarkable of my experiences at the sitting.

I am, etc.,   Gavin Fleming.

August 15, 1913.

An Instance of Spirit Persistence

Mr. William B——, a gentleman of Norse ancestors, came from the north of Aberdeen. He was a stranger to me, but, being duly vouched for, joined us in our sittings at Rothesay, July 13, 14, and 15, 1913. As the case was a remarkable one, I have selected it for "The Voices" without further comment than this. I have permission to do so, withholding correct name and address; but these can be furnished to any of your readers entitled to know.— James Coates.

I cannot give every detail of what occurred in these séances, but will give some instances indicating the difficulties of spirit communion and the efforts of the departed to make their presence known. Mr. B—— struck me as a man deeply in earnest, sterlingly honest; the reverse of credulous, and, I thought, slow in thought. This was due to his caution and the desire for accuracy. He was deeply interested in all he heard and saw, and was impressed with the fact—during his first séance—that others were receiving convincing evidence. When he was addressed by someone over the psychophone, he either did not hear, or did not understand, what was said, or reply with promptness. Sometimes names are difficult to give, or the meaning of the statements were not caught at the time. So there was uphill work on both sides. When I spoke to him, after the first sitting, he said: "It is all so new and strange; I don't know what to make of it." The intelligences interested in him were so patient and determined that they actually forced their identity upon him. It is remarkable what efforts are made by these spirit-people to get at those who are sincere on the earth- plane. Inability to understand or grasp what is presented is not so difficult to overcome as stupid scepticism.

Mrs. Wriedt said: "I see a man who has been injured on the head by the kick of a horse." To Mr. B——: "He is for you. Do you know him?" "No," said this gentleman: "I am not sure." The psychic gave a further description of the place and the circumstances, and then said: "The name is James; do you know one like that?" "No." (He knew a person of the name, but was not sure it was the same.) Without going into further details, Mrs. Wriedt said: "I guess he's for you."

Singing was suggested, and "Annie Laurie" was sung with right goodwill; with the singing there was a fine cornet accompaniment by some invisible player. Dr. Sharp was thanked for this manifestation. After some voices had spoken and been recognised, Dr. Sharp addressed this gentleman and said; "There is someone here who says that he passed out of your mother's family three years ago—an old man of the name of Robert. Do you know him?" "No; there was no one of that name." This was said reflectively. Afterwards Mr. B—— wrote; "My guide, who claims to be an old minister, bore the name of Robert." So far there was not much progress. Again a voice addressed him, but he did not catch the name. One sitter after another tried to help him, but without much success.

The voice plaintively; "Dae ye no hear me?" "No; I can't make out what you say." Was the response. "Oh, dear, I'm Harrie." This was managed after Dr. Sharp made it clear there was a lady here of the name of Harrie." And a man named "John." Our friend acknowledged he had a brother of that name, but he was not sure that it was he who spoke, saying: "I do not recognise the voice."

Dr. Sharp explained, if the friends were not so timid and gave time, the voices would become clearer. "You must mind that this woman is not speaking with the aid of her own bodily organs. We have to draw from the sitters and materialise a thorax with vocal chords, which the friends, by our aid, use. It is not, 'Do you recognise the voice,' but, 'Do you recognise what the voice says?'" "Yes," he admitted, he did recognise the names and what was said. He appeared fearful to be drawn, and certainly did not take up what was said. He was evidently waiting for more detail before he was satisfied. Who shall blame him? One, however, can be too cautious.

Dr. Sharp, in his loudest and cheeriest tones, delivered a lecture on spiritualism, "as the oldest religion in the world," and announced they were going to build a spiritual temple in Glasgow. He wanted money to buy bricks, etc. As a psychophone message it had the advantage over the telephone; not only all in the room heard it, but, if there was anyone in the avenue outside, they might have heard it too.

A voice in a low key, but clear enough to be heard, said: "How are you, Willy?" "It is for you," I said as Mr. B—— was a little slow in responding. "Who are you?" he asked. After some trials "Harrie" was given. "Yes," he replied. Then came forward some family details about an "Alec." "What Alec?" "Your nephew Alec" was the clear and definite response. "Well, I had a nephew Alec, but have not seen him for a long time." (I never met one slower to make admissions. This was not done deliberately, but arising from not being fully satisfied.)

On Sunday, July 13, our friend's wife tried to manifest, but did not give enough to be recognised. In speaking to him she referred to the changes since she left; to certain people, and how the world had gone with him. All true enough, but he wanted more. Yet no one in that room could have told him what this voice had done. The medium knew nothing of himself nor of his family. Yet "the voice," claiming to be that of his wife, evidently did know; but he was not satisfied. He told me he wanted to be sure, as he had heard of evil and personating spirits. He was not sure; it might not be she. This conversation took place after the séance was over. I told him to leave all these ideas outside the séance-room door. When addressed by a voice, to respond and encourage speaking; the more he spoke and the more kindly, the better. Instead of harping at "What's your name?" or "I don't know you," keep talking, as to a friend. Hear the tale, and two things will follow——you will get the name all right, or the person whom you say you do not know will be able to tell you of someone whom you both know, and thus establish the identity. As to evil spirits, why prejudice those who come to you and hinder their utterance by that attitude of mind? You are a good, straightforward man. It is time enough to think of evil spirits when they invite you to do evil or bring evil to your door. The man was honest; he had the training and the experience of a life-time behind him. These manifestations were new and wholly outside his experience. He said he would take my way of it, and speak more freely to "the voices."

On Monday (July 14), at 11 a.m.., Several things came out, and one was that "dourness in th' uptak was maistly on his ain side," and on the other, that love and patience of the spirit friends brought recognition. He learned that he had been in error in rejecting on the previous day the voice claiming to be that of his wife, who did not say she lived with him thirty years. The voice: "Harrie; my name is Harrie. Yes, Willy. I did not say I lived with you for thirty years. You thought that. It is thirty years since we lived together." This was correct. "We were so happy together; we had a pleasant time then, only it was so short." Then the man and the woman exchanged thoughts across the borderland. Home and family were talked about; how her husband had changed in thirty years. He had learned, too, about a brother who had been away; and so the story went on.

"Alec is here; yes, your nephew Alec." A.: "I know." "He will speak for himself." Someone else comes and cries, "Uncle William." Q.: "Who are you?" A.: "Uncle John is here. It was he who told me you were here; how is aunty?......Father is here. ......We're all here. Goodbye......;" and so the identity was established.

Touching on some of the perplexities of spirit communion. The spirit of John spoken of, and who manifested in an earlier sitting, intimated, "I see Ellen every day." Mr. B. did not think this was correct, as "the only Ellen in our family is still with us." There should be little difficulty in this. It might mean that the uncle in spirit was seeing his niece Ellen in the body every day, just as he was seeing his brother William every day. This brother in spirit had a daughter Elinor, who predeceased him, and might have been the one spoken about. But it appeared to me that it was Ellen in the body, and at home, who was spoken about. If it was Elinor, the name Ellen was a fair attempt to give that name. It was someone on the connection of that name that this spirit was referring to; whether daughter or niece, there could be no mistaking the reference.

Shortly after the foregoing an etherealised form appears and moves toward us. I was sitting near this gentleman, taking notes. There was no mistaking the female form. The voice of his wife coming clearer out of the darkness, as if gaining greater power and confidence, said: "Do you see me Willy? I am trying to show myself." "Yes: I see you, but I cannot very well make you out." The etherealised form became more defined, and we saw the figure of a medium-sized woman with a child in her arms. How wonderful the patience of the spirit people! The identity was established. The little one in the arms of that luminous figure signified the cause of his wife's passing out.

Dr. Sharp who had explained matters more than once, said: "Your great-grandmother cannot come to you, she has gone to another plane; but this little woman comes; she has followed you for years......She is earth-bound." I interposed with an objection; when it was explained, "She is earth-bound; bound to earth by those she loves, and she is always with you. She brought you here, and tells me that she is helping to care for one in your house—smoothing her way till her body returns to our mother earth. You know that there is one at home who needs care? This dear woman, who loves you, has told me to tell you this— your wife, Harrie. Do you understand?" "Yes I understand," was the quiet answer of one thankful for the convincing manifestations. There in that room—out of the thick darkness—came a voice claiming to be that of his wife, telling him of things which he alone knew; in that room appeared a slightly luminous female with a child in its arms, claimed by the "voice" to be that of herself. Striking evidence; valuable persistence. Not less valuable were Dr. Sharp's cogent commentary to the effect that his wife and the spirit friends were like Christian Endeavour workers. They were healing the sick, comforting the mourner, and bringing immortality to light. "When your wife has done her work she will go to the seventh sphere." He concluded by sympathising with this man in his loneliness, his thoughts, sufferings, and private struggles. His wife was well and happy, but would be happier when she realised that she had got him to know that "Immortality and endless progress are true, and it is for you to know it; and she comes back to help you to understand. That is why you are here."

I must now summarise. Mr B. said that he had a nephew named Alec. Dr. Sharp said: "What he had heard about him was all wrong." Then came out the story of this Alec having gone abroad. Out—up the river—trading with natives—Natal way. Wes, he had passed out. No, he had no quarrel with his housekeeper, and was not killed by her. He had no cause to shoot or kill anybody. No; he had not killed himself. "He has told me all about it," said Dr. Sharp. "He says he is your nephew. I will let him talk for himself."

Another voice said: "Uncle William, I was ashamed, and could not have spoken unless I had been helped. My troubles came about through heavy drinking. Had I kept straight, things would have turned out all right. I am not the only innocent man who has left home and fallen into bad ways. I never forgot my people, and am thoroughly ashamed for all the trouble I gave them. Well, this is how it happened. Two natives came to the store and wanted goods without money, but I would not give them. They were abusive, and I ordered them out. They will not fight, but are very vindictive. They went their way, but watched their chance when I was in liquor and nobody about to mark me. They came again; I had been drinking, and was not myself. I ordered them out; these two came for me with knives, and slashed at me, meaning to mark my face. One cut my jugular vein; that finished me. I was found where I was left. The authorities did not examine my body properly, or they would have found the cuts there......My housekeeper had nothing to do with it. She was a native woman who looked after the place......No; she was not in league with the boys......She had nothing to do with it. They cleared out, and the woman cleared out, being afraid she would be caught and would have to tell on the boys what she knew. She knew if she did her life would not be worth a brass farthing. I had no need to kill myself; I did not commit suicide. Uncle, do you believe me?"

The above is but a brief outline of a sordid and tragic story. The uncle, putting together what he had heard with what he was now told by his nephew in spirit, did believe, and all the more so as the nephew's identification was made emphatic by his reference to his poor father, mother, and others. There was an aunt referred to, and the speaker had met his father in spirit life. Dr. Sharp gave advice about an ailing person in the sitter's home, and, while intimating that a change would do her good, said she would not recover. Other references were made and their correctness admitted.

This report has been received and read by Mr. William B——. He consents to publication on the condition that his anonymity be respected. He has travelled from Free Kirkism to enlightened Agnos-ticism, and is now a sincere spiritualist; but never in his life has he had a similar experience or witnessed such startling manifestations of spir-it power like these recorded. When one takes into consideration that this stranger from the north met Mrs. Wriedt for the first time in our home, where all present were strangers to him, one must admit that the evidence for supernormal knowledge—aye, and for spirit commu-nion—was most convincing.

MRS. WRIEDT AT ROTHESAY
By Vice Admiral W. Usborne Moore

From Light, August 16, 1913. Mrs. Wriedt left Cambridge House, Wimbledon, on July 1, and, after giving certain séances at Glasgow on the 3rd and following days, arrived at Rothe-say on the 8th.

Owing to the courtesy of Mr. and Mrs. Coates, I was privileged to attend four circles in their well-ventilated séance-room. Though each séance lasted about two hours, there was no feeling of closeness or op-pression, and the conditions were pleasant and harmonious. I sat be-tween Mr. and Mrs. Coates on every occasion.

The first was on July 16, and it lasted two hours. The night was wet, but that did not seem to affect the mediumship of Mrs. Wriedt. I did not count accurately the number of spirits who manifested, but, in-cluding those who came to me, I heard at least twenty-five. There were seventeen sitters besides the psychic.

The chief feature of this sitting was the visit of a repentant son in spirit life to his mother, Mrs. M. He had died by his own hand three years ago. When he manifested he briefly told his story, expressing the utmost contrition for the errors of his life and the rash act that termi-nated it, and which had broken the heart of his father. I understood that this was the first time he had unburdened himself to his widowed mother. In answer to her questions, he said that he was now happier than he had been since he had passed over. Up to this time—so Mrs. M. told me—she had heard of him "in the gray," but he had not been allowed to speak to her.

There came to me my spirit companion Iola, who has been in the higher life thirty- nine years. I could see her, but not so plainly as Mrs. Coates. Her mother also came, bringing with her my little grand-daughter, who perished in an accident in April, 1911. Two other spirits conversed with me—one, Captain Dunlop, R.N., who expressed in a jocular way his surprise at finding me "going in for this sort of thing"; the other, Mr. Douglas Murray, who said, among other items: "I have found my arm." (Douglas Murray was a friend who belonged to the same dining club in London, and died about two years ago. During one of his visits to Egypt his dragoman had desecrated a mummy to obtain a case for his employer. Shortly after this Murray lost his right arm. The mummy case was brought home, and eventually found a home in the British Museum, after various adventures. It is said that all who handled this case suffered death or misadventure.)

Both Dunlop and Murray had lived in England so many years that they spoke without any Scotch accent. Except in the case of my friends, it seemed to me that all the spirits spoke Scotch, some an odd dialect not in present use.

The next séance I attended was on July 20 (2 to 4 p.m.) There were fifteen persons in the circle besides the psychic. I estimated that over twenty spirits manifested. The principal event of this afternoon was the meeting of Mr. David Wright with his Irish niece in spirit life, who had passed over at the age of seventeen. Mr. W. said to her; "can you sing to me any of those songs you used to sing?" A.: "I will try." She then sang a verse or two of three songs, which I understood were his favourites. Iola spoke to me, and, after a short conversation, she said, loud enough for the circle of friends to hear: "I am always glad to meet the Admiral's friends." This spirit never uses the trumpet. Mr. Coates welcomed her to the Rothesay circle. This time I did not see Iola, but Mrs. Coates did. Two other acquaintances spoke to me. The Scotch voices were more remarkable throughout this séance than in that of July 16.

My third general séance was on July 21 (2 to 3.40 p.m.). Sixteen sitters besides the psychic. Iola was the first to manifest. I saw her form standing plainly in front of Mr. Coates and myself. We had a short talk. The principal evidence was afforded by the manifestation of a daughter of Mr. and Mrs. P., who had "passed" but six weeks before, at the age of twenty-five. Her father reminded her that before her death he had taught her what he knew about spirit life. She replied: "Yes, father, but I have learnt far more since I came over; in fact, you know nothing of the glories of this plane." She expressed herself as very happy; it was an affecting scene. Mr. James Robertson, of Glasgow, was present at this séance. His son-in-law manifested, and spoke most naturally and evidentially, addressing him as he did in life. Andrew Jackson Davis came and spoke to him and to me for some minutes. We had quite a discussion about Professor William James. The Scotch voices again remarkable.

July 22 (8.20 to 10 p.m.). Once more I had the privilege of attending Mr. Coates's circle. There were sixteen sitters besides the psychic. Among the was a Mr. F., a very tall man, who was quite new to the subject. It was to this gentleman the strongest evidence came.

First there was a good deal of loud singing, in which Dr. Sharp and another spirit joined. While this was going on Iola spoke to me. It was impossible for her to make more than two or three words clear, on account of the noise. I expect this was done as a test, to prove that it was possible to hear two spirits singing and one talking simultaneously.

A spirit came asking for a "Mrs. Wriedt, Admiral," evidently known to us two only; but he could not give his name. Dr. Sharp said "Admiral, that was Sam Jones." Then the spirit returned, and we had a conversation about his friends in London. (Mr. Samuel Jones was Mayor of Toledo, Ohio, U.S., some years ago. Neither Mrs. Wriedt nor myself knew him in life, but we both knew his widow. He had manifested in Detroit to his widow and two of her friends when I was present. These friends landed in England for the first time on July 3, and were at this moment in the Hotel Cecil, Strand, London, where I saw them two days later.)

Presently a tall figure of a woman etherealised in the cabinet, walked in the direction of Mr. F., and bowed. Later he was visited by a son, who called himself "Jimmy." Not long after Iola came again, and told me all was well at home, and my wife was preparing for her trip to Switzerland. I said: "But she is not going till the end of the month." Answer: "By the time you get home it will be the inside of a week." (When I reached home, at 9 p.m. on July 24, I found that on July 22 Mrs. Moore had been engaged in some very necessary preparations for leaving home. She started at 9 a.m. on July 31.) My guide went on to refer to the state of our nephew, who was dying, and then said: "Will you tell that newspaper man [Mr. F.] that it was his sister that came out of the cabinet and bowed to him? She has been taking care of his son." Mr. F. said, "I had no sister," but almost at once corrected himself by adding: "I remember now that there was an infant girl in my family who died before I was born." (I saw Mr. F. for a minute, for the first time, just before entering the séance-room, and did not know his occupation until this incident occurred.) The Scotch language very much in evidence.

It appeared to me that every sitter obtained some personal evidence of spirit return at each of these four séances. The impression made upon me was profound, chiefly on account of the Scotch voices, so natural and yet so entirely different from the English voices to which I was accustomed. There was but one trumpet used, yet I frequently heard two, occasionally three, voices speaking at the same instant.

Mr. Coates was good enough to allow me to sit in private with Mrs. Wriedt three times. The information gained at these séances meant a good deal to me, but would be of no interest to your readers. Iola spoke without the aid of a trumpet, and the psychic did not hear a single word. On one occasion she fell asleep while the conversation was going on.

CONCLUSIONS

In putting forward these few abridged narratives describing the experiences of some forty or fifty persons with one medium for the direct voice phenomena, I have, I am aware, only scratched the surface of a stupendous problem. The writers who have been good enough to send me their notes for publication represent only about one- eighth of the total number who have experienced the pleasure of hearing and seeing these marvels in England and Scotland in 1912-1913; and even they have been restricted from divulging more than a portion of what they have absorbed in their search for truth. The startling revelations made by the voices in the séance-room, unsolicited, and dealing with facts not within the consciousness of the sitter at the time, some of them of the most intimate private character, have not been revealed. It would be impossible for those who received them to surrender such secrets, even if belief in the phenomena themselves were prevalent in the country.

The most striking instance of spirit return which has come under my notice has not been mentioned at all. It was a case of parents who had lost their only child. When I approached them on the subject, and pointed out the good they might do to sorrowing fellow-creatures by allowing me to include their testimony, I was met with a flat refusal, notwithstanding I explained that their names should, if necessary, be withheld. I think it is much to be regretted.

Probably about half the inhabitants of this country do not believe in spirits at all. Certainly but a few realise their proximity. It would be waste of time trying to undeceive them: it is not for this class that the book is written. These narratives are collected for the encouragement of those who feel that some help must be forthcoming in the dire distress which almost paralyses them in its intensity, and yet unwilling to put themselves into a position where they might encounter deceit, which they would naturally regard as sacrilege: but who are desirous of finding consolation in any honest quarter. The churches have told them nothing which affords the slightest alleviation of their pain. In prosperous times, when all is well in the home, they drift on, repeating the Church services and imagining they believe in a Day of Judgment and in the reunion of relatives and friends at that distant period. Presently a shock comes: there is a vacant chair; a loved one has been torn away, and all is blank misery. To whom shall the sufferer turn for relief? He can only speak of the advantages of extinction, and mutter wordy platitudes about the existence of nothing but what your senses can tell us. Shall he go to the parson? The parson assures him that all is well; that God is good: and that, if only he trusts in faith, he shall rejoin the object of his affection at the end of the world. But wait! There is a condition: he shall rejoin his loved one after these millions of years only if he has led a good life. If this is not the case, he will, on that awful day, be again torn from her, unless she, indeed, has also been frail, when the two will accompany one another into hell.

Poor comfort all this! If the bereaved man has a decent education and average natural understanding, he is revolted by this doctrine. He finds, however, that he cannot contradict the parson out of the Prayer Book, and he is, if possible, more miserable than before.

Presently a friend comes to him by stealth and whispers: "There are no dead. She whom you imagine to be dead is alive: there is only a veil between you; you will be reunited. Her corpse lies in the grave; but she herself is in the spirit world. Come with me and I will prove this to you.'" The stricken man follows listlessly, not much impressed. He is taken to a room where ten men and women are sitting in a circle. After some singing a voice is heard, then another and another, each one greeting some member of the party, giving names and identifying themselves as certain personalities. No voice addresses the man of sorrow. He is concentrating all his thoughts on the dead. He has not yet reached that platform of self-elimination which enables him to be actively interested in another's joy, though he admits to himself that there seems to be something very real in what is going on. Later on, for a whole five minutes, he forgets his trouble, no longer concentrating on the one subject, and leans forward listening. Ah! What is that still small voice? "My name," he exclaims; "who is speaking?" A.: "I am your wife." "Is it possible?" he cries; but the voice does not respond, and there is no more that night.

His next step is to pay a visit to the Society for the Prevention of Research, where he relates the strange happenings of the previous evening to the courteous secretary, who looks at him with a pitying glance and says: "Poor man; it is sad. Are you sure that you were not hallucinated?" At this his spirit is up, and he replies: "These may be coincidences; but I was certainly not a victim of hallucination." "Ah!" says the sapient secretary, "but do you not know that these mediums have detectives all over the place, and know your name, the name of the relative you mourn, and all about you?" The visitor is now thoroughly aroused, and he replies: "But I went on the spur of the moment with my friend Mr. Sertain." "Yes, yes (with a faint smile) we know him; he believes in what he calls 'spirit return.' Only one spirit has ever returned, and we have copyrighted him. Next time take a conjurer with you, and he will tell you how the trick is done. "Yes, yes; goodbye. So glad we can help you in any way."

But our mourner, oddly enough, is not impressed by the secretary; some instinct tells him that he does not ring true. He goes again to the medium by himself. Again he is addressed by the same voice as before: "Fred, Fred, do you remember when I lost your ring?" He asks: "Where?" "In Sydney," is the reply. Fred cannot remember anything about the loss of a ring in Sydney. "How long ago?" he asks. A.: "In 1888." Q.: "Do you mean at a ball?" A.: "Yes, yes, yes"(eagerly). Fred now recollects that a year after his marriage his wife lost a small guard ring that he had given her; but, while he is considering, the opportunity for further conversation is lost. The séance soon after is over. He leaves the house much impressed, and hoping to hear more in the future. Possibly he visits the Society again, and this time is met by the Rejecting Officer, Miss Blight, who, on hearing his story, says: "Yes, yes, very interesting, but you knew about the loss of the ring." He says: "I had the greatest difficulty in recalling the incident to my mind." "Quite so, but it was in your subliminal. Read Myers, dear sir, and next time you attend Mrs. Right's séance-room take a conjurer." Poor Fred cannot for the life of him see how a conjurer could assist him so far, and goes instead to his original introducer, Mr. Sertain, who advises him to sit with Mrs. Right again; to try and keep his mind a perfect blank, and listen. He obeys, and during the next interview a voice is heard: "Jane, Jane" (this is the name of his wife); "Fred, ask mother for Uncle Tom's Cabin." He is puzzled, but remembers having heard of an old book of that name, and writes to Sydney to ask his mother-in-law is she knows if her daughter ever possessed such a book. The reply is that she never heard of it, but that it is possible she might have left more than one book at her school in

Shropshire, where she was educated between the ages of fourteen and eighteen. The schoolmistress is appealed to, and, after some delay, ferrets out a copy of Uncle Ton's Cabin, which she sends. In the flyleaf he finds the name of Jane—(her maiden name) —1883. Feeling somewhat elated by this discovery, Fred interviews Miss Blight once more. She receives him with her usual urbanity, and takes note of what he tells her. To his inquiry, "How do you account for this madam?" she answers "But, of course, you knew of your wife having read this book?" "I can swear that I never heard of it" is his instant reply. Miss B.: "Very well, but her mother knew of it?" Fred: "She declares she never heard her daughter mention it." Miss B.: "But the school-mistress knew of it?" Fred: "It was another lady who was mistress when my wife was there, and she died ten years ago." Miss B.: "Surely somebody living knew of it; one of your wife's Schoolfellow perhaps?" Fred: "Possibly, there may be some alive." Miss B.: "Oh, then, the explanation is easy. Are you aware that a medium in trance can tap any source of earthly information?" Fred: "Really! No I did not know that; but you see Mrs. Right is never in trance. I never saw anyone more alert in my life. She was chattering while the voice that I believe emanated from the spirit of my wife was speaking in very low tones to me." Here there is a very long pause, while Miss Blight looks out of the window. Slowly Fred comes to the unhappy conclusion that he is not believed, and rises to depart. But Miss Blight says: "We can put you on the right path for learning something about spirit communication. Have you read any of our Cross Purposes?" "No madam, I have not." "Well come to the meeting tomorrow night. Mr. Kington is going to address us on A hitherto unsuspected meaning on Mrs. Dream's automatic script on How Johnnie got home from the fair. Here is a card. The Right Hon. Mr. Gerard will follow with Notes on a bit of bonnie blue ribbon." Our Fred is, by this time, moving towards the door. With a hasty "Goodbye," and an expression very like the name of the smallest piece of European money, he disappears, never to enter these rooms again.

But, although Fred does not again trouble the Society for the Prevention of Research, he pays three or four more visits to Mrs. Right, and has long conversations with Jane, who gives him, bit by bit, absolute certainty of her identity and continued existence.

The above is a fictitious narrative; but I defy any old investigator to say that it does not fairly represent, in the form of a parable, the vicissitudes of many bereaved people today in their search for some help in their terrible trouble.

It is not part of my scheme to decry any religion. Every faith not accompanied by barbarity is of use to those who believe in it and act up to it. There are many roads to New York; we all get there in time. I am a believer specially in the beneficent effects of the Roman Catholic doctrine as a social factor of vast importance. There are hundreds of thousands of feeble men and women trembling over the precipice of reason who are buffeted about by the caprices of fortune. One evil happens to them after another until they know not which way to turn, nor whence to look for relief, from their torturing doubts and fears. The Roman Catholic Priest steps in and says with a confident, impressive air: "Come to us, and we will guide your steps; all we require is that you shall surrender your will and obey all our behest's, and you shall be safe." "They follow the priest, and feel no longer responsible for their own salvation. I am sure if it were not for Roman Catholicism there would be countless suicides, and the madhouses would be full.

But this is not meat for the strong man who jealously guards his own individuality, who is true to himself, and is temporarily stunned by some crushing sorrow. He wants assurance that his dead are alive; he is determined not to be lulled into a false security.

If he searches diligently for it, he will find that there is a way of communing with those he has lost; and in spiritism he finds peace.

I do not deny that communication with the spirit world is full of perplexities. Answers to questions put to spirits are often contradictory and apparently misleading. Generally, this is owing to the difficulty experienced in describing to beings who are functioning in three dimensions what is taking place in a region inhabited by those who are functioning in four or more. But the essential points are gained quickly by the earnest investigator; he soon learns that he is destined to live again; that immortality is a fact; that he can commune without much difficulty with those whom the world calls dead. For the rest, he is content to wait till he passes into the new life.

I am not a philosopher, and do not pretend to be able to give any satisfactory solution of all the difficulties which arise almost daily in this interesting study. Moreover, during the last two years, since I published *Glimpses of the Next State*, I have learned only a little more than I had then acquired. I am merely a collector of facts, and have no theories to offer, though I may now and then interpolate my personal views upon what has taken place. The difficulty of our spirit visitors in communicating at all must be enormous. We ply them with questions, the majority of which they are not able to answer because they have not yet reached the higher spheres; they make the attempt by stating what they have heard from others, and are, doubtless, often incorrect. If you ask a spirit who is in the third sphere to describe to you what is a "Realm," you may get some answer, but it is sure to be wrong, as he is in too low a stage of advancement to know anything at all about it.

Then, again, the higher spirits are hampered by the personality of the medium. To us it is highly important that the medium should be an ignorant person, unable to form any theories for herself, so that we shall receive the undiluted message. But there is another side to the question. When the psychic is densely ignorant it appears to be impossible, at times, for the spirit to get through any lofty ideas; I have watched this often.

Every spirit comes into the circle with a set speech. It is plain to any close observer that they have to prepare themselves for the ordeal, and protect themselves from the effects of entering our sense atmosphere of low vibrations. "I am so glad to see you this morning," or "I thank you for giving me the opportunity of talking this morning," is rather commonplace when it goes on for six days running; but these, or some other equally tedious speech, is usually the commencement of your sitting. One started, the conversation may go on for half an hour with scarcely a break. Even Dr. Sharp, or John King, often begin with a stereotyped greeting, apparently got up beforehand.

However, if we have to choose, it is better to employ the uneducated psychic, for, if a strong spirit bursts through with lofty ideas and delicate sentiments, you feel at once assured that the psychic has no part or parcel in the communication. Who is there that has read Stainton Moses's automatic script, and does not suspect that there is much of the personality of the scribe in the text?

We hear much that is far beyond the faculties of the medium, and that is because the strength to manifest is drawn from the sitters. Undoubtedly, the spirits, or the controls, draw from our throats. For weeks after Mrs. Wriedt came to England in 1912 I went about with a slight cough, an irritation in the throat. I have heard sitters say to me, "That last spirit which came spoke in your voice." The ingredient supplied by the medium which makes this phenomenon possible is a complete mystery, and I doubt if it will be discovered, at any rate in our generation.

The direct voice is the highest spiritualistic phenomenon yet discovered, and when it can be obtained without the use of the trumpet, and without the medium hearing what is said, we have reached the most advanced stage of manifestation. Nothing that I have investigated is equal in delicacy, or conviction, to the still small voice which I, alone, can hear.

It is objective; there is no clairaudience about it, but it is rare. In the narratives, it will be noticed that M.E., Mrs. Findlay Smith, Mrs. Richards, and a few others have attained this plane of investigation besides myself. On at least fifty occasions I have enjoyed this privilege. I have been spoken to for long periods—from twenty to forty minutes—without Mrs. Wriedt hearing a single word

A subject which is little understood is the importance of the mental attitude of the sitters. If they are hostile to the psychic, it is needless to say that nothing occurs. But this is not usually the case; people do not pay to sit with a medium in whom they do not believe. Suppose they thoroughly trust the psychic, there may yet be failure. Their minds may be upset by some circumstance that has nothing to do with the séance; they may be angry with someone they have met two hours before; they may be ill, or think they are. Any jar will upset them. The only chance of success is when medium and sitters are in pleasant humour and have emptied their minds of everything, even of those whom they desire to see or to hear.

Why, I hear some ask, is the direct voice of so much importance; why does it rank so high in spiritualistic phenomena? The answer is: Because the possibility of fraud is removed one stage further off than it is in any other phase of manifestation; and, in the case of the independent voice without the trumpet and only just audible to the person for whom it is intended, is entirely eliminated. Above all the direct voice gives you information, some of which may be in your consciousness, some in your subliminal mind, but much which you have never heard and have to confirm at a distance from the séance-room. In any case the medium is excluded as a factor in the knowledge acquired. In some mysterious way which we do not know anything about, she must aid in the production of the voices, because we cannot hear them when she is out of the house. But the facts given have no reference whatever to her personality.

This has been proved in a number of ways. Two voices have been frequently heard by me and others talking simultaneously to two sitters in the circle about matters entirely unknown to the psychic or to each other; occasionally three; and at very rare intervals, four—one using the trumpet and two or three without. The medium, when talking, is often interrupted by a voice, and for a second or two both have been heard to speak together. A voice has been heard to sing and another speak simultaneously. Certain privileged sitters have heard the voice in full light with the medium eight feet from them; I have heard it when she was eighteen feet from me, in full electric light. Some of us have heard it when the French windows were open; and one gentleman has heard it in the dark when the woman was downstairs in the drawing-room. I do not deny that experienced spirits like Dr. Sharp and John King can read the minds of the sitters, but I do deny that casual spirit visitors can do so, or that a medium not in trance can know anything about the supraliminal, or subliminal, minds of her clients. This American woman is never in trance. She is ignorant of the significance of the messages given under her nose, even if she hears them, which is not always the case when the trumpet is used; never, when it is not.

Then we have the coarser physical phenomena: trumpets thrown about, chairs are turned upside down, tables are moved many feet, vases of flowers are transported from place to place, flowers are taken out of bowls and given to sitters. Often, these things happen in dead silence, and frequently while they are performed the hands of the medium are held by a sitter. There is no bungling, no article is injured, no one is hurt. All this appears to a superficial investigator to be senseless. But is it so? Are these phenomena as meaningless as they seem? Personally I do not like them, as they generally indicate that sufficient power is not available for spirit communication; but they have a purpose. They show intelligence and exercise of force by beings who are not mortal; they do not help to the identification of our spirit friends, but they show what can be done by the denizens of another state of consciousness.

My work would be incomplete if I did not say something about the personality of Mrs. Wriedt. In *Glimpses of the Next State* I have not shirked the question of evils attending the daily exercise of mediumship. Mrs. Wriedt is no exception to the general rule. I have had opportunities of watching her narrowly, and find her a most interesting psychological problem. It is unfair to judge professional psychics by rules that we are in the habit of applying to ordinary members of the human family. They are entirely abnormal. In the séance-room they hear spirits talking, sitters conversing together; outside of it, in the house and elsewhere, they hear all sorts of talk, good, bad, and indifferent. Partly dazed by what is taken from them during the exercise of their gift, they mix everything up together in their brains, and become guilty of many terminological inexactitudes. In the case of educated, cultured psychics, the disastrous consequence of the exercise of occult powers is kept in check by common sense, environment, and temperance in the exercise of their gift; but with professionals it is not so, and they gradually slip into habits of gross inaccuracy; they are subject (and the more powerful are the worst) to grave hallucinations.

If Mrs. Wriedt were an ordinary woman, I should be obliged to describe her as untruthful. As she is not, I prefer to say that she is irresponsible in the ordinary affairs of life. Vacillating to a most remarkable degree, she alters her plans twenty times in a week, and only one thing is certain about her—that if she says, say, on Monday, that she intends to do something on the following Friday, that particular project will not be accomplished on that day. All powerful professional psychics are subject to the same peculiarity.

In essential she is as true as steel. Those who know her are aware that she is warm- hearted, sympathetic, and would do anything for a fellow mortal in distress. It is a passion with her to be the means of giving consolation to those who require it. I have noticed that those who have lost children are they who most quickly benefit by her passive ministrations. I am not speaking of credulous people who give themselves away, and take the initiative in conversation with spirits, but sane men and women who know the elementary rules of psychic investigation, and who regard personation as sacrilege and fraud on this side with the utmost horror, and who are on their guard to detect dishonesty on either this plane or the next.

I know of one man past middle life, high up in his profession, and a stranger to me and Mrs. Wriedt, whom I took to Cambridge House in May. He had recently lost his only child. Before we entered the house I warned him to be as passive as he could, and to try and empty his mind of every thought when the door of the séance-room closed upon him. He returned to me in the drawing-room in an hour, having arrived at a stage of psychic understanding which had taken me four years to reach. The explanation is simple: he was in urgent need of consolation; I required none. He told me all he had experienced. His narrative is not in this book, but I hope he will publish it before a year is out.

Mrs. Wriedt does not permit herself to be investigated by merely curious people, or those who are known to be out simply in search of fraud; who, in short, have no constructive purpose in view. She says she went through all this a quarter of a century ago, and that it is not reasonable to expect her to start her mission in every town by being gagged, tied up, and physically tested by strangers, some of whom may be entirely ignorant of the business in hand. If the evidence of identity which come out in such profusion during her séances do not appeal to those who hear them, she is content to let the sitters think what they like. She has no objection whatever to the really open-minded sceptic.

I wish to say here and now that with this attitude I entirely agree, and I desire to add that there is no conceivable circumstance which could now shake my conviction of the genuineness of her gift. Her control Dr. Sharp, has so arranged matters that I have received a hundred proofs, at least, without his medium being aware of what was going on.

As I have said elsewhere, a woman who has been the means of conferring so much consolation upon hundreds of people here and in the United States is apt to be spoilt, and come to regard herself as the "Gift," and not merely the highly privileged instrument of the higher powers who control her destiny. It requires a very strong head to remain balanced when so many are overwhelming her with praises and gifts. I earnestly hope that she may so control her mental equipoise as to render possible the maintenance of her powers. Though not the only direct-voice medium in America, she is the most highly developed, and I do not hesitate to say that if she tempted Dr. Sharp to withdraw his guidance, and she was blotted out, it would be a serious misfortune to the western world.

When all are so good, it is difficult to say in this collection of narratives which is the most important. If I had to chose, I can think of nothing more convincing than those in Scotland, and more especially in Rothesay. Mr. Coates welcomed to his séance-room Englishmen as well as Scotchmen. No English spoke in Scotch, and no Scotch spirit spoke in English, unless—as in some cases I know—he had lost his accent by long residence in England before he died. Some of the Scotch spoken was that of early Victorian days, and one or two spirits used Gaelic. There were a number of languages spoken in Mrs. Wriedt's séances, but to me, who am unacquainted with any language except my own, the Rothesay circles were of the highest significance.

What is a medium? Answer: "Nobody knows." I am sure that I can hazard a guess as well as anyone living, for I have enjoyed the leisure to investigate, and have psychics in my family. My theory is as follows: All human beings have a dual personality—a physical body and a spiritual body. In the case of nine people out of ten, the two are inextricably mixed, and the psychic or spiritual body never separates from the natural or physical body, except under harmonious conditions in the séance-room, when, I am of opinion, most of us function chiefly with our spirit bodies. Now, in the case of the tenth person—the psychic—I believe there is a constant separation, and that he or she as the case may be, is unconsciously living in both this state and the next all the time.

In the séance-room this spirit body is made use of by the controls to interpret the messages which come through from the selected spirit visitors. The controls gather from the sitters the necessary strength to form the voices. Should the medium be entranced, as is the case with Susannah Harris, she is assisted by her subliminal mind being able to communicate with the subliminal minds of the sitters; but in the case of Mrs. Wriedt, who is always alert, her spirit body alone is able to be used to attain success. Hence I say that Mrs. Wriedt" gift is of an unique kind, and affords us a satisfaction which we do not derive from any other form of mediumship.

It is not wise for young people, hysterical people, or those engaged in arduous brain- work, to attend these séances. The conviction of identity comes so suddenly, it is enough to upset the mental balance of any but seasoned, level-headed men and women. And I think everybody who attends such circles ought to be carefully prepared by reading the works of those who have made earnest investigation into such phenomena. Dr. G. F. Oldham wrote to me after his first séance in May 1913:—

It was all so astounding and convincing; yet half an hour later, when I was mixing with the London democracy in the underground, I could hardly believe it true. After twenty-five years of scientific education and thought it is exceedingly hard not to feel that perhaps there is some other explanation. The only plausible one I can suggest is that Mrs. Wriedt can project some kind of a secondary personality into the room endowed with marvellous powers of imitating deceased persons, and reading their and the sitter's minds; but this seems very far-fetched and as wonderful as the normal explanation. Of one thing I am sure—that the whole occurrences are strong meat, and very unfitted for any but those who have strongly balanced minds. I can well believe it is not desirable for the ordinary run of person, and will not be for many a long year......

I do not go quite so far as Dr. Oldham, but I am positive that preparation is necessary. The absence of it led to serious difficulties in Christiania in 1912, and those were not lessened by the fact that the gentleman who took charge of the circles was nearly stone deaf. As to a "Secondary personality" marching around with omnipotent faculties, I think we may leave that to my Society for the Prevention of Research.

I will close with a brief reflection on the problem ever before us: "What are these voices?" Remember, there is only one rational alternative to the assumption that they are what they profess to be—the utterances of the minds of personalities that once lived on the earth-plane, and who gather strength to be heard by drawing from the physical bodies of the sitters. It is this: that they are prompted by personators—beings from a society of cunning, depraved spirits whose delight and diabolical purpose it is to deceive mankind. This hypothesis is held by a very large body of people, and cannot be ignored, though it is, in the highest degree, unsavoury. All Roman Catholics believe it, and many estimable members of the Anglican Church. But is it reasonable? Is not the bible full of psychic phenomena from cover to cover? Is it not the standard work on spiritism?

"But," urges the priest, "our spirits—those mentioned in Holy Writ—are all good spirits; yours are all bad." We ask: "What is your authority for that statement?" and we get no answer. The fact is, the statement itself is gross presumption, and cannot bear scrutiny. For what object would the Supreme Intelligence allow such purposeless wickedness? Are any level-headed men or women the worse for listening and holding communion with these voices? Does it alter their character, make them less charitable or less worthy of respect than they were before? Do the voices counsel wrong or prompt any evil actions? Do they condemn anyone? Assuredly not. Do they not ever speak of loving kindness, sympathy, forgiveness of wrong, hope for the wrong-doer who repents for his sins? Assuredly yes" In the main they appear to have one object in view—to teach objectively the immortality of the soul, and to confirm the precepts, though not the literal text, of the Bible.

It is my conviction that spiritism is a Divine institution permitted by the Almighty to meet the growing materialism of the age, and that sooner or later the Church will have to come into line with it. If it does not, so much the worse for the church.

APPENDIX A

INSTANCES OF THE DIRECT
VOICE IN THE BIBLE

It is extremely difficult in the Bible to distinguish between the direct voices, voices in visions, and clairaudience; but I am inclined to think that most readers will consider that the following cases should be included in the list of instances of the direct voice:——

Genesis iii, 9; iv, 9; vi, 13; xii, 1-8; xvi, 8; xvii, l; xviii, 5; xviii,17; xix 2; xxi, 17; xxii, 11; xxvi, 2; xxvi, 24; xxxii, 26; xxxv, 1; xxxv, 9.

Exodus iii, 4; iv, 2;; iv, 27;chs. Vi-xii frequent; ch. Xix; xxxiii, 9. Numbers xii, 4; xvi, 20; xx, 7; xxii, 28. Duteronomy xxxi, 14; xxxiv, 4. Joshua v, 14.

Judges vi, 12; xiii, 3. 1 Samuel iii, 4; xv, 10; xvi, 7. 2 Samuel ii, 1. 1 Kings ix, 3; xvii, 3; xix, 9-12. Ezekiel I, 28; ii, 3. St. Matthew iii, 17; xvii, 5; xxviii, 5; xxviii, 18. St. Mark ix, 7;xvi, 14, 15. St. Luke I, 13; I, 28; ii, 10; iii, 22; xxii, 43; xxiv, 5; xxiv, 17; xxiv, 36-50 St. John xx, 13; xx, 19; xxi, 5-23. Acts I, 11; viii, 26; ix, 4; xii, 7; xxvii, 24. 1 Corinthians xii, 10. 2 Corinthians xii, 4.

APPENDIX B

A SPIRIT'S PROPHESY FULFILLED

Earlier in the book it will be seen that Iola told me that she would speak to me again. At that time there was not the smallest probability of another opportunity of sitting with Mrs. Wriedt, as she had refused an invitation from some of her friends in Southsea to go to them, and I had no intention of coming to London for more than a month, by which time I had good reason to suppose she would be back in America.

However, on Saturday, September 13, I was reading the proofs of the description of the séance related on p. 243 and had just got to the bottom of that page, when the telephone-bell rang, and a friend in the town told me that Mrs. Wriedt had arrived at his house. Mrs. Wriedt then spoke, and we arranged a private séance for 11 o'clock the following morning. It appeared she had returned suddenly from the Continent, and, in her spasmodic way, had rushed down with an American friend for the week- end.

The private sitting which I had with her on the Sunday morning was remarkable. The room was not wholly dark; I could see chairs and other objects in the room. I had conversations with four spirit friends, among them Iola, who talked for over twenty minutes without the medium hearing a single word. John King controlled, and amused me very much by his first remark: "What about Oliver Lodge?" (Four days before the president of the British Association for the Advancement of Science had delivered his famous pronouncement at Birmingham.)

On this morning I learnt some entirely new facts about the psychic properties of the trumpet, which are interesting; but I must wait for further experiments before publishing results. Dr. Sharp did not manifest.

APPENDIX C

ADVICE TO THOSE WHO SIT
WITH TRUMPET MEDIUMS

When a voice is heard addressing you ask the name once, and if you do not hear it given clearly do not repeat the question, but go on talking about other subjects, thus: "Are you a friend or a relative?" "Where did we last meet?" "How old were you when you passed over?" "Have we any mutual friends?" "Did you pass over by an accident?" "Did you pass over by disease?" "How long is it since you passed over?" "Were you married?" "Is your widow on this plane?" and so forth. Say anything, but go on talking to the spirit. In a little time you will find that the voice will become louder and clearer. You will gain nothing by repeating the same question.

Enter the séance-room with your mind as far as possible a blank. If you concentrate on a particular personality, you will fail.

When sitting in company with others never ask questions of the control which involve a discussion. Avoid all argument about Reincarnation, Vivisection, Vaccination, or any other subject which might be expected to be a matter of different opinions among the sitters. Remember that your companions have come with the hope of hearing the voices of their relatives and friends in spirit life, and not to argue about anything.

Do not cross your legs, nor fold your arms, nor close your mouth. Sing if you are invited to do so.

Do not take any professional medium to a séance as a guest. It leads to want of harmony, as the control of such medium wishes to exhibit his or her special gift, and this interferes with the manifestations.

Do not talk while a spirit voice is addressing another sitter.

Address your spirit friends precisely as you would if they had not passed over, with just that degree of respect or familiarity which you accorded to them during their lives.

W. U. M.

APPENDIX D

CORRECTION TO GLIMPSES OF THE NEXT STATE MR. HEREWARD CARRINGTON AND THE BANGS SISTERS

From Light, December 14, 1912

Sir,—As you have closed the correspondence on the above subject, I am not going to enter into any controversial matter, but merely to make a statement as an act of justice to Mr. Carrington.

In Appendix (C) to my book I have thrown out doubts of Mr. Carrington having been inside the Bangs Sisters' houses. After discussing the pros and cons I wound up with the following sentence: "However, I would fain believe that, owing to so long a time having elapsed...... the Bangs sisters may possibly have forgotten what sitters they received on a certain date......Let us try and credit that he did go into the séance room......"(p. 625). I am pleased to say that this pious wish has been translated into fact. A mutual friend remonstrated with me for doubting Mr. Carrington's bona fides, and I suggested to him that there was a simple way of proving that his friend had sat with May Bangs. If Mr. Carrington would procure from Dr. Funk's executors the original letter that he found between the closed slates, I would compare the handwriting with that of my letters obtained in a somewhat similar way. This letter has been sent, and I have compared it: the writing, in my opinion, is practically the same as in my letters.

I am, therefore, prepared to assert that Mr. Carrington did sit with May Bangs, and, in reply to a letter from himself to his "Dearest mother, Jane Thompson" (who never existed), did receive a reply addressed to "Dearly Loved Son Harold," in affectionate terms, from his "devoted mother, Jane Thompson."

As I took a number of precautions that Mr. Carrington did not, which included sitting between May Bangs and the suspected door, and using my own chemical ink, slates, marked paper, and so forth, I am as certain that my letters are genuine spirit manifestations as I am that his was intended to make a fool of him.

Unless Mr. Carrington desires to pursue the controversy in some other journal, I do not propose to refer to the matter again. Dr. Funk is dead. The Annals of Psychical Science (English version) is also defunct, and few investigators care a button about the matter. In the next edition of *Glimpses of the Next State* I shall delete those passages which contain doubts as to Mr. Carrington having been inside the house.

W. Usborne Moore.

Paperbacks also available from
White Crow Books

Marcus Aurelius—*Meditations*
ISBN 978-1-907355-20-2

Elsa Barker—*Letters from
a Living Dead Man*
ISBN 978-1-907355-83-7

Elsa Barker—*War Letters
from the Living Dead Man*
ISBN 978-1-907355-85-1

Elsa Barker—*Last Letters
from the Living Dead Man*
ISBN 978-1-907355-87-5

Richard Maurice Bucke—
Cosmic Consciousness
ISBN 978-1-907355-10-3

G. K. Chesterton—*Heretics*
ISBN 978-1-907355-02-8

G. K. Chesterton—*Orthodoxy*
ISBN 978-1-907355-01-1

Arthur Conan Doyle—*The
Edge of the Unknown*
ISBN 978-1-907355-14-1

Arthur Conan Doyle—
The New Revelation
ISBN 978-1-907355-12-7

Arthur Conan Doyle—
The Vital Message
ISBN 978-1-907355-13-4

Arthur Conan Doyle with
Simon Parke—*Conversations
with Arthur Conan Doyle*
ISBN 978-1-907355-80-6

Meister Eckhart with Simon Parke—
Conversations with Meister Eckhart
ISBN 978-1-907355-18-9

Kahlil Gibran—*The Forerunner*
ISBN 978-1-907355-06-6

Kahlil Gibran—*The Madman*
ISBN 978-1-907355-05-9

Kahlil Gibran—*The Prophet*
ISBN 978-1-907355-04-2

Kahlil Gibran—*Jesus the Son of Man*
ISBN 978-1-907355-08-0

Kahlil Gibran—*Spiritual World*
ISBN 978-1-907355-09-7

D. D. Home—*Incidents
in my Life Part 1*
ISBN 978-1-907355-15-8

Mme. Dunglas Home; edited,
with an Introduction, by Sir
Arthur Conan Doyle—*D. D.
Home: His Life and Mission*
ISBN 978-1-907355-16-5

Edward C. Randall—
Frontiers of the Afterlife
ISBN 978-1-907355-30-1

Lucius Annaeus Seneca—
On Benefits
ISBN 978-1-907355-19-6

Rebecca Ruter Springer—*Intra
Muros: My Dream of Heaven*
ISBN 978-1-907355-11-0

Leo Tolstoy, edited by Simon
Parke—*Forbidden Words*
ISBN 978-1-907355-00-4

Leo Tolstoy—*A Confession*
ISBN 978-1-907355-24-0

Leo Tolstoy—*The Gospel in Brief*
ISBN 978-1-907355-22-6

Leo Tolstoy—*The Kingdom
of God is Within You*
ISBN 978-1-907355-27-1

Leo Tolstoy—*My Religion:*
What I Believe
ISBN 978-1-907355-23-3

Leo Tolstoy—*On Life*
ISBN 978-1-907355-91-2

Leo Tolstoy—*Twenty-three Tales*
ISBN 978-1-907355-29-5

Leo Tolstoy—*What is Religion*
and other writings
ISBN 978-1-907355-28-8

Leo Tolstoy—*Work While*
Ye Have the Light
ISBN 978-1-907355-26-4

Leo Tolstoy with Simon Parke—
Conversations with Tolstoy
ISBN 978-1-907355-25-7

Vincent Van Gogh with
Simon Parke—*Conversations*
with Van Gogh
ISBN 978-1-907355-95-0

Howard Williams with an
Introduction by Leo Tolstoy—*The*
Ethics of Diet: An Anthology
of Vegetarian Thought
ISBN 978-1-907355-21-9

Allan Kardec—*The Spirits Book*
ISBN 978-1-907355-98-1

Wolfgang Amadeus Mozart
with Simon Parke—
Conversations with Mozart
ISBN 978-1-907661-38-9

Jesus of Nazareth with
Simon Parke—*Conversations*
with Jesus of Nazareth
ISBN 978-1-907661-41-9

Thomas à Kempis with Simon
Parke—*The Imitation of Christ*
ISBN 978-1-907661-58-7

Emanuel Swedenborg—
Heaven and Hell
ISBN 978-1-907661-55-6

P.D. Ouspensky—*Tertium Organum:*
The Third Canon of Thought
ISBN 978-1-907661-47-1

Dwight Goddard—*A Buddhist Bible*
ISBN 978-1-907661-44-0

Leo Tolstoy—*The Death*
of Ivan Ilyich
ISBN 978-1-907661-10-5

Leo Tolstoy—*Resurrection*
ISBN 978-1-907661-09-9

Michael Tymn—*The*
Afterlife Revealed
ISBN 978-1-970661-90-7

Guy L. Playfair—*If This Be Magic*
ISBN 978-1-907661-84-6

Julian of Norwich with
Simon Parke—*Revelations of*
Divine Love
ISBN 978-1-907661-88-4

Maurice Nicoll—*The New Man*
ISBN 978-1-907661-86-0

Carl Wickland, M.D.—*Thirty Years*
Among the Dead
ISBN 978-1-907661-72-3

Allan Kardec—*The*
Book on Mediums
ISBN 978-1-907661-75-4

John E. Mack—*Passport*
to the Cosmos
ISBN 978-1-907661-81-5

All titles available as eBooks, and selected titles available in Hardback and Audiobook formats from www.whitecrowbooks.com